NEWCOMER'S
HANDBOOK ®

FOR MOVING TO AND LIVING IN

LOS ANGELES

Including Santa Monica, Pasadena,
Orange County, and the San Fernando Valley

5th Edition

503-968-6777
www.firstbooks.com

FIRST BOOKS

Author: Joan Wai

Editors: Emily Horowitz, Linda Franklin

Series Editor: Linda Franklin

Cover design: Erin Johnson Design and Jillian Gregg

Interior design: Erin Johnson Design and Tricia Sgrignoli/Positive Images

Interior layout and composition: Tricia Sgrignoli/Positive Images

Maps provided by Scott Lockheed and Jim Miller/fennana design

Transit map courtesy of the Los Angeles County Metropolitan Transportation Authority (Metro). Used with permission.

ISBN-13: 978-0-912301-91-4

ISBN-10: 0-912301-91-0

Published by First Books®, 503-968-6777, www.firstbooks.com.

What readers are saying about Newcomer's Handbooks:

I recently got a copy of your Newcomer's Handbook for Chicago, and wanted to let you know how invaluable it was for my move. I must have consulted it a dozen times a day preparing for my move. It helped me find my way around town, find a place to live, and so many other things. Thanks.

– Mike L.
Chicago, Illinois

Excellent reading (Newcomer's Handbook for San Francisco and the Bay Area) ... balanced and trustworthy. One of the very best guides if you are considering moving/relocation. Way above the usual tourist crap.

– Gunnar E.
Stockholm, Sweden

I was very impressed with the latest edition of the Newcomer's Handbook for Los Angeles. It is well organized, concise and up-to-date. I would recommend this book to anyone considering a move to Los Angeles.

– Jannette L.
Attorney Recruiting Administrator for a large Los Angeles law firm

I recently moved to Atlanta from San Francisco, and LOVE the Newcomer's Handbook for Atlanta. It has been an invaluable resource—it's helped me find everything from a neighborhood in which to live to the local hardware store. I look something up in it everyday, and know I will continue to use it to find things long after I'm no longer a newcomer. And if I ever decide to move again, your book will be the first thing I buy for my next destination.

– Courtney R.
Atlanta, Georgia

In looking to move to the Boston area, a potential employer in that area gave me a copy of the Newcomer's Handbook for Boston. It's a great book that's very comprehensive, outlining good and bad points about each neighborhood in the Boston area. Very helpful in helping me decide where to move.

– no name given (online submit form)

TABLE OF CONTENTS

CONTENTS

101 **Finding a Place to Live**
Finding and renting apartments; shares and sublets; leases, security deposits and rent control; tenant resources; renter's/homeowner's insurance; buying a home; the buying process

119 **Moving and Storage**
Truck rentals; interstate and intrastate movers; storage; moving with children; moving-related tax deductions

131 **Money Matters**
Banking; credit cards; credit reports, taxes; moving or starting a business

139 **Getting Settled**
Utilities; telephones, internet; garbage and recycling; print and broadcast media; driver's licenses and state IDs; automobile registration, parking; voter registration; passports; obtaining a library card; finding a physician; pet laws and services; safety and crime

163 **Helpful Services**
Rental services, domestic services; mail and shipping services; consumer protection; services for people with disabilities; immigrant newcomers; gay and lesbian life

175 **Childcare and Education**
Daycare, babysitting, nannies; parent resources; public and private schools; nearby colleges and universities

CONTENTS

AT FIRST GLANCE, LOS ANGELES APPEARS TO BE A SPRAWLING metropolis, with no clear demarcations from one municipality to the next, let alone distinct neighborhoods. It takes time and patience to navigate this town and to understand the subtle qualities that make Santa Monica different from Venice, or Silverlake from the Fairfax district, but after a while, you will find neighborhoods in Los Angeles have different characteristics. Exploring LA's communities is easy and fun, and for newcomers especially, it's encouraged—just expect to spend at least some of the time sitting in traffic.

While cruising through the city you will no doubt encounter the "strip mall" phenomenon; that is, the appearance of one- to three-story mini-malls on every other block. While some consider these modern strip malls architectural eyesores, these neighborhood commerce centers usually provide a needed service or product.

Los Angeles's problems of crime and violence may be notorious, but in reality they reflect the nation's urban woes, and are certainly no better or worse here than in other major US cities. In fact, in the latest survey of FBI crime statistics, which ranked violent crime levels of the 300 largest metropolitan areas in the country, Los Angeles didn't even make the top 70. As in any city, a good dose of street smarts and common sense will help steer you away from trouble, and, as safety experts are fond of reminding us, always be aware of your surroundings. Certain high-crime neighborhoods such as South-Central and Watts are not recommended for outsiders or newcomers, but there are plenty of safe and affordable areas in which to live, work, and play.

In terms of climate, the warmest temperatures and worst air pollution occur in the summer months and, in general, you can expect the climate and air quality to be hotter and smoggier the further east you go. The Los Angeles metropolitan area reliably ranks at or near the top of ozone pollution lists, so if smog-related illnesses are a particular concern, choose your location carefully. For detailed information on the air quality in the areas you are considering calling home, contact the **South Coast Air Quality Management District** at 909-396-2000, www. aqmd.gov.

The City of Los Angeles is the second most populous city, behind New York City, in the USA, with an estimated population of over 4 million in 2007. Los Angeles County is comprised of 10.2 million residents and alone would rank as the eighth most populous state.

LA is a multi-ethnic, multicultural society as diverse as any city in the world. The ethnic breakdown of students enrolled at LA Unified School District (the largest district in the USA after New York) tells you just how diverse it is here: 72.8% Hispanic, 11.2 % Black, 8.9% White, 3.7% Asian, and the balance include American Indian, Filipino, and Pacific Islander. People from more than 140 countries live in Los Angeles County, including the largest population of Mexican, Armenian, Korean, Filipino, Salvadoran, and Guatemalan communities outside their respective home nations. The city is so large you can fit St. Louis, Milwaukee, Cleveland, Minneapolis, San Francisco, Boston, Pittsburgh, and Manhattan all within the municipal boundaries!

For decades, people around the world have been attracted to Los Angeles for its promises of fame and fortune, and excellent year-round weather. While only a sliver of the population is famous and wealthy, the good weather here is no myth. Average temperatures range from 58 degrees Fahrenheit in December to 76 degrees in September, and it's not uncommon to have an 80-degree day at the beach in February, while much of the rest of the country shivers under a layer of snow. Our annual precipitation is just under 15 inches, with an average of 291 sunny days a year.

Some fun facts you may want to know about LA: Downtown is considered the largest government sector outside of Washington DC, hosting over 45,000 public sector jobs. The three largest non-governmental employers in the county are Kaiser Permanente and aerospace manufacturers Northrop Grumman Corporation and Boeing. To keep up the "beautiful people" here, 200 board-certified plastic surgeons call this county home. There are over 2,200 stars on the Hollywood Walk of Fame. The city flower is the Bird of Paradise and the Coral Tree is the official city tree.

Due to the vastness of LA County, this guide does not attempt to cover every neighborhood, but it does cover many. Some profiled communities, while very much a part of LA, are incorporated cities in their own right; others are distinct neighborhoods within the City of Los Angeles proper. What follows are comprehensive yet concise descriptions of neighborhoods and cities that would be appropriate to those relocating to LA or its environs. We start on the Westside with the beach communities and then move east, more or less, through downtown, and then north, covering the Valley. In this latest edition we have profiled twelve significant Orange County communities as well.

Including the City of LA, Los Angeles County consists of 88 cities, such as Glendale, West Hollywood, and Beverly Hills. (There are usually signs posted on major thoroughfares identifying the border of a particular city.) Each city has an independent city council and provides municipal services. Many residents proudly identify with their municipality and its reputation—taking offense when referred to as "Angelenos." Neighborhoods within the City of LA, which measures roughly 470 square miles or 11.5% of the county, include Fairfax, Westwood, West LA, Hollywood, Downtown, and North Hollywood. The city's patchwork quilt–like composition resulted from battles over a surprisingly simple commodity during its formation: water. Municipalities that were annexed by the City of LA because of their water supplies often retained their community name. Many of the major streets in town are named after people who helped shape this city (Mulholland Boulevard, Doheny Drive, Chandler Boulevard); you'll be introduced to them in the brief history section later in this chapter.

Other useful information such as area codes: 213 (downtown); 323 (areas surrounding downtown, including Hollywood); 310 and 424 (Westside and South Bay); 562 (Long Beach); 818 (the Valley, Glendale, and Burbank) (a 747 split or overlay is proposed for the West Valley areas like Van Nuys and Canoga Park but has yet to be implemented); 661 (Santa Clarita); 626 (Pasadena); 949 and 714 and 657 (Orange County); as well as zip codes, post offices, district police stations, neighborhood hospitals, public libraries, community resources, and public school districts follows each neighborhood description. In some cases, the neighborhood boundaries are approximations, since areas that are not distinct cities tend to blend into one another.

Unless otherwise noted, housing statistics included in the neighborhood profiles are derived from Dataquick, www.dqnews.com (same resource used by the *LA Times*). In fourth quarter 2007, the National Association of Realtors' ranking of the US metropolitan areas with the highest median sale price for existing single-family homes placed Los Angeles fifth, at $589,200, and Orange County at number three, with a median price of $699,600. In itself, this number doesn't tell the full story since homes vary widely in price here, but dropping prices by double-digit percentages are a good indicator of increasing affordability in the LA market…at least until the trend reverses.

Greater Los Angeles's traffic is perhaps the most famous negative among her many pluses. If it feels like you're always sitting in your car, you may be right. According to the latest Census figures, the average LA commute runs 29 minutes. And 3% of LA commuters do "extreme commutes," that is, spend 90 minutes or more driving to work. Urban sprawl is a major contributor to traffic, requiring many people to get in their car to reach everything from the grocery store to the gym. Probably the only time driving may be a breeze in LA is on a federal or Jewish holiday as a noticeably shortened commute is the reward for those who still have to work. Short of these reprieves, allowing plenty of commute time to reach your destination, whether it be a weekday or weekend, is just a fact of life here. But as someone once said of LA, "If this is hell, why is it so popular?" For those who choose to call Los Angeles "home," she welcomes you with a wealth of opportunities.

LOCAL QUIRKS & LINGO

- Sorry, no "secret" language exists in this melting pot of a city, unless you count Spanish. And it is helpful to have some knowledge of Spanish pronunciation since many major street names are in Spanish: Cahuenga (pronounced "ca-weng-ga") and La Cienega ("la see-en-ne-ga").
- OK, maybe there's one local phrase newcomers should familiarize themselves with. "I gotta go over the hill" is something commuters say when traveling between LA proper and the San Fernando Valley; the hill refers to the Hollywood Hills. Most people use Laurel Canyon, Coldwater Canyon, or the 101 to "go over the hill" in either direction.
- While the Bay Area likes to refer to their freeways without the word "the," you'll sound like an outsider if you don't call it "the 10" or "the 405." By the way, that's "the four - oh - five" and "the one - oh - one."
- You can be ticketed for driving too slowly on *the* 405 (or any other freeway) here.
- In California, it is illegal to leave your pet unattended in a car "under conditions that endanger the health or well being of an animal...that could reasonably be expected to cause suffering, disability, or death to the animal" (such as a hot car).
- Certain cities, such as Burbank and Beverly Hills, forbid overnight parking on its streets without a permit. If you're planning on staying with a (new) friend overnight, make sure you read posted signs carefully.
- If the city issues a "red flag day" alert, parking is prohibited on certain streets within high fire hazard areas. This is to allow fire trucks to navigate tight turns and narrow streets more easily. Typically a red flag day, characterized by 15% humidity or less, wind speeds above 25 mph, and elevated temperatures, occurs three to seven days a year. These areas are marked with street signs. The fire department's web site, www.lafd.org/redflag, has posted maps of these areas.
- In an effort to reduce waste, Santa Monica is drafting an ordinance to outlaw single-use plastic grocery bags and require retailers to charge consumers if they want to use paper bags at every store and restaurant in the city. Currently, take-out food and beverages must be served in recyclable containers.

WHAT TO BRING

- **A car**; if it isn't obvious by now that a car culture dominates LA, it will be when you get here. Although LA has a large bus transit system and an underground subway and light rail system that are slowly growing, LA is simply too big to get around effectively without a car. And, public transportation by bus often means an even longer commute time than if you drove yourself. Small, compact model cars are the most economical and ideal for maneuvering LA's tight parking spots. Be prepared to shell out the bucks for insurance coverage; the cost for auto insurance in LA is among the nation's highest.

- **A map**; it'll take newcomers a while to create a mental map of where one community is in relation to another, and to figure out how much time is necessary to get from one place to another. Traffic patterns create situations where the shortest route is not always the fastest. Although many city streets are laid out in a grid, there are plenty of exceptions with streets that cross over, change names, and create not four, but five junctions at an intersection. If you don't want to buy a GPS system, then a *Thomas Guide* street map (loose-leaf books of detailed LA neighborhood road maps) is perfect for finding alternate routes around gridlocked freeways. The *LA County, LA County/Ventura*, and *LA County/Orange Thomas Guides*, veritable LA bibles, can be purchased through First Books at www.firstbooks.com or at most local bookstores.
- **A cell phone**; good for multi-tasking while you're sitting in traffic or telling people you're meeting that you're running late. However, as of July 2008, you may only use your cell phone in your car with a hands-free device (such as a headset). If you're under 18, you are prohibited from using a cell phone or any texting device at all while driving.
- **An open mind and positive attitude**; if this is your first time in Los Angeles, be prepared to interact with many different cultures and ethnicities. In general, Californians are famous for their laid-back attitudes, and Angelenos are no exception; however, the pace of life here is faster and more energetic than in smaller cities—but that's what makes it so fun!

While this *Newcomer's Handbook® for Moving to and Living in Los Angeles* will introduce you to the area, nothing compares to discovering the area's many beautiful facets yourself. Welcome and enjoy.

STREET ADDRESS LOCATOR

Most major Los Angeles streets follow a standard grid pattern, running east-west and north-south, but there are plenty that snake around, stop at one block, then continue down another with little rhyme or reason. We offer a general guide to LA's thoroughfares and city layout. Nearby cities may have their grids laid out differently. Ultimately, the best way to figure out where you are, or where you want to go, is to pull out your trusty *Thomas Guide* or use an online map. And, unless you're in a tough part of town, don't be shy about asking for directions. Every Angeleno has gotten lost at one time or another in this sprawling metropolis. If you are uncomfortable asking strangers for directions, try calling 411 on your cell phone—many providers offer concierge services that include giving directions.

Roads that run east-west are usually boulevards (Pico Boulevard) and if they're numerical, they're streets (Third Street). Those that run north-south are avenues (but there are plenty of exceptions like Westwood Boulevard). The grid pattern extends to downtown, except the grid is tilted about 45 degrees to Hoover Street. Continue south, and downtown returns to an upright grid at Martin Luther King Junior Boulevard. (The east-west street numbers continue through South Central.)

The approximate center of the grid is downtown at Main Street and First Street. All streets that run north-south below First Street increase in number as you travel south. For north-south streets above First Street, the numbers increase in number as you head north. For example, La Brea Avenue is one long north-south street. First Street bisects La Brea Avenue into South La Brea Avenue (south of First) and North La Brea Avenue (north of First) in Hancock Park—but most Angelenos refer to a street without the "south" or "north." So an address like 1400 La Brea Avenue can be in Culver City or Hollywood. (Always ask for a cross street when getting the address of a new location.) The same goes for many of the streets that run east-west. If the east-west street runs west of Main Street, "West" is attached to the street moniker and the numbers increase as you head further west; if the east-west street runs east of Main Street, "East" is the modifier and the street numbers increase as you head further east of Main Street.

Outside of downtown, some numbered streets make up the side streets, while main thoroughfares have names such as Wilshire Boulevard or Beverly Boulevard. Beyond that, there is little logic behind the names of city streets. Until you familiarize yourself with the city, keeping a map in the car is almost as important as your insurance card.

The lack of a formal system in street planning might be blamed on the fact that many of the communities came into being before incorporating with the City of Los Angeles. Fortunately, the city's main thoroughfares are easy to identify—they're heavy with traffic because they're used as alternatives to the freeways. Some of the **main arteries** include:

- **Santa Monica Boulevard**: begins in Silverlake at Sunset Boulevard and runs west, ending in Santa Monica on Ocean Avenue. This is a heavily traveled street on the Westside.
- **Wilshire Boulevard**: begins at Grand Avenue, downtown, and ends at Ocean Avenue on Santa Monica Boulevard. It is heavily traveled throughout its length.
- **Ventura Boulevard**: this valley-based street begins in Universal City where Cahuenga Boulevard ends and runs west to Woodland Avenue in Woodland Hills.
- **Sepulveda Boulevard**: begins at San Fernando Boulevard in Mission Hills (in the Valley) and runs south, paralleling the 405 Freeway into the 91 Artesia Freeway in Manhattan Beach; often used by commuters looking for an alter-

native to the 405 Freeway, especially along the "Sepulveda Pass," the passage that joins the Valley with LA.

• **Laurel Canyon Boulevard:** begins at Sunset Boulevard in Hollywood and runs north into the Valley to Webb Avenue. A popular (but winding) alternative to the 101 and 405 freeways because it's centrally located, making it easy to go between the Valley and LA proper.

A BRIEF LOS ANGELES HISTORY

This is El Pueblo de Nuestra Señora la Reina de Los Angeles (in English, the town of our lady the queen of the angels). That's the name the Spanish gave to this city in 1781 when 44 village settlers made their home in what is now downtown Los Angeles. The end of the US-Mexican war was marked by the Treaty of Cahuenga, signed in 1847 at a structure called Campo de Cahuenga, still standing today in Universal City. The name Cahuenga likely was inspired by the nearby Indian American village called "Kaweenga." This treaty, signed in 1847, ended the war in California, thus the campo earned the nickname "birthplace of California." The Treaty of Guadalupe Hidalgo, signed a year later, had Mexico agreeing to cede Los Angeles and the balance of California to American Territory for $15 million. About a decade later, Campo de Cahuenga became a stagecoach station along the longest route in the world, and eventually a major mail route stop for California.

The annexation of California brought even more gold prospectors to Sutter's Mill in the town of Coloma (north of Sacramento) in 1848. Following the end of the Civil War, LA experienced a large influx of immigrants from England, France, Spain, Mexico, and China. The division of many large Mexican ranches created the communities of Compton, Santa Monica, and Pasadena. During the 1860s a marketing campaign telling people to "Go West" started a speculative land frenzy. The real estate market collapsed, however, and a chamber of commerce was created to lure people back. The city's population in 1890 was 50,000. In 1892, Edward Doheny discovered oil near what is now Dodger Stadium. Enough oil was discovered that LA became a major oil producer in the early 1900s, creating a black gold rush. The wealthy Doheny built Greystone Mansion as a wedding gift for his son. This meticulously maintained 55-room Tudor in Beverly Hills hosts concerts, garden tours, and weddings today.

With growing city prosperity comes the growing need for water. The efforts of the LA Water Department's (which eventually became the LADWP) chief engineer, William Mulholland, and others helped convince (some say trick) farmers to give up water rights to their land in the San Fernando Valley. Early residents too were persuaded of the need for the construction of a massive aqueduct. When it was completed in 1913, the Owens Valley Aqueduct System was the largest in the world. It brought precious water to the desert and enabled agriculture to thrive. By the 1920s, groves of oranges, lemons, and olives characterized the

San Fernando Valley. The arrival of the Pacific Electrical Railway, spearheaded by Henry E. Huntington, continued to fuel the city's growth.

The movie industry had its beginnings in the arrival of director D.W. Griffith and actress Mary Pickford, who started making movies in this little village called Hollywood in the early 1900s. The constant sunshine was ideal for these early film cameras, which required a lot of light, so this factor lured additional filmmakers. *LA Times* publisher Henry Chandler paid to erect the sign "Hollywood Land" on the Hollywood Hills to advertise a real estate development he was invested in. In 1949, the sign was shortened to "Hollywood" for city pride.

LA came into its own when it hosted the summer Olympic Games in 1932. The LA Memorial Coliseum was enlarged to accommodate 100,000+ Olympic spectators. (We hosted the Olympic Games once more in 1984, being the first and only city to ever host two summer Olympic games.) In May of 1937, Amelia Earhart departed from Burbank Airport and was never heard from again. The city's population grew to 1.5 million by 1940, and by twenty years later, swelled to 2.4 million.

During WWII, LA became a center for the production of aircraft and war supplies. Lockheed Aircraft Corporation built planes in Burbank until 1990 (the Empire Center stands there today, with an airplane as part of the mall's logo). LA's electric streetcars (famously known as the red cars) thrived as an efficient and popular mode of public transportation. The reason behind their demise is the stuff of movies. Conspiracy theorists allege that big business conspired to purchase all the street cars and dismantle them to force cities to purchase buses and commuters to buy automobiles and tires. Another, less controversial but more likely theory is that the streetcars were suffering diminishing ridership as increasing numbers of commuters fell in love with a more private, faster mode of transportation—the automobile.

LA experienced a post-war boom during which many of its communities sprung up to receive soldiers returning to make babies. During the 1950s, city planners decided to remove the height limit on buildings in a downtown area known as Bunker Hill, which paved the way for downtown's skyscrapers. The United California Bank Building (later called the First Interstate Tower, now the Aon Tower), was the tallest building in town when it completed construction in 1973.

The redevelopment of Bunker Hill and downtown is still ongoing. The birth of the Cathedral of Our Lady of Angels church and the Walt Disney Concert Hall served as anchors in the master plan. With development of a Civic Park that stretches from Grand Avenue, at the top of Bunker Hill, to Spring Street at the bottom of the Hill, the hope is to make a central park (and nearby City Hall) relevant to residents. Mixed residential housing (where the first floor of residential housing is filled with commercial services) is taking root now with the approval of the $2.5 billion Grand Avenue Project. LA Live, an entertainment campus dubbed "Times Square West," is under construction next to the Staples Center and Nokia

Theater. The campus is scheduled to house ESPN's west coast broadcasting center, restaurants, and a club. Two major hotels are also planned for construction. Envisioning a pedestrian-friendly area with lots of affordable high-rise housing, the City Council dreams of transforming and reviving the city's center as a place to be and go to. These major improvements happening downtown are a healthy indication of this city's thriving and exciting future. The current mayor, Antonio Villaraigosa, likes to joke that the construction crane is the unofficial city bird. How very true for the heart of this city.

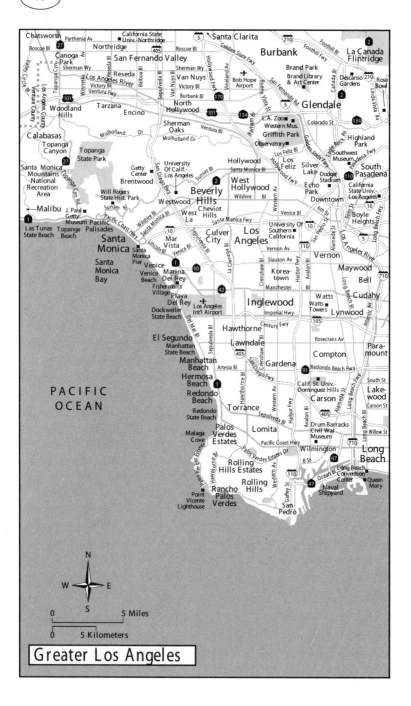

Greater Los Angeles

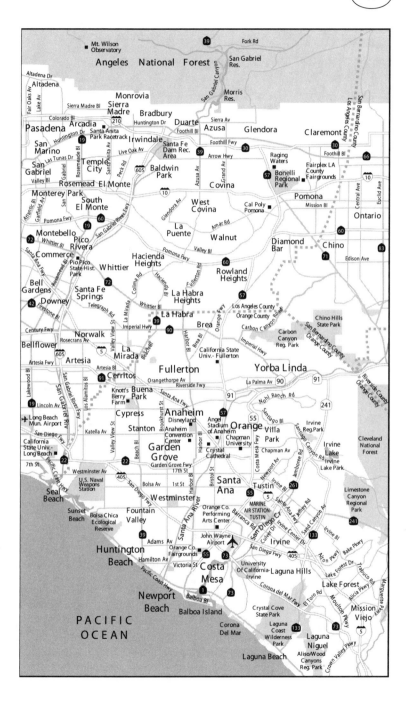

LA NEIGHBORHOODS & COMMUNITIES—WEST

MALIBU

Boundaries: North: Mulholland Highway; **East**: Tuna Canyon Road, Saddle Creek Road; **South**: Santa Monica Bay; **West**: Mulholland Highway

"Malibu—it's a state of mind." This message seen on license plate holders across Los Angeles may leave you scratching your head and wondering what it all means...until you get to the City of Malibu. Once you've traveled the twenty miles northwest of Santa Monica on the Pacific Coast Highway (PCH) you'll find Malibu is not so much a place as a peaceful vibe, something often absent in other parts of the region.

In fact, initially Malibu may not be so impressive. You'll find the usual fast-food stands, small shopping centers, and surf shops, sprinkled with a few fancy restaurants. The pretty Malibu Pier offers fishing and food. Most nonresidents come to Malibu for the beaches, which are some of the loveliest and cleanest (both sand and water) in the Los Angeles area. Zuma Beach is the most visited, nearby Point Dume is a bit less crowded, and Leo Carrillo, a 1,600-acre beach situated farther northwest, features three campgrounds. Surfrider Beach is still popular with surfers, as it was in the 1950s and '60s when Annette Funicello and Frankie Avalon frolicked here in their Beach Blanket Bingo movies. Even Pepperdine University has an ocean view in Malibu.

As for residents, Malibu is the home, or second home (or third, or fourth) to the rich and famous, who enjoy its scenery and privacy. Particularly popular with celebrities is the Malibu Beach Colony, a gated community right on the sand. Note: While the streets and homes in the Colony are not accessible to outsiders, the ocean is. The tidelands in California, defined as the area below the mean high tide, are considered public land. Hence, you can park along the road before or

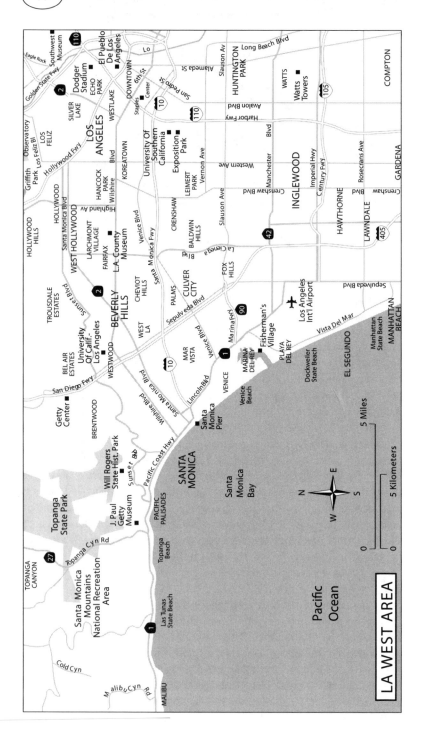

LA WEST AREA

after the Colony property (or, for that matter, almost any other private beach area in the state) or park in the Malibu Lagoon parking lot and walk west. As long as you stay on the wet, packed sand, you'll be able to get a look at the beachside villas in this celebrity enclave. A few private beach communities have guards that will chase you off the dry, sandy part of the beach, but stick to the hard, wet sand along the tide line and you should be fine. Another word of warning, alcohol and smoking are prohibited on all Malibu beaches and are citable offenses.

Aside from the famous folks, Malibu has a fair share of successful professionals, surfer dudes and dudettes, and just plain beach lovers calling it home. As you might imagine, rents and house prices in Malibu are most expensive at the coast, a couple million (beachfront property easily sells for more), and then decrease as you move inland, into the canyons. While the area is mostly owner-occupied, a diligent hunter can locate a sprinkling of apartments, condominiums, guesthouses, and townhomes for rent.

Because much of Malibu is hilly, dry canyon country, almost every summer brush fires are a problem; in 2007 four mansions were lost. Then in the winter, in places where hillside vegetation has been burned, rains can cause landslides, which then cause flooding. During heavy rains, rockslides are responsible for the occasional closures of the Pacific Coast Highway, the main artery in and out of Malibu. Through it all, most residents say the privacy and beauty of Malibu make residing here worthwhile.

Web Site: www.ci.malibu.ca.us

Area Code: 310, 424

Zip Codes: 90264, 90265

Post Offices: Main Post Office, 23648 Pacific Coast Hwy; La Costa Station, 21229 Pacific Coast Hwy; Point Dume Station, 29160 Heathercliff Rd

Police District: Malibu is served by the Los Angeles County Sheriff's Department, 27050 Agoura Rd, Agoura, 818-878-1808, www.lasd.org

Emergency Hospitals: Malibu Urgent Center, 23656 Pacific Coast Hwy, 310-456-7551; Santa Monica UCLA Medical Center, 1250 16th St, Santa Monica, 310-319-4000, www.healthcare.ucla.edu

Libraries: Malibu Library, 23519 W Civic Center Way, 310-456-6438, www.cola publib.org; Palisades Library, 861 Alma Real Dr, 310-459-2754, www.lapl.org

Public School Education: Santa Monica-Malibu Unified School District, 1651 16th St, Santa Monica, 310-450-8338, www.smmusd.org

Community Resources: Pepperdine University, 24255 W Pacific Coast Hwy, Malibu, 310-506-4000, www.pepperdine.edu; Malibu Bluffs Park, 24250 Pacific Coast Hwy, 310-317-1364; Malibu Equestrian Park, 6225 Merritt Dr, 310-317-1364; Charmlee Wilderness Park, 2577 S Encinal Canyon Rd, 310-457-7247; Malibu Parks and Recreation Department, 310-456-2489, www.ci.malibu. ca.us

Public Transportation: call 800-COMMUTE or visit www.mta.net, for specific bus route schedule and information.

TOPANGA CANYON

Boundaries: North: Mulholland Drive; **East:** Topanga State Park; **South:** Santa Monica Bay; **West:** Los Flores Canyon

Curvy mountain roads, tangled trees and vines, an occasional hippie-type hitch-hiking alongside the canyon passageway—are we in LA? Nestled in the Santa Monica Mountains between Santa Monica and Malibu, Topanga Canyon hardly seems like a part of a major metropolis. Its roots are firmly planted in the hippie, artist, and other alternative communities that have populated this unincorporated part of Los Angeles County for decades.

It's easy to see why people choose to live in Topanga Canyon. For starters, there is the beautiful, natural setting, complete with vistas (in some spots) of the Pacific Ocean. Another bonus is the relatively low cost of housing. Residences run the gamut from mountain cabins to newer, high-end houses, and rents and home prices are much lower compared with nearby, chic Malibu. Most area housing was built after 1950, and much is filled by newcomers, many of whom previously were residents of the City of LA. Yes, the word is out, Topanga is more than just a good state park to take a day hike; hence today your next-door neighbor here is as likely to be a Hollywood producer as a stained-glass artist.

However, people accustomed to the convenience of home-delivered Chinese food or 2 a.m. grocery shopping should think twice about living in Topanga Canyon. Although only a few miles up the Pacific Coast Highway from Pacific Palisades, Topanga feels remote. At the crest of Old Topanga Canyon Road, a commercial strip caters to the basics like food and gas, but for the most part, once you've driven up the hill towards home, you've probably left the day's errands behind. Beyond stargazing, nightlife is limited to a handful of local restaurants. And that's just the way locals like it.

Hikers frequent Topanga Canyon, especially along the beautiful, hilly trails at Topanga State Park. Within Topanga Canyon is Topanga Creek, the third largest watershed draining into Santa Monica Bay. (Look out for the turtle crossing sign in the neighborhood.) Another fun spot in the canyon is the Will Geer Theatricum Botanicum, a rustic outdoor theater that now includes the S. Mark Taper Foundation Youth Pavilion. It is a place where, on a warm summer evening, you can have a romantic, candle-lit picnic and then sit under the stars on comfy throw pillows and view a Shakespearean drama or other play or musical production. Music lovers will appreciate their annual Topanga Days music and art celebration, focusing on independent sounds and bluegrass and rock.

Finally, it's worth noting that if heavy rains hit during the winter, certain sections of Old Topanga Canyon Road and Topanga Canyon Boulevard, the primary arteries serving this community, are prone to closure due to landslides, especially along the creek beds. City crews are quick to bring in bulldozers, so the residents consider this a minor nuisance in exchange for more relaxed mountain living.

Web Site: www.topangaonline.com

Zip Code: 90290

Area Codes: 310, 424

Post Office: 101 S Topanga Canyon Blvd, 800-275-8777

Police District: Topanga Canyon is served by the Los Angeles County Sheriff's Department, 27050 Agoura Rd, 818-878-1808, www.lasd.org.

Emergency Hospitals: Saint John's Hospital and Health Center, 1328 22nd St, Santa Monica, 310-829-5511, www.stjohns.org; Santa Monica - UCLA Medical Center, 1250 16th St, Santa Monica, 310-319-4000, www.uclahealth.org

Libraries: Malibu Library, 23519 W Civic Center Way, Malibu, 310-456-6438, www.colapublib.org; Palisades Library, 861 Alma Real Dr, Malibu, 310-459-2754, www.lapl.org

Public School Education: LA Unified School District, 333 S Beaudry Ave, LA, 213-241-1000, www.lausd.k12.ca.us

Community Resources: Topanga State Park in the Santa Monica Mountains National Recreation Area, 310-455-2465, www.parks.ca.gov; Topanga Community House, 1440 Topanga Canyon Blvd, 310-455-1980, www.topangacommunityclub.org; Will Geer Theatricum Botanicum, 1419 N Topanga Canyon Blvd, 310-455-3723, www.theatricum.com

Public Transportation: call 800-COMMUTE or www.mta.net for specific Metro bus route and schedule information.

SANTA MONICA

PACIFIC PALISADES
RUSTIC CANYON

Boundaries: North: San Vicente Boulevard; **East:** Centinela Avenue; **South:** Dewey Street; **West:** Santa Monica Bay, Pacific Ocean

Nicknamed "Santa Moscow" for its liberal city politics, Santa Monica, which is its own municipality, was once a highly coveted neighborhood for its rent-controlled, seaside apartments. However, rent control has ended and in its place is "vacancy decontrol" (started in 1999—see **Finding a Place to Live**), which allows landlords to set rent at whatever price they deem appropriate, once a formerly rent-controlled apartment has been vacated. Rental prices now reflect the higher price tag expected of seaside living.

To soften the blow for renters, the City of Santa Monica maintains some level of control over the amount rent may be increased. Each year, at the beginning of September, the City's Rent Control Board determines the maximum percentage by which landlords may raise rent. So, while newcomers moving into an apartment will shell out some dollars to live here, annual rental increases are typically held in check. Typically, the general adjustment agreed upon by the board varies between 3% and 4%. In Santa Monica, Rent Control Board determinations apply only to multiple-unit dwellings built before April 10, 1979. The majority of the rental units qualify. With so much potential for confusion, the rent control office provides special coordinators (310-458-8751, www.smgov.net/rentcontrol) to help renters determine what their legal rent should be.

Potential home buyers with low to moderate incomes can seek assistance from the **Santa Monica Housing and Redevelopment Department**, 310-458-2251, www.smgov.net, an organization designed to provide affordable housing options, including low-cost housing for seniors and the disabled.

Committed to social and environmental sensitivity, Santa Monica has become one the first US cities to make it a matter of city policy to rely on sustainable or renewable resources, overseen by the Environmental Programs Division of the Environmental and Public Works Management Department. Electricity (generated by sustainable sources) and natural gas are the primary sources of energy within the city. There is also a recycling program in place for homeowners and renters, and aggressive campaigns to encourage residents to use water- and energy-efficient devices. The city's Civic Center parking structure is the world's first sustainable public parking lot (solar powered, reduced water usage), located at 333 Civic Center Drive.

These environment-friendly policies must be having an effect. Area residents like to brag that the air is cleaner and the weather cooler here than anywhere else in LA, and it's true. While summer temperatures in Los Angeles can hover in the eighties and nineties, it's not uncommon for Santa Monica to sport temperatures that are fifteen degrees cooler than downtown or the Valley. Many apartments do not have air conditioners. The city is more recently making headlines with their attempts to ban plastic grocery bags. They drafted an ordinance in 2008 which the city is expected to pass.

Approximately 20% of the housing stock in Santa Monica is composed of single-family homes; the rest consist of multi-unit apartments and condos. Not surprisingly, 70% of residents are renters. Residential streets are lined with either rows of mature magnolia trees or towering palms. The area north of upscale shopping street Montana Avenue features some of LA's most beautiful (and priciest) homes, most built in the early 1960s. For those less financially endowed, the area south of Santa Monica Avenue offers mostly apartments and condominiums, while still boasting easy access to the area's cafés, coffeehouses, and shops. Be aware, street parking is extremely difficult to procure, especially in apartment neighborhoods, and is one of the drawbacks of residing here. The city operates a web site with a real-time map that displays available spaces in its public parking lots at http://parking.smgov.net.

Main Street is probably the hippest and beachiest area in this small city. The art galleries, restaurants and bars with patio seating, shops, and coffeehouses overflow with ever-so-chic singles (the median age here is 39) or young families with strollers in tow. To the west of Main Street are several walking lanes lined with some nice and some run-down beach cottages, but regardless, prices are high due to the proximity to the ocean. The hilly neighborhood just east of Main Street consists of apartments and condominiums with a few funky houses mixed in.

The focus in downtown Santa Monica is the lively outdoor mall, Third Street Promenade, with shops, restaurants, and a multitude of theaters attracting huge crowds (and enterprising street performers) on weekends. The Santa Monica Place Mall is on the southern end of the promenade and currently closed for remodeling, but it is scheduled to reopen in fall of 2009. Walk just a bit west to the Santa Monica Pier, which is the western end of famed Route 66. A remodeled Santa Monica Civic Center, Santa Monica College, Swim Center, and Santa Monica Municipal Airport are some of the amenities located nearby. A lively arts scene thrives here too as evidenced by the many galleries dotting the area. Well-tended community parks, active neighborhood watch programs, and strongly supported social services for the elderly and disabled round out this seaside neighborhood's offerings, making Santa Monica a favorite for families and singles, both young and old.

A small suburb of Santa Monica is **Pacific Palisades**. This seaside community, part of Los Angeles City, is surrounded by six major canyons and has the look of a posh small town. Upscale shops, restaurants, and grocery stores are clustered village-style on Sunset Boulevard and patronized by well-to-do residents who live nearby in multimillion-dollar homes. Housing stock ranges in size from mansions to older and smaller houses to apartments and condos. Local amenities include the Tennis Center (inside the Palisades Park Recreation Center) and the Riviera Country Club. Next door is an even more secluded enclave called **Rustic Canyon**. Aptly named, the canyon neighborhood consists of a little over 200 homes in the densely wooded forest.

Web Sites: www.smgov.net, www.cityofla.org, www.co.la.ca.us
Area Code: 310, 424
Zip Codes: 90401–6, 90272
Post Offices: Santa Monica Main Office, 1248 5th Street; Colorado Station, 1025 Colorado Ave; Will Rogers Station, 1217 Wilshire Blvd; Pacific Palisades, 15209 W Sunset Blvd
Police District: Santa Monica Police Headquarters, 333 Olympic Dr, 310-458-8411, www.santamonicapd.org
Emergency Hospitals: Saint John's Hospital and Health Center, 1328 22nd St, 310-829-5511, www.stjohns.org; Santa Monica - UCLA Medical Center, 1250 16th St, 310-319-4000, www.uclahealth.org

Libraries: Main Library, 601 Santa Monica Blvd, 310-458-8600; Fairview branch, 2101 Ocean Park Blvd, 310-450-0443; Montana Ave branch, 1704 Montana Ave, 310-829-7081; Ocean Park branch, 2601 Main St, 310-392-3804; www. smpl.org

Public School Education: Santa Monica-Malibu Unified School District, 1651 16th St, Santa Monica, 310-450-8338, www.smmusd.org

Community Resources: Santa Monica City Information Desk, 310-458-8411; parking permits, 310-458-8291; Santa Monica College, 1900 Pico Blvd, 310-434-4000, www.smc.edu; Lincoln Park, 1150 Lincoln Blvd; Memorial Park, 1401 Olympic Blvd; Santa Monica Recreation Division, 310-458-8300, www.smgov. net; Santa Monica Pier, 310-458-8900, www.santamonicapier.org; Santa Monica Swim Center, 2225 16th St, 310-458-8700, www.smgov.net/aquatics; Palisades Tennis Center, 851 Alma Rea Dr, 310-573-1331, www.palitenniscen ter.com

Public Transportation: the affectionately named Big Blue Bus serves Santa Monica residents. Call 310-451-5444 for specific Santa Monica Municipal Bus Line routes and schedule information, or check www.BigBlueBus.com.

VENICE

Boundaries: **North**: Dewey Street; **East**: Walgrove Avenue; **South**: Washington Street; **West**: Santa Monica Bay, Pacific Ocean

The funkiest of Los Angeles's beach communities, Venice is an eclectic mix of artists, surfers, bodybuilders, and sightseers. It was founded in 1900 by Abbot Kinney, whose dream was to foster a cultural renaissance in America by recreating an Italian "Venice" here. Some of the area's original Venetian-style architecture still stands near the boardwalk, as do a few of the canals (located between Washington Boulevard and Venice Boulevard at Dell). Despite these Venetian touches, it is doubtful that Abbot Kinney had any idea just what kind of culture Venice would become known for. Yes, men and women in skimpy bathing suits do roller-blade down the streets here, and yes, burly muscle men and women do perform their workouts and flex for tourists at Muscle Beach, and yes, that skateboarding bulldog you've seen online does its thing here, but Venice is also home to a strong and thriving artists' community, composed of first-rate studios, galleries, and artists' residences. The heart of the area is Ocean Front Walk (known as the boardwalk), a beachfront collection of shops, outdoor cafés, street performers, jewelry and sunglasses stands, and the liveliest place in town to get your palm read, hair braided, or back massaged. Since space is at a premium, housing runs the gamut from beach cottages to jam-packed apartments to oceanfront villas that, in total, support a residential population of over 31,000. Prices and quality vary greatly, but generally the closer you are to the ocean, the more you pay.

East of the boardwalk is Abbot Kinney Boulevard. While this street hasn't caught on like Santa Monica's Main Street (and some think that's just fine), it features an interesting mix of art galleries, antique stores, restaurants, and shops. The surrounding homes and apartments are somewhat run down as the mode of lifestyle here suggests comfort over polish. More recently, some homebuyers, who have to shell out an average of a million dollars for a home, are opting to tear down the old house and start fresh. Rentals, however, especially bungalows, more readily dot the main thoroughfares like Abbot Kinney Boulevard and Pacific Avenue and its side streets.

Each spring, artists open their studios and homes for the Venice Artwalk, an area fundraiser. The Canal Neighborhood, located between Venice and Washington boulevards east of Pacific Avenue, offers a unique and charming living situation. The houses along the canals vary from ramshackle cottages to newly built mini-mansions. Many residents have their own rowboats for tooling through the area, and visiting romantics can even rent a gondola for a little taste of Italy, LA style.

While Venice's proximity to the beach and boardwalk and general outdoor lifestyle are definite pluses, beware that crime here is higher than average, and east of Sixth Avenue is a rough neighborhood called Oakwood. Bounded by California Avenue, Lincoln Boulevard, Rose Avenue, and Abbot Kinney Boulevard, the area is known for gang activity.

As Venice is one of the most popular tourist attractions in California, the City of Los Angeles is addressing the crime situation with increased patrol efforts, especially on weekends.

Web Sites: www.cityofla.org, www.grvnc.org

Area Code: 310, 424

Zip Code: 90291

Post Office: Main Post Office, 1601 Main St; Venice Carrier Annex Station, 313 Grand Blvd

Police District: Pacific Division, 12312 Culver Blvd, 310-482-6334, www.lapd.org

Emergency Hospital: Centinela Freeman Regional Medical Center, 4650 Lincoln Blvd, 310-823-8911, www.centinelafreeman.com

Library: Venice-Abbot Kinney Memorial branch, 501 S Venice Blvd, 310-821-1769, www.lapl.org

Public School Education: LA Unified School District, 333 S Beaudry Ave, LA, 213-241-1000, www.lausd.k12.ca.us

Community Resources: Venice Recreation Center, 1531 Ocean Front Walk, 310-399-2775, www.laparks.org; Westminster Park, 1234 Pacific Ave; Pacific Resident Theatre, 703 Venice Blvd, 310-822-8392, www.pacificresidentthe atre.com; Penmar Recreation Center, 1341 Lake St, 310-396-8735, www.laparks.org

Public Transportation: call 800-COMMUTE or visit www.mta.net for specific Metro bus route and schedule information.

MARINA DEL REY

Boundaries: **North**: Washington St; **East**: Centinela Boulevard; **South**: Ballona Creek; **West**: Santa Monica Bay, Pacific Ocean

Situated around the world's largest manmade small-boat harbor, Marina del Rey has a reputation as a singles area, many of whom enjoy the Marina's waterfront locale and proximity to boating, sailing, windsurfing, water-skiing, tennis, and jogging and bicycling paths. And foodies will appreciate the over 60 sit-down restaurants packed into a two-mile radius, making it a popular evening destination among locals and visitors alike.

In Marina del Rey, the area known as the Marina Peninsula, a strip of land between the ocean and the boat harbor, is composed of streets and walkways that run perpendicular to the beach. Locals use the alphabetically arranged nautical street names, "Anchorage" down to "Yawl," to refer not only to the streets themselves but also to the beaches they abut. The Marina Peninsula offers small condominiums and apartments but has recently seen an explosion of high-rise condos. Upscale mini-mansions are another offering. In fact, real estate is at such a premium here that almost 90% of the residential buildings in Marina del Rey are multi-unit housing. Less than 3% are single detached homes, and these are primarily beach cottages. All are priced over a million dollars.

There is an abundance of modern, high-rise apartments, many built since the 1980s, throughout the rest of Marina del Rey. Gyms, swimming pools, and tennis courts are common features. At the western end of the 90 Freeway, you'll find million-dollar condos offering sweeping views of the city and ocean, complete with the finest amenities within their slender towers. However, it's the **Del Rey Arts District** (bordered by Beach Avenue to the north, Maxella Avenue to the south, Del Rey Avenue to the west, and Redwood Avenue to the east) that more people will find more affordable (at least by LA standards). Formerly full of warehouses, the area now features recently built lofts and condos that have become very trendy among advertising and entertainment industry folk. Overall, housing prices in Marina del Rey lean toward the high end, so many young professionals fresh out of college team up here as housemates.

Web Sites: www.cityofla.org, www.visitmarina.com
Area Code: 310, 424
Zip Code: 90292
Post Office: Marina del Rey branch, 4766 Admiralty Way
Police District: Pacific Division, 12312 Culver Blvd, 310-482-6334, www.lapd.org.
Emergency Hospital: Centinela Freeman Regional Medical Center, 4650 Lincoln Blvd, 310-823-8911, www.centinelafreeman.com

Library: Marina del Rey branch, 4533 Admiralty Way, 310-821-3415, www.cola publib.org

Public School Education: LA Unified School District, 333 S Beaudry Ave, LA, 213-241-1000, www.lausd.k12.ca.us

Community Resources: Fisherman's Village, 13723 Fiji Way, 310-301-6000; UCLA Marina Aquatic Center, 14001 Fiji Way, 310-823-0048, www.marinaaquatic center.org; LA County's Department of Beaches and Harbors, 13837 Fiji Way, 310-305-9504, http://beaches.co.la.ca.us

Public Transportation: call 800-COMMUTE or visit www.mta.net for Metro bus route and schedule information.

PLAYA DEL REY

Boundaries: North: Ballona Creek; **East**: Lincoln Boulevard; **South**: Manchester Avenue; **West**: Pacific Ocean

Tucked in between Marina del Rey and LAX, residents say Playa del Rey (Spanish for "King's Beach") is their little private hideaway. Isolated from the rest of Los Angeles by wetlands and featuring a shack-style downtown strip of mom-and-pop restaurants and shops, Playa del Rey has the feel of a small California beach town. Since there are no public parking lots and street parking is limited, the beaches here are relatively uncrowded, even during the hot summer months.

Housing in Playa del Rey is approximately 45% owner-occupied and 55% renter-occupied. **Lower Playa del Rey** consists of the few streets right along the beach, and features mostly modern townhomes, condominiums, and apartments. Heading east on Manchester Avenue is **Upper Playa del Rey**, and with the exception of some housing that offers magnificent views, this residential area is considered a bit less desirable than the spots right down by the water. On the other hand, if you're looking to rent or buy a house, you'll have more opportunities in this upper area. Another plus, homes here tend to be newer than those found in other communities; many were built in the 1980s.

Playa del Rey is located just north of LAX, a fact that can be a plus or minus, depending on your needs. Frequent travelers will appreciate the easy commute to the airport, but the noise, especially in Upper Playa del Rey, can be a nuisance. Plus, talk of LAX expansion, which would encroach on this area, surfaces every so often. On the eastern border of this community is the Catholic Loyola Marymount University. Founded in 1865, it is the first college built in Los Angeles, and it offers entertainment and educational opportunities to the public. Golf fans will notice the Westchester Golf Course is also adjacent.

Prospective residents might also like to know that Playa del Rey is the site of the Hyperion Treatment Plant, a sewage treatment facility at 12000 Vista del Mar. The Department of Public Works assures that state-of-the-art technology is used both to monitor the environmental impact of the plant and to maintain safe standards (visit ww.lacity.org/SAN/htp.htm for more information about the plant). If you would like more information on the environmental monitoring of the plant, contact **Heal the Bay**, 310-451-1500, www.healthebay.org, a volunteer organization that monitors the health of the Santa Monica Bay.

For years, there was talk of developing the wetlands, once owned by Howard Hughes, with an office/residential park or movie production facilities such as Dreamworks Studios, but in 2001, the California Wildlife Conservation Board purchased the wetlands to protect it from development, making this nature preserve an effective and now permanent barrier from the rest of the city. The scaled-down development area is now known as **Playa Vista**. This controversial development has ambitious plans to accommodate around 13,000 residents but has been bogged down off and on for years by litigation examining environmental concerns, risk of methane gas, and soil liquefaction fears, all of which have been addressed by the planners. The first phase now houses about 4,000 people in a mix of condos, townhomes, and single-family homes. The second phase, approved by the LA City Council in 2005, plans to create 2,600 new residential units, in addition to office and retail space. The new LA Clippers'Training Center here is expected to open in 2008.

Web Sites: www.cityofla.org, www.co.la.ca.us, www.playavista.com
Area Code: 310, 424
Zip Code: Playa del Rey: 90293; Playa Vista: 90094
Post Office: Playa del Rey branch, 215 Culver Blvd; Playa Vista branch, 7381 La Tijera Blvd
Police District: Pacific Division, 12312 Culver Blvd, 310-482-6334, www.lapd.org
Emergency Hospital: Centinela Freeman Regional Medical Center, 4650 Lincoln Blvd, 310-823-8911, www.centinelafreeman.com
Library: Marina del Rey branch, 4533 Admiralty Way, 310-821-3415, www.cola publib.org
Public School Education: LA Unified School District, 333 S Beaudry Ave, LA, 213-241-1000, www.lausd.k12.ca.us
Community Resources: Loyola Marymount University, Loyola Blvd at W 80th St, 310-338-2700, www.lmu.edu; Del Rey Lagoon Park, 6660 Esplanade; Los Angeles City Department of Recreation and Parks, 213-473-7070, www.laparks. org; Westchester Senior Recreation Center, 8740 Lincoln Blvd, 310-649-3317; Westchester Golf Course, 6900 W Manchester Ave, 310-649-9168, www.west chester.americangolf.com
Public Transportation: call 800-COMMUTE or visit www.mta.net for specific Metro bus route and schedule information.

EL SEGUNDO

Boundaries: **North**: Imperial Highway; **East**: Aviation Boulevard; **South**: Rosecrans Boulevard; **West**: Vista del Mar Boulevard

Located directly south of Los Angeles International Airport and fourteen miles southwest of downtown LA, the city of El Segundo, Spanish for "the second," is so named because in 1911, Standard Oil Company selected it as the site of its second oil refinery. In fact, a 1920s newspaper advertisement described the town as "the Standard Oil payroll city." The 1,000-acre refinery, now run by Chevron USA, is still a major part of El Segundo, encompassing the southwestern quadrant of the city. The rest of the city is 80% zoned for commercial/industrial use and 20% is composed of the tranquil residential enclave west of Sepulveda Boulevard.

In addition to the oil refinery, El Segundo is the long-time home to Mattel Toys, Northrop Grumman, Unocal, and Computer Sciences Corporation. Many people commute to this community to work. In fact, its daytime population exceeds approximately 70,000, compared with its resident population of about 15,000. A 1980s hot spot for aviation and defense industry companies, the Los Angeles Air Force Base (modernized in 2006) and its Space and Missile Systems Center are still based here.

You can expect most of the housing here to be modern—generally built between 1950 and 1980, but rather nondescript. The need for housing by corporate execs wanting to keep their commutes short has pushed home prices higher, but price tags remain cheaper than the surrounding areas. Apartments are rare, but when available are more affordable than most Westside communities. El Segundo residents love the small-town atmosphere and the fact that it has its own school district. However, due to its proximity to LAX, overhead noise can be distracting for those living in the north. Also, intermittent fumes from the Hyperion sewage treatment plant (see section on Playa del Rey) have given the area the nickname "El Stinko." On the upside, big business has provided the community with the means for recreational amenities including The Lakes at El Segundo Golf Course, a recreational park located at East Pine Avenue and Eucalyptus Drive, and the Toyota Sports Center, which features a public ice skating rink. Between Sepulveda and Aviation boulevards on Rosecrans Avenue are a large office park and a movie theater. The city also put some money into improving its downtown in 2003, and Main Street is populated with eateries. Serviced by the 405 San Diego and 105 Century/Glen Anderson freeways and the Metro Green Line, access to the southwestern part of LA and its beaches is second to none.

Web Site: www.elsegundo.org

Area Codes: 310, 424

Zip Code: 90245

Post Offices: El Segundo branch, 200 Main St; Airport Station, 9029 Airport Blvd, Los Angeles

Police District: El Segundo Police Headquarters: 348 Main St, 310-524-2200, www.elsegundo.org/police

Emergency Hospital: Centinela Freeman Regional Medical Center, 4650 Lincoln Blvd, 310-823-8911, www.centinelafreeman.com

Library: El Segundo Public Library, 111 W Mariposa Ave, 310-524-2728; www. elsegundo.org/library

Public School Education: El Segundo Unified School District, 641 Sheldon St, El Segundo, 310-615-2650, www.elsegundousd.com

Community Resources: The Lakes at El Segundo Golf Course, 400 S Sepulveda Blvd, 310-322-0202, www.golfthelakes.com; Recreation Park, E Pine Ave and Eucalyptus Drive; El Segundo Parks and Recreation Department, 310-524-2300, www.elsegundo.org; Toyota Sports Center, 555 N Nash St, 310-535-4400, www.toyotasportscenter.com

Public Transportation: call 800-COMMUTE or visit www.mta.net for specific Metro Green Line and Metro bus route and schedule information.

MANHATTAN BEACH

Boundaries: North: Rosecrans Avenue; **East**: Aviation Boulevard; **South**: Artesia Boulevard; **West**: Pacific Ocean

Manhattan Beach is a clean, affluent beach community. It may be a bit more of a commute to work, but the youthful residents, generally in their thirties, think the beautiful beaches and lively shops, restaurants, and bars are worth the drive.

Upscale beach life here centers around The Strand, a cement promenade popular with skaters, joggers, and walkers, and the South Bay Bicycle Trail, which also runs along the beach. The white sand draws droves of sunbathers and volleyball players, who can choose their game site from among over 100 courts located just steps away from beachfront homes.

A short walk from the city's sandy beach is the vibrant and charming shopping district, centered around Manhattan Avenue and Manhattan Beach Boulevard. The area is densely packed with cafés, bars, bookstores, and clothing shops. Weekend nights can take on the feel of a college town as scores of young hipsters walk the streets to take in the local bar and restaurant scene. Polliwog Park is popular with families for its grassy expanse and children's play areas. The city hosts an annual free catch-and-release fishing derby here. Next door to the park is the Begg Pool.

Housing options near the ocean include quaint beach cottages with porches or balconies that open right onto the sandy strip and multi-unit apartment buildings, most of which were built during the 1950s. Manhattan Beach is on a slight hill, so many parts, especially the district called the Hill Section, boast ocean views. Rents for these units are higher than if not comparable to LA's other beach communities. The area east of Ardmore Avenue, called the Tree Section, is more family oriented, with mostly single-family houses. The trend in recent years has seen the typical homeowner opting to tear down old housing to build a new custom home.

As with many beach communities, residential streets are narrow and parking is impossible, especially on weekends when beachgoers flock to the area. It is important to note that, although Manhattan Beach is located only about 20 miles southwest of downtown Los Angeles, the weekday commute to downtown can be as long as 45 minutes to over an hour, each way. If your job requires a lot of flying, though, Manhattan Beach is conveniently located near LAX.

Web Site: www.ci.manhattan-beach.ca.us

Area Code: 310, 424

Zip Code: 90266

Post Offices: Main Post Office, 1007 N Sepulveda Blvd; Substation, 425 15th St

Police District: Manhattan Beach Police Headquarters, 420 15th St, 310-802-5140, www.citymb.info

Emergency Hospital: (nearest) Little Company of Mary, 4101 Torrance Blvd, Torrance, 310-540-7676, www.lcmhs.org

Library: Main Library, 1320 Highland Ave, 310-545-8595, www.colapublib.org

Public School Education: Manhattan Beach Unified School District, 325 S Peck Ave, Manhattan Beach, 310-318-7345, www.manhattan.k12.ca.us

Community Resources: Marine Avenue Park, Marina Ave and Redondo Ave; Live Oak Park, N Valley Drive and 21st St; Polliwog Park, Manhattan Beach Blvd and N Peck Ave; Manhattan Beach Parks & Recreation Department, 310-802-5410, www.ci.manhattan-beach.ca.us; Begg Pool, 1402 N Peck Ave, 310-802-5428; Manhattan Village Mall, 3200 N Sepulveda Blvd, 310-426-6313, www.shop manhattanvillage.com.

Public Transportation: call 800-COMMUTE or visit www.mta.net for specific Metro bus route and schedule information.

INGLEWOOD

Boundaries: North: 64th Street; **East**: Van Ness Avenue; **South**: Imperial Highway; **West**: 405 Freeway

Sports fans remember the City of Inglewood as the home of The Great Western Forum (at Prairie Avenue and Manchester Boulevard), the original site of the Los Angeles Lakers, Kings, and Clippers before their move to the Staples Center downtown. In late 2000, the Great Western Forum was purchased by the Faithful Central Bible Church of Inglewood to provide Sunday worship services to its 10,000-member, primarily African-American, congregation. The church continues to allow concerts and other entertainment events to book the Forum, now called the LA Forum. Inglewood is also the site of the Hollywood Park horse race track and casino. Planes departing and approaching nearby LAX are quite apparent, and security bars and gates are a must in this urban neighborhood. The eastern side, called Morningside Park (between Hyde Park and Century Boulevard), is generally thought of as more secure with its gated streets. A handful of multi-unit apartment buildings are also located here. It's recommended that potential renters locate vacancies that include secured parking.

Housing in Inglewood consists of two- and three-bedroom homes, the majority built between 1940 and 1960. Some neighborhood streets seem to be waging an ongoing fight with graffiti and litter; others are much neater and tidier. An exciting development, appropriately called Inglewood Renaissance, is on Pincay Drive, between Crenshaw Boulevard and Prairie Avenue. Adjacent to the Hollywood Park Racetrack, the area features over 350 new homes that started construction in 2005. The city has also made a concentrated spruce-up effort to draw more commercial office developments along the Century Boulevard corridor.

Downtown Inglewood is centered around the shopping district of Market Street and Manchester Avenue, offering day-to-day amenities such as grocery stores, pharmacies, and hair salons. The largest patch of green in the community is the Inglewood Park Cemetery, located to the north of the racetrack. The 405 San Diego Freeway borders the western edge, and the relatively new 105 Transit Highway, which is elevated above Inglewood, creates an unwelcome forest of concrete pillars along Inglewood's southern border.

Web Site: www.cityofinglewood.org, www.inglewood.now

Area Code: 310, 424

Zip Codes: 90301–5

Post Offices: Main Post Office, 300 E Hillcrest Blvd; Lennox branch, 4443 Lennox Blvd; Morningside Park Station, 3212 W 85th St; North Station, 811 N La Brea Ave

Police District: Inglewood Police headquarters, 1 Manchester Blvd, 310-412-5200, www.inglewoodpd.org

Emergency Hospital: Centinela Freeman Regional Medical Center, 4650 Lincoln Blvd, 310-823-8911, www.centinelafreeman.com

Libraries: Main Library, 101 W Manchester Blvd, 310-412-5380; Crenshaw-Imperial branch, 11141 Crenshaw Blvd, 310-412-5403; Morningside Park branch, 3202 W 85th St; 310-412-5400, www.cityofinglewood.org/depts/library

Public School Education: Inglewood Unified School District, 401 S Inglewood Ave, Inglewood, 310-419-2700, www.inglewood.k12.ca.us

Community Resources: Hollywood Park Racetrack and Casino, 1050 S Prairie Ave, 310-419-1500, www.hollywoodpark.com; Centinela Park, 700 Warren Lane; Rogers Park, N Oak St and N Eucalyptus Ave; Inglewood Parks and Recreation Department, 310-412-8750, www.cityofinglewood.org; Centinela Adobe Complex, 7643 Midfield, 310-412-8750; Inglewood Senior Citizens Center, 111 N Locust St, 310-412-5338

Public Transportation: call 800-COMMUTE or visit www.mta.net for specific Metro Green Line and Metro bus route and schedule information.

MAR VISTA, PALMS, CHEVIOT HILLS

Boundaries: North: 10 Santa Monica Freeway; **East**: Motor Avenue; **South**: Venice Boulevard; **West**: 405 Freeway

Located within the City of LA, Mar Vista and Palms, just northwest of Culver City, attract those looking for reasonably priced housing (for the Westside), both for rent and purchase. These more urban neighborhoods with Spanish exteriors may not be as well manicured as nearby pricier communities, but many young, ethnically diverse families appreciate the break on their pocketbook. This easy-to-access Westside location not only offers plenty to choose from in terms of housing, but its small commercial center with a good selection of neighborhood restaurants and easy shopping along Motor Avenue is popular with the locals as well.

Palms is the oldest community on the Westside; the first streets were laid down in 1886. The Palms Depot first served the Southern Pacific Railroad and then the Pacific Electric Railway. In the 1920s, Laurel and Hardy often filmed their comedy flicks in Palms, using its famous Red Cars on the railroad as a backdrop. Over time, this historic depot, a rare example of that period's Victorian "Eastlake" style architecture, fell into disrepair, but in 1975 it was moved to and restored by the Heritage Square Museum. Today, this modest middle-class town offers mostly rental housing in an urban setting. The Metro Expo Line, once it opens in 2010, will connect Palms to downtown.

Between Palms and **Mar Vista**, the latter is more geared toward family living, offering a bigger selection of single-family homes and fewer apartment buildings. Affordable home prices in Mar Vista attract many young families. A few streets running atop the hill in Mar Vista boast ocean and city views. As evidence of the population in this area, the lovely Mar Vista Park at McLaughlin and Palms is usually filled with families (or kids with nannies). The park's recreation department caters to children, offering summer camps, gym classes, and toddler programs.

The Santa Monica Airport, which sits on the northern border of Mar Vista, can be a noise nuisance. (Those viewing Mar Vista should know that many people often confuse this neighborhood with the housing project located west of Culver City called Mar Vista Gardens.)

Venice Boulevard, the southernmost boundary for both Palms and Mar Vista, is a commercial strip seemingly overflowing with businesses where you can find everything from ethnic food to discount futons to auto parts. A short drive or walk north on Motor Avenue just under the 10 Freeway leads to lovely **Cheviot Hills**, a hilly residential enclave of mostly vintage Southern California homes. Continuing north on Motor Avenue will lead to the popular Cheviot Hills Park, offering 14 lit tennis courts, archery, swimming, basketball courts, and baseball diamonds, and to Rancho Park, reputed to be one of the busiest public golf courses in the country. Motor Avenue continues north into the Twentieth Century Fox studio lot, and although it's closed to the public, you may spot the old movie set street from *Hello, Dolly* as you drive by.

Web Sites: www.palms-california.us, www.cityofla.org, www.co.la.ca.us

Area Code: 310, 424

Zip Code: 90034

Post Offices: Mar Vista Station, 3826 Grand View Blvd; Palms Station, 3751 Motor Ave

Police District: Pacific Division, 12312 Culver Blvd, 310-482-6334, www.lapd.org

Emergency Hospital: Brotman Medical Center, 3828 Delmas Terr, Culver City, 310-836-7000, www.brotmanmedicalcenter.com

Libraries: Mar Vista branch, 12006 Venice Blvd, 310-390-3454; Palms-Rancho Park Library, 2920 Overland Ave, 310-840-2142; www.lapl.org

Public School Education: LA Unified School District, 333 S Beaudry Ave, LA, 213-241-1000, www.lausd.k12.ca.us

Community Resources: Mar Vista Recreation Center, 11430 Woodbine St, 310-398-5982; Palms Recreation Center, 2950 Overland Ave, 310-838-3838; Cheviot Hills Park and Recreation Center, 2551 Motor Ave, 310-837-5186, www.laparks.org; Rancho Park Golf Course, 10460 W Pico Blvd, 310-838-7373; Hillcrest Country Club, 10000 W Pico Blvd, 310-553-8911

Public Transportation: call 800-COMMUTE or go to www.mta.net for specific Metro bus routes and schedule information. Santa Monica's Municipal Big Blue Bus has lines in the area; call 310-451-5444, www.bigbluebus.com for route and schedule information. For the Culver City Municipal Bus Line, call 310-253-6510, www.culvercity.org/bus/bus.asp

CULVER CITY

Boundaries: North: Venice Boulevard; **East**: Jefferson Boulevard; **South**: Slauson Avenue; **West**: 405 Freeway

Culver City is the original and current home to several major movie studios, including the landmark site of Metro-Goldwyn-Mayer (now the location of Raintree Plaza mall). Such movie classics as *Citizen Kane, King Kong, ET,* and the scene of Atlanta burning in *Gone with the Wind* were all filmed on the lots of Culver City movie studios. Today Sony Pictures and several other major film and television producers are located here.

Though only five square miles and bordered on all sides by parts of LA, Culver City is its own municipal entity. It is bisected by Ballona Creek, which empties into the Pacific Ocean. The majority of Culver City is zoned for commercial, industrial, and light industrial business; however, those looking to reside here can find pockets of single-family homes. The majority of homes are simple, two- or three-bedroom homes, generally built between 1950 and 1980. Because Culver City did not begin developing until the 1940s, homes in this community are newer than those in many other Los Angeles neighborhoods. Apartment rentals are pricey due to its Westside location, but are less than what might be found in Santa Monica.

The lively commercial district of Culver City has over three million square feet of shopping space. Retailers include the 140-store Fox Hills Mall, a handful of auto dealerships, and the historic Helms Bakery Building (which houses furniture retailer HD Buttercup). The city has recently become an art destination—the Culver City Art District, clustered along La Cienega Boulevard between Venice and Washington boulevards, is packed with galleries. As a workplace hub, the old industrial area known as the Hayden Tract, located between National Boulevard and Higuera Street and north of Ballona Creek, now consists of a collection of art and design studios, high-tech marketing firms, and architecture offices. Two unique buildings designed by award-winning architect Eric Owen Moss, one on National Boulevard and another on Hayden Avenue, have also focused attention on this area for their eye-catching appearance.

On weekends, residents take to the sidewalk cafés and retail stores along Washington Boulevard, while kids head to the Culver City Skateboard Park or Culver Ice Arena. Dog owners, with pooches in tow, head to "the boneyard," the city's only off-leash dog park. Both the skateboard and dog parks are located within the 45-acre Culver City Park. During the weekday, the wide thoroughfares of Venice, Washington, and Culver boulevards provide alternatives to the 10 Santa Monica Freeway into Marina del Rey and Santa Monica. After rush hour, when Culver City's daytime workforce population has left, area residents are able to enjoy a less hurried pace.

Web Site: www.ci.culver-city.ca.us, www.ccgalleryguide.com

Area Code: 310, 424

Zip Code: 90230, 90232

Post Offices: Main Post Office, 11111 Jefferson Blvd; Gateway Station, 9942 Culver Blvd

Police District: Culver City Police headquarters, 4040 Duquesne Ave, 310-837-1221, www.culvercity.org/police/police.asp

Emergency Hospital: Brotman Medical Center, 3828 Delmas Terr, 310-836-7000, www.brotmanmedicalcenter.com

Library: Culver City Library, 4975 Overland Ave, 310-559-1676, www.colapublib.org

Public School Education: Culver City Unified School District, 4034 Irving Place, Culver City, 310-842-4220, www.ccusd.k12.ca.us

Community Resources: Veterans Memorial Park, 4417 Overland Ave; Culver City Park, Duquesne Ave and Jefferson Blvd, 310-558-8638; Culver City Recreation Department, 310-253-6650, www.culvercity.org; Culver City Dog Park, www.culvercitydogpark.org; Culver City Skateboard Park, 310-558-8638

Public Transportation: for the Culver City Municipal Bus Line, call 310-253-6510 or visit www.culvercity.org/depts_bus.html. Call 800-COMMUTE, or visit www.mta.net for specific Metro bus route and schedule information. Santa Monica's Big Blue Bus has lines in the area; call 310-451-5444, www.bigblue bus.com for route and schedule information.

WEST LOS ANGELES

Boundaries: **North**: Santa Monica Boulevard; **East**: Beverly Glen Boulevard; **South**: Pico Boulevard; **West**: Centinela Avenue

While still centrally located on the Westside, the area known as West LA tends to be less expensive than nearby Westwood, Brentwood, and Santa Monica. Here, the streets are more urban, dotted with convenience shops, gas stations, and strip malls, many of which could use a new coat of paint.

Housing stock mainly consists of bunched together, nondescript, three-story apartments dating from the 1960s and '70s. Many do not have air conditioners, though the air is cooler here, with the ocean just a stone's throw away in the beach community of Santa Monica. Like much of Los Angeles, new condo developments have been dotting the area. One of the tallest mixed-use residential buildings on the Westside, once completed, will be a 25-story condo building at Wilshire Boulevard and Barrington Avenue. Traditionally, most renters rely on street parking, but some buildings provide back-alley parking spaces, though many are not gated. The positives for this Westside location include convenient access to major freeways, including the 10 Santa Monica and 405 San Diego, and mid-range rental rates. The area certainly makes up for in affordability what it lacks in architectural charm, creating a good choice for people on a budget who want to live on the Westside.

Aficionados of Japanese food and culture should check out Sawtelle Boulevard north of Olympic Boulevard, where a number of Japanese restaurants, groceries, and Japanese-owned nurseries can be found. Also worth a visit is the funky Art Deco movie house called the Nuart (on Santa Monica Boulevard just west of the 405 Freeway), which features foreign and alternative films, plus a weekly Saturday midnight showing of *The Rocky Horror Picture Show*.

Parents will enjoy the greenspace in Westwood Park, which features two playgrounds, playing fields, and picnic tables. Shoppers from all over come to West LA, the locale of two major malls. The indoor Westside Pavilion mall offers typical shopping amenities, plus a 2007 expansion added a 12-screen movie theater with a wine lounge. The upscale outdoor Westfield Century City mall is currently undergoing a remodel and redesign. It caters to a fashion-conscious crowd and even offers valet parking. The Century City mall's movie theater complex is especially popular with Westsiders and is frequently sold out on weekends. The weekday lunch crowd—business-suited men and women from the nearby work district (heavy in the entertainment and law fields)—frequents the mall's food court.

According to recent demographic statistics by the US Census Bureau, the Westside comprises only 3% of Los Angeles County's total land area, yet 7% of the county's population and 13% of the county's jobs are in this coveted part of town—explaining why the bordering 405 San Diego Freeway is such a heavily used (and frequently clogged) thoroughfare.

Web Sites: www.cityofla.org, www.co.la.ca.us

Area Code: 310, 424

Zip Code: 90025

Post Offices: West Los Angeles branch, 11420 Santa Monica Blvd; West Los Angeles branch, 11270 Exposition Blvd Fl. 2; Village Station, 11000 Wilshire Blvd; Westside Pavilion, 10800 W Pico Blvd #389

Police District: West Los Angeles Division, 1663 Butler Ave, 310-575-8402, www.lapd.org

Emergency Hospital: UCLA Medical Center, 10833 LeConte Ave, 310-825-9111, www.uclahealth.org

Library: West Los Angeles branch, 11360 Santa Monica Blvd, 310-575-8323, www.lapl.org

Public School Education: LA Unified School District, 333 S Beaudry Ave, LA, 213-241-1000, www.lausd.k12.ca.us

Community Resources: Westwood Park, 1350 S Sepulveda Blvd; Los Angeles City Department of Recreation and Parks, 213-473-7070, www.laparks.org; Westside Pavilion Shopping Mall, Overland Ave and Ayres Ave, 310-474-6255, www.westsidepavilion.com; Westfield Century City, 10250 Santa Monica Blvd, 310-277-3898, www.westfield.com

Public Transportation: call 800-COMMUTE or visit www.mta.net for specific Metro bus route and schedule information. Santa Monica's Big Blue Bus has lines in the area; call 310-451-5444, www.bigbluebus.com for route and schedule information.

BRENTWOOD

Boundaries: North: Sunset Boulevard; **East**: 405 Freeway; **South**: Wilshire Boulevard; **West**: Centinela Avenue

The lushly planted, upscale Brentwood exudes prestige for those with the means to live here. Brentwood's central position on the Westside and numerous apartment buildings make it a natural choice for new and established professionals. What this community may lack in character, it makes up for with a vanilla-safe environment. Running through Brentwood's center, the busy coral tree–lined San Vicente Boulevard offers brand-name clothiers, upscale restaurants, bookstores, coffee shops, and gourmet groceries. The boulevard also acts as a divider for area residences, with houses located to the north of it, and stylish contemporary apartments and condominiums to the south. The northwestern-most part, called Brentwood Circle, is an affluent, gated residential area of palatial homes on shady streets. Go south of Sunset, west of the 405, and you'll find a neighborhood called Brentwood Glen, featuring more modest houses and apartments. Multiple bedrooms, i.e., more than three, are typical in these custom homes tucked on quiet streets that curve through hills. These hillside residences translate into big price tags (often in the millions). Higher-end rent also applies to Brentwood's apartments.

The area around Brentwood Village, the quaint shopping area where Barrington Avenue meets Sunset Boulevard, includes the Brentwood Country Mart, cafés, bakeries, hair salons, a post office, and park. Many joggers and dog walkers especially love the wide, grassy median that makes up San Vicente Boulevard, which, for the truly motivated, will take exercisers all the way west to the coastline in Santa Monica.

Brentwood is also home to the Getty Center, a billion-dollar "campus" of buildings housing, among other art-related programs and institutions, the late J. Paul Getty's collection of European antiquities and art. Designed by noted architect Richard Meier, the mountain-top museum has been a hit with locals and visitors alike who are treated to a great view of the 405 San Diego Freeway in a meandering electric tram ride up the mountain.

Proximity to the 405, the main north/south artery in and out of Brentwood, can be both a blessing and a curse. Commuters spill over from the frequently sardine-packed 405 into Sepulveda Boulevard and nearby parallel streets in a mad dash to trim minutes from their rush-hour drive.

Web Sites: www.cityofla.org, www.co.la.ca.us

Area Code: 310, 424

Zip Code: 90049

Post Office: Brentwood Main Office, 18 Oak St; Barrington Station, 200 S Barrington Ave

Police District: West Los Angeles Division, 1663 Butler Ave, 310-575-8402, www.lapd.org

Emergency Hospital: UCLA Medical Center, 10833 LeConte Ave, 310-825-9111, www.uclahealth.org

Library: Brentwood branch–Donald Bruce Kauffman Library, 11820 San Vicente Blvd, 310-575-8273, www.lapl.org

Public School Education: LA Unified School District, 333 S Beaudry Ave, LA, 213 241-1000, www.lausd.k12.ca.us

Community Resources: The Getty Center, 1200 Getty Center Dr, 310-440-7300, www.getty.edu; Barrington Recreation Center, 333 S Barrington Ave, 310-476-3866, www.laparks.org; Brentwood Country Club, 590 Burlingame Ave,

310-451-8011; Los Angeles City Department of Recreation and Parks, 213-473-7070, www.laparks.org

Public Transportation: call 800-COMMUTE, or visit www.mta.net for specific Metro bus route and schedule information. Santa Monica's Big Blue Bus has lines in the area; call 310-451-5444, www.bigbluebus.com for route and schedule information.

WESTWOOD

Boundaries: North: Sunset Boulevard; **East**: Beverly Glen Boulevard; **South**: Santa Monica Boulevard; **West**: 405 Freeway

South of the tony hills of Bel Air lies Westwood, most famous for being the home of the University of California Los Angeles (UCLA). The area around the campus is filled with fraternities, sororities, and student-inhabited apartment buildings, but non-students also enjoy the proximity to Westwood Village's many shops, restaurants, and movie theaters, as well as the sporting and cultural events held on campus.

Westwood doesn't quite hum with the same amount of enthusiasm as in its heyday in the eighties, but this college town has a healthy nightlife that's supported by plenty of twenty-somethings. That must explain the dense population of big-screen movie theaters here. In fact, many feature films make their star-studded debut here.

Apartment rentals in Westwood are expensive due to the student population's voracious need for housing. Especially during the school year, it is not unusual for students to double up in a one-bedroom, or bunk four to a two-bedroom.

For those newcomers to Westwood with a car and no garage, a word of warning: hunting down street parking in Westwood requires diligence and a lot of patience. And beware the meter maids—Westwood has some of the quickest ticket writers in the county.

In the northern portion of Westwood, you'll find custom-built homes along winding, eucalyptus-lined streets, many on culs-de-sac. With the exception of the city's meticulously groomed National Cemetery located between Veteran Avenue and the 405 Sepulveda Freeway, Westwood is surrounded by affluence. The Bel Air Country Club lies just to the north, the Los Angeles Country Club and posh neighborhood of Holmby Hills are to the east, and the slick outdoor shopping mall, Century City Center, is to the south. The price of comfort and convenience isn't cheap; housing prices are on par with Santa Monica.

Prices ease up a bit as you move farther away from campus, especially going south toward the 10 Santa Monica Freeway. There's a little less green (both the kind you grow and the kind you earn) found south of Wilshire Boulevard, the trade-offs here being cheaper housing and easier parking. As you head closer to

Los Angeles, apartments and houses are still modern and clean, but mingle with commercial zones, making for heavier traffic. Many professionals and singles reside and work in the area. Also in the southern part of Westwood Boulevard is "Little Persia." You'll find a cluster of Persian restaurants and stores dotting this street.

The Federal Office Building, where many of the city's federal offices are housed, is at Wilshire and Sepulveda boulevards, and the high-profile Getty Museum is a stone's throw across the 405 Sepulveda Freeway in neighboring Brentwood. The always congested 405 has been undergoing an expansion through this area, and commuters will have to deal with the construction until at least 2009.

Web Sites: www.cityofla.org, www.co.la.ca.us

Area Code: 310, 424

Zip Code: 90024

Post Offices: Wilshire branch, 10920 Wilshire Blvd Ste. 150; UCLA Medical branch, 308 Westwood Plaza; Village Station, 11000 Wilshire Blvd

Police District: West Los Angeles Division, 1663 Butler Ave, 310-575-8402, www.lapd.org

Emergency Hospital: UCLA Medical Center, 10833 LeConte Ave, 310-825-9111, www.uclahealth.org

Library: West Los Angeles branch, 11360 Santa Monica Blvd, 310-575-8323

Public School Education: LA Unified School District, 333 S Beaudry Ave, LA, 213-241-1000, www.lausd.k12.ca.us

Community Resources: Westwood Park, 1350 S Sepulveda Blvd; Holmby Park, 601 Club View Drive; Los Angeles City Department of Recreation and Parks, 213-473-7070, www.laparks.org; Los Angeles Country Club, 10101 Wilshire Blvd, 310-276-6104; UCLA-Armand Hammer Museum, 10889 Wilshire Blvd, 310-443-7000, www.hammer.ucla.edu

Public Transportation: call 800-COMMUTE or go to www.mta.net for specific Metro bus route and schedule information. Santa Monica's Big Blue Bus has lines in the area; call 310-451-5444 or visit www.bigbluebus.com for route and schedule information. LADOT also operates here; call 310-808-2273 or visit www.ladottransit.com for commuter route and schedule information.

BEVERLY HILLS

TROUSDALE ESTATES

BEL AIR ESTATES

Boundaries: **North**: hills above Sunset Boulevard; **East**: Doheny Drive; **South**: Whitworth Drive; **West**: Whittier Drive

The above boundaries are rough outlines of Beverly Hills—residents are very particular about what constitutes a Beverly Hills address. There's even something called "Beverly Hills P.O.," which refers to areas that may not look as meticulously groomed as Beverly Hills, but fall within the coveted Beverly Hills postal code, therefore entitling such residents to the city's civic amenities. Even the popular networking internet site MySpace is headquartered here. One reason that locals are so concerned about who's in and who's out is that, as its own city, and a well-funded one at that, Beverly Hills' municipal services (police, fire, public education, etc.) are considered top notch in Los Angeles County. Even the well-stocked Beverly Hills public library requires its patrons have library cards (that are gold-colored, by the way) separate from the Los Angeles Public Library's system.

With a worldwide reputation as the home of the rich and famous, the many multi-bedroomed residences in the Beverly Hills housing market feature hefty price tags. The tree-rich **Trousdale Estates** is another exclusive community of custom-built homes tucked in the winding hills north of Beverly Hills, and **Bel Air Estates** sports mansions nestled in canyon country to the west. Apartments, though similar in look and style to much of West Los Angeles (i.e., Spanish stucco), are harder to find and understandably pricier too. Tenacious bargain hunters may find more affordable pricing in the area known as "below the tracks." Though long since removed, train tracks once ran through Beverly Hills along Santa Monica Boulevard, and the site serves to demarcate the high rent from the not-so-high rent district of the city.

Downtown Beverly Hills (including the famous Rodeo Drive) starts south of Santa Monica Boulevard and continues south to Wilshire Boulevard. Along Wilshire Boulevard are high-rise office buildings, large upscale department stores (Neiman Marcus, Saks Fifth Avenue), and the stately Four Seasons Beverly Wilshire Hotel. South of Wilshire Boulevard is the area where more affordable apartments and flats are located. The majority of these buildings were constructed before the 1940s, and many offer hardwood floors and molded ceilings. Harder to find but worth hunting for are the gatehouses and apartments over garages that are part of many of the Beverly Hills homes in "the flats," the palm tree–lined residential streets between Sunset and Santa Monica boulevards, and to a lesser extent in the hills above Sunset Boulevard.

Beverly Hills streets are kept clean and have strict parking rules that nearly fill the length of the lampposts on which they're posted. No freeways are immediately accessible from Beverly Hills, which means surface streets such as Wilshire Boulevard and Santa Monica Boulevard serve as surrogate freeways in and out of this city—preserving the exclusivity of the neighborhood, just the way residents like it.

For housing leads in Beverly Hills try the classifieds in the local *Beverly Hills Courier* (310-278-1322, www.thebeverlyhillscourier.com).

Web Sites: www.beverlyhills.org
Area Codes: 310, 424

Zip Codes: 90210–2

Post Offices: Main Post Office, 325 N Maple Drive; Crescent branch, 323 N Crescent Drive; Beverly branch, 312 S Beverly Drive;

Police District: Beverly Hills Police headquarters, 464 N Rexford Drive, 310-550-4951, www.beverlyhills.org

Emergency Hospital: Cedars-Sinai Medical Center, 8700 Beverly Blvd, 310-423-3277, www.csmc.edu

Library: Beverly Hills Library, 444 N Rexford Drive, 310-288-2220, www.beverlyhills.org

Public School Education: Beverly Hills Unified School District, 255 S Lasky Drive, Beverly Hills, 310-551-5100, www.bhusd-facilities.org

Community Resources: Beverly Hills parking permits, 310-285-2548; La Cienega Park Community Center, 8400 Gregory Way, 310-550-4625; Roxbury Park Community Center, 471 S Roxbury Drive, 310-550-4761; Beverly Gardens Park, Santa Monica Blvd and Beverly Drive, 310-285-2537, www.beverlyhills.org

Public Transportation: call 800-COMMUTE or go to www.mta.net for specific Metro bus route and schedule information.

NEIGHBORHOODS — EAST

WEST HOLLYWOOD

Boundaries: North: Sunset Boulevard (to the west), Fountain Avenue (to the east); **East:** La Brea Avenue; **South:** Beverly Boulevard (to the west), Willoughby Avenue (to the east); **West:** Doheny Drive

Although only 1.9 square miles in size with 37,000+ residents, West Hollywood proudly displays public art and rainbow flags along a median down Santa Monica Boulevard. The city is well known for its gay and lesbian community, particularly on the western side. The area is also home to a large Jewish community and a Russian immigrant population that both cluster on the southern and eastern borders. Jewish immigrants were the first group to come to the area, spilling west from the Fairfax District where they had settled after World War II. The gay community was next to discover "WeHo." Some were attracted to the growing design community here and others by the relative security of living in this then-unincorporated area in LA County, which was under the jurisdiction of the county sheriff and not the Los Angeles Police Department (said to frequently raid gay clubs).

On a stroll through Plummer Park on Santa Monica Boulevard, you can see the mosaic of neighbors who make up the area. As an example of how the local government is responsive to its citizenry, West Hollywood was the first US city to declare Yom Kippur (the Jewish Day of Atonement) a legal holiday, and the social and politically minded residents of this community were responsible for paving

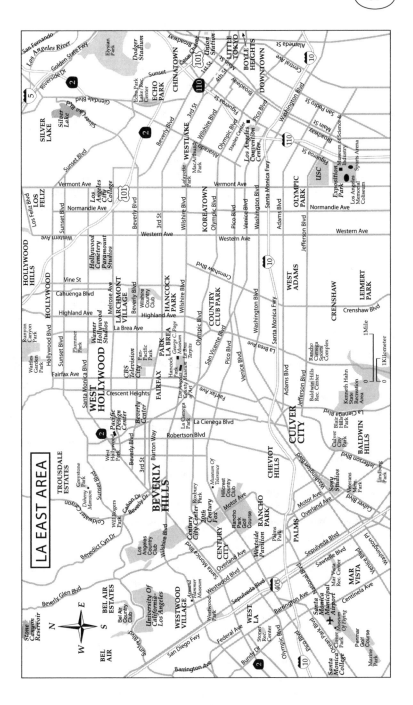

the way to outlaw discrimination against people with AIDS. One weekend every June the city plays host to one of the largest gay pride festivals in the country.

Residents enjoy numerous amenities in this pedestrian-friendly city, including chic shopping and dining, and the beautiful Spanish-style architecture that graces many West Hollywood streets. Santa Monica Boulevard runs the length of the city and has a business base as diverse as the community itself. On the western end of the street there are many retail stores, cafés, and nightclubs catering to the GLBT (gay, lesbian, bisexual, and transsexual) community. A burgeoning group of gyms and related fitness and beauty businesses have transformed the area near city hall into Health Row. East of Fairfax Avenue, radiating from the boulevard, you can see the entrepreneurial efforts of and residences to West Hollywood's thriving immigrant community. Head south to Melrose, between Fairfax Avenue and Doheny Drive, you'll find many more trendy retailers including Elixir Tonic & Teas, 8612 Melrose Avenue, which features a lab-coated Asian herbalist concocting restorative tonics.

West Hollywood is also the site of the Pacific Design Center (www.pacificdesigncenter.com, note it is only open to professional interior designers), a huge collection (1.2 million square feet) of interior design showrooms that anchors the myriad interior decorating businesses along Melrose, Beverly, and Robertson boulevards. The center itself is affectionately known as "the blue whale," due to the large scale and bright blue hue of the original building. Added later was an equally large and bright green building, Center Green, with even more showrooms. Farther south on La Cienega Boulevard is the chic Beverly Center, a multi-level indoor mall, and its humbler sister the Beverly Connection, a smaller outdoor mall.

The northernmost part of West Hollywood features some of the trendiest sites on Sunset Boulevard, including nightclubs like House of Blues, Whisky a Go Go, and The Laugh Factory. On weekend nights you'll find this section of the Boulevard choked with traffic and exhausted car valets as club-goers cruise the scene, hoping for a peep through the windows of Larry Flynt's Hustler Hollywood. Farther west is Sunset Plaza, a tony strip of sidewalk cafés and designer label retailers, where celebrity sightings are not unusual.

Clean and well-tended apartments and condominiums make up the majority of residences lining the leafy streets radiating out from the night scene section of Santa Monica Boulevard. The buildings are a mix of older Spanish-style homes and the modern but boxy three- to four-story stuccos. A handful of retirement/assisted living apartments are also located in the area.

While the "vacancy decontrol," phased-in in 1996 by the Costa-Hawkins bill (which allows landlords to raise rent in a previously rent-controlled apartment to market value, after a tenant vacates the apartment), is in effect for all of California, including West Hollywood, prospective renters will be interested to know that the City of West Hollywood has a strict and intricate rent control law that regulates the maximum percentage (typically around 1.5% or less) that a landlord may raise rent. This adjustment is based on the consumer price index and is released every July. Rent control does not apply to single-family dwellings, some condominiums, and any apartments that received a certificate of residency after 1979. Apartment vacancies are not difficult to find and the stock of available condominiums is especially healthy. Only 8% of the housing in West Hollywood consists of detached homes. West Hollywood's **Department of Rent Stabilization** publishes a list of residential units available for rent. Call their 24-hour **Rental Referral Service Hotline** 323-848-6419 for more information. Limited street parking dictates the use of parking permits. Weekend parking is made scarcer by Angelenos of all persuasions looking for a night on the town in West Hollywood.

Web Site: www.weho.org

Area Code: 310

Zip Code: 90069

Post Office: West branch, 820 N San Vicente Blvd; Cole branch, 1125 N Fairfax Ave

Police District: West Hollywood contracts with the County of Los Angeles Sheriff's Department, 780 N San Vicente Blvd, 310-855-8850, www.wehosheriff. com.

Emergency Hospital: Cedars-Sinai Medical Center, 8700 Beverly Blvd, 310-423-3277, www.csmc.edu

Library: 715 N San Vicente Blvd, 310-652-5340, www.colapublib.org

Public School Education: LA Unified School District, 333 S Beaudry Ave, LA, 213-241-1000, www.lausd.k12.ca.us

Community Resources: West Hollywood Permit Parking Division, 323-848-6392, www.weho.org; Department of Rent Stabilization, 323-848-6450; www.weho. org; Convention and Visitor Bureau, 800-368-6020, www.visitwesthollywood. com; West Hollywood Recreation Department, 323-848-6308, www.weho. org

Public Transportation: the West Hollywood CityLine/DayLine offers shuttle services within the city of West Hollywood; call 800-447-2189 or 323-848-6375 for specific route and schedule information. Santa Monica's Big Blue Bus services West Los Angeles and Santa Monica; call 310-451-5444 or visit www. bigbluebus.com for route and schedule information. For all other areas, call 800-COMMUTE, or visit www.mta.net for specific Metro bus route and schedule information.

FAIRFAX DISTRICT (MID-WILSHIRE)

Boundaries: North: Willoughby Avenue; **East:** La Brea Avenue; **South:** Pico Boulevard; **West:** La Cienega Boulevard

Long the center of Los Angeles's Orthodox Jewish community, the Fairfax District includes a blend of cultures and lifestyles, including Indian, Ethiopian, African-American, and urban hip mixed in with the daytime office folk. Indeed, Fairfax

Avenue itself is a cultural mish-mash where one can find family-run kosher butchers, Ethiopian restaurants, African artifacts, and Indian spice shops. Even Canter's Delicatessen reflects the diversity of the neighborhood, serving up matzo ball soup to elderly Jewish residents by day while featuring jazz and other music in the adjoining "Kibitz (Yiddish for 'chat') Room" at night.

The Farmers' Market at Fairfax Avenue and Third Street is a favorite for tour bus stops and Fairfax District locals who come for fresh, picture-perfect fruits and vegetables and cafés. It's also a busy lunch spot for business people, especially the nearby television and movie industry executives (CBS's Television City is right next door and the Writers Guild of America is across the street). The Grove, an outdoor pedestrian mall that opened in 2003, is right next door to the Farmers' Market. This bustling mall consists of flagship stores from several major retailers and a 14-screen movie theater with an art deco entrance. Intimate and polished, this upscale mall also features an on-site concierge, a small fountain, and a clanging cable car that transfers tourists and locals the short distance between the mall and market at no charge. A large development of new luxury apartments, The Palazzo at Park La Brea Apartments, has popped up on the other side of Third Street.

A retail district along Third Street between La Cienega Boulevard and Crescent Heights is dotted with new and used clothing and furniture stores, and La Brea Avenue to the east boasts several trendy furniture stores and eateries, as well as some of the area's most well kept Spanish-style apartment buildings along Sycamore Avenue, just east of La Brea. Finally, there is the famous, incense-infused Melrose Avenue. Melrose, on the Hollywood border, is LA's funkiest shopping street and the place to go to find the latest chic fashion and food items. The street's denizens are some of LA's most urban and cutting-edge, with pierces, tattoos, and the latest body art practically *de rigueur*.

Besides the interesting mix of local residents in the Fairfax District, the architecture of much of the housing here is another plus. You can find reasonably priced rentals in everything from multi-unit apartment buildings to small houses. If it's within your budget and you're lucky enough to locate a vacancy, the real gems are the 1920s and '30s duplexes. Usually two-story stuccos, with one unit on the top and another below, many of these duplexes feature such touches as hardwood floors, built-in cabinetry, leaded or stained glass windows, ceramic-tiled bathrooms and kitchens, and spacious rooms. It's typical for the landlord to live in one unit and rent out the other, and often the backyard is available for shared access.

Web Site: www.fairfaxla.com
Area Codes: 310, 213
Zip Codes: 90035, 90211, 90048, 90036, 90019
Post Office: Bicentennial Station, 7610 Beverly Blvd; 5350 Wilshire Blvd

Police District: (north of Beverly Blvd) Hollywood Division, 1358 N Wilcox Ave, 213-485-4302; (south of Beverly Blvd) Wilshire Division, 4861 Venice Blvd, 213-485-4022, www.lapdonline.org

Emergency Hospital: Cedars-Sinai Medical Center, 8700 Beverly Blvd, 310-423-3277, www.csmc.edu

Libraries: Fairfax branch, 161 S Gardner St, 323-936-6191; Wilshire branch, 149 N Saint Andrews Pl, 323-957-4550, www.lapl.org

Public School Education: LA Unified School District, 333 S Beaudry Ave, Los Angeles, 213-241-1000, www.lausd.k12.ca.us

Community Resources: Parking Permits, 310-843-5936, www.lacity-parking.org; Wiltern Theatre, 3790 Wilshire Blvd, 213-380-5005; Kodak Theatre, 6801 Hollywood Blvd, 323-308-6300, www.kodaktheatre.com; The Grove, 189 The Grove Drive, 323-900-8080, www.thegrovela.com; Los Angeles City Department of Recreation and Parks, 213-473-7070, www.laparks.org

Public Transportation: call 800-COMMUTE, or visit www.mta.net for specific Metro bus route and schedule information.

HANCOCK PARK

LARCHMONT VILLAGE

Boundaries: North: Melrose Avenue; **East**: Western Avenue; **South**: Wilshire Boulevard; **West**: La Brea Avenue

Hancock Park is noted for its rolling, well-groomed front lawns and stately pre–WW II homes, previous residences of Los Angeles's powerful elite. Some of the area's oldest and grandest homes may be viewed here. Hardwood floors and built-in cabinetry are typical features of homes in this area. The posh Wilshire Country Club begins just north of Third Street, and residents enjoy the proximity to the business district along Wilshire Boulevard. Miracle Mile, as the boulevard is called, was developed during the 1930s when art deco was in its heyday, and many buildings display this historical architectural influence. However buildings like the Wiltern Theater, preserved in all its art deco glory, are slowly giving way to modern developments. The LA County Museum of Art has been purchasing neighboring buildings for expansion, and their Broad Contemporary Art Museum just opened in 2008. Tony Beverly Hills is located to the west, much to the delight of "shopaholics." And for all you bread lovers, the La Brea Bakery, 624 South La Brea Avenue, is known for its artisan breads, including a fresh baked chocolate cherry creation, and scrumptious rectangular toasting bread. Banks, gas stations, and bus stops are conveniently dotted throughout the area. Hancock Park is popular with Jewish families, and a number of orthodox and conservative synagogues are located within walking distance.

Bordered by Koreatown to the east and Mid-City to the south, Hancock Park offers homes that are a little less expensive than what can be found on the Westside. Pricey modern apartments are clustered in Park La Brea, a gated and grassy community just east of Hancock Park. Parking within Hancock Park is never easy for visitors as many streets are restricted and require permits after business hours.

More affordable apartments and flats—and slightly more relaxed parking regulations—may be found near quaint **Larchmont Village**, located along Larchmont Boulevard between Beverly Boulevard and Third Street. Within Larchmont Village, you'll find a string of one-of-a-kind retail businesses and restaurants. Like many of Los Angeles's more trendy neighborhoods, people and their pets can be spied enjoying a meal at sidewalk tables in between boutique shops. Business owners can be seen sweeping their sidewalks and addressing their customers by name. No tourist attractions here, just tidy residences with well-kept lawns and small florists, dry cleaners, bookstores, eateries, and the like. Just east of the village is a district called **Windsor Square**, featuring homes from the same era as Hancock Park, but slightly more modest in scale. Mature tulip trees and grassy lawns create a sense of lushness in neighborhood streets. The Mayor's official residence, the Getty House, was built in 1921 and is located on Irving Boulevard.

Web Sites: www.cityofla.org, www.co.la.ca.us, www.larchmont.com, www.windsorsquare.org

Area Codes: 323, 213

Zip Codes: 90004–5, 90010, 90019–20, 90036

Post Office: Oakwood Station, 265 S Western Ave; Sanford Station, 3751 W 6th Street

Police District: (north of Beverly Blvd.) Hollywood Division, 1358 N Wilcox Ave, 213-972-2971; (south of Beverly Blvd.) Wilshire Division, 4861 Venice Blvd, 213-473-0476, www.lapdonline.org

Emergency Hospitals: Hollywood Presbyterian Medical Center, 1300 N Vermont Ave, 213-413-3000, www.hollywoodpresbyterian.com; Children's Hospital of Los Angeles, 4650 Sunset Blvd, 323-660-2450, www.childrenshospitalla.org

Libraries: Memorial branch, 4625 W Olympic Blvd, 323-938-2732; Wilshire branch, 149 N Saint Andrews Pl; 323-957-4550; Fairfax branch, 161 S Gardner St, 323-936-6191, www.lapl.org

Public School Education: LA Unified School District, 333 S Beaudry Ave, LA, 213-241-1000; www.lausd.k12.ca.us

Community Resources: Parking Permits, 310-843–5936, www.lacity-parking.org; Pan Pacific Recreation Center, 7600 Beverly Blvd, 323-939-8874, www.laparks.org; Los Angeles County Museum of Art (LACMA), 5905 Wilshire Blvd, 323-857-6000, www.lacma.org; Los Angeles City Department of Recreation and Parks, 888-LA-PARKS, www.laparks.org

Public Transportation: call 800-COMMUTE, or visit www.mta.net for specific Metro bus route and schedule information.

HOLLYWOOD

HOLLYWOOD HILLS

Boundaries: North: Mulholland Drive (in the west), Griffith Park (in the east);
East: Vermont Avenue; **South:** Melrose Avenue; **West:** North La Brea Avenue

With images from Hollywood's golden era often in newcomers' minds, many come to Hollywood expecting to rub elbows with the stars and find work in the studios. The reality is that only a handful of studios, Paramount among them, remain in Hollywood, and most working actors try to avoid the tourists. In fact, much of Hollywood has become a budget-rent apartment district and tired tourist destination, dotted with souvenir shops and strip clubs, and is further tarnished by the urban realities of homelessness and crime. The closest most get to a star is at the Walk of Fame where the celebrities' names are engraved in stars lining the sidewalk. The good news, however, is the presence of transients has been greatly reduced and some glamour restored to Hollywood, thanks to an aggressive revitalization effort.

The famous Sunset Boulevard ("the Strip") runs through the heart of Hollywood, providing access to neighboring West Hollywood, a place known for its bustling nightlife. Along Hollywood Boulevard is Hollywood and Highland (at the intersection of the same name), a multi-story outdoor mall that, from its third-floor pedestrian bridge, offers the best view anywhere of the Hollywood sign. It is anchored by the hip Hollywood Renaissance Hotel and classy Kodak Theatre (host to the annual Academy Awards). Step out onto the Boulevard for a sample of local entertainment: actors dressed as famous celebrities for photo ops and street performers all vie for your tips. Thanks to the mall's success as a destination, the intersection of Hollywood and Highland is very congested on weekend evenings. You'll also find a cluster of twenties-era theaters: Mann's Chinese, the Egyptian, and the El Capitan, popular among movie lovers for opening night. Many die-hard movie fans will happily stand in line two or more hours for seats and costume themselves according to the movie's theme.

To be content to call Hollywood home, you must love the energy and edginess of the area. Most apartment complexes in central Hollywood were built in the 1950s and '60s, and despite the area's lack of garages and tight street parking, these apartments are filled with many budget-minded singles pursuing their American dream. Amenities much appreciated by the locals include plentiful laundromats, car washes, and cheap eats.

In sharp contrast, the exclusive **Hollywood Hills** is but a few minutes north of Sunset Boulevard. The Hills feature some of Los Angeles's most sought-after residential areas (Hollywood Knolls, Lakeridge Estates, and Hollywood Manor), and many in the entertainment business call the neighborhood home. Here you'll find million-dollar custom-built homes located on windy, twisting hillsides, complete with the prerequisite Lexus or Mercedes-Benz, or both. A warning: coyotes can pose a danger to unprotected/unattended small pets here. The Lake Hollywood Reservoir provides beautiful lakeside views and jogging trails for residents within the Hills. Formerly used for chlorinated water storage, the open reservoir was retired from service (due to concerns with water quality from nearby runoff) but will remain full, to be tapped only in case of emergency.

Nestled at the base of the Hills is the Hollywood Bowl, summer home of the Los Angeles Philharmonic and a popular attraction among Angelenos of all ages. The summer series includes orchestral, jazz, and popular tunes, and some nights a fireworks show accompanies the performance. And if these entertainment amenities aren't enough, the Hollywood Hills location also offers quick access to neighboring Beverly Hills and the Westside via Sunset Boulevard.

Outside the Hills and south of the apartments, but just north of hip Melrose Avenue, a pocket of charming, Santa Fe style homes run along tree-lined sidewalks. Rental and housing prices tend to be high, due to the proximity to Melrose Avenue's trendy shopping boutiques and restaurants.

Overall, Hollywood is tiered into a geographic hierarchy of the entertainment business, with those who have "made it" living in the Hills north of Franklin Avenue and those still trying, living south. In-between the hills and the flats, you'll find a few gentrified bohemian enclaves, but overall, Hollywood's population is a mix of working class folk, professionals, artists, and aspiring actors.

Web Sites: www.hollywoodchamber.net, www.cityofla.org, www.hollywood knolls.org

Area Code: 323

Zip Codes: 90028, 90068, 90078

Post Office: Hollywood Station, 1615 N Wilcox Ave

Police District: Hollywood Division, 1358 N Wilcox Ave, 213-972-2971, www.lap donline.org

Emergency Hospitals: Kaiser Permanente Hospital, 4867 Sunset Blvd, 323-783-4011, www.kaiserpermanente.org; Hollywood Presbyterian Medical Center, 1300 N Vermont Ave, 213-413-3000, www.hollywoodpresbyterian.com

Libraries: Frances Howard Goldwyn Hollywood Library, 1623 N Ivar Ave, 323-856-8260; John C. Fremont branch, 6121 Melrose Ave, 323-962-3521; www.lapl.org

Public School Education: LA Unified School District, 333 S Beaudry Ave, LA, 213-241-1000, www.lausd.k12.ca.us

Community Resources: Lake Hollywood Reservoir, northern end of Weidlake Drive, 323-463-0830, www.ladwp.com; Barnsdall Art Park, 4800 Hollywood Blvd, www.barnsdallartpark.com; Hollywood and Highland, 6801 Hollywood, Blvd, 323-467-6412, www.hollywoodandhighland.com; Kodak Theatre, 6801 Hollywood Blvd, 323-308-6300, www.kodaktheatre.com; Los Angeles City Department of Recreation and Parks, 888-LA-PARKS, www.laparks.org

Public Transportation: call 800-COMMUTE, or visit www.mta.net for specific Metro bus route and schedule information.

LOS FELIZ, SILVERLAKE, ECHO PARK

Boundaries: **North**: Mulholland Drive (in the west), Griffith Park (in the east); **East**: Vermont Avenue; **South**: Melrose Avenue; **West**: Crescent Heights

More affordable than the Westside, these are the funky communities that hug the Santa Monica Mountains, between Hollywood and Dodger Stadium. Los Feliz, Silverlake, and Echo Park residents vary greatly, from white-collar entertainment industry executives to the working class. The appearance of residential (a near 50-50 mix of houses and apartments) and commercial zones is likewise varied, ranging from mansion-sized homes with well-tended lawns to modest residences with security bars.

Los Feliz defines the start of East Los Angeles and is the farthest north among these three communities. Residents here are typically well off financially and are sometimes a colorful lot with outrageous hairdos, pierced tongues, and cutting-edge urban fashion quite the norm. Los Feliz residents enjoy the closest proximity to Griffith Park, the largest publicly owned park in the United States. The park occupies 4,400 acres in the hills and features the Los Angeles Zoo, the Griffith Park Observatory Planetarium and Laserium, the Greek Theater, Travel Town Train Park, and the Gene Autry Western Heritage Museum. There are also picnic areas, a soccer field, and 50 miles of hiking and horseback riding trails. Along Hillhurst Avenue near Los Feliz Boulevard is Los Feliz Village, the site of bookstores, trendy eateries, and clothing boutiques to the stars. Speaking of trendy, many wing-tipped dancers frequent The Derby, 4500 Los Feliz Boulevard, a bar and restaurant that offers free swing lessons in the evenings. Residents also host an annual street fair in June.

Located along Franklin Avenue, the two-story, multi-bedroom homes, built in the old-style of Hollywood mansions, attract many a budding starlet. Madonna once resided behind wrought iron gates with the letter "M" sculpted on it. Area architecture varies greatly from stucco to medieval, but the majority of the residences feature 1930s opulence. The houses are of mansion proportions with price tags to match. Homes in Los Feliz cost a good deal more than those in Silverlake or Echo Park, and street access to residences is occasionally congested by people heading in and out of Dodger Stadium or the Greek Theater in Griffith Park.

Silverlake, located farther south, offers several shopping districts with the usual cafés, antique stores, and bookstores along Vermont and Hyperion avenues. A number of private residences designed by 1930s architect Richard Neutra line the 2200 block of East Silverlake Boulevard. Lucky residents even get a view of the tree-lined Silverlake Reservoir. The well-kept Spanish-style homes seem modest when compared with their neighbors to the north. Silverlake's gay enclave too is toned down when compared with West Hollywood, but gay and lesbian residents enjoy their own cluster of bars and clubs in the area, and trans-sexuals, cross-dressers and other alternative lifestylists seem to prefer Silverlake. The 5 Golden State Freeway borders the northeast section of Silverlake.

Farther southeast is **Echo Park**. Established in the 1920s, this largely blue-collar, Latino community hugs the base of the hills, facing a man-made lake that offers paddle boating on sunny weekends. Well-preserved Victorian and Crafts-man-style homes, built when the area was in its heyday, are clustered along Carroll Avenue in an area called Angelino Heights. Boxy apartments, square bungalows, and cottages make up the rest of the selection in the neighborhood's housing stock. Since this neighborhood came to be before the rise of the automobile, you'll find a number of tight "staircase streets," and some hillside residences are accessible only by foot via these stairs. The Avalon Stairways, at Echo Park Avenue and Avalon Street, are one such example, with the longest being the 230-step Baxter Stairway (at Baxter Street), which leads to Elysian Park. Street parking is very difficult. However, within walking distance are a variety of mom-and-pop shops and restaurants in Echo Park offering the latest in Latino pop music and the best in Mexican and Spanish food and wares.

Also located in Echo Park is Dodger Stadium (near Elysian Park Avenue and West Sunset Boulevard), which can make navigation into these communities difficult during sporting events, and Elysian Park, second in size only to Griffith. Proximity to downtown LA (just hop onto the nearby 110 Pasadena Freeway) is a plus for local commuters. Heat and smog become especially noticeable dur-ing the summer, but nothing air conditioners can't handle. Housing prices in this urban neighborhood tend to be reasonable, and architecturally interesting older homes abound. Graffiti and security, however, may be a concern, and many hom-eowners elect to subscribe to private patrols to supplement the city's.

Web Sites: www.losfelizvillageonline.com, http://silverlake.org, http://historic echopark.org, www.cityofla.org, www.co.la.ca.us

Area Code: 323

Zip Code: 90026

Post Office: Edendale station, 1525 N Alvarado St

Police District: Northeast Division, 3353 San Fernando Dr, 213-485-2563, www. lapdonline.org

Emergency Hospitals: Children's Hospital of Los Angeles, 4650 Sunset Blvd, 323-660-2450, www.childrenshospitalla.org; Hollywood Presbyterian Medi-cal Center, 1300 N Vermont Ave, 213-413-3000, www.hollywoodpresbyterian. com

Library: Los Feliz branch, 1874 Hillhurst Ave, 323-913-4710; Echo Park branch, 1410 W Temple St, 213-250-7808; www.lapl.org

Public School Education: LA Unified School District, 333 S Beaudry Ave, LA, 213-241-1000, www.lausd.k12.ca.us

Community Resources: Barnsdall Park, 4800 Hollywood Blvd, www.barnsdallart park.com; Echo Park Lake and Recreation Center, Bellevue Ave and Glendale Blvd, 213-250-3578; Elysian Park Therapeutic Recreation Center, 929 Academy Rd, 323-226-1402, www.laparks.org; Dodger Stadium, 1000 Elysian Park Ave, 323-224-1507, http://dodgers.mlb.com; The Derby, 323-663-8979, www.clubderby.com.

Public Transportation: call 800-COMMUTE, or visit www.mta.net for specific Metro bus route and schedule information.

LEIMERT PARK

BALDWIN HILLS
CRENSHAW

Boundaries: North: Martin Luther King Jr. Boulevard; **East:** Leimert Boulevard; **South:** Vernon Avenue; **West:** Crenshaw Boulevard

Located seven miles southwest of downtown LA and nestled in the Crenshaw District, Leimert Park is one of the first planned communities in Los Angeles. Development here began in the early 1930s and grew around the park itself (located at the triangular intersection of Leimert and Crenshaw), created by Olmsted & Olmsted, a later incarnation of the same firm that designed New York's Central Park. The surrounding area of shops, 1940s-style duplexes, and Spanish Colonial style houses on wide, tree-lined streets is known as Leimert Park Village.

Leimert Park is characterized by its lovely homes and close-knit African-American community. Most residences in Leimert Park consist of homes and duplexes boasting 1930s and 1940s architecture, which is not found in many other parts of the city. Housing costs are moderate, with a typical home price comparable to that of East Los Angeles communities like Echo Park and Silverlake.

Stroll down Degnan Boulevard and you will find galleries, art centers, jazz & blues clubs, and bookstores, all highlighting African-American themes. The World Stage at 4344 Dugan Avenue hosts regular workshops and performances of jazz and literature. In August, an annual jazz festival here draws music lovers from all over the city. The large Baldwin Hills Crenshaw Plaza mall offers convenient shopping.

In comparison, the nearby Crenshaw neighborhood, distinguishable by its gridded city streets, has a more urban feel, with wrought iron security bars on houses and businesses a common sight. This neighborhood gained notoriety as the flashpoint for the infamous 1992 Los Angeles riots.

The LAX airport, located a few miles to the southwest, is a convenience to those who fly frequently, and a noise nuisance to others.

Neighboring to the west is the community of Baldwin Hills, an unincorporated patch of oil-rich, but hilly land dotted with working oil pumps. Nicknamed the "African American Beverly Hills," the area houses many well-to-do families, especially in the neighborhood known as the Baldwin Hills Estates. Bordered by the Kenneth Hahn State Recreation Area, richly landscaped hillside homes are treated to views of the LA basin. Home prices are reasonable considering the hillside locale, comparable to that of Echo Park. The state park's amenities include a fishing lake, hiking trails, picnic tables, and baseball fields.

Web Sites: www.leimertparkvillage.org, www.fotbh.org, www.cityofla.org, www. co.la.ca.us

Area Code: 213

Zip Code: 90008

Post Offices: Crenshaw Station, 3894 Crenshaw Blvd; Baldwin Hills branch, 3650 W Martin Luther King Jr Blvd

Police District: Southwest Division, 1546 W Martin Luther King Jr Blvd, 213-485-2582, www.lapdonline.org

Emergency Hospitals: LA County - USC Medical Center, 1200 N State St, 323-226-2622, www.usc.edu/patient_care/hospitals/lac_usc; Centinela Freeman Memorial Hospital, 333 N Prairie Ave, 310-674-7050, www.centinelafreeman. com

Libraries: Angeles Mesa branch, 2700 W 52nd St, 323-292-4328; Baldwin Hills branch, 2906 S La Brea Ave, 323-733-1196; Exposition Park branch, 3665 S Vermont Ave, 323-732-0169; www.lapl.org

Public School Education: LA Unified School District, 333 S Beaudry Ave, LA, 213-241-1000, www.lausd.k12.ca.us

Community Resources: Leimert Park Village, 43rd Pl and Crenshaw Blvd, 213-694-1499; The World Stage, 323-293-2451, www.theworldstage.org; Baldwin Hills Crenshaw Plaza, 3650 W Martin Luther King Jr Blvd, 323-290-6636, www. crenshawplaza.com; Rancho Cienega Park, 5001 Rodeo Rd, 323-290-3141, www.laparks.org; Kenneth Hahn State Park, 4100 S La Cienega Blvd, 323-298-3660, www.parks.ca.gov

Public Transportation: call 800-COMMUTE, or visit www.mta.net for specific Metro bus route and schedule information.

DOWNTOWN

WESTLAKE
BOYLE HEIGHTS
CHINATOWN
LITTLE TOKYO

Boundaries: North: Montana Street (in the west), Washington Boulevard (in the east); **East:** west of Michilinda Avenue; **South:** Columbia Street (in the west), California Boulevard (in the east); **West:** Hills west of Linda Vista Avenue

For many years, downtown was considered a business district, not a residential neighborhood. During the day, a large number of employees in law, finance, and advertising would occupy the tightly packed high-rise office buildings. At night, after most day-timers have gone home and retailers have pulled down iron gates over storefronts, the streets would take on a ghost-town feel. Now, re-vitalization is breathing life into downtown, especially noticeable along Figueroa Street between the 10 and 101 freeways. New high-rise residences have started to squeeze out the city's homeless population, but they're still a presence here. LA's Skid Row—nicknamed "The Nickel" because it is centered on Fifth Street, roughly between Third and Seventh streets and Alameda and Main streets—is easily identified by the makeshift cardboard box homes and brimming grocery carts. The district's homeless, estimated at 5,000, seek refuge in the city's cluster of homeless shelters and soup kitchens located here. A downtown Los Angeles homeless map can be seen on the web: http://homeless.cartifact.com. LA County's homeless population, though decreasing, is the largest in the country and estimated at over 68,800.

Outside of The Nickel, you'll see many of the city's finest cultural institutions are situated here. The Arata Isozaki–designed Museum of Contemporary Art (MOCA), the Music Center, the Dorothy Chandler Pavilion, LA's restored Central Library, the Downtown Convention Center (the largest on the West Coast), and the gleaming Frank Gehry–designed Disney Concert Hall are all located downtown. The new Nokia Theater built next to the Staples Center sports arena along with more hotels and shops currently under construction are destined to form "Times Square West." Also calling these environs home is the University of Southern California, a compact but beautiful private college campus. The 110 Harbor Freeway, 10 Santa Monica Freeway, and 101 Hollywood Freeway all border downtown, making entry to and exit from this area easy, albeit slow during rush hour.

Downtown is where you'll find the city's flower, jewelry, textile, garment, toy, and produce districts. While primarily a wholesale district, many businesses do retail to the public, which makes for beaucoup savings for savvy bargain hunters unmindful of the no-frills display of wares. The ethnic hamlets of Chinatown, Little Tokyo, and the Mexican village–style Olvera Street are also situated in downtown.

In 1993, Los Angeles opened the first phase of the long-awaited subway, the Metro Red Line. Starting at the beautiful, historic Union Station on North Alameda Street, riders zip through most of downtown in seven minutes. The Red Line extends to Hollywood through Universal City and ends in North Hollywood. The Blue Line transports passengers from Downtown to Long Beach; the Green Line serves LA International Airport; and the Gold Line route goes to Pasadena. (See the Metro Rail map at the end of this book.) Although these established lines have been well received by riders, in 1998, LA County voters, angry with management and funding troubles, banned local tax revenues from funding any future subway tunnel construction, effectively freezing any further development of the subway.

Downtown planners have very ambitious plans to make the heart of the city a place where you'd want to take up residence. Until a few years ago, housing in downtown had been limited mostly to low-rent single-occupancy hotels and apartments and artists-in-residence and loft-type housing like those found at the large Santa Fe Art Colony at 2401 South Santa Fe and The Brewery at 1920 North Main Street. Today there has been rapid construction of new apartments, lofts, and condominiums and conversions ("adaptive reuse") of former office and bank buildings into housing. The boxy and cheery Market Lofts at Ninth and Hope streets is a typical example of the high-density, mixed-use residences now found here. The Downtown Business Improvement group organizes tours of downtown housing every Saturday; visit their web site (www.downtownla.com) for more information.

Those wanting a central locale might also consider the business districts in the ethnically diverse neighborhoods of **Westlake** (west of Alvarado Street), **Boyle Heights** (east of the Los Angeles River), **Chinatown** (slightly north of Cesar E. Chavez Avenue), or **Little Tokyo** (east of San Pedro Street) to locate housing. Blue- and white-collar families and recent immigrants (mostly Hispanic, Chinese, and Japanese) are the majority of residents in these neighborhoods. The quality of housing is uneven, varying from aging buildings in need of improvement to the well preserved or newly built. Most, if not all, of the stores and restaurants are bilingual and cater to the tastes of area residents. **Little Tokyo** is easily the most polished of these enclaves. Despite its proximity to litter-ridden parts of downtown LA, tidy apartments and well-tended streets reflect the residents' sense of pride in their neighborhood. Japanese ex-pats seeking the tastes and comforts of home have an array of dining and shopping choices in the Japanese Village Plaza and Little Tokyo Mall. The Japanese American Cultural & Community Center at 244 South San Pedro Street, with its Japan America Theatre, an 880-seat performance space, and the Japanese American National Museum on East First Street round out the cultural offerings in the Little Tokyo cityscape.

Web Sites: www.downtownla.com, www.visitlittletokyo.com, www.chinatownla.com, www.co.la.ca.us; www.cityofla.org

Area Code: 213

Zip Codes: 90012–15, 90017, 90057

Post Offices: Textile Finance Station, 100 W Olympic Blvd; Alameda Station, 760 N Main St; Arcade Station, 508 S Spring St; Market Station, 1122 E 7th St; Little Tokyo Station, 406 E 2nd St

Police District: Hollywood Division, 1358 N Wilcox Ave, 213-485-4302, www.lapdonline.org

Emergency Hospitals: Good Samaritan Hospital, 1225 Wilshire Blvd, 213-977-2121, www.goodsam.org; White Memorial Medical Center, 1720 E Cesar Chavez

Ave, 323-268-5000, www.whitememorial.com; LA County-USC Medical Center, 1200 N State St; 323-226-2622, www.usc.edu/patient_care/hospitals/lac_usc

Libraries: Central Library, 630 W 5th St, 213-228-7000; Little Tokyo branch, 203 S Los Angeles St, 213-612-0525; Chinatown branch, 639 N Hill St, 213-620-0925

Public Schools: LA Unified School District, 333 S Beaudry Ave, LA, 213-241-1000, www.lausd.k12.ca.us

Community Resources: Los Angeles Conservancy provides downtown walking tours, 213-623-2489, www.laconservancy.org; Exposition Park at Figueroa St and Exposition Blvd, www.laparks.org; University of Southern California at Figueroa St and Jefferson Blvd, 213-740-2311, www.usc.edu; Los Angeles Memorial Coliseum, 3911 S Figueroa St, www.lacoliseum.com; Dodger Stadium, 1000 Elysian Park Ave, 323-224-1507, http://dodgers.mlb.com; Staples Center, 1111 S Figueroa St, 213-742-7100, www.staplescenter.com; Japanese American Cultural & Community Center, 244 S San Pedro St, 213-628-2725, www.jaccc.org; Japanese American National Museum, 369 E First St, 213-625-0414, www.janm.org; Los Angeles City Department of Recreation and Parks, 213-473-7070, www.laparks.org

Public Transportation: call 800-COMMUTE or 800-371-LINK for specific Metro bus or Metro Rail (respectively) route and schedule information (www.mta.net). The DASH is a $.25 fare mini-bus that runs exclusively in downtown between the area's major tourist stops and office buildings; call 213-808-2273 for route and schedule information.

NEIGHBORHOODS — SOUTH

Fifty years after Columbus came upon the shores of America, Cabrillo and his crew of explorers anchored along the shore of what is present-day Long Beach, and by the late 1700s, Spanish settlements and missions began to shape this part of the country. In fact, much of the southern end of Los Angeles County started out as a Spanish ranchero. When the Southern Pacific Railroad's "iron horse" laid railroad tracks through the land in the 1870s, mass transportation brought in hordes of settlers. Shrewd developers like John G. Downey and the brothers Atwood and Gilbert Sproul correctly predicted that the sprouting communities along the railroad lines would become flourishing towns. Downey developed a section of his rancho into a town and gave the community his family name, and the Sproul brothers demanded successfully that passenger trains stop in Norwalk, or "North-walk" as it was called then. Long Beach too saw masses of settlers disembarking at its station. The surrounding undeveloped countryside serviced the cattle and farm industries. Some of the largest sugar beet farms in the state were in Norwalk. The discovery of oil in the southern end of Los Angeles during the 1920s and '30s rocketed the area's growth toward industry and manufactur-

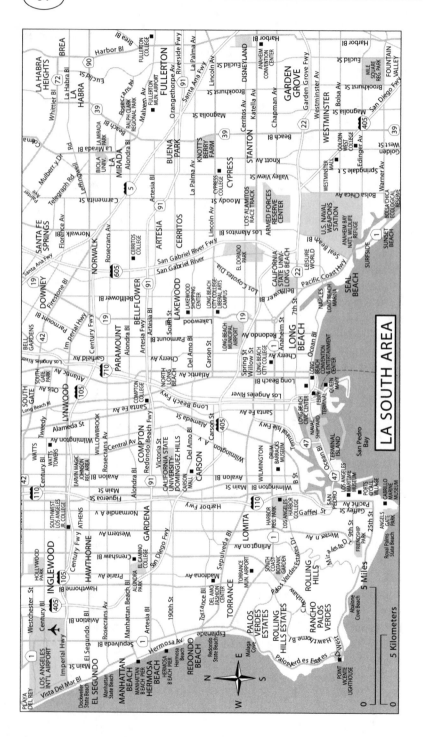

LA SOUTH AREA

ing. Much of this area—the southwest peninsula of LA County as well as Long Beach—is usually referred to as the South Bay.

The biggest housing boom in southern LA came after WW II when the Lakewood Park Company started developing what would become the nation's first post-war housing tract: 17,500 homes on about 3,500 acres, transforming Lakewood from a sugar beet field into a planned community. In 1954, Lakewood residents rejected annexing to the neighboring City of Long Beach. They voted instead to incorporate as a city, with the novel idea of continuing to contract with Los Angeles County for county services such as road maintenance, utility services, and fire protection. This "Lakewood Plan" was so successful it served as a blueprint for incorporating many future cities in the state and across the country.

DOWNEY

BELLFLOWER
LAKEWOOD

Boundaries: North: Telegraph Road; **East:** San Gabriel River; **South:** Forest Road (in the east), Gardendale Street (in the west); **West:** the Rio Hondo River

A southern suburb of Los Angeles, the **City of Downey** is a self-contained community with its own downtown, civic theater, school district, and fire and police departments. A majority of the housing is owner-occupied, with two to three bedrooms, and built between 1950 and 1980.

Despite its tract housing origins, many homes here have since been customized. Remodeling styles vary, and the presence of security bars and doors appears to be the exception rather than the rule. While 40% of the housing stock consists of apartments and condos, the single-family home dominates here at 60%, making this a comfortable south–of–central LA community for first-time homebuyers.

Historically, this traditionally working class community's biggest employer was the Rockwell International Space Division, near Lakewood Boulevard off the 105 Century Freeway. However, cutbacks in the aerospace industry caused the company to scale down its workforce drastically and to eventually close its doors in 1999. Today, Rancho Los Amigos Hospital, a spinal injury treatment center, and the home improvement stores All American Home Center and Home Depot make up the area's biggest employers. Bordered by the 710 Long Beach Freeway to the west and the 5 Santa Monica Freeway to the east, Downey offers quick access to the southern border of Los Angeles County, explaining why more than three-quarters of its residents work outside of Downey in other parts of LA County. The busy international Port of Long Beach/Los Angeles is approximately 12 miles away and equally close is the northern border of Orange County.

The Civic Theater in downtown Downey presents Broadway shows and musicals and is home to the Downey Symphony Orchestra and the Downey Civic Light Opera. Typical of other downtowns, there are a number of restaurants, hotels, and office buildings to be found here. For strolling, the intersection of Florence Avenue and Paramount Boulevard is a busy commercial hub dotted with bookstores, restaurants, gift shops, grocery stores and offices. The Stonewood Center Mall at Firestone and Lakewood boulevards, completely remodeled in 2005, is a large enclosed shopping mall with over 170 stores. The prominent presence of parks (nearly 100 acres), playgrounds, and movie theaters typifies this family-centered community. In fact, children of all ages can boast that Downey is home to the oldest McDonald's still in operation, at Lakewood Boulevard and Florence Avenue. The fast-food icon also operates a museum and gift shop.

Farther south, heading toward Long Beach, is the cozy, 6.4-square-mile **City of Bellflower**. In terms of housing, it is similar in composition to Downey; however, the presence of overhead power and telephone lines is noticeable here, especially down the wide thoroughfares that define Bellflower's city blocks. (Some LA cities route their power lines underground.) These imposing steel posts fade away, however, once you turn off onto the side streets. Lots of green yards and trees complement the tidy, single-story homes in this ethnically diverse working-class community. The housing stock is dominated by three-bedroom homes, most built in the '70s and '80s.

A story similar to Bellflower can be told of the **City of Lakewood**, located to the south, 25 miles southeast of LA. Defined by the San Gabriel River to the east and Long Beach to the south, Lakewood is slightly larger, occupying nearly 10 square miles. Having celebrated 50 years in 2004, this city, it can be said, defines suburbia. Now home to 88,000+, it was built in the early 1950s for working-class families, many of them returning G.I.'s. A unique attribute of this city is that in residential areas, frontage roads parallel main thoroughfares and access from the frontage roads to the thoroughfares is infrequently spaced. Although sidewalks are showing signs of wear and commercial buildings could use some sprucing up, most residents are pleased to call Lakewood home. The very first Denny's opened here in 1959. And Lakewood Center is one of the more popular malls in the neighborhood. The city-sponsored Lakewood Beautiful Awards, recognizing well-groomed homes, only hints at the area's civic pride. The neighborhood around Lakewood High School is especially picturesque, and a number of parks dot the primarily residential neighborhood. There's also the Lakewood Center Mall for shopping. According to the 2000 Census, almost 40% of Lakewood households have school-aged youngsters and 85% of the housing here consists of single-family detached homes. Several non-Lakewood school districts cover this area, although Lakewood residents have been trying to form their own school district for some time. Just to the east, past the river, runs the 605 San Gabriel River Freeway for easy access into Orange County.

Web Sites: www.downeyca.org, www.bellflower.org, www.lakewoodcity.org

Area Code: 562

Zip Codes: Downey: 90241–2, Bellflower: 90706, Lakewood: 90712–3

Post Offices: Downey branches: 10409 Lakewood Blvd, 13003 Dahlia St, 7911 Imperial Hwy, 8111 Firestone Blvd.; Bellflower branch, 9835 Flower St; Lakewood branch, 5200 Clark Ave

Police District: Downey is patrolled by its own police force, Downey City Police, 10911 Brookshire Ave, 562-861-0771, www.downeypd.org. The cities of Bellflower and Lakewood contract with the Los Angeles County Sheriff's Department for law enforcement services. Lakewood Sheriff's Station, 5130 N Clark Ave, 562-623-3500; Bellflower substation, 16615 Bellflower Blvd, 562-925-0124; www.lasd.org.

Emergency Hospitals: Downey Regional Medical Center, 11500 Brookshire Ave, 562-904-5000; Kaiser Foundation Hospital - Bellflower, 9400 Rosecrans Ave, 562-461-6085, www.kaiserpermanente.org; Lakewood Regional Medical Center, 3700 E South St, 562-531-2550, www.lakewoodregional.com

Libraries: Downey, 11121 Brookshire Ave, 562-904-7360, www.downeylibrary.org; Norwalk: Alondra Library, 11949 E Alondra Blvd, 562-868-7771; Bellflower: Clifton M. Brakensiek, 9945 E Flower St, 562-925-5543; Lakewood: Angelo M. Iacoboni Library, 4990 Clark Ave, 562-866-1777; George Nye Jr Library, 6600 Del Amo Blvd, 562-421-8497; www.colapublib.org

Public School Education: Downey Unified School District, 11627 Brookshire Ave, Downey, 562-469-6500, www.dusd.net; Bellflower Unified School District, 16703 Clark Ave, Bellflower, 562-866-9011, www.busd.k12.ca.us. For Lakewood, consult the following districts: Bellflower Unified School District (see above); Long Beach Unified School District, 1515 Hughes Way, Long Beach, 562-997-8000, www.lbusd.k12.ca.us; and LA Unified School District, 333 S Beaudry Ave, LA, 213-241-1000, www.lausd.k12.ca.us.

Community Resources: Heritage Park, 12100 Mora Dr; Dennis the Menace Park, 9125 Arrington Ave, 310-904-7127; Furman Park, 10419 S Rives Ave; Downey Recreation Parks and Department, 562-904-7238, www.downeyca.org; Los Amigos Golf Course, 7295 Quill Dr, 562-869-0302, http://parks.co.la.ca.us/los_amigos.html; Downey Museum of Art, 10419 S Rives Ave, 562-861-0419; Downey Civic Theatre, 8345 Firestone Blvd, 562-904-7230, www.downeytheatre.com; Stonewood Center Mall, 251 Stonewood St, 562-861-9233, www.shopstonewoodcenter.com; Lakewood City Information Line, 562-925-4357.

Public Transportation: call 800-COMMUTE, or visit www.mta.net for specific Metro bus route and schedule information. This area is also serviced by Downey LINK, 562-529-LINK; the Metro Greenline 800-COMMUTE; and the Bellflower Bus, 562-865-7433, www.bellflower.org.

LA MIRADA, NORWALK

Boundaries: North: Leffingwell Road; **East:** Beach Boulevard; **South:** Alondra Boulevard; **West:** San Gabriel River

The **City of La Mirada** is a modest southern suburb of Los Angeles, on the northern border of Orange County. This relatively new community (incorporated in 1960) occupies just 7.8 square miles and includes the large La Mirada Park and Golf Course and the private, theologically conservative Biola University. An island of Republicanism in a largely Democratic county, La Mirada is known for its civic beauty, landscaped streets, and lush greenbelts, with pine, palm, and other trees lining its residential streets. The city's cultural and sporting amenities have started to blossom. In addition to the La Mirada Theatre for the Performing Arts, there's now the new Splash! La Mirada Regional Aquatics Center, and a community gymnasium with regularly scheduled activities for an annual membership fee. A clear sign the city is dedicated to keeping crime low: residents are enjoying protection from a brand-spanking-new 6,000-square-foot sheriff's substation behind city hall.

More recently built tract housing communities along Visions Drive feature three- and four-bedroom homes. The median range for existing three-bedroom, single-story homes is slightly lower than the median for the county, and La Mirada is one of the few California cities that does not levy a property tax above the 1% levy by the County of Los Angeles. La Mirada operates its own school district, but receives some city services (such as fire) from Los Angeles County. Typical of many new or yet-to-be-developed communities with land to spare, residences are comfortably spaced apart. The 5 Santa Ana Freeway borders La Mirada's southern edge, making access easy to downtown LA.

Directly west of La Mirada is the **City of Norwalk**, a working-class community dating back to the nationwide housing boom of the 1940s. Correspondingly, the houses tend to be modest single-story, two- and three-bedroom homes, similar in composition to neighboring Downey. Area homes are neat and well-kept, but more tightly packed together compared with La Mirada. Some homes share driveways, but most everybody has a front or back yard. Architecturally speaking, most of these 1950s homes are unremarkable, but their affordability, slightly less expensive than homes in La Mirada, appeals to many first-time, budget-minded homeowners. Security doors and windows are visible. Typically, the breadwinners of Norwalk commute to neighboring commercial districts such as Downey for work. Norwalk civic amenities include Cerritos College, located on the southwest corner of Norwalk, the Norwalk Sports & Arts Complex, and the Norwalk Entertainment Center at Civic Center Drive. The LA County Register/Recorder's office manages the county's voters, real estate documents, and birth and marriage records here. The city also boasts great freeway access; it's served by the 91 Riverside Freeway to the south and the 605 San Gabriel Freeway to the west; interstates 5 Santa Ana Freeway and 105 Century Freeway pass through the community.

Web Sites: www.cityoflamirada.org, www.ci.norwalk.ca.us

Area Code: 562

Zip Codes: 90638, 90650

Post Offices: La Mirada, 14901 Adelfa Dr; Norwalk: 12415 Norwalk Blvd; 14011 Clarkdale Ave

Police District: La Mirada and Norwalk contract with the Los Angeles County Sheriff's Department for law enforcement services. La Mirada Sheriff's station, 13716 La Mirada Blvd, 562-902-2960; Norwalk Sheriff's station, 12335 Civic Center Dr, 562-863-8711, www.lasd.org

Emergency Hospitals: Kindred Hospital - La Mirada, 14900 E Imperial Hwy, 562-944-1900, www.kindredlamirada.com; Norwalk Community Hospital, 13222 Bloomfield Ave, 562-863-4763, www.norwalkcommunityhospital.com;

Libraries: La Mirada Library, 13800 La Mirada Blvd, 562-943-0277; Norwalk Library, 12350 Imperial Hwy, 562-868-0775; Alondra Library, 11949 E Alondra Blvd, 562-868-7771; Norwalk Regional Library, 12350 Imperial Hwy, 562-868-0775; www.colapublib.org

Public School Education: Downey Unified School District, 11627 Brookshire Ave, Downey, 562-469-6500, www.dusd.net; Norwalk-La Mirada Unified School District, 12820 Pioneer Blvd, Norwalk, 562-868-0431, www.nlmusd.k12.ca.us

Community Resources: La Mirada Park, 13701 S Adelfa Rd; Biola University, 13800 Biola Ave, 562-903-6000, www.biola.edu; La Mirada Theatre for Performing Arts, 14900 La Mirada Blvd, 562-944-9801, www.lamiradatheatre. com; La Mirada Community Gymnasium, 15105 Alicante Rd, 562-902-2938, www.cityoflamirada.org; Cerritos College, 11110 Alondra Blvd, 562-860-2451, www.cerritos.edu; Norwalk Sports & Arts Complex, 13000 Clarkdale Ave, 562-929-5566, www.ci.norwalk.ca.us; Norwalk Aquatic Pavilion, 12301 Sproul St, 562-929-5622, www.ci.norwalk.ca.us/parksandrecfaclist.asp; Norwalk Nature Center, 13000 Clarkdale Ave, 562-929-5702

Public Transportation: call 800-COMMUTE, or visit www.mta.net for specific Metro bus route and schedule information. This area is also serviced by Downey LINK, 562-529-LINK and the Metro Greenline 800-COMMUTE. Norwalk is also serviced by the Norwalk Transit System, 562-929-5550, www.ci.norwalk.ca.us

CITY OF LONG BEACH

CITY OF PARAMOUNT

Boundaries: North: Carson Street; **East:** 605 San Gabriel River Freeway; **South:** Pacific Ocean; **West:** 710 Long Beach Freeway

With 35 miles of beach, in a city of 50 square miles, it's easy to see why this city, incorporated in 1888, was called "Long Beach." From a population of 1,500 and an area of just three square miles in those early years, the city has grown to an estimated 460,000, making it the second most populous city in LA County. As host to the busiest port on the west coast, the Port of Los Angeles/Long Beach and the Long Beach Marina (this largest city-run marina in the country, with nearly 4,000 slips, was renovated in 2007), many area residents are employed in the shipping industry. Visitors come to tour the dry-docked luxury cruise ship of yesteryear, the *Queen Mary*, and the popular Aquarium of the Pacific. Opened in 1998, the Aquarium was part of a $650 million renovation of the Long Beach waterfront. Adjacent is downtown Long Beach, a pleasant outdoor shopping village of New England–style buildings, known as Shoreline Village, and the Long Beach Convention & Entertainment Center, which was expanded to triple its original size in the early 1990s. Along the coast, favorable sailing waters with offshore breakwaters and a natural bay host the Congressional Cup, Transpac, and Olympic trial races. Farther inland are three major golf courses and a country club. Hugging the 405 San Diego Freeway is the Long Beach Municipal Airport (see **Transportation**). The city is a popular and convenient weekend getaway for Angelenos who come to enjoy a sparkling waterfront and all the amenities of a full-fledged city without the urban grit.

Considering the city's proximity to the coast, homes prices span a healthy range, from just under a million dollars to the mid-$350,000's (as of early 2008). Residents are almost equally divided between renters and owners. Over 40% of the single-family dwellings were constructed between 1940 and 1960, and 40% of total housing stock consists of single-family detached homes. The residential streets and main thoroughfares of Long Beach are well tended and tree lined. The quality of housing differs from other beachfront communities in that older, lower-income neighborhoods surround the water and downtown, and homes get newer and costlier as you move inland toward Cal State University Long Beach. The City Place Long Beach (at Fourth Street and Long Beach Boulevard) is a nice example of the mixed-use zoning that's popping up in many urban neighborhoods; below its many apartments and lofts are lots of independent retail and entertainment options for evenings out. This is located within an area referred to as the **East Village Arts District**. The Pike at Rainbow Harbor (95 South Pine Avenue) is another entertainment district featuring restaurants, movie complex, and a Ferris wheel.

Getting in and out of Long Beach can be a bit of a hassle because the 710 Long Beach Freeway, which runs north-south, is narrow and often clogged with trucks taking shipments in and out of the port; running east-west is the perpetually busy 405 San Diego Freeway. In an effort to ease local congestion, the nation's first public bike station was constructed at First Street and The Promenade (for more info, call 562-436-2453 or visit www.bikestation.org). Billed as a bike-transit facility, members (who pay a $20 administrative fee and $96 for a year's membership) can rent cruiser-type bicycles and lockers at a reduced fee. There are more than 30 miles of shoreline and riverside bicycle paths in the city. The public bus and light rail also make stops at this bike facility. While the 30-mile commute to downtown LA may be an inconvenience, it is often viewed as a relatively minor trade-off by those seeking affordable housing in a bustling seaside community.

The **City of Paramount** is north of Long Beach and is best known as the birthplace of the Zamboni ice resurfacing machine and the Paramount Iceland rink—training ground of skating great Dorothy Hamill. Today, the city has been tarnished somewhat by blight and crime, but over the last two decades the city has cracked down on gangs and been able to lower its crime rates. Several years ago, the city spent $62 million on city improvements, including upgrading/adding parks, fountains, and landscaping. Outdoor art sculptures spruce up public spaces around town. Housing prices have recently trended past the low end of the Long Beach price spectrum, making it attractive for many first-time homebuyers. The city's turnaround has been especially noticeable in the commercial districts, with big business chains like Home Depot setting up shop in the area.

Web Sites: www.ci.long-beach.ca.us, www.paramountcity.com

Area Code: 562

Zip Codes: 90802–46, 90723

Post Offices: 1920 Pacific Ave; 2727 E Anaheim St; 300 N Long Beach Blvd

Police District: Long Beach Police Department, 100 Long Beach Blvd, Long Beach, 562-570-7260, www.longbeach.gov/police. Paramount contracts with the Los Angeles County Sheriff's Department for law enforcement services: Paramount Station, 15001 Paramount Blvd, 562-220-2002, www.lasd.org

Emergency Hospitals: Community Hospital of Long Beach, 1720 Termino Ave, 562-498-1000, www.chlb.org; Long Beach Memorial Medical Center, 2801 Atlantic Ave, 562-933-2000, www.memorialcare.org; Pacific Hospital - Long Beach, 2776 Pacific Ave, 562-997-2500, www.phlb.org; St. Mary Medical Center, 1050 Linden Ave, Long Beach, 562-491-9000, www.stmarymedicalcenter. com

Libraries: Long Beach Public Library, 101 Pacific Ave, 562-570-7500; Alamitos Neighborhood Library, 1836 E Third St, 562-570-1037; Bay Shore Neighborhood Library, 195 Bay Shore Ave, 562-570-1039; Mark Twain Neighborhood Library, 1325 E Anaheim St, 562-570-1046; Burnett Neighborhood Library, 560 E Hill St, 562-570-1047; www.lbpl.org

Public School Education: Long Beach Unified School District, 1515 Hughes Way, Long Beach, 562-997-8000, www.lbusd.k12.ca.us; Paramount Unified School District, 15110 California Ave, Paramount, 562-602-6000, www.paramount. k12.ca.us

Community Resources: Shoreline Park, E Shoreline Drive and Pine Ave; Bixby Park, Cherry Ave and E Ocean Blvd; Long Beach Parks and Recreation, 562-570-3232, www.ci.long-beach.ca.us/park; CityPlace Long Beach, Fourth St

and Long Beach, www.longbeachcityplace.com; E Village Arts District, www.
eastvillagelive.com; The Pike at Rainbow Harbor, 95 S Pine Ave, 562-432-8325,
www.thepikeatlongbeach.com; Skylinks Golf Course, 4800 Wardlow Rd, 562-
421-3388; Virginia Country Club, 4602 Virginia Rd, 562-424-5211; Paramount
Iceland, 8041 Jackson St, 562-633-1171, www.paramounticeland.com

Public Transportation: call 800-COMMUTE, or visit www.mta.net for specific
Metro bus route and schedule information. The Metro Blue Line runs between Long Beach and downtown LA; call 213-626-4455 for Metro schedule
information. For Long Beach Transit, call 562-591-2301 or visit www.lbtransit.
com for route and schedule info. The Long Beach Passport Bus Shuttle is a
free downtown bus shuttle, 562-591-2301. The Long Beach Bikestation is at
105 The Promenade North; call 562-436-2453 or go to www.bikestation.org
for more information. The Paramount Easy Rider Shuttle transports residents
along a fixed route; call 562-981-6300 for information.

Additional South Bay communities you might want to consider…

- **Hermosa Beach**, just south of Manhattan Beach and north of Redondo Beach,
  is the only one of the three to own its own beach. Spanish for "beautiful," this
  beach city features a strong surfer community and is also known as the "Beach
  Volleyball Capital of the World." Condos dominate apartment offerings, and
  both dot neighborhoods west of the Pacific Coast Highway. Three-bedroom
  homes are typical here, and many are beachside, which translates into million-
  dollar price tags: 310-318-0239, www.hermosabch.org
- **Redondo Beach**, south of Hermosa Beach, has a similar beach lifestyle vibe
  to that of Hermosa Beach. It's divided in two segments, referred to as North
  and South, where South Redondo refers to the pier, marina, and the cleanest
  part of the city. North Redondo is mostly residential and commercial. North
  Redondo homes tend to be slightly cheaper than those in South Redondo:
  310-372-1171, www.redondo.org
- **Torrance**, south of Redondo Beach, is the fourth largest city in LA County and
  supports a lot of industry. The ExxonMobil Refinery is situated in the northern
  part of town and supplies much of Southern California's gasoline. The American headquarters of Toyota and Honda are based here, which explains the
  large Japanese-American population. And the Del Amo Fashion Center is one
  of the largest malls in America. Housing runs in a variety of price ranges, depending on proximity to the ocean, with the most affordable housing tending
  to be in the north and east: 310-328-5310, www.ci.torrance.ca.us
- **City of Palos Verdes Estates**, south of Torrance, on the Palos Verdes peninsula,
  ranked as 47th most expensive place to live by Forbes.com in 2007. This well-
  to-do community enjoys city-run amenities such as a golf club, tennis club,
  beach & athletic club, and stables. A slight majority of homes here are single
  family, and median prices are similar to what you'd find in other beachside cities: 310-378-0383, www.palosverdes.com/pve

- **City of Rancho Palos Verdes,** also on the Palos Verdes peninsula, like Palos Verdes Estates, is another prestigious community that enjoys breathtaking views of the Pacific Ocean. The Trump National Golf Club opened in 2006 and a luxury housing development, "The Estates at Trump National," is onsite. Median prices here run slightly below that of Palos Verdes Estates: 310-377-0360, www.palosverdes.com/rpv

SAN FERNANDO VALLEY AND OTHER POINTS NORTH

Just north of the Hollywood Hills, via either the 405 San Diego Freeway or 101 Hollywood Freeway, is a large, flat basin called the San Fernando Valley, known as "the Valley," a stronghold of suburban middle and upper-middle class neighborhoods. Its earliest settlers, the Gabrielino Indians, and later the missionaries who founded the San Fernando Rey de Espana Mission in 1797, recognized the Valley's great qualities, grooming its fertile land into prosperous farming and ranching communities, which became world-famous for their orange, lemon, walnut, and persimmon groves. Following WW II, housing tracts sprouted across the Valley and the area became a working model for the American dream. By the 1950s, the Valley was a bastion of suburbia, offering Los Angelenos affordable homes complete with two-car garages and a patch of lawn to call their own. Today, nearly four million people live in the Valley. (In 1999, some Valley residents started a secession measure to make the Valley its own municipality. Measure F went before voters citywide in 2002, where only 51% of Valley voters cast votes in favor of it, and Los Angeles voters soundly rejected it.)

So what, you ask, does the Valley offer that is so different from its southerly neighbor? Generally, the Valley's living options are more suburban in feel, more spacious, but still with close proximity to many businesses, including the entertainment studios and related businesses in the eastern communities of Burbank, Glendale, and Universal City. Homebuyers typically find that they can get more house for their money in the Valley and, while the temperatures are hotter (by 10 to 20 degrees) and the smog worse, the 'burbs lifestyle is what many seek. In addition, this formerly white enclave has taken on a more racially and ethnically mixed flavor, with a steady influx of African-American, Asian, and Latino residents.

Ventura Boulevard, a thriving business and restaurant strip, runs east-west through the southern portion of the Valley. All forms of housing are represented; single-family homes tend to be located on the side streets that run east and west while apartments and condos line the main streets going north and south. Ventura Boulevard (running parallel to the 101 Hollywood Freeway) begins in Studio City, and heads west through Sherman Oaks, Van Nuys, the City of Encino, Woodland Hills, and the City of Calabasas (the latter three are known as the West

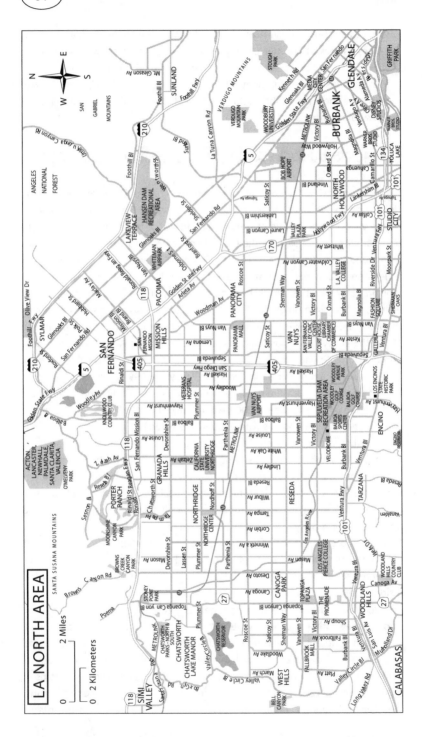

Valley). Continuing northeast from the western border of the Valley are the communities of West Hills, Reseda, and Northridge (the East Valley).

The well-established planned communities of the West Valley have been so well tended they still feel new. There are occasional pockets of redevelopment where new homes have been built over old, but they're rare. People looking for newly built homes now search westward in the neighborhoods of Ventura County, which offer the planned and gated communities of Thousand Oaks and Westlake Village. Others search northward in the City of Santa Clarita, where the communities of Valencia and Newhall occupy the northernmost border of LA County. The commute from these northern areas can be an hour-plus for those who work in Los Angeles proper, but for many, the suburban lifestyle offered by these environs makes the hours spent behind the wheel worthwhile.

The eastern communities of LA County (that is, east of the 5 Golden State Freeway) defy easy categorization as they're not part of the San Fernando Valley nor are they technically part of the City of LA. These communities start with the City of Burbank, City of Glendale, and include the City of Pasadena, City of South Pasadena, and unincorporated Altadena. The freeways that service these areas are confusing. The 134 Ventura Freeway runs east-west and eventually becomes the 210 Foothill Freeway in Pasadena. The northern tip of the 110 Harbor Freeway begins in Pasadena, but this wide strip of pavement isn't really a freeway and is also known as South Arroyo Parkway, which is also a leg of the Historic Route 66. This busy road and bustling commercial strip transforms in South Pasadena to a true freeway (the 110), which takes commuters downtown. To add more confusion, the 210 Foothill Freeway also runs north (at the junction that the 134 Ventura Freeway becomes the 210) and yet still has the same name as its twin, the other 210 Foothill Freeway, which runs east. (Just be sure to buy a *Thomas Guide*!)

But enough about freeways, let's look at the communities...

WEST VALLEY

ENCINO
WOODLAND HILLS
SHERMAN OAKS
VAN NUYS

Boundaries: **East**: 405 San Diego Freeway; **South**: Santa Monica Mountains; **North**: 101 Ventura Freeway; **West**: Reseda Boulevard

Pretty and lined with old growth oaks, Encino (which means "oak tree" in Spanish) is located on the north side of the Santa Monica Mountains, facing the San Fernando Valley. Adjacent and to the west is another well-tended community, Woodland Hills, and to the northeast is Van Nuys, a busy but more middle-class community in comparison. Homey Sherman Oaks is Encino's eastern neighbor and not as modest as Van Nuys, but not quite as new as Encino or Woodland Hills either. The bordering 405 San Diego and 101 Ventura freeways provide easy access for commuters.

Encino and **Woodland Hills** are similar in that they're both upper-middle-class, homogeneous communities. Streets are clean and homes well maintained. A number of celebrities reside in these family-oriented neighborhoods that feature modern or Spanish-style architecture. Most of the houses are one-story three- or four-bedroom homes, with prices higher in Encino than in Woodland Hills. The reason for the difference, Woodland Hills is not as fully developed as Encino, but that gap will certainly close as growth here continues. The business districts of Encino and Woodland Hills, the bulk of which line Ventura Boulevard and Warner Center, boast the greatest number of banks and savings and loans of any Valley community, and retail districts are being developed or expanded, especially in Woodland Hills. Two large indoor malls, Topanga Plaza and The Promenade at Woodland Hills, are within a few blocks of each other. A Westfield Village of outdoor shops, restaurants, and 360-unit apartment complex to bridge the two malls along Topanga Canyon Boulevard is currently in the planning stages. Residents are privy to six golf courses and there are several parks in the area. The Sepulveda Dam Recreation Area offers two thousand acres of open space and is popular for hiking, picnicking, biking, and paddle boating. The Los Encinos State Historical Park offers five acres dedicated to the preservation of the area's history, including a building that is over 150 years old. Bicycling enthusiasts can enjoy watching races and attending training programs at the Encino Velodrome, an outdoor bike racing track that was first built in 1963.

Van Nuys is host to the Anheuser-Busch Brewery and to the Van Nuys Airport, which does not take commercial flights, but serves as home base for private and corporate jets and helicopters. Car dealerships cluster along Van Nuys Boulevard, just north of Riverside Drive, and discount retailers located farther north on the same street blare Mexican pop music, reflecting the preferences of many area residents. The LA Valley College campus is also here. Most Van Nuys residences are in the form of apartments, with only about 30% of housing in the form of single-family residences. Housing here is much cheaper than neighboring Encino, and the affordability has made this community attractive to recent immigrants and blue-collar workers, many employed by the manufacturing and industrial assembly plants nearby. Upkeep of residences varies greatly; some streets show a lot of care while others sport security bars and could use sprucing up. To meet the issue of neighborhood neglect, one particular Van Nuys neighborhood formed its own neighborhood association and beautification committee, naming the area **Valley Glen** in 1996. Its borders are Victory Boulevard on the north, Coldwater Canyon on the east, Burbank Boulevard on the south, and Hazeltine Avenue on the west. As a result of this concentrated community effort, Valley Glen property values are slightly higher than the surrounding area.

Sherman Oaks is a mix of flat and hilly land. Residential streets south of Ventura Boulevard wind into the hills, where the neighborhoods and housing styles are less protypical suburbia and sport higher price tags than much of the Valley. It is north of Ventura Boulevard where you will find more middle-class homes lining the side streets and a respectable choice of apartments along main thoroughfares. Residential architecture varies from ranch homes to boxy stuccos. Many have back and front yards that are tended by hired gardeners who mow and trim their way from one house to the next. Housing prices are comparable to those found in Encino; apartments are also not too difficult to find. In the Northridge earthquake of 1994 (Northridge is northwest of Sherman Oaks), scattered parts of Sherman Oaks were hard hit, especially along Hazeltine Avenue. But with the rebuilding of apartments and homes, life has returned to normal. Typical of many neighborhoods in the Valley, the majority of area businesses line Ventura Boulevard, including a pleasant mall called Westfield Fashion Square, chain grocery stores, banks, restaurants, and a variety of other retailers serving the needs of the local community. Weekend evenings find the locals, their children, and the family dog out on the sidewalks of Ventura Boulevard just west of Van Nuys Boulevard for dinner, ice cream, and window gazing.

Web Sites: www.cityofla.org, www.valleyglen.org, www.encinochamber.org, www.sohainfo.com, http://lacounty.info

Area Code: 818

Zip Codes: Encino: 91316, 91436; Woodland Hills: 91364–7; Van Nuys/Valley Glen: 91401–35; Sherman Oaks: 91401

Post Offices: Encino branch, 5805 White Oak Ave; Woodland Hills Main Post Office, 22121 Clarendon St; Van Nuys Main Post Office, 15701 Sherman Way; Sherman Oaks branch, 14900 Magnolia Blvd

Police District: Encino and Woodland Hills are patrolled by the LAPD's West Valley Division: 19020 Vanowen St, 818-374-7611; Van Nuys and Sherman Oaks are patrolled by the LAPD's Van Nuys Division: 6240 Sylmar Ave, 818-374-9500; www.lapdonline.org.

Emergency Hospitals: Encino Tarzana Regional Medical Center - Encino Campus, 16237 Ventura Blvd, 818-995-5000, www.encino-tarzana.com; Kaiser Permanente Woodland Hills Medical Center, 5601 De Soto Ave, 818-719-2000, www.kaiserpermanente.org; Van Nuys Hospital, 15220 Vanowen St, 818-787-0123; Valley Presbyterian Hospital, 15107 Vanowen St, Van Nuys, 818-782-6600, www.valleypres.org; Sherman Oaks Hospital & Health Center, 4929 Van Nuys Blvd, 818-981-7111, www.shermanoakshospital.com

Libraries: Encino-Tarzana Library, 18231 Ventura Blvd, 818-343-1983; Woodland Hills Library, 22200 Ventura Blvd, 818-226-0017; Platt branch Library, 23600 Victory Blvd, 818-340-9386; Van Nuys Library, 6250 Sylmar Ave, 818-756-8453; Sherman Oaks Library, 14245 Moorpark St, 818-205-9716; www.lapl.org

Public School Education: LA Unified School District, 333 S Beaudry Ave, LA, 213-241-1000, www.lausd.k12.ca.us

Community Resources: Sepulveda Basin Recreation Area, 17017 Encino Blvd, 818-756-8060, www.laparks.org; Los Encinos State Historic Park, 16756 Moorpark St, 818-784-4849, http://los-encinos.org or www.parks.ca.gov; Encino Velodrome, 17301 Oxnard St, 818-881-7441, www.encinovelodrome.org; Encino Community Center, 4935 Balboa Blvd, 818-995-1690, www.laparks. org; Van Nuys-Sherman Oaks Park, 14201 Huston St, 818-783-5121, www. laparks.org

Public Transportation: call 800-COMMUTE or visit www.mta.net for specific MTA bus route and schedule information.

EAST VALLEY

WEST HILLS
CANOGA PARK
RESEDA
NORTHRIDGE

Boundaries: **East**: Shoup Avenue; **South**: Victory Boulevard; **North**: Nordhoff Street; **West**: Ventura County

The eucalyptus trees that are a common sight in much of California are said to have descended from the ones first planted in **West Hills** by an English immigrant named Alfred Workman, who imported the fragrant tree from Australia. Today, all kinds of greenery line the well-tended streets of this community. The West Hills Neighborhood Council helped separate West Hills from **Canoga Park** in 1988 to develop a distinct identity, and the Council continues to actively support residents. The area's largest business is the West Hills Hospital.

Canoga Park (originally called Owensmouth) has a scruffier urban feel with busy and crowded Sherman Way being the main thoroughfare. Its retail stores look a little faded and the area is dotted with small industrial areas and office parks. West Hills is cleaner, greener and embraces a more suburban vibe. Housing consists of a mix of your typical '50s-style stucco bungalows, ranch-style houses from the '60s and '70s, and custom homes with Mediterranean architecture. The homes along the western edge, such as the Stonegate neighborhood, tend to be more upscale, and residential streets undulate among the rolling hills. A three-bedroom, two-bath house is typical. Families strolling with their kids or pets are a common sight. Home prices tend to run a little higher than neighboring Canoga Park. Local shopping options include Platt Village (Platt and Victory) and Fallbrook Center mall (22950 Vanowen Street). Knapp Ranch Park offers basketball and tennis courts, a children's play area, and picnic tables.

East of Canoga Park is **Reseda**, an early Valley suburb that is showing its age in places. This urban neighborhood has taken on an East Los Angeles feel as recent immigrants find the working class community's affordability attractive. Among its rows of residential streets, the aging housing stock would benefit from sprucing up. But, the price of homes here is less than what you'd pay in Canoga Park. Local amenities feature a three-acre duck pond and community center inside Reseda Park.

Northridge is to the north. Most people remember this community from the Northridge Earthquake of 1994. Its epicenter was on Reseda Boulevard, a main thoroughfare here. Driving around today, it's difficult to tell that this was one of the hardest hit communities. A number of homes and apartments benefited from facelifts or new construction following the aggressive rebuilding effort. Housing prices vary, lower toward the south due to proximity to the Van Nuys Airport (private planes only), just southeast of this neighborhood. Then home prices rise slightly as you head north. There are pockets of new housing proposals, including a development of 30+ new homes proposed for White Oak Avenue between Lassen and Superior.

Among the concrete here is an oasis called Northridge Park & Recreation Center. Within the park is a house once owned by Clark Gable that's popular for weddings. Over 170 stores are located in the Northridge Fashion Center. This indoor mall was severely damaged in the quake, rebuilt shortly after, then modernized and expanded in 1998. Nearby is CalState University Northridge, serving 34,000 students. Their on-campus amenities such as the fitness center with gym and pool and a 1.5-acre botanic garden are open to residents. On the southeast corner of campus is a small orange grove lovingly tended by the school since the campus's initial construction in the 1950s. These citrus trees could be the oldest remnant of the massive orange groves that used to flourish all over Valley.

Web Sites: www.canogaparknc.org, www.westhillsnc.org, www.resedacouncil. org, www.northridgecouncil.org, www.northridgeeast.com, http://lacounty. info

Area Code: 818

Zip Codes: Canoga Park: 91304; West Hills: 91304, 91307; Reseda: 91325, 91328, 91335; Northridge: 91324–30, 91343

Post Offices: Canoga Park Station, 8201 Canoga Park Ave; West Hills Station, 23055 Sherman Way; Reseda Station, 7320 Reseda Blvd; Northridge Station, 9534 Reseda Blvd

Police District: Devonshire Division (for north of Roscoe Blvd): 10250 Etiwanda Ave, 818-832-0633; West Valley Division (for south of Roscoe Blvd): 19020 Vanowen St, 818-374-7611, www.lapdonline.org

Emergency Hospitals: West Hills Hospital & Medical Center, 7300 Medical Center Dr, 818-676-4000, www.westhillshospital.com; Northridge Hospital Medical Center, 18300 Roscoe Blvd, 818-885-8500, www.northridgehospital.org

Libraries: Canoga Park branch, 20939 Sherman Way, 818-887-0320; West Valley Regional branch, 19036 Vanowen St, 818-345-9806; Northridge branch, 9051 Darby Ave, 818-886-3640; www.lapl.org

Public School Education: LA Unified School District, 333 S Beaudry Ave, LA, 213-241-1000, www.lausd.k12.ca.us

Community Resources: Knapp Ranch Park, 25000 Kittridge St, 818-883-9370, www.laparks.org; Reseda Park & Recreation Center, 18411 Victory Blvd, 818-881-3882, www.laparks.org; Northridge Park & Recreation Center, 18300 Lemarsh St, 818-349-7341, www.laparks.org; Northridge Fashion Center, 9301 Tampa Ave, 818-701-7051, www.northridgefashioncenter.com; CalState Northridge, 18111 Nordhoff St, 818-677-1200, www.csun.edu

Public Transportation: call 800-COMMUTE or visit www.mta.net for specific MTA bus routes and schedule information.

NORTH HOLLYWOOD

TOLUCA LAKE
STUDIO CITY

Boundaries: **East**: Cahuenga Boulevard; **South**: Ventura Boulevard; **North**: Saticoy Street; **West**: Van Nuys Boulevard

North Hollywood, located within the Valley, is great for affordable apartments and easy access to almost any place in LA without actually being in Los Angeles proper—as long as you have a car. Serviced by the 101 Hollywood Freeway (driver beware, this schizophrenic freeway goes both north-south and east-west), the largely Hispanic North Hollywood neighborhood is a working-class enclave. You'll find rents are more affordable as you go north, though proximity to industrial and commercial zones makes for noisier and grittier living. If you stick close to main thoroughfares like Riverside Drive or Moorpark Street (the southern end of North Hollywood) you will find residences that combine North Hollywood's affordability with the neighboring security of the Toluca Lake (to the east) and Studio City (to the west) communities.

Available street parking runs the gamut and depends on whether the street you live on is crowded with apartments or homes. The good news is permits are not required, street parking is usually unrestricted, and most apartments provide gated parking spaces.

Vacancies in apartments or homes are not hard to find. Among other things, rents here depend on proximity to the more prestigious Toluca Lake and Studio City zip codes. Affordable housing and easy access to the studios make North Hollywood a good bet for transplants interested in the entertainment business.

Judging by the large selection of individual serving–sized portions of food in neighborhood grocery stores, this town is home to a significant singles population. Grocery shopping abounds, with every major supermarket chain represented in the area. For those on the move, dry cleaners and gas stations can be found on virtually every street corner. Used bookstores and thrift shops dot the area, convincing many a bargain hunter they've died and gone to heaven.

Eateries to satisfy every stomach and wallet size, from the cellphone-armed executive with a fat expense account to the would-be-starlet, abound. Actors, writers, and producers, with their irregular work schedules, keep stores and restaurants hopping throughout the week and weekend.

The renovation of NoHo, North Hollywood's arts district, has yielded a collection of small actor's theaters, coffee shops, used bookstores and eclectic retail stores along Lankershim Boulevard. The Academy of Television Arts and Sciences also calls this one-square-mile-wide district home. The subway's red line ends in NoHo. Many new apartments, condos, and townhomes have sprouted near this and the Universal Studios subway stations.

A pleasant place for a stroll is City Walk at nearby Universal Studios. It's a self-contained outdoor "entertainment complex" (read: theme restaurants, stores, and movie theaters) drawing tourists and locals alike, especially on weekends. (Residents who live within qualifying zip codes may request a booklet of free parking passes from Universal's corporate communications office at 818-777-3591.) Natives who like to keep up with the latest movie releases will appreciate the selection at Odyssey Video or Eddie Brandt's Saturday Matinee on Vineland Avenue.

The neighboring communities of **Toluca Lake** and **Studio City** are higher-income neighborhoods with plush apartments, recently built condos, and single-family homes hidden among leafy trees. The fact that Toluca Lake and Studio City are just minutes from the media districts of Burbank and Universal City means that a lot of entertainment industry people live in the area. Comedian Jay Leno, an avid car collector, can sometimes be seen hanging with fellow grease monkeys at the oldest remaining Big Boy Restaurant, Bob's Big Boy, 4211 Riverside Drive, which hosts antique car shows and car hop service on weekends.

Within Studio City, you'll find a mix of owners and renters. Single-family residences that cluster behind magnolia trees south of Ventura Boulevard (the main thoroughfare) are slightly more expensive than the homes lining streets that run east-west, just north of Ventura Boulevard. Apartments and condos are grouped to the north of Ventura along north-south running streets. Ventura Boulevard is a long, bustling street with a wide variety of restaurants and retail merchants—a great place to meander and browse or just people watch.

Web Site: www.nohoartsdistrict.com, www.gtlnc.org, www.scnc.info, http://laco unty.info

Area Code: 818

Zip Codes: 91601–91606

Post Offices: North Hollywood Station, 7035 Laurel Canyon Blvd; Chandler Station, 11304 Chandler Blvd; Toluca Lake Station, 10063 Riverside Drive; Studio City Station, 3950 Laurel Canyon Blvd

Police District: North Hollywood Division: 11640 Burbank Blvd, 818-623-4016, www.lapdonline.org

Emergency Hospitals: hospitals serving this area are located within neighboring communities: Providence Saint Joseph Medical Center, 501 S Buena Vista Ave, Burbank, 818-843-5111, www.providence.org; Sherman Oaks Hospital & Health Center, 4929 Van Nuys Blvd, Sherman Oaks, 818-981-7111, www.sher manoakshospital.com

Libraries: North Hollywood Regional branch, 5211 Tujunga Ave, 818-766-7185; Valley Plaza branch, 12311 Vanowen St, 818-765-9251; Studio City branch, 12511 Moorpark St, 818-755-7873; www.lapl.org

Public School Education: LA Unified School District, 333 S Beaudry Ave, LA, 213-241-1000, www.lausd.k12.ca.us

Community Resources: North Hollywood Recreation Center & Senior Center, 1143 Chandler Blvd, 818-763-7651; Studio City Recreation Center, 12621 Rye St, 818-769-4415; www.laparks.org; Laurel Canyon Dog Park, 8260 Mulholland Drive, 818-769-4415

Public Transportation: call 800-COMMUTE or visit www.mta.net for specific MTA bus routes and schedule information.

BURBANK, GLENDALE

Boundaries: East: 5 Golden State Freeway; **South**: 134 Ventura Freeway; **North**: Verdugo Mountains; **West**: Clybourn Avenue

One of the oldest Los Angeles suburbs, the **City of Burbank** began life as a humble sheep pasture. Named after Dr. David Burbank, a sheep-ranching dentist, it wasn't until 1928 with the development of a small airplane manufacturing site owned by Alan Loughead (who changed the spelling to Lockheed) that modern Burbank began to form. Around the same time, a motion picture studio laid roots here and was eventually acquired by Warner Brothers. Today, Burbank's big industry is entertainment, home to NBC's West Coast headquarters, Disney Studios, Nickelodeon Animation Studios, and a host of other entertainment-related businesses. City leaders, in a campaign to establish Burbank as the "Media Capital of the World," have nicknamed the town Media City. However, since NBC's acquisition of Universal Studios, they have announced plans to sell off its Burbank facility once construction of new facilities in Universal City is completed in 2011.

With an older town, you might expect worn architecture and fully filled out lands. By those standards, Burbank hardly reveals its true age. Most of its existing homes were built in the 1960s and have been well cared for. The residences here are well tended and often display the unique characteristics of their owners.

While this community may not be as leafy as others, many of the stucco homes, built to maximize the land allotted to them, sport lush lawns. The housing stock is nicely balanced between renters and homeowners; about 45% are single-family homes and the remaining 55% are townhomes, condos, and apartments. Many condos have been recently built; apartments, however, range from the recently built to the well preserved. Rents vary; you'll find bargain rates for a one-bedroom in an older building but you can expect to pay more to live in the same in a new building. Prospective homebuyers might want to check nearby **Verdugo Hills** (dubbed the Burbank Hills) for newly built multi-bedroom Spanish architecture homes, complete with panoramic views.

The cost of living in Burbank is slightly lower than in many of Los Angeles County's upper-middle class communities; and business taxes and licenses cost less. The Bob Hope Airport (formerly called the Burbank-Glendale-Pasadena Airport) offers travelers the choice of some major airlines (see **Transportation**), without the congestion of LAX. The airport was trying to establish a new passenger terminal, but area residents who did not want the additional noise pollution opposed it. To date, airport authorities have agreed to put off building a new passenger terminal until after 2014. However, they have built a collection of new fast food restaurants at the entrance of the airport.

Starting in the mid 1990s, community leaders revamped the city's 22 parks (including three senior centers), built a brand new police and fire headquarters, and opened a three-story, indoor mall, the Burbank Town Center at 201 East Magnolia Boulevard. Just on the other side of the mall is "Burbank Village," San Fernando Boulevard in downtown Burbank, a popular evening hangout for its stores and restaurants, not to mention a large AMC theater complex. A couple of new residential developments are here, Burbank Village Walk (just east of the Village) and The Burbank Collection (right next to the theater). The huge Swedish discount furniture store, IKEA, is located here, providing put-it-together-yourself furniture at reasonable prices. Horse lovers should note that Burbank has a residential area zoned for horses, the Rancho Equestrian area located near Keystone Street, south of Alameda Avenue. The lovely Los Angeles Equestrian Center is in Burbank. Neighborhood restaurants lean toward comfort food rather than gourmet-type fare.

With a small-town feel, clean streets, and one of the most responsive police departments around, Burbank also feels contemporary and metropolitan. It is this city's charm, affordability and total lack of attitude common to other LA towns that makes Burbank a stand-out for young families and senior citizens.

Adjacent to Burbank, just east of the 5 Golden State Freeway, is the **City of Glendale**. It too has undergone a great deal of change in the past two decades, becoming an ethnically diverse population of over 200,000 people in its 30 square miles. Glendale, the third largest city in Los Angeles County, has a more urban feel and pace than Burbank, but housing prices are comparable.

Single- and multi-family units were once the predominant housing type here, but today, multi-family units comprise 60% of the city's housing stock. In fact, Glendale has one of the highest percentages of multi-family dwelling units, many of which were built in the 1980s, of any city in California. Most apartment buildings are clustered around downtown—a bright and cheery business district located just south of the 134 Ventura Freeway. Some of the newest two-story, stucco, red-tiled homes are poised above Chevy Chase Drive, east of Highway 2. Most existing homes were built between 1950 and 1980 and can be found north of Foothill Boulevard.

Glendale has attracted a large Asian, Middle Eastern, and Mediterranean population. The nation's largest Armenian population resides here. Recognizing residents' love for chess, the city built a chess "park" in 2004 at 227 North Brand Boulevard near the Alex Theatre. Between two retail stores is a passageway lined with 16 cement tables with inlay chess boards. Glendale's main thoroughfare, the recently redeveloped Brand Avenue, is lined with charming restaurants and sumptuous bakeries of many ethnic persuasions. Overall, streets are clean, business districts well tended, and social amenities abundant, including the large indoor mall, Glendale Galleria, and 32 city parks. Across the street from the Galleria, The Americana at Brand, a mixed-use development set to open in 2008, will feature shops, restaurants, "apartment homes," and high-end condos situated around a courtyard. The city's civic beautification efforts on Brand Avenue and tree plantings along Colorado Boulevard have paid off handsomely. Kenneth Village, a quaint row of 1920s storefronts on Kenneth Road at Granville Avenue, features picturesque retail stores. Another gem within the city is its main library, holding an impressive collection of over 20,000 books.

Web Sites: www.ci.burbank.ca.us; www.ci.glendale.ca.us, http://lacounty.info
Area Code: 818
Zip Codes: Burbank: 91501–91523; Glendale: 91201–91213
Post Offices: Burbank Main Post Office, 2140 N Hollywood Way; Glendale Main Post Office, 313 E Broadway St; many more locations
Police District: Burbank and Glendale operate their own municipal police forces: Burbank Police Headquarters: 200 N Third St, 818-238-3000, www.ci.burbank. ca.us/police; Glendale Police Department: 140 N Isabel, 818-548-4840, www. ci.glendale.ca.us/police/default.asp
Emergency Hospitals: Providence Saint Joseph Medical Center, 501 S Buena Vista Ave, Burbank, 818-843-5111, www.providence.org; Glendale Memorial Hospital and Health Center, 1420 S Central Ave, Glendale, 818-502-1900, www.glendalememorialhospital.org
Libraries: Main Burbank Library, 110 N Glenoaks Blvd, 818-238-5600; Buena Vista branch, 300 N Buena Vista, 818-238-5620; Northwest branch, 3323 W Victory Blvd, 818-238-5640; www.burbank.lib.ca.us; Main Glendale Library, 222 E Harvard St, 818-548-2030; Brand Library & Art Center, 1601 W Mountain

St, 818-548-2051; Casa Verdugo branch Library, 1151 N Brand Blvd, 818-548-2047; Chevy Chase branch, 3301 E Chevy Chase Dr, 818-548-2046, Grandview branch Library, 1535 Fifth St, 818-548-2049; Pacific Park branch Library, 501 S Pacific Ave, 818-548-3760; ww.brandlibrary.org

Public School Education: Burbank Unified School District, 1900 W Olive Ave, Burbank, 818-729-4400; www.burbank.k12.ca.us; Glendale Unified School District, 223 N Jackson St, Glendale, 818-241-3111, http://gusd.net

Community Resources: Olive Recreation Center and George Izzay Park, 1111 W Olive Ave, 818-238-5385; Verdugo Recreation Center, 3201 W Verdugo Ave, 818-238-5390; Burbank Tennis Center, 1515 N Glenoaks Blvd, 818-843-4105, www.burbanktenniscenter.com; Johnny Carson Park, 400 S Bob Hope Dr; Burbank Starlight Bowl, 1249 Lockheed View Dr, 818-525-3721, www.starlightbowl.com; De Bell Municipal Golf Course, 1500 E Walnut Ave, 818-845-5052/0022; Burbank Family YMCA, 321 E Magnolia Blvd, 818-845-8551, www.burbankymca.org; Burbank Parks and Recreation Department, 818-238-5300, www.ci.burbank.ca.us; Los Angeles Equestrian Center, 480 Riverside Dr, 818-840-9063, www.la-equestriancenter.com; Glendale Central Park, E Colorado St and S Louise St, 818-548-2000, http://parks.ci.glendale.ca.us/parks.htm.

Public Transportation: call 800-COMMUTE, or visit www.mta.net for specific MTA bus routes and schedule information. Downtown Glendale has a shuttle known as the "Beeline"; call 818-548-3968, or visit www.glendalebeeline.com for route and schedule information

PASADENA

ALTADENA
SAN MARINO
SOUTH PASADENA

Boundaries: North: Montana Street (in the west), Washington Boulevard (in the east); **East:** West of Michilinda Avenue; **South:** Columbia Street (in the west), California Boulevard (in the east); **West:** Hills west of Linda Vista Mountain Way

Pasadena's claim to fame is the always-sunny New Year's Day Tournament of Roses Parade and Rose Bowl, but this city's roots, like much of the Valley, are in agriculture. Pioneers who came to this area in the late 1800s found success growing oranges and olives, and named their community Pasadena (derived from an Ojibwa word and translated into "Crown of the Valley").

By the turn of the 20th century, the town had become a winter retreat for wealthy Midwesterners such as David B. Gamble of Procter & Gamble and chewing gum magnate William Wrigley Jr. Through the next several decades it was known as a quiet, pretty, and conservative place in which to raise a family. By the way, the ornate Wrigley mansion, built between 1908 and 1914, serves as the offices of the Pasadena Tournament of Roses Association today.

Over the past few years, a revitalized "old town" has sparked new interest in the area. Colorado Boulevard is Pasadena's main artery, and the heart of Old Pasadena. The city's original business district, Old Pasadena is bounded by Pasadena Avenue, Walnut Street, Arroyo Parkway, and Green Street; restored historic buildings offer a unique array of retailers, art galleries, movie theaters, antique shops, restaurants, and offices. On weekend nights, the sidewalks are brimming with people. The outdoor pedestrian mall, Paseo Colorado, opened in 2002, adds to the area's shopping possibilities.

Those arriving in Pasadena via the 134 Ventura Freeway are greeted by a magnificent view of the intricate and recently restored Colorado Street Bridge (Colorado Boulevard at Arroyo Seco). Carefully preserved, turn-of-the-century homes grace the streets, and Pasadena residents take pride in the city's small town atmosphere. At first glance, single-family homes appear to make up the majority of the residential offerings; however, about half of the city's residents are renters. Most homes were built in the 1950s, with about 30% constructed before 1939. Housing prices in Pasadena start above the county median and go up from there. The neighborhood is clean, palm tree-lined, with plenty of grassy front yards. "Pah-sad-na," as some intentionally but affectionately mispronounce the name, is a lovely place to own a home. An indication that residents are mindful of keeping their city beautiful, $127 million was spent in 2007 restoring city hall (built in 1927).

Would-be homebuyers who fall in love with Pasadena may elect to buy in the neighboring, yet-to-be-incorporated **Altadena**, just north of Pasadena. Residents of this leafy suburb find they can still enjoy the benefits of Pasadena without the higher price tag; homes here hover just above the county median. Suburban to its core, Altadena still has plenty of room for development. Some homeowners keep horses on their land and many backyards open right onto mountain trails. Paved sidewalks and apartment buildings are scarce. In a tradition that dates back to 1920, every holiday season, residents are known to deck out the giant cedar trees along Santa Rosa Avenue between Woodbury Road and Altadena Drive with lights.

If money is not a concern, try the **City of San Marino**, Pasadena's southern neighbor, which also offers a cozy community with beautiful, rolling tree-lined streets. The posh Langham Huntington Hotel & Spa offers pampering to the ladies who lunch—they number more than a handful here. The main library, which has been redone into a "state of the art" complex, reopened in early 2008. The picture-perfect, multiple-bedroom homes are in the million-dollar to millions of dollars range—more expensive than Pasadena. This storybook neighborhood was featured in the Steve Martin film *Father of the Bride*.

To the south of Pasadena is—surprise—the **City of South Pasadena**. It too features Craftsman-style and Mission Revival architecture. Located between

Pasadena and Los Angeles, it acts as a buffer between these two environs, and consequently some streets aren't as well tended as those of its northerly sister. Despite its more urban feel, homes here fetch prices that approach those in Pasadena.

In the commercial districts of these residential neighborhoods, boutique shops and gourmet grocery stores mingle with general retailers, providing plentiful shopping options. South Lake Avenue is where you'll find designer label boutiques. Preservation of area historic sites adds to the village-like feel of these communities. Pasadena's public library is housed in a Renaissance-style building. One of the country's oldest soda fountains, the Fair Oaks Pharmacy and Soda Fountain (1526 Mission Street, South Pasadena), still dishes out malts and egg creams much like it did back in the 1920s.

The Jet Propulsion Laboratory, Cal Tech, Pasadena Center (the city's convention center), Pasadena Playhouse (built in 1917), the lavish Huntington Gardens and Library, and the privately owned Norton Simon Museum, featuring Western European painting and Asian sculpture, round out the first-rate cultural and educational offerings in the area.

Depending on where you work, Pasadena, serviced by the 210 Foothill and 134 Ventura Freeways, can be a half-hour commute to downtown Los Angeles or parts of the Valley—or a long haul if you need to head to the western and southern communities of Los Angeles. A car is definitely needed here, unless you plan to work in an area easily accessed by public transportation or your own two feet. The Metro also runs the Gold Line from downtown Los Angeles to Pasadena. When South Pasadena residents complained about excessive noise from the Gold Line, the MTA responded by building a sound wall between the Mission and Fillmore stations in 2007.

On the downside, Pasadena, nestled as it is in the foothills of the San Gabriel Mountains, can get hot and smoggy. Still, Pasadena and its neighboring cities remain a wonderful place to call home…just be on the lookout for central air conditioning when house hunting here.

Web Sites: www.ci.pasadena.ca.us, www.pasadenacal.com, www.ci.south-pasadena.ca.us, www.altadenatowncouncil.org, www.cityofsanmarino.org, http://lacounty.info

Area Code: 626

Zip Codes: Pasadena: 91101–91126; South Pasadena: 91030; San Marino: 91108; Altadena: 91001

Post Offices: Pasadena Main Post Office, 600 N Lincoln Ave; S Pasadena Main Post Office, 1001 Fremont Ave; Altadena Main Post Office: 2271 Lake Ave; many more locations

Police District: Pasadena Police Headquarters, 207 N Garfield Ave, 626-744-4501, www.ci.pasadena.ca.us/police; South Pasadena Police Headquarters, 1422 Mission St, 626-403-7270, www.ci.south-pasadena.ca.us; San Marino Police

Department Headquarters, 2200 Huntington Dr, 626-300-0720, www.cityof
sanmarino.org/smpd

Emergency Hospitals: Huntington Memorial Hospital, 100 W California Blvd,
626-397-5000, www.huntingtonhospital.com; Methodist Hospital, 300 W
Huntington Dr, 626-898-8000, http://methodisthospital.org

Libraries: Main Library, 285 E Walnut St, 626-744-4066, www.ci.pasadena.ca.us/
library; South Pasadena Public Library, 1100 Oxley St, 626-403-7330, www.
ci.south-pasadena.ca.us; San Marino Public Library, 1890 Huntington Drive,
626-300-0777, www.sanmarinopl.org or http://brandnewlibrary.org; Altadena Main Library, 600 E Mariposa St, 626-798-0833, http://library.altadena.
ca.us

Public School Education: Pasadena Unified School District, 351 S Hudson Ave,
Pasadena, 626-795-6981, www.pasadena.k12.ca.us; South Pasadena Unified
School District, 1020 El Centro St, South Pasadena, 626-441-5810, www.spusd.
net; San Marino Unified School District, 1665 West Dr, San Marino, 626-299-
7000, www.san-marino.k12.ca.us; Altadena is part of the La Canada Unified
School District, 5039 Palm Dr, La Canada, 818-952-8300, www.lcusd.net

Community Resources: Norton Simon Museum, 411 W Colorado Blvd, Pasadena,
626-449-6840, www.nortonsimon.org; Huntington Library, Art Collections &
Botanical Gardens, 1151 Oxford Rd, San Marino, 626-405-2100, www.hunting
ton.org; Pacific Asia Museum, 46 N Los Robles Ave, Pasadena, 626-449-2742,
www.pacificasiamuseum.org; Tournament House & Wrigley Gardens, 391 S
Orange Grove Blvd, 626-449-4100, www.tournamentofroses.com; Rose Bowl,
991 Rosemont Blvd, Pasadena, 626-577-3100, www.rosebowlstadium.com;
Brookside Park, 360 N Arroyo Blvd, Pasadena; Pasadena Human Services &
Recreation Department, 626-744-7290, www.ci.pasadena.ca.us/humanser
vices/default.asp; California Institute of Technology, 1201 E California Blvd,
Pasadena, 626-395-6811, www.caltech.edu.

Public Transportation: call 800-COMMUTE, or visit www.mta.net for route and
schedule information for MTA bus and the Metro Gold Line. Foothill Transit
contributes regular and express bus service here, 626-967-3147, www.foothill
transit.org. LADOT also operates commuter express lines here, 800-363-1317,
www.ladottransit.com. Free Pasadena ARTS Buses shuttle the shopping and
entertainment districts; inquire with Transit Operations at 626-398-8973,
www.ci.pasadena.ca.us/artsbus for routes and hours.

SANTA CLARITA

NEWHALL
VALENCIA
LANCASTER
PALMDALE
ACTON

Boundaries: East: Angeles National Forest; **South:** Junction of the 5 Golden State and 14 Antelope Valley Freeways; **North:** Angeles National Forest; **West:** 5 Golden State Freeway

Santa Clarita became a city only in 1987. But since then, it has been frequently recognized as a kid-friendly suburban city. In fact, in 2006, CNN/*Money* Magazine selected the city among the 20 best places to live, and among cities in California, Santa Clarita was tops. The community's low crime, nice climate, and amenities figure in as factors. In fact, the city claims its schools consistently rank in the top 10% in California.

Fifty-two square miles in size and with a population of over 177,000, Santa Clarita is the fourth-largest city in LA County. It is located 35 miles north of downtown Los Angeles, in between the 5 Golden State and the 14 Antelope Valley freeways, near the Six Flags Magic Mountain Theme Park (incidentally, the city's largest employer). The established community of Newhall and the newer tract-housing community of Valencia are both within Santa Clarita.

Much of Santa Clarita's existing housing was built in the 1960s; however, during the late 1990s the city experienced another housing boom. Prices here are reasonable, primarily due to Santa Clarita's far-flung location, making it one of the fastest growing cities in the county. While 26 miles may not sound far, with traffic, an hour-plus commute into central LA would not be unusual. (You could opt for the Metrolink, which takes residents to Burbank, Glendale, or downtown LA.) Despite the longer-than-average commute to LA, many newcomers are drawn to Santa Clarita's affordable housing and newness. And, according to FBI statistics, Santa Clarita is the safest city of its size in the state and the nation.

Typical housing in Santa Clarita consists of newer four-bedroom/two-story homes. Newly built condominiums run about two-thirds the price of a new home. Rentals, with a slightly lower vacancy rate than the rest of the county, are moderately priced. Young families make up a large segment of the population—the median age here is about 34. Santa Clarita sponsors Pride Week every April, an organized effort to keep the community clean (call organizers at 661-255-4918 for more details). A word of warning to newcomers from cold climates, Santa Clarita is in desert country and gets quite hot during the summer.

"New" seems to be the best adjective to describe the communities of Santa Clarita. New apartment complexes have gone up around Town Center Drive. Three of their newest parks are only a few years old: 17-acre Canyon Country Park; 5-acre Begonias Lane Park (both in Canyon Country); and the 8-acre Creekview Park in Newhall. The city's commitment to creating a family-friendly environment is obvious, with its latest effort involving the new Aquatics Center, which hosts frequent youth swimming races. The city also operates a "park mobile" that visits various parks to provide games and crafting activities (call 661-284-1465).

Revitalization efforts and civic dollars are also being invested in downtown **Newhall**. The typical chain restaurants, houseware stores, and grocery stores can be found in the myriad of recently built strip malls. Old Town Newhall features restaurants and shops. School buildings here are also new. (Note that separate districts represent elementary schools and high schools here.) The California Institute of the Arts (Cal Arts), the Disney-sponsored arts college where many top animators graduate, is located in Newhall, and a new theater complex and major recreation area and skateboard park in adjacent Canyon Country are some of the more recently available community offerings.

In **Valencia**, community amenities are similar to neighboring Newhall's but the buildings appear even newer. Valencia residents are especially keen on preserving the neighborhood's spacious environs. Oak trees and generous greenbelts are plentiful here, supported by residents who pay an annual assessment for public landscape upkeep. (Not so in other nearby communities, where *au naturel* tends to be the rule.) This tract-housing community is also noted for excellent traffic flow within its well-planned streets and an extensive series of scenic walkways and bikepaths. Their indoor mall, Westfield Valencia Town Center, recently announced plans to expand.

Farther north of Santa Clarita are the City of Acton, the City of Lancaster, and the City of Palmdale. All three are located in Antelope Valley, with Lancaster and Palmdale bordering Edwards Air Force Base. This is truly desert country, spacious flat land, hot dry air, no smog, and bargain-priced homes garnished with freshly planted trees. The commute to LA is even longer than what it would be from Santa Clarita. Metrolink riders frequently pass animals grazing the wild animal nature preserve called Shambala Preserve. **Acton**, nearly 50 miles from LA, is the most southern of the trio. Acton originally sprung up as a mining town when gold, copper, and titanium were found in the late 1800s. Homes in this intimate equestrian community are the most expensive of the three. Many of the ranch-style homes in this area were built in the mid 1980s. The older residences date from between 1950 and 1970. Rentals make up a modest 27% of the housing stock here. Three- to four-bedroom homes are sprouting up all over with commercial districts blossoming alongside.

Lancaster is the second largest city on the California side of the Mojave Desert. The affordability of land here has attracted distribution centers for companies such as Rite Aid. The Lancaster Performing Arts Center, founded in 1989, supports local artists and provides a nice concert venue for the city's diverse residents. In 1996, the city constructed Clear Channel Stadium, which now hosts the city's minor league baseball team.

Palmdale too is enjoying new amenities as it continues developing; a large Sheriff's Station opened in 2006 and the Palmdale Regional Medical Center is scheduled to open in 2009. Air Force Plant 42 is situated here, and Edwards Air Force Base is the largest employer in the city. The prices of these homes run well below the county median, with Palmdale slightly higher than Lancaster. These towns make lovely selections for first-time homebuyers who enjoy desert suburban life.

Web Sites: www.santa-clarita.com, www.cityofacton.org, www.cityoflancasterca. org, www.cityofpalmdale.org, http://lacounty.info

Area Code: 661

Zip Codes: Santa Clarita: 91300–99; Acton: 93510; Lancaster: 93534; Palmdale: 93550

Post Offices: Santa Clarita Main Post Office, 24355 Creekside Rd; Acton Main Post Office, 3632 Smith Ave; Lancaster Main Post Office: 1008 W Ave J2; Cedar Station, 567 W Lancaster Blvd; Palmdale Main Post Office, 38917 20th St E; Palmdale branches: 2220 E Palmdale Blvd, 37167 Sierra Hwy, 829 W Palmdale Blvd; many more locations

Police District: all communities are patrolled by the LA County Sheriffs. The Santa Clarita Valley station is at 23740 Magic Mountain Pkwy, 661-255-1121, www.scvsheriff.com; Lancaster station: 501 W Lancaster Blvd, 661-948-8466; Palmdale Station: 750 E Ave, 661-272-2400, www.lasd.org.

Emergency Hospitals: in Valencia and Newhall, Henry Mayo Newhall Memorial Hospital, 23845 W McBean Pkwy, 661-253-8000, www.henrymayo.com; for Lancaster and Acton: Antelope Valley Hospital Medical Center, 1600 W Ave J, 661-949-5000, www.avhospital.org; LAC-High Desert Multi-Service Ambulatory Care Center, 44900 N 60th St W, 661-948-8581; Lancaster Community Hospital, 43830 10th St W, 661-948-4781, www.lancastercommunityhospital. net; in Palmdale: South Valley Health Center, 38350 40th St E, 661-272-5000, www.avph.org.

Libraries: Valencia Library, 23743 W Valencia Blvd, 661-259-8942; Newhall Library, 22704 W 9th St, 661-259-0750; Santa Clarita Valley Bookmobile for Acton, 661-260-1792; Lancaster Library, 601 W Lancaster Blvd, 661-948-5029; www. colapublib.org; Palmdale City Library, 700 E Palmdale Blvd, 661-267-5600, www.palmdalelibrary.org;

Public School Education: Saugus Union School District, 24930 Ave Stanford, Santa Clarita, 661-294-5300, www.saugus.k12.ca.us; William S. Hart Union High School District, 21515 Centre Pointe Pkwy, Santa Clarita, 661-259-0033, www.hartdistrict.org; Newhall School District, 25375 Orchard Village Rd, Valencia, 91355, 661-291-4000, www.newhallschooldistrict.net; Acton-Agua Dulce Unified School District, 32248 N Crown Valley Rd, Acton, 93510, 661-269-5999, www.aadusd.k12.ca.us; Antelope Valley Union High School District, 44811 Sierra Hwy, Lancaster, 661-948-7655, www.avdistrict.org; Lancaster School District, 44711 N Cedar Ave, Lancaster, 661-948-4661, www.lancaster. k12.ca.us; Palmdale School District, 39139 N 10th St East, Palmdale, 661-947-7191, www.psd.k12.ca.us

Community Resources: Santa Clarita Activities Center, 20880 Centre Pointe Pkwy, 661-284-1476, www.santa-clarita.com; Santa Clarita Aquatics Center, 20850 Centre Pointe Pkwy, 661-250-3766, www.santa-clarita.com; Newhall Park, 24923 Newhall Ave, 661-286-4000; Valencia Meadows Park, 25671 Fedala Rd, 661-286-4000; Canyon Country Park, 17815 W Soledad Canyon Rd,

Santa Clarita; Santa Clarita Park, 27285 Seco Canyon Rd, 661-799-1198, www.
santa-clarita.com; Santa Clarita City recreation programs, 661-250-3700; Cal
Arts, 24700 McBean Pkwy, Valencia, 661-255-1050, www.calarts.edu; Acton
County Park, Syracuse Ave and Crown Valley Rd, www.cityofacton.org/park.
htm; Lancaster Performing Arts Center, 750 Lancaster Blvd, 661-723-5950,
www.lpac.org

Public Transportation: Antelope Valley Transit Authority route and schedule information: 661-945-9445, www.avta.com; Santa Clarita Transit/Bus route and
schedule information: 661-294-1287, www.santa-clarita.com/cityhall/field/
transit; for Metrolink information, 800-371-LINK, www.metrolinktrains.com.

NEIGHBORHOODS—ORANGE COUNTY

Disneyland is what many people think of when Orange County is mentioned,
that and orange groves, many of which can still be seen from Interstate 5. This
sleepy agricultural community between Los Angeles and San Diego, long
ignored through the years, has been discovered and then rediscovered, transformed by farmers, entrepreneurs, and families, many of whom in more recent
years have been squeezed out by the ravenous housing demands in Los Angeles
and San Diego.

Orange County was established in 1889, formally breaking off from the
County of Los Angeles. Known for its crops of Valencia oranges, lemons, avoca-
dos, and walnuts, Orange County was named, logically enough, after its bountiful
orange groves. In the early 1900s, Buena Park farmer Walter Knott founded a farm
stand and restaurant, which eventually evolved into the Knott's Berry Farm Theme
Park. And in 1955, Walt Disney opened the Magic Kingdom in nearby Anaheim. It
was in the 1960s when some of Los Angeles County's population began spilling
over into Santa Ana Valley that Orange County really began to boom.

Today, Orange County consists of 798 square miles, 42 miles of coastline, 34
cities, and a population of three million. Orange County is ranked as the second
largest county in California. Oranges are still grown here, but nursery stock and
cut flowers are the main agricultural breadwinners now. In the last decade or so,
the OC has developed into a desirable, affluent, and ethnically diverse suburban community. According to the National Association of Realtors, in the fourth
quarter of 2007, the median price of homes in Orange County ran well over the
half million mark, more than $110,000 over LA County's median, but under San
Francisco's median price of $805,400. Sales have started out unusually sluggish
in 2008, with the number of homes sold fallen by 40% compared to the previous year. The high cost of housing combined with the difficulty in obtaining a
large loan is partially to blame for the slow-down. Bad news aside, area amenities
abound: The Orange County Performing Arts Center in Costa Mesa, the Orange
County Museum of Art in Newport Beach, and the Verizon Wireless Amphithe-

atre in Irvine are some of the cultural venues here. Also calling this county home is the Crystal Cathedral, a twelve-story Christian nondenominational church in Garden Grove, famous for its Christmas and Easter services inside the glass and steel sanctuary.

Many OC cities are worth investigating for newcomers. Along the shore, where median prices for homes trend toward the millions, you will find the communities of Newport Beach, Corona del Mar, and Laguna Beach. The beach lifestyle is prominent, drawing people who love residing just a few steps from the sand, surf, and sun. Some of the priciest real estate in California and the nation is along this coastline. Farther inland, the more urban communities of Anaheim, Santa Ana, and Irvine offer much more in the way of affordable to middle-range housing. Although most residents of the OC work locally, some do drive the hour-plus commute to LA. Below we have profiled some of the more developed Orange County communities that are particularly noteworthy for their variety of housing, cultural resources, and city amenities.

IRVINE

Boundaries: East: Interstate 5 San Diego Freeway; **South**: 73 San Joaquin Hills Freeway; **North**: Barranca Parkway and Portola Parkway; **West**: MacArthur Boulevard

James Irvine, one of four sheep ranchers in this sleepy backlands south of Los Angeles, acquired hundreds of thousands of acres of land for his ranching operations. It was his son, James Irvine Jr., who in 1894 created The Irvine Company, changing from ranching to growing orchards of olives and citrus. When the company was passed down to his son, Myford, in 1947, urban development became the focus. The University of California purchased a thousand acres from The Irvine Company in 1959 to build UC Irvine, and an additional 500 acres surrounding its campus was purchased to develop a master community plan for 50,000 people called The Irvine Ranch. The Irvine Business Complex and the neighborhoods of Turtle Rock/University Park, Culverdale, The Ranch, and Walnut soon followed. Architect William Pereira, best known for designing the Transamerica Building, was the head of this master plan, which was so large in scope that today it remains one of the nation's largest planned communities. In 1971, residents voted to incorporate their community and an even larger radius of land, for a total of 55 square miles, to create the City of Irvine. The Irvine Company continues to develop Irvine from its headquarters in Newport Beach.

The relative newness of this city is apparent in the clean lines of its modern architecture and the tidiness of both its business and residential sections. Open land continues to give way to new business parks and residential developments, making it possible to buy a brand new home in the city's many "villages"—as the neighborhoods here are called. In particular, those looking for a new home

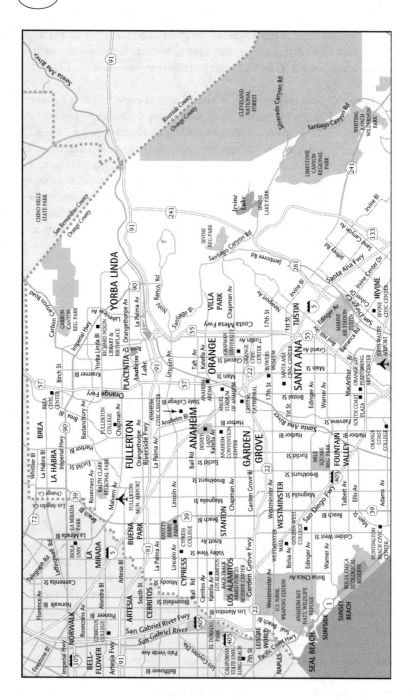

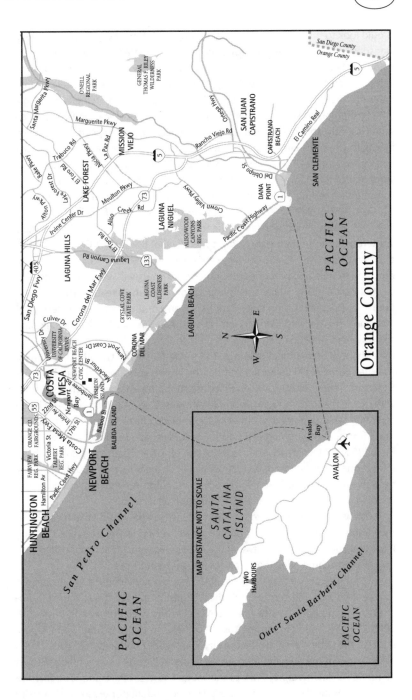

Orange County

should look to the Villages of **Portola Springs** and **Woodbury**. Visit www.thevil
lagesofirvine.com to keep abreast of village development. Housing demand in
Irvine has been growing due to its relative affordability and convenient location
in the center of Orange County. Many folks, drawn to the pricey coastal communities of Costa Mesa and Newport Beach that sit just west of Irvine, find living a
little farther inland slightly easier on their pocketbooks. Homes in Irvine, which
sell at slightly above the county's median price, span the spectrum of apartments, townhomes, larger family homes (the average home has five bedrooms),
and custom estates. The City of Irvine has an affordable housing office that provides assistance to lower-income households, with a number of master planned
communities setting aside a portion of housing for lower income residents. Call
949-724-7456 or 949-724-7454 or visit www.cityofirvine.org for a brochure.

The villages here are family-friendly, with parks and recreation centers
scattered throughout. The city is so kid-friendly that they have a Child Care Coor-
dination Office (949-724-6632, www.cityofirvine.org/depts/cs/childcare) to help
provide referrals and parent education. Dog owners will want to take note of
Central Bark, a nearly 3-acre enclosed park for off-leash recreation. The Disc Golf
Course at Deerfield Community Park has been popular with disc golfers since
1980, and the Harvard Sk8 Park on Harvard Avenue features bowls, rails, and
spines where skateboarders show off their stuff day and night. Adults too have
their share of recreational offerings. The Irvine Museum at 18881 Von Karman
Avenue specializes in California art from the Impressionist period, and the Irvine
Spectrum Center and The Market Place are shopping-entertainment complexes
with movie theaters, restaurants, and retail stores (see listings below). And if you
can't find what you need at either of these places, head to neighboring Costa
Mesa for the newly remodeled South Coast Plaza at 3333 Bristol Street, Costa
Mesa (800-782-8888, www.southcoastplaza.com). A shopper's day is easily filled
here at one of the largest malls in America, which includes over 300 shops, many
exclusive to California. The California Scenario Sculpture Garden by Isamu Nogu-
chi, next to the mall, is a wonderful destination on its own.

Following a trend toward increasing density within residential areas, high-
rise condominium towers are springing up all over Irvine. The latest are 3000 The
Plaza and The Plaza Irvine, between the 405 Freeway and 73 toll road. Filled with
modern resort amenities, these condos are priced at $1 million.

As for the college that started it all, UCI has blossomed into a well-respected
four-year college and the county's third largest employer. It was the first public university to have faculty win two Nobel Prizes in chemistry and physics. In
2008, UCI was listed among the top 50 colleges in *U.S. News and World Report*;
it is also the largest employer in the city. The student population of over 27,000
drives some of the demand for housing in the University's surrounding villages
of **Turtle Rock/University Park** to the south, and **West Park** and **Woodbridge**
to the east. Housing that is most coveted by the student population is University
Town Center, a collection of apartments and condos (with its own shopping area

and cinema) connected to campus by a pedestrian bridge. Rents for apartments in these areas tend to increase every year, compelling some forward-thinking parents to buy a home or condo for their child to reside in during his or her school years and then sell it after graduation.

Web Sites: www.ci.irvine.ca.us, www.cityofirvine.org, www.thevillagesofirvine. com

Area Code: 949

Zip Codes: 92602–20

Post Offices: Main Office, 15642 Sand Canyon Ave; East Irvine, 14982 Sand Canyon Ave; Harvest Station, 17192 Murphy Ave; University Station, 4255 Campus Dr, Ste A100

Police District: Irvine Police Department, 1 Civic Center Plaza, Irvine, 949-724-7000, www.ci.irvine.ca.us/ipd/default.asp

Emergency Hospitals: Irvine Regional Hospital and Medical Center, 16200 Sand Canyon Ave, 949-753-2000, www.irvineregionalhospital.com; UC Irvine Health Care, 101 The City Dr S, 714-456-7890, www.healthcare.uci.edu

Libraries: Heritage Park Regional Library, 14361 Yale Ave, 949-551-7151; University Park Library, 4512 Sandburg Way, 949-786-4001; Katie Wheeler Library, 13109 Old Myford Rd, 714-669-8753; www.ocpl.org

Public School Education: Irvine Unified School District, 5050 Barranca Pkwy, Irvine, 949-936-5000, www.iusd.org; Tustin Unified School District, 300 S C St, Tustin, 714-730-7301, www.tustin.k12.ca.us

Community Resources: Heritage Park Community Center, 14301 Yale Ave, 949-724-6750; University Community Park, 1 Beech Tree Ln, 949-724-6815; Woodbridge Community Park Senior Center, 20 Lake Rd, 949-724-6900; www. ci.irvine.ca.us; Turtle Rock Community Park, Sunny Hill and Turtle Rock Dr, 949-724-6750; Deerfield Community Park Disc Golf Course, 949-724-6620, www. ci.irvine.ca.us; Laguna Niguel Regional Park, 28241 La Paz Rd, Laguna Niguel, 949-923-2240, www.ocparks.com; South Coast Plaza, 3333 Bristol St, Costa Mesa, 800-782-8888, www.southcoastplaza.com; Harvard Skateboard Park, 14701 Harvard Ave, 949-337-6577, www.ci.irvine.ca.us; Irvine Museum, 18881 Von Karman Ave, 949-476-2565, www.irvinemuseum.org; Irvine Spectrum Center, Irvine Center Drive and I-405, 949-753-5180, www.shopirvinespectrumcenter.com; The Market Place, 2777 El Camino Real, 714-730-4124, www.shopthemarketplace.com; Newcomers Club of Irvine (women only), 949-387-3710, www.newcomersclub.com; Central Bark, 6405 Oak Canyon, 949-724-MUDD, www.cityofirvine.org.

Transportation: Orange County Transportation Authority (OCTA), 714-636-7433, www.octa.net; TRIPS (disabled & senior transportation), 949-724-RIDE, www. cityofirvine.org

NEWPORT BEACH

BALBOA ISLAND
CORONA DEL MAR

Boundaries: East: 73 San Joaquin Hills Freeway; **South:** Crystal Cove State Park; **North:** Irvine Avenue and Upper Newport Bay; **West:** Pacific Ocean

Newport Beach, the largest coastal city in Orange County, is a homogeneous, upper-class community. Known for its yacht clubs and beachfront property, it was also the setting for the popular TV series *The O.C.*, which elevated the Newport Beach lifestyle to the stuff of legend. Leafy coral trees and purple bougainvilleas, the city's official tree and flower, decorate the picturesque residential streets. Temperatures are impressively moderate year-round, with high temperatures averaging 75 degrees in the summer and 65 degrees in the winter. With an average annual rainfall of only 12 inches, the sunny weather makes this city an ideal resort town. The exclusive Balboa Bay Club & Resort and Four Seasons are just two of many resorts in the area. Newport Beach's average population of 76,000 swells to 100,000+ in the summer due to an influx of tourists and visitors. Many Angelenos trek the 50 miles south from LA for weekend getaways here.

This beachside city consists of 59% owner-occupied residences; the rest are renters. Most of the single-family homes were built between the 1960s and 1970s, and condos, townhomes, and villas round out the offerings. Home sales start at one and go up to three million dollars plus; anything under is a "steal." Rental rates are consistent with rates found at any upper-class beachside community. A newer luxury residential development with breathtaking views of the Pacific Ocean, the Newport Coast features an arch along the PCH that marks your entrance into this affluent neighborhood. The Pelican Hill Golf Club is next door for those who want to be close to the putting greens.

A number of private estates and beach houses line Newport Harbor. This huge sparkling marina is home to more than 9,000 boats and yachts, making it one of the world's busiest small boat harbors. More than a handful of yacht clubs call it home. Boating is the main draw, but there is also fishing, swimming, and volleyball.

The primary shopping district for Newport Beach is Fashion Island, an upscale open-air mall that occupies a small man-made island. The annual Taste of Newport is a popular September event; 70,000 locals and visitors sample the best of local dining over three days. The Orange County Museum of Art is also in Newport Beach. Exhibits emphasize modern works of art, and curators frequently showcase emerging artists from the state. Newport University, a private college founded in 1976, features a school of business administration, behavioral sciences, and law.

The man-made **Balboa Island,** located just a five-minute ferry ride from the Balboa Peninsula or a short drive over a bridge at the end of Jamboree Boulevard, is an intimate, exclusive, and picturesque neighborhood. The ferry ride is especially popular during the summer season, and waits to board the ferry (which transports people and cars) can run as long as an hour. Marine Avenue and accompanying side streets are popular for shopping and dining. The island itself, including the bridge, is a mere 2.6 miles. Since land is at a premium here, many of the houses, most with extraordinary bay views, are packed close together—reminiscent of San Francisco. When the island was developed during World War I, land parcels were doled out for $250. Today, if you can find a cottage for sale, you're easily looking at a million dollars and more. That said, the island is widely popular among UCI students for its fully furnished rentals and, sitting only six miles from campus, its convenient location. The close-knit population of 3,000 maintains the island's storybook character with streets named after gems like Sapphire and Ruby and an annual Christmas boat parade (running since 1908). The peninsula side has a "Fun Zone" as well as a Pavilion where you can board ships to Catalina Island.

On the southern end of Newport, about four miles southwest of UCI, is **Corona del Mar** (Spanish for "Crown of the Sea"). This Orange County jewel starts at the base of the San Joaquin Hills and runs east of Avocado Street to the city limits. The seaside village's small-town allure comes with a big-city price tag. House hunters can expect to pay close to two million dollars plus for estates of varying architectural styles. Rentals are limited and run slightly higher than rentals on Balboa Island. The main commercial drag is California State Route 1, dotted by galleries, restaurants, and boutiques. The community even has its own beach, the **Corona del Mar State Beach**, which is well groomed and popular with swimmers and sunbathers.

Web Sites: www.city.newport-beach.ca.us, www.balboa-island.com, www.cdm chamber.com

Area Code: 949

Zip Codes: Newport Beach: 92660–3; Corona del Mar: 92625; Balboa Island: 92662

Post Offices: Main Office, 1133 Camelback St; Bay Station, 191 Riverside Ave; Balboa Station, 204 Main St; Balboa Island Station, 206 Marine Ave; Corona del Mar Main Office, 406 Orchid Ave

Police District: Newport Beach Police Department, 870 Santa Barbara Dr, Newport Beach, 949-644-3681, www.nbpd.org

Emergency Hospitals: Hoag Memorial Hospital Presbyterian, One Hoag Dr, 949-764-4624, www.hoaghospital.org; Newport Bay Hospital, 1501 E 16th St, 949-650-9750, www.newportbayhospital.com

Libraries: Central Library, 1000 Avocado Ave, 949-717-3800; Crean Mariners branch, 2005 Dover Drive, 949-644-3078; Corona del Mar branch, 420 Marigold Ave, Corona del Mar, 949-644-3075; Balboa branch, 100 E Balboa Blvd, Balboa, 949-644-3076; www.newportbeachlibrary.org

Public School Education: Newport-Mesa Unified School District, 2985-A Bear St, Costa Mesa, 714-424-5000, www.nmusd.k12.ca.us

Community Resources: Newport Beach Recreation & Senior Services, 949-644-3152, Newport Beach Harbor Resources, 949-644-3034, www.city. newport-beach.ca.us; Newport Harbor, 18712 University Dr, Irvine, 949-923-2250, www.ocparks.com; Sherman Library & Gardens, 2647 E Pacific Coast Hwy, Corona del Mar, 949-673-2261, www.slgardens.org; Orange County Museum of Art, 850 San Clemente Dr, 949-759-1122, www.ocma.net; Upper Newport Bay (Peter & Mary Muth Interpretive Center), 2301 University Dr, 949-923-2290, www.ocparks.com; Corona del Mar State Beach, Ocean Blvd and Iris Ave, 949-644-3151, www.parks.ca.gov; Pelican Hill Golf Club, 22651 Pelican Hill Rd S, 877-735-4226, www.pelicanhill.com; Fashion Island, Pacific Coast Hwy and Newport Center Dr, 949-721-2000, www.shopfashionisland. com; Newport University, 4101 Westerly Pl, 800-345-3272, www.newport. edu

Public Transportation: Orange County Transportation Authority (OCTA), 714-636-7433, www.octa.net

TUSTIN

Boundaries: East: Jamboree Road; **South**: Barranca Parkway; **North**: Irvine Boulevard; **West**: 55 Costa Mesa Freeway

The City of Tustin, about ten miles north of UCI, has been slowly but steadily growing. Its allure: outright affordability in comparison to the coastal cities. Easy access to I-5 and I-15, plus the 55 and 91 freeways, is another perk. Residents of this conservative city, which occupies just 11 square miles, make up a little over 2% of the county's population. Sycamore, eucalyptus, pepper, palm, pine, and oak trees were once so plentiful in Tustin that it dubbed itself the City of Trees. Some of these trees gave way to the El Toro Marine Corps Air Station in WW II, the establishment of which helped fuel Tustin's early growth.

The newer and more popular residential area is east of downtown at **Tustin Ranch**, which consists of single-family homes and condos. A lavish Tustin Ranch Golf Club and shopping centers, like the nearly mile-long The Marketplace and the more intimate Tustin Courtyard and Plaza, have added to its popularity. Median homes prices run an additional $300,000 above the county's median price, and condos run significantly less than that, making them a hot commodity. Farther north, million-dollar estates dot the hillsides next to Peters Canyon Regional Park and Reservoir, which come with panoramic views of the Saddleback Mountains and Pacific Coast. Outside of Tustin Ranch, homes are selling at the county median. In the south central part of town, **Laurelwood** is a 50-50 mix of condominiums and detached homes. The majority of Tustin's existing housing stock, generally consisting of two- to four-bedroom homes, was built in the 1960s or later. Single-family homes are slightly edged out in number by multi-family dwellings, but that's likely to change as land developers ramp up construction of new homes. Rentals, usually in the one- or two-bedroom range, are favored by UCI students and by workers from local industry—Ricoh Electronics, Inc. and Dawn Food Products are the two biggest manufacturers in the area. Many business parks are situated on and around Red Hill Avenue between Edinger Avenue and Barranca Parkway. Sycamores and other trees grace many of the city streets.

With the closure of the 1,500-acre El Toro Marine Corps Air Station (MCAS) in 1999, the land was renamed Tustin Legacy, and city planners established an ambitious community plan regarding its use. Urban parks, schools, residential villages, and commercial zones are part of the plan. Tustin Field, a 29-acre parcel between Harvard Avenue and Jamboree Road and adjacent Edinger Avenue, was the first phase to be completed. This fledgling neighborhood features a mix of traditional detached houses, urban-style row houses, and cluster townhouses meant to resemble a village square. After being delayed by clean-up of soil and water contamination left behind by the closure of the MCAS, construction has finally started at a furious pace to build an additional 4,000 new homes over former military housing. **North Tustin** is still unincorporated and has plenty of room for expansion and development.

Possibly the county's oldest "old town" is in Tustin on Main Street and El Camino Real. Well-preserved commercial buildings, some dating back to the 1880s, and a Victorian mansion are still standing. The Tustin Museum documents the street's evolution from a blacksmith store and Wells Fargo Express stop to present day. More modern commercial districts are in the Marketplace on El Camino Real, which it shares with Irvine.

Web Site: www.tustinca.org
Area Code: 714
Zip Codes: 92780-2
Post Offices: Main Office, 340 E 1st St
Police District: Tustin Police Department, 300 Centennial Way, 714-573-3200, www.tustinpd.org
Emergency Hospital: Tustin Hospital and Medical Center, 14662 Newport Ave, 714-669-5880, Healthsouth Tustin Rehabilitation Hospital, 14851 Yorba St, 714-832-9200, www.healthsouth.com
Library: Tustin branch, 345 E Main St, 714-544-7725, www.ocpl.org
Public School Education: Tustin Unified School District, 300 S C St, Tustin, 714-730-7301, www.tustin.k12.ca.us
Community Resources: Peppertree Park, 230 W 1st St, 714-573-3326; Tustin Parks and Recreation, 714-573-3326, www.tustinca.org; Tustin Museum, 714-731-5701, www.tustinhistory.org; Peters Canyon Regional Park and Reservoir, 714-973-6611, www.ocparks.com; Tustin Ranch Golf Club, 12442 Tustin Ranch Rd, 714-734-2104, www.tustinranchgolf.com; Tustin Chamber of Com-

merce, 714-544-5341, www.tustinchamber.com; Tustin Legacy Planning, 714-573-3000, www.tustinlegacy.com; The Marketplace, 2777 El Camino Real, 714-730-4124, www.shopthemarketplace.com, Family & Youth Center, 14722 Newport Ave, 714-573-3370, www.tustinca.org

Transportation: Orange County Transportation Authority (OCTA), 714-636-7433, www.octa.net

ANAHEIM, COSTA MESA

Boundaries: East: Riverside County line; **South:** Orangewood Avenue; **North:** 91 Freeway; **West:** Brookhurst Street

When German grape farmers founded a 200-acre community in 1857, they named it "Ana-heim," which loosely means home by the Santa Ana River in German. A plague 20 years later wiped out the vineyards, so citrus trees became the crop of choice. These orange groves would be the first commercially produced crops in Orange County. Covering 50 square miles today with 324,000+ residents, **Anaheim**, the second largest city in Orange County, is best known as home to "the happiest place on earth." Over 40 million visitors a year visit the Anaheim Resort district, which consists of Disneyland, Disney's California Adventure, Downtown Disney, and the Anaheim Convention Center—billed as the largest on the West Coast. The entire city has undergone a facelift over the years with newly planted trees, repaved streets, and a widened 5 Freeway to support its number one industry: tourism. As the city's largest employer, Disney continues to create outstanding retail and dining destinations for visitors and residents alike with its latest urban oasis, Anaheim Gardenwalk, featuring a manicured garden theme.

In addition to the famed Angel Stadium, resident sports fans enjoy a rich selection of venues here: Arrowhead Pond, the Honda Center (home of the Anaheim Ducks), and American Sports Centers. The Grove of Anaheim, a 1,700-seat indoor concert venue, is at the northwest corner of Angel Stadium. And rounding out the cultural offerings for residents is a new museum called the Muzeo (714-956-8936, www.muzeo.org). Billed as an urban cultural center since the gallery is sandwiched among loft-style apartments, the Muzeo features traveling exhibits.

Residents here consist of 57% owners and 43% renters. **West Anaheim** is the most mature part of town, having built up during the '50s. The price tags of homes here are comparable to the rest of Anaheim, falling under the county median. To the east is affluent **Anaheim Hills**, a master-planned community well known for the professional athletes that live there. Local residents earn a median income that is the highest in all of Orange County. The Anaheim Hills Golf Course is the centerpiece of this community. Probably the only downside is that wildfires are a hazard in these hills, sparking up an average of once a year. An additional 2,500 new homes are planned for the area called **Mountain Park**, located between the Eastern Transportation Corridor (Route 241) and Coal Canyon Road. This expansion will push right up against the eastern border to Riverside County. Originally the development had ambitions to build 8,000 homes, but residents successfully petitioned against overdevelopment.

The area around Angel Stadium, called the **Platinum Triangle,** is also being revitalized. The city is hoping to transform this formerly industrial area into a regional hub of housing and jobs, so they have zoned the space for high-density, mixed-use districts (consisting of condos and loft apartments and retail). Planners promise mini-blocks that are pedestrian friendly for modern urban dwellers. Construction is scheduled to start sometime in 2008, but this ambitious reinvention already looks promising for newcomers.

Southeast of Anaheim is what some call the "heart of the OC," the city of **Costa Mesa**, Spanish for "tableland coast." Cattle from the Mission San Juan Capistrano used to graze this land, which was originally a semi-rural farming community. The Estancia Adobe, a waystation for the herd tenders that was built in the early 19th century in the northwestern part of the city, still stands today at 1900 Adams Avenue.

Sixteen square miles make up this city, which 113,000+ residents call home. Much like the surrounding communities, temperatures are mild in the winter and warm in the summer. City planners dictate that 48% of the land be designated for residential use and 14% for commercial zoning, 14% for industrial, and 24% for "public and semi-public uses." The Auto Club of Southern California is the city's largest employer. The largest economy is retail, with the South Coast Plaza Mall of particular note due to the high sales volume it generates annually. Wandering the city, you may notice a lot of new car dealerships and pet supply stores. The slick Orange County Performing Arts Center recently expanded to include the Segerstorm Center for the Arts concert hall. Also nearby this cultural center are the South Coast Repertory and the massive Orange County Fairgrounds.

Median home prices here hover around the median price for the county. About 48% of the residences here are single-family homes, the rest consisting of multi-unit housing. This explains why a little over half of the housing is renter occupied. The majority of local housing stock consists of three- to four-bedroom homes, built between 1950 and 1979, most of it in the '60s. Much of the land is already built out, so there is not a lot of new housing activity except for the construction of multi-family dwellings. The newest apartment complex can be found at The Enclave at South Coast, a gated community built in 2007 and within walking distance of South Coast Plaza Mall.

The Costa Mesa Redevelopment Committee sponsors a Homebuyer's Assistance Program (www.cmredevelopment.org/rda-programs.htm) for would-be homebuyers of low and moderate income. Every April, the city organizes a Neighbors for Neighbors Spring Clean-up where good citizens gather to help clean Fairview Park and do exterior touch-ups and weeding yards of low income and senior homes. Fairview Park is popular for model airplane flyers, horseback riding, and hiking.

Web Site: www.anaheim.net, www.anaheimoc.org, www.ci.costa-mesa.ca.us

Area Code: 714, 858, 949

Zip Codes: Anaheim: 92800–99, Costa Mesa: 92626–8

Post Offices: Main Office, 701 N Loara St; 5505 E Santa Ana Canyon; 2255 W Ball Rd

Police District: Anaheim Police Department, 425 S Harbor Blvd, 714-765-4300, www.anaheim.net; Costa Mesa Police Department, 99 Fair Rd, Costa Mesa, 714-754-5033, www.ci.costa-mesa.ca.us

Emergency Hospital: Anaheim General Hospital, 3350 W Ball Rd, 714-827-6700; Anaheim Memorial Hospital, 1111 W La Palma Ave, 714-774-1450, www.memorialcare.org; Western Medical Center Anaheim, 1025 S Anaheim Blvd, 714-533-6220, www.westernmedanaheim.com

Library: Anaheim Central Library, 500 W Broadway, 714-765-1880; Haskett Library, 2650 W Broadway, 714-821-0551; Euclid Library, 1340 S Euclid Ave, 714-765-3625, Sunkist Library, 901 S Sunkist, 714-765-3576, Canyon Hills Library, 400 Scout Trail, Anaheim Hills, 714-974-7630, www.anaheim.net; Costa Mesa Library branch, 1855 Park Ave, Costa Mesa, 949-646-8845, www.ocpl.org

Public School Education: Anaheim Union School District, 501 Crescent Way, Anaheim 714-999-3511, www.auhsd.k12.ca.us; Buena Park School District, 6885 Orangethorpe Ave, Buena Park, 714-522-8412, www.bpsd.k12.ca.us; Orange Unified School District, 1401 N Handy St, Orange, 714-628-4000, www.orangeusd.k12.ca.us; Newport-Mesa Unified School District, 2985-A Bear St, Costa Mesa, 714-424-5000, www.nmusd.k12.ca.us

Community Resources: Anaheim Gardenwalk, 321 W Katella Ave, 858-613-1800, www.anaheimgardenwalk.com; Honda Center, 2695 E Katella Ave, 714-704-2400, www.hondacenter.com; American Sports Centers, 15000 S Anaheim Blvd, 714-917-3600, www.americansportscenters.com; Anaheim Parks Maintenance, 714-765-5155; The Grove of Anaheim, 2200 E Katella Ave, 714-712-2700, www.thegroveofanaheim.com; The Muzeo, 241 S Anaheim Blvd, 714-956-8936, www.muzeo.org; Oak Canyon Nature Center, 6700 E Canyon Rd, 714-998-8380, www.anaheim.net/ocnc; Featherly Regional Park, 24001 Santa Ana Canyon Rd, 714-771-6731, www.ocparks.com; Orange County Performing Arts Center, 600 Town Center Drive, Costa Mesa, 714-556-8984, www.ocpac.org

Transportation: Orange County Transportation Authority (OCTA), 714-636-7433, www.octa.net

LAGUNA BEACH

Boundaries: **East**: Aliso/Woods Canyons; **South**: South La Senda Drive; **North**: Laguna Caynon; **West**: Pacific Ocean

This seaside artists' colony is nestled in eucalyptus-filled rolling hills that overlook the ocean. Even early on, the picturesque seascapes appealed to summer vacationers and landscape painters like Norman St. Clair and William Wendt. Artist Edgar Payne started a gallery in 1918 that was so successful it grew to become one of the first art museums in California, the Laguna Art Museum. Robert Wyland's signature whale paintings can be seen around town today. Local artisans often exhibit their wares right on their front porch. Surfers may be interested to know that it was during the 1950s that Hobie Alter was making wood Hobie surfboards out of his garage here in Laguna. A gate built in 1935 that still stands today at Forest and Park Avenues has an inscription that explains Laguna Beach's allure: "This gate hangs well and hinders none, refresh and rest then travel on."

An air of exclusivity is maintained by the Laguna Greenbelt (undeveloped land that surrounds the community) and the fact that there are only two paths in, the Pacific Coast Highway and Route 133. And that's just the way the environmentally conscious locals like it. This relaxed, homogeneous resort town only covers 9.1 square miles and with 7 of it being coastline, combing tide pools and whale watching are popular activities. This was the first city on the West Coast to assign officers to policing its tide pools to protect wildlife. During the busy summer season, the city hosts lots and lots of art festivals: the Sawdust Festival, the Art-A-Fair, the Plein Air Painting Invitation, but the big enchilada is the Festival of the Arts/Pageant of the Masters. The Pageant uses local actors to stage brief recreations of famous art works to the tunes of live music before a live audience. Three million people visit the resort throughout the year, the majority during the summer.

Beachside living comes with an understandably higher price tag, and homes here run at a median price of $1.5 million. The lack of available land among hilly terrain for new construction also contributes to the high real estate values. Housing growth has eked by on an average of 2% a year. Laguna Beach's housing permit department is famously particular when reviewing new construction and remodels, keeping growth in check as a result. A majority of residences here (62%) are single-unit detached homes with three to four bedrooms. And 70% of the structures here were built between 1939 and 1979. Residences in downtown tend to be beach cottages and bungalows. But go into the hills and you'll see many gravity-defying custom homes designed to capture glimpses of the ocean. There are no master planned divisions here. A wide variety of architectural styles are represented since the majority of houses were designed to owner specifications (and whims). The most recent, and likely final, development of new luxury homes is in the gated community located in Emerald Bay, the city's northernmost point.

Hillslides are a rare but real hazard here. The most recent serious slide occurred in 2005. Significant rainfall that winter took its toll and 17 houses were lost, and another 11 were seriously damaged in the Bluebird Canyon area. All these homes have since been rebuilt, a testament to how much residents love it here.

Web Site: www.lagunabeachcity.net, www.lagunabeachinfo.org

Area Code: 949

Zip Codes: 92600–99

Post Offices: Main Office, 29911 Niguel Rd; Playa branch, 350 Forest Ave; South Laguna branch, 31677 Virginia Way

Police District: Laguna Beach Police Department, 505 Forest Ave, 949-497-0701, www.lagunabeachcity.net

Emergency Hospitals: South Coast Medical Center, 31872 Coast Hwy, 949-499-1311, www.southcoastmedcenter.com; Saddleback Memorial Medical Center, 24451 Health Center Drive, Laguna Hills, 949-837-4500, www.memorialcare.org

Library: Laguna Beach branch, 363 Glenneyre St, 949-497-1733, www.ocpl.org

Public School Education: Laguna Beach Unified School District, 550 Blumont St, 949-497-7700, www.lbusd.org

Community Resources: Laguna Coast Wilderness Park, 20101 Laguna Canyon Rd, 949-923-2235, www.ocparks.com; Laguna Art Museum, 307 Cliff Dr, 949-494-8971, www.lagunaartmuseum.org; Festival of the Arts/Pageant of the Masters, 800-487-3378, www.foapom.com; Laguna Playhouse, 606 Laguna Canyon Rd, 949-497-2787, www.lagunaplayhouse.com

Transportation: City of Laguna Beach Transit Department, 949-497-0746, Orange County Transportation Authority (OCTA), 714-636-7433, www.octa.net

WESTMINSTER, FOUNTAIN VALLEY

Boundaries: **East**: Magnolia Street; **South**: Edinger Avenue; **North**: State Route 22; **West**: Bolsa Chica Street

After Anaheim, the city of **Westminster** was the next city to be founded in Orange County. Taking advantage of the generous water tables at the time, the town started up as an agricultural community in 1870, expanding until it experienced a decline during the '70s, but it recovered due to a large influx of Vietnamese immigrants after the Vietnam War. Now matured into a bedroom community, commuters enjoy easy access to the Garden Grove Freeway (State Route 22), which defines the northern border, and the 405 Freeway, which bisects the city. Community amenities include the Westminster Mall, Buckingham Public Park, and the Westminster Museum. The Liberty Skate Park is popular among younger residents. The 419-seat Rose Center Theater is a recent addition to the local cultural scene.

Occupying 10.2 square miles, this compact working-class community features 60% owner-occupied units; the balance are renters. The majority (81%) of its housing stock was built between the '50s and the '70s, with single-story three-bedrooms the norm here. Many homes are tidy stucco ranch style, but showing their age. Still, their prices are in pace with the county median's.

The largest Vietnamese enclave within the US is in Westminster's Little Saigon, located on Bolsa Avenue between Magnolia and Ward streets. This one-mile stretch of Bolsa Avenue, which includes the two-story Asian Garden Mall, represents the largest concentration of ethnic strip malls and mom-and-pop retailers outside of Vietnam. The very active Vietnamese-American community hosts an annual Tet Festival celebration (Vietnamese new year) that draws many visitors.

Southeast of Westminster is the city of **Fountain Valley**. Consisting of 8.9 square miles, this is a quiet suburban community with lots of flat land. The few remaining strawberry fields dotting the area are giving way to industrial development. Hyundai Motor America is headquartered here. Homes, 75% owner occupied, are priced slightly above the county's median. Apartment and condo complexes tend to cluster by the 405 freeway. City officials follow a master plan that dates back to the 1960s when the city experienced its first growth spurt. For this reason, city officials boast that theirs is one of the best master planned communities in the OC.

Fruits of this planning are evident as the community is well organized into square-shaped neighborhoods. Each square typically includes a park, and shopping malls are within walking distance of each residential neighborhood. Detached family homes make up 68% of housing here, and about 16% are multi-family units of 5+. Fountain Valley built about 40% of its current housing stock in the 1960s and 42% in the 1970s. New housing construction is rare since the city is fully mature.

Residents have a wonderful urban park, The Mile Square Regional Park, which contains three golf courses, two soccer fields, an archery range, and two fishing lakes. Home buyers may want to check out the city's New Home rehabilitation and first-time home buyer's assistance programs.

Web Site: www.ci.westminster.ca.us, www.fountainvalley.org

Area Code: 714

Zip Codes: Westminster: 92683–5; Fountain Valley: 92708, 92728

Post Offices: Westminster Main Office, 15030 Goldenwest, Fountain Valley branch, 17227 Newhope St

Police District: Westminster Police Department, 8200 Westminster Blvd, 714-898-3315, www.westminster-ca.gov; Fountain Valley Police Department, 10200 Slater Ave, 714-593-4485, www.fvpd.org

Emergency Hospitals: Kindred Hospital - Westminster, 200 Hospital Circle, 714-893-4541, www.khwestminster.com; Fountain Valley Regional Hospital, 17100 Euclid St, 714-966-7200, www.fountainvalleyhospital.com; Orange Coast Memorial Medical Center, www.memorialcare.org, 714-378-7000

Library: Westminster branch, 8180 13th St, 714-893-5057, Fountain Valley branch, 17635 Los Alamos, 714-962-1324, www.ocpl.org

Public School Education: Westminster School District, 14121 Cedarwood Ave, 714-894-7311, www.wsd.k12.ca.us; Fountain Valley School District, 10055 Slater Ave, 714-843-3200, www.fvsd.k12.ca.us

Community Resources: Westminster Museum, 8612 Westminster Blvd, 714-891-2597, www.nwpr.bc.ca; Westminster Mall, 1025 Westminster Mall, 714-898-2558, www.simon.com; Rose Center Theater, 14140 All American Way, 714-793-1150, www.rosecentertheater.com; Buckingham Park, 6502 Homer St, 714-895-2860; Liberty Skate Park, 13900 Monroe St, 714-895-2860; Asian Garden Mall, 9200 Bolsa Ave, www.asiangardenmall.com; Mile Square Regional Park, 16801 Euclid Ave, 714-973-6600, www.ocparks.com

Transportation: Orange County Transportation Authority (OCTA), 714-636-7433, www.octa.net

YORBA LINDA, FULLERTON

Boundaries: East: Chino Hills State Park; **South**: Esperanza Road; **North**: Chino Hills State Park; **West**: Rose Drive

By the northern border of Orange County, north of Anaheim, you'll find the well-groomed city of **Yorba Linda**. CNN rated "The Land of Gracious Living" as the number two best California city in which to live in the US in 2006. The crime rate is among the lowest in the county. In fact, Yorba Linda does not maintain its own police force, but contracts with the Brea Police Department. Also as the birthplace of former president Richard Nixon, the city is home to Nixon's Presidential Library.

As affluent as this city is (a six-figure income is the norm), their first-ever high school broke ground only in 2007 and plans to open by 2009 at Bastanchury Road and Fairmont Boulevard. Currently, most teens attend Esperanza High School in neighboring Anaheim. An interesting quirk of the town, there are no movie theaters within the city's 20 square miles. On the spiritual front, one of only six Buddhist temples in the US, the Shinnyo-en Buddhist USA Temple, is here, and the Yorba Linda Friends Church is the largest Quaker church in the world. Every October, residents celebrate the community's heritage with their annual Fiesta Days Parade and Family Fair. Their Community and Senior Center actively supports its more senior residents with daily scheduled activities for an annual membership of only $5.

Over 64,000 residents call Yorba Linda home, with 85% of them being homeowners. Median prices here run $200,000 to $300,000 above the county's, but the stucco homes are set on roomy lots and 78% of them are three or four bedrooms. Condos, townhomes, and gated apartment complexes round out the other housing options here. The bulk of residences were built during the '70s and '80s, and 78% of the housing stock are single-family detached homes. An active equestrian community means many houses have a private stable. Over 100 miles' worth of well-tended local trails are popular with hikers as well as horses and their riders. There's a good balance of flat land with gentle hills for much of the area, but new, more expensive homes balance on steep hills on the east side. A unique characteristic of homes here is that their exteriors feature slate or brick and they enjoy great views of the Santa Ana River. To the north is a planned "golf community," Vista del Verde, where some of the newest upscale homes in the city are centered around the Black Gold Golf course and complemented by public art sculptures. They also offer townhomes, condominiums, and "paired homes." More modest housing can be found to the west, the older section of town, but even this section would be considered upper middle class.

The neighboring city of **Fullerton** got its moniker from George H. Fullerton, the man responsible for routing the Santa Fe Railway through the city in the early 1900s. In 1934, the original Hawaiian Punch recipe was dreamed up by three Fullerton residents. The city is nicknamed "Education City" because five colleges and universities are based here among strip malls and suburban housing tracts within Fullerton's 22 square miles. Students representing Troy High School frequently place number one or two at the National Science Bowl (sponsored by Jet Propulsion Labs, no less).

Recent beautification efforts have revived downtown, centered at Harbor Boulevard and Commonwealth Avenue. Nightlife south of Commonwealth Avenue has become so vibrant that occasional unruliness has caused the OC Weekly to dub the area "Bourbon Street West." The hardcore punk music scene originated here and is still thriving thanks to fans among local college students.

Like Yorba Linda, Fullerton has its share of equestrian estates, clustered in a community called Sunny Hills. Nearby Laguna Lake Park houses an equestrian center. Ameriage Heights, on the western part of town, features some of the newer homes and commercial districts in the area, having completed construction in 2004. Driving through the city, you'll note architectural styles vary from Craftsman to custom mansions. Median prices for homes here span a range from approximately 18% below county median to about 10% above the median.

A new housing development of 540 single-family homes and 205 townhomes has been proposed for the northern tip of town, West Coyote Hills (between Rosecrans Avenue and Euclid Avenue). However, due to its proximity to the Robert E. Ward Nature Preserve, some controversy surrounds this and an environmental impact report was recently prepared. This development is still awaiting approval from the City Council, which has a history of advocating new development.

Amenities residents enjoy here include the Fullerton Arboretum on the campus of Cal State Fullerton, the Fullerton Civic Light Opera, the Janet Evans Swim Complex, and fishing at Laguna Lake. A noteworthy annual event is First Night, an alcohol-free, family-oriented New Year's Eve celebration. Commuters may appreciate plans to create the Fullerton Transportation Center, a major transportation hub at 120 East Santa Fe Avenue, which is already a major Orange County Transit Authority bus depot and train station.

Web Site: www.ci.yorba-linda.ca.us
Area Code: 714
Zip Codes: Yorba Linda: 92885–7; Fullerton: 92831–8
Post Offices: Yorba Linda Main Office, 4770 Eureka Ave; Fullerton Main Office, 1350 E Chapman Ave
Police District: Yorba Linda contracts with the Brea Police Department, 1 Civic Center Circle, 714-990-7623, www.ci.brea.ca.us; Fullerton Police Department, 237 W Commonwealth Ave, 714-738-6800, www.ci.fullerton.ca.us
Emergency Hospitals: Placentia Linda Hospital, 1301 N Rose Drive, Placentia, 714-993-2000, www.placentialinda.com; St. Jude Medical Center, 101 E Valencia Mesa Drive, Fullerton, 714-871-3280, www.stjudmedicalcenter.org
Library: Yorba Linda Public Library, 18181 Imperial Hwy, 714-777-2873, www.yorbalindalibrary.com; Fullerton Public Library Main branch, 353 W Commonwealth Ave, 714-738-6334, http://fullertonlibrary.org
Public School Education: Placientia-Yorba Linda Unified School District, 1301 Orangethorpe Ave, Placentia, 714-996-2550, www.pylusd.org; Fullerton Unified School District, 1401 W Valencia Drive, Fullerton, 714-447-7400, www.fsd.k12.ca.us
Community Resources: Richard Nixon Presidential Library, 18001 Yorba Linda Blvd, 714-993-5075, www.nixonlibraryfoundation,org; Travis Ranch Activity Center, 5200 Via del le Escuela, 714-961-7167, www.ci.yorba-linda.ca.us; Yorba Linda Community Center & Senior Center, 4501 Casa Loma Ave, 714-961-7185, www.ci.yorba-linda.ca.us; Fullerton Museum Center, 301 N Pomona Ave, 714-738-6545, www.ci.fullerton.ca.us; Fullerton Civic Light Opera, 714-879-1732, www.fclo.com; Janet Evans Swim Complex, 801 W Valencia Ave, 714-773-5788, www.fastswimming.net; Laguna Lake Park, 3120 Lakeview Drive, 714-738-6576, www.ci.fullerton.ca.us
Transportation: Orange County Transportation Authority (OCTA), 714-636-7433, www.octa.net

Additional OC cities you might want to consider...

- **Huntington Beach**, 714-536-5486, www.ci.huntington-beach.ca.us
- **Mission Viejo**, 949-470-3000, www.cityofmissionviejo.org
- **City of Orange,** 714-744-5511, www.cityoforange.org
- **San Juan Capistrano**, 949-493-1171, www.sanjuancapistrano.org
- **Santa Ana**, 714-647-5200, www.ci.santa-ana.ca.us
- **Seal Beach**, 562-431-2527, www.ci.seal-beach.ca.us

A S IN ALL MAJOR METROPOLITAN AREAS, YOU CAN FIND APARTMENTS, condos, single-family homes, mansions, and everything in between in Los Angeles. Your choice will depend on your needs and your financial resources.

Unless you're moving here from New York, San Francisco, or San Diego, brace yourself for sticker shock. In fourth quarter 2007, the National Association of Realtors' ranking of the US metropolitan areas with the highest median sale price for existing single-family homes placed Los Angeles fifth, at $589,200, and Orange County at number three, with a median price of $699,600. After years of the median cost of an LA house increasing by double-digit percentages, the sales figures have started to go down by double-digit percentages. How long this will last is anybody's guess. But the good news is in 2007, Los Angeles was rated by *Money Magazine* to be the 4th best place in the USA in which to live. According to another survey, Los Angeles has dropped from the 29th in 2006 to the 42nd most expensive city in the world in 2007. Since fewer people are opting to buy a home, there has been an increased demand for rentals. Between 1998 and 2007, rental vacancies in the city declined from 7% to 4.4%.

As far as rentals, it's impossible to state what the "average" rents are for one-bedroom apartments in Los Angeles since the locale, area resources, and building amenities greatly affect the going rates. Keep in mind, location can mean the difference between a cramped single with ancient appliances in Santa Monica and a cheery one-bedroom with central air and a fireplace in Van Nuys— and the Santa Monica place would cost more! Speaking in very general terms, beachside community rentals tend to consist of two- or three-level apartment buildings (sometimes cramped and usually pricier due to their proximity to the Pacific Ocean); inland architecture fluctuates from duplexes in Beverly Hills to modern, major complexes like those downtown and in the Fairfax District, to quirky art-deco units and apartments in the modern clean lines of the 1960s and

'70s, which are scattered throughout the county. Prices are generally tied into a neighborhood's prestige and general upkeep. Housing around the major universities, particularly UCLA and USC, is tight because of the student population. The recent trend toward revitalization has seen a sprinkling of new buildings throughout the city, especially downtown, as landowners raze old deteriorating units to build new complexes. If you're looking to own, condominiums are typically less expensive than a townhouse or detached house. Condos and townhouses are popular choices here for would-be homeowners who find the down payment for a single-family detached home out of their means. Another option is the high-end condo, which costs more than a house and feels like a mansion... once you step inside. Be warned however that in the latest Realtor's report on median sale prices for condos, Los Angeles ranked as the second most expensive after San Francisco.

New or old home? If you're looking for a new home within greater LA, you'll have better luck finding a recently built condo rather than a new house. Residential land in Los Angeles is fully built out and buyers will have to look at the suburbs, often outside of LA County, if they want a newly built home. Some homebuyers who want to stay in the city opt to purchase an existing home with the intent of remodeling it or tearing it down to build anew.

To get the most current information on what homes are going for in various southern California communities, visit **DataQuick's** site at www.dqnews.com. The **US Department of Housing and Urban Development (HUD)'s** web site is a good clearinghouse of information for prospective homeowners and renters in California: www.hud.gov. The Los Angeles HUD branch can be reached at 213-894-8000. To compare quality-of-life and cost-of-living data for about 3,000 US cities and towns, including 300 metropolitan areas, log onto **BestPlaces**, www.bestplaces.net.

RENTING

Finding an apartment in the Los Angeles area can be simple or difficult, depending on where you are looking and your budget. Rental market conditions within the greater Los Angeles area vary. More units are available in luxury, high-end complexes; in the more economical units, vacancies are harder to come by. The best bet for a new and relatively affordable apartment may lie in downtown LA. The Downtown Center Business Improvement District boasts that since 1999, over 9,000 units of housing have been added, with an additional 2,000 under construction. And the first grocery store to open downtown in over 50 years just opened in the summer of 2007.

Before hitting the internet, the newsstands, or the pavement to look for an apartment, first determine how much money you are willing to spend on your monthly rent and what size apartment you want. If you need a two-bedroom place but can only afford $1,000 per month, you can cross Beverly Hills off your list. Since competition for the lower-rent one-bedroom units is high, the next best thing is to opt for a two-bedroom, two-bath, and split the rent with a roommate; you may even spend less in this scenario.

APARTMENT HUNTING

Once you have determined your housing budget and desired apartment size, walk or drive through the neighborhoods in which you would like to live. Not only will this give you a feel for the areas, but often you can find "For Rent" signs posted on available apartments. Finally, ask around. Co-workers and friends may know of vacancies in their buildings, and landlords are often quite willing to take a referral from a trustworthy tenant. Below are the resources available to you as you search for the perfect place to call home.

NEWSPAPER CLASSIFIED ADVERTISEMENTS

A key resource for those hunting for an apartment is the classifieds. The *Los Angeles Times* lists pages of rentals, with the largest selection in its Sunday edition; web-goers: www.latimes.com. (Tip: most grocery and convenience stores and newsstands get an early Sunday edition of the *Los Angeles Times*, including the classified ads, on Saturday morning.) Smaller regional and weekly alternative newspapers like the *LA Weekly*, the *Santa Monica Outlook*, *Beverly Hills Courier*, and *The Tolucan Times* also have rental ads (see **Newspapers and Magazines** in **Getting Settled** for contact information for these publications). For those looking at mid- to higher-end apartments, you can pick up free, monthly apartment listing directories from Von's and Ralph's grocery stores, 7-Eleven stores, AM-PM Mini Markets, and other convenience stores, motels and hotels, real estate agents, banks, moving companies, and airports. Look for the *Apartment Guide*, www.apartmentguide.com (no fee), or the *Original Apartment Magazine*, www. aptmag.com (no fee).

RENTAL AGENTS

Using a real estate agency for apartment rentals is not the norm here, as area agents generally are used for those trying to locate townhouses, condos, or houses for sale. However, apartment-listing services, which let you browse for free but require a fee before they'll release the contact information for the rental, are common. These services have become so popular among landlords/managers that they have significantly reduced the rental ads that landlords/managers used to place in the local papers.

- **Westside Rentals**, 800-RENT-005, www.westsiderentals.com; for a $60 fee, you can view their 19,000+ listings for 60 days.
- **Rent Times**, 323-653-RENT, www.rentimes.com; $49 fee, offers online listings that include vacancies and sublets, including houses and guest homes for three months.
- **4 Rent in Los Angeles**, 310-276-4197, www.4rentinla.com, a $39 fee gets you 30 days of access to their listings.
- **Crown Relocation**, 714-898-0955, www.crownrelo.com; specializes in corporate employee relocations. But for a fee, individuals can hire a moving consultant to do all the legwork of locating a home based on preferences and lifestyle.

SHARING

Sharing a two-bedroom with a roommate is often more economical than getting a one-bedroom by yourself. The same classified ads sources mentioned above also have a "Rentals to Share" section. A roommate service may also be an option. Similar to rental agencies, a fee is charged to conduct a search for a compatible roomie. Consider one of the following:

- **Roommate Matchers**, 323-653-ROOM, www.roommatematchers.com; for a $49 membership fee, they will match you up with compatible roommates for 12 weeks. You can also browse pictures of potential roomies and descriptions of their housing.
- **Roommate Express**, 800-487-8050, www.e-roommate.com; $29 membership fee, will match you with a roommate looking to rent or one who already has a place to share.
- **Roommate Access**, 866-823-2200, www.roommateaccess.com; fee-based matching service.

SHORT-TERM/SUBLETS

If you prefer to take your time finding just the right place, consider a **sublet**. Some UCLA and USC students who are departing for the summer months as well as landlords desiring to fill student apartments during the summer may offer sublets. If you are interested in finding a temporary housing arrangement, go the same route as apartment seekers (above). In particular, local papers like the *Los Angeles Times*, the *LA Weekly* (http://losangeles.sublet.com), and roommate-matching services (listed above) are great resources for sublet listings. In addition, sublet seekers will do well to check for notices posted on college kiosks (or via college housing services directly) and neighborhood notice boards (at laundries, cafés, metro stops, etc.) Short-term rental opportunities might include a weekly or monthly rental situation. See the **Temporary Lodgings** chapter near the end of this guide for additional ideas.

OTHER PLACES TO LOOK

Keep your eyes peeled. Many neighborhood coffee shops, grocery stores, pet stores, and laundries have bulletin boards or wall space devoted to posting neighborhood announcements. Tucked between flyers for yoga classes and dog walkers, you may find notices of apartment or house rentals. More often, you'll find flyers for apartment shares. Some of the best rental bargains are advertised only with a sign on the window or front yard of an apartment building. The web sites of the city or neighborhood you're interested in may have leads as well. (Refer to the neighborhood profiles at the beginning of the book.)

ONLINE RESOURCES—RENTING

Los Angeles is well covered in terms of online sites for those seeking rentals. Many sites post apartment listings only; others help match roommates, and/or supply moving-related information or links to other moving-related sites. Here are a few:

- **Apartment Access**, www.apartmentaccess.com; listings for large metropolitan areas in the USA, including Los Angeles. Skim their listings of apartments; then, if it looks promising, pay a flat rate of $40 to use the service. Since landlords can list their units at no cost, your subscription buys you access to updated listings of apartments that you can lease without an agent fee.
- **Apartment Ratings**, www.aptratings.com; not an apartment listing service but rather a nationwide rating service. Residents of the Los Angeles area post assessments of where they live for the benefit of those in search of an apartment.
- **Craig's List**, http://losangeles.craigslist.org; the Los Angeles component of this popular web site posts listings for fee and no-fee apartment rentals, roommates, and sublets.
- **Rent.com**, www.rent.com, is free to search apartments in the Los Angeles area and they give you $100 if you sign a lease from their posting.
- **Move.com**, www.move.com; comprehensive web site where you can find apartments, homes (both sales and rentals), and roommates in Los Angeles. Free to renters.
- **Roommates**, www.roommates.com; pay $5.99 for a three-day trial, $19.99 for 30 days, and $29.99 for 60 days for listings from this roommate-matching company.

CHECKING IT OUT

It's two months into your lease and, suddenly, that cozy budget bachelor pad you found is feeling claustrophobic and the police choppers buzzing overhead are keeping you awake at night. To avoid this scenario we suggest you bring a checklist of your musts and must-nots. In addition, you should make a quick inspection to make sure the apartment's beauty is not just skin deep. A little time and a few questions asked now can save you a lot of time, money, and headaches later. Specifically, you may want to look for the following:

- Are the kitchen appliances clean and in working order? Do the stove's burners work? How about the oven? Is there enough counter and shelf space? Be aware, apartments in Los Angeles do not usually come with refrigerators, and you may need to buy or rent your own. Some landlords offer rentals on refrigerators they have in the building.
- Do the windows open, close, and lock? Do the bedroom windows open onto a noisy or potentially dangerous area? Is there an air-conditioning unit or central air?
- Are there enough closets and is there enough storage space?
- Are there enough electrical outlets for your needs? Do the outlets work?
- Are there any signs of insects?
- What about laundry facilities? Are they in the building or nearby?
- How did the building fare in the last earthquake? Superficial cracks along the walls or ceiling don't necessarily indicate a serious structural problem. The city's Department of Building and Safety (213-977-6941 or 888-LA4BUILD) can provide you with information if you are unsure.
- Outside, do you feel comfortable? Will you feel safe here at night? Is there secured parking? How many spaces? If two, are they tandem (so that one car blocks the other) or side by side? Is there an extra fee for parking? What about public transportation and shopping?
- Are you responsible for paying gas, water, and/or electricity? This policy varies from place to place, and paying any combination or none at all is possible.
- How quick to respond is the landlord or manager to work orders for repairs in the apartment? If possible, ask current tenants about this. Does the manager live on the premises?

Ed Sacks' *Savvy Renter's Kit* contains a thorough renter's checklist for those interested in augmenting theirs.

If it all passes muster, be prepared to stake your claim without delay!

STAKING A CLAIM

While it is not necessary to wear your Sunday best, coming on time and appearing neat and well-kept, no matter how superficial, is certain to give a good impression to a prospective landlord. Also come with checkbook in hand. Often the person who is willing to put down a deposit first will get the apartment. Have ready access to your references, both credit and personal, and bring your rental history with you: previous residence addresses, manager contact information, and length of tenancy for the past five years or more to fill out a rental application.

LEASES, SECURITY DEPOSITS, AND RENT CONTROL

The lease is a legally binding contract that outlines both your obligations to your landlord and your landlord's obligations to you. Of course, you should read your lease carefully, and get a full written explanation for anything that does not make sense to you, *before* signing. If you have any questions regarding your lease, security deposit, or rent control, contact your rent stabilization board (see below).

Here are some things to consider in your lease:

- Is this a month-to-month rental, or a one- or two-year lease?
- Are pets allowed?
- Are water beds allowed?
- Are you allowed to barbecue on the property?
- Can you sublet your unit?

Under California law, in most instances the security deposit cannot exceed two months' rent for an unfurnished unit or three months' rent for a furnished unit. The deposit can be collected in addition to the first month's rent. In some cities, for instance in West Hollywood or Santa Monica, landlords are required to pay interest on your security deposit as stipulated by rent control. Check with your rent board for specifics in your city. In addition, your landlord cannot raise your rent during a lease period unless it is so stated in your lease—read carefully before signing. If your landlord is increasing your rent by 10% or less, you must be given 30-days' notice. If your landlord is increasing your rent by more than 10%, you must be given 60-days' notice.

LANDLORD PROBLEMS

You should try to resolve any problems with your landlord first. However, if your efforts are fruitless, there are a number of city and state housing advocates available:

- **California Department of Fair Employment and Housing**, 800-233-3212, www.dfeh.ca.gov; handles discrimination claims.
- **City of LA Tenant & Landlord Information Line**, 213-808-8888 or 866-557-RENT, http://lahd.lacity.org, has a free downloadable Landlord Tenant Handbook on their web site, and helps handle landlord-tenant disputes including information on eviction procedures. If you reside in another city,

contact the housing department or general information line of your city for a referral.

- **LA County Department of Consumer Affairs**, 213-974-1452, http://dca. lacounty.gov, their web site has useful information about renter's rights.
- **Coalition for Economic Survival**, 213-252-4411, www.cesinaction.org; specializes in legal problems with regards to tenants' rights.
- **Fair Housing Council of San Fernando Valley**, 818-373-1185, http://fhcsfv. org; investigates housing discrimination in the Valley.
- **Legal Aid Foundation of Los Angeles**, 213-640-3881, www.lafla.org; can refer a lawyer for handling disputes.
- **Neighborhood Legal Services of LA County**, 800-433-6251, www.nls-la.org; provides information and assistance to low-income renters regarding evictions and landlord problems.
- **US Department of Housing and Urban Development**, 800-669-9777, www. hud.gov; handles discrimination and other housing problems.

RENT STABILIZATION

In an effort to offer affordable rental housing, several cities in the Los Angeles area have enacted rent stabilization. Rent control laws and their effects vary according to city. In Los Angeles City, for example, rent stabilization is applicable only to buildings built before 1979. If you're renting in a building built after this date, the landlord can issue annual increases at whatever amount he/she pleases, with notice.

The most recent development in rent control, and one that is more beneficial to the landlord than to the tenant, is the Costa-Hawkins Bill (also known as "vacancy decontrol"), which went into effect in 1999. This bill allows landlords to raise the rents of vacated rent-controlled units to current market value, which has resulted in a significant loss of bargain-priced rentals. It is worth noting that rental units affected by the Costa-Hawkins Bill are still covered by rent control in terms of how much rent may be raised from year to year during a tenancy. However, this type of rent control does nothing to prevent the rent of recently vacated apartments from being immediately raised to current market value. Cities with rent control have counselors who can help a renter sort it all out. Contact the following rent stabilization boards to learn how rent control works in your area.

- **Beverly Hills Rent Information Office**, 455 N Rexford Dr, 310-285-1031, www. beverlyhills.org
- **City of LA Department of Housing**, 3550 Wilshire Blvd, 213-808-8888 or 866-557-RENT, http://lahd.lacity.org

- **Santa Monica Rent Control Board**, 1685 Main St, Rm 202, 310-458-8751, www.smgov.net/rentcontrol
- **West Hollywood Department of Rent Stabilization**, 8611 Santa Monica Blvd, 323-848-6450, www.weho.org

RENTER'S/HOMEOWNER'S INSURANCE

Renter's insurance provides a relatively inexpensive policy against theft, water damage, fire, and in many cases personal liability. Earthquake insurance usually has to be purchased separately. Renter's insurance does not cover structural damage to the building, only personal belongings. Go for the replacement value over cash-value policy. As with all insurance, be sure you understand your policy completely and ask questions. While most insurance companies offer renter's insurance, call to be sure. (Check with your auto insurance agency to see if they offer renter's insurance—many agencies offer discounts for multiple policy holders.) AAA, Farmers, and State Farm are some of the larger insurance agencies offering coverage in the area. Homeowners in need of financing will be required to obtain a homeowner's insurance policy as part of the home buying process. Insurance customer satisfaction ratings and comparisons are possible at www.insure.com; also the **State of California Department of Insurance** does an annual survey of homeowner insurance providers in Los Angeles: Go to www.insurance.ca.gov 800-927-4357. After the 1994 Northridge earthquake, some companies stopped selling earthquake insurance altogether. In response, in 1996, the California Legislature established the **California Earthquake Authority** (916-325-3800, www.earthquakeauthority.com), which is a privately funded, publicly operated organization to provide earthquake coverage to Californians. This coverage is not required, but certainly recommended. Due to the variances in local geography, additional natural disasters that may pose some risk to your home include wildfires, landslides, flooding, and environmental hazards—all should be disclosed in your title inspection report to help you determine which additional protections you might need. A thorough home inspection will address the home's structural integrity as well. When you obtain insurance, many insurance companies will require that you provide a detailed inventory of your possessions. Photograph or videotape your furniture, jewelry, electronics, and anything else of value to supplement your documentation. Store this inventory separate from your home, in a safe-deposit box or with a family member or trusted friend. To order your CLUE (Comprehensive Loss Underwriting Exchange) report, call **ChoiceTrust**, 866-312-8076, or order one through their web site: www.choicetrust.com. This national database of consumers' automobile and homeowner's insurance claims is used by insurers when determining rates or denying coverage. Contact ChoiceTrust if you find any errors in your report.

BUYING

In Southern California's tight housing market, becoming a homeowner can be a good financial investment. Over the long term, the cost of renting can exceed that of owning, especially in high-rent districts. If you expect to spend at least seven years in one place and if you can afford it, purchasing a home is worth investigating. That said, a newcomer to Los Angeles would be well advised to rent or sublet for at least one year before buying, giving time to learn about various neighborhoods, commuting issues, and local schools. Realtors recommend that buyers get pre-qualified for a loan before house hunting (see **The Buying Process**). Sellers who entertain multiple bids are not so common in today's marketplace. But still, making a good impression on the seller when viewing a house could be to your advantage. The search for a condo, townhome, or house requires resourceful and aggressive search tactics. Your best bet is to work with an attentive broker who has access to homes waiting to be listed with the Multiple Listing Service. Assisting your broker's efforts by browsing the "Real Estate" section of the Sunday *Los Angeles Times* as well as the numerous home-for-sale listings on the web, such as www.OpenHouses.com, is a good idea. Free real estate guides—*Homes & Land* (800-277-7800, www.homes.com), *The New Home Buyers Guide* (800-273-HOUSE, www.homebuyersguideusa.com), and *Coldwell Banker Homes* (800-733-1380 or 800-589-9866, www.californiamoves.com)—can be found on racks at grocery stores, pharmacies, and newspaper stands. City web sites (see **Neighborhoods**) will often offer links to real estate options.

REAL ESTATE BROKERS

Most people selling a home in Los Angeles use a real estate broker/agent, which is helpful for buyers. An agent is knowledgeable about the maze of legal paperwork required in California and will have access to brand-new listings. The real estate broker takes a percentage of the sale, usually 5% to 6% of the price of the home (paid by the seller) to cover services, which include writing and making an offer, guiding the buyer through escrow and settlement, and answering questions.

RECOMMENDATIONS FOR FINDING A REAL ESTATE BROKER

Seek the referrals of friends, family, and co-workers, and/or browse the classifieds and/or internet for a broker who handles listings in neighborhoods that appeal to you. Any search should include a visit to the **www.realtor.com** site, since working with a licensed broker ensures a certain level of professionalism.

(Do not rely on the Realtor symbol on the real estate broker's business card as sole proof that they're Realtor licensed.) Investigate the vicinity in which you're interested and look for offices in the area—that broker is likely to have more intimate knowledge of the neighborhood than a broker whose office is in another community. Call a realty agency or check their web site for a field office in the community in which you're interested.

Of concern to some, many real estate brokers alternate between representing a buyer or seller at different times. For those looking for an agent that specializes in representing only buyers, seek out an accredited Buyer's Representative via the **Real Estate Buyer's Agent Council** of the National Association of Realtors (800-648-6224, www.rebac.net) or contact **Buyers Broker** (888-302-0001, www.homesoflosangelescounty.com and www.homesoforangecounty.com).

Some of the larger real estate agencies offer **concierge** or **relocation services**. Expect an organized network of prescreened local vendors to provide every service a homebuyer could need, from locksmiths to maid service to upholstery cleaning, often offered at a discount. Inquire with your realtor to see if they offer this service.

THE BUYING PROCESS

PRE-QUALIFICATION/PRE-APPROVAL

The first thing you need to consider when buying a house is how much you can spend. Start with your gross monthly income, then tally up your monthly debt load: credit cards, car loans, personal debt, child support, alimony, etc. For revolving debt (like credit card debt), use your minimum monthly payment for the calculation. For the purposes of this calculation, ignore any debts you expect to have paid off entirely within six months' time. As a rule, your monthly housing costs shouldn't exceed 28% of your total monthly income, and your debt load shouldn't exceed 36% of it. That said, these days lenders might tailor the 28/36 ratio depending on your situation (assets, liability, job, credit history). When calculating your budget, don't forget to factor in closing costs, which include insurance, appraisals, attorney's fees, transfer taxes, and loan fees. Fees normally range from 3% to 7% of the purchase price. Likewise, when figuring out your budget, be sure to factor in the additional monthly outgoes of homeowner's insurance, property taxes (tax deductible), utilities, condo fees, improvements, and maintenance.

Lenders suggest that you "pre-qualify" or, better still, get "pre-approved" for a loan. **Pre-qualification** is, in essence, an educated guess as to what you'll be able to afford for a loan. To be **pre-approved**, your loan officer will review your financial situation (by running a credit check, going over your proof of employment, savings, etc.) and then you will be given a letter documenting that the bank is willing to lend you a particular amount based on your proven financial situation. Pre-approval is a bit more labor-intensive for you and the lender, but sellers and real estate agents will take you more seriously if you show up with a pre-approval letter in hand.

For either pre-qualification or pre-approval of a loan, go to your lender with documentation of your financial history and a list of your debt load, and contact the three major credit bureaus (listed below) beforehand to make sure your credit history is accurate. You will need to provide your name, address, previous address, and social security number with your request. Contact each company for specific instructions, or visit **www.annualcreditreport.com** for online access to all three. A credit report will list your credit activity for the past seven years, including your highest balance, current balance, and promptness or tardiness of payments. After seven years, the slate is wiped clean for any credit transgressions, except in the case of bankruptcy and foreclosure, which will appear on your record for 10 years. If you find your credit score is not as good as it could be, keep in mind that lenders are more concerned with your most recent track record than how you behaved seven years ago. It's best to try to pay all your bills in full and on time for at least a year before you apply for a loan, and be aware that even if you pay your bills on time, having too much credit can be a problem. Even if your credit report isn't stellar, you most likely can still get a loan, though your rates (interest and fees) may be higher. A substantial down payment can counteract credit flaws as well.

It's best to get a copy of your credit report from each bureau, as each report may be different. (For contact information on the major **credit bureaus**—Experian, Equifax and TransUnion—see "Credit Reports" in the **Money Matters** chapter). Your credit report will have a FICO (Fair Isaac and Company). Typically, lenders will give a standard loan for scores of 650+; if your score is lower, you'll probably get a sub-prime loan (from a non-major lender and with a higher interest rate). If you discover any inaccuracies on your credit report, you should contact the service immediately and request that it be corrected. By law, credit bureaus must respond to your request within 30 days. If you have questions about your credit record, call Fannie Mae's non-profit credit counseling service at 800-732-6643 before you apply for a mortgage. Be aware that too many credit record inquiries can lower your credit status.

FINANCING

Most buyers need a **mortgage** to pay for a house. A typical house mortgage is for either 15 or 30 years and consists of four parts, commonly referred to as "PITI" (principal, interest, taxes, and insurance). The **principal** is the flat sum of money that you borrowed from the lender to pay for the property. The larger the down payment, the less you will need to borrow to meet the total purchase price of your home. The lender charges **interest**, a percentage of the principal, as repayment for the use of the money that you've borrowed. (Points, each one equal to 1% of the amount you borrow for your mortgage, might also contribute to the interest.) Your community charges you **taxes** based on a percentage of your property value, which you'll continue paying even after your mortgage is paid off. The final component of PITI is house **insurance** against calamities such as fire, theft, and natural disasters. In many cases, people deposit funds into an escrow or trust account to cover insurance and taxes. Within three business days of applying for your loan, your lender must give you a "good faith estimate" of how much your closing costs will be.

There are many loan programs around. Search the internet, newspapers, and books, and speak with financial planners, real estate agents, and mortgage brokers to find out what's available. Direct lenders (banks) and mortgage brokers are the most common places to go for a loan. A **direct lender** is an institution with a finite number of in-house loans, whose terms and conditions are controlled by the lender. A **mortgage broker**, on the other hand, is a middleman who shops around to various lenders and loan programs to find what's best for your needs. Because brokers shop around for the best interest rates, it's often worth paying their fee. Most major lenders and brokers have their own web sites. For a list of local banks, look in the **Money Matters** chapter.

When educating yourself about mortgages, be sure to take the time to research institutions' loan costs and restrictions: interest rates, broker fees, points, prepayment penalties, loan term, application fees, credit report fees, and cost of appraisals. The **Bank Rate Monitor** (www.bankrate.com) offers pages of information on mortgages and interest rates at over 2,000 banks. It may pay to shop around.

DOWN PAYMENT

Down payments vary. Some lenders offer programs that require as little as 5% down or even zero down. An example of these programs is Fannie Mae's three/two loan program, which gives a first-time buyer 95% of the price of a home. The buyer is required to supply 3% of the down payment; the other 2% can be a gift from family, a government program, or a non-profit agency. Zero-down mortgages have returned to pariah status due to a number of banks suffering losses from the borrower defaulting. If you do manage to obtain a loan with no down payment, the interest will be about 2% higher than what you'd pay at 20% down. The best interest rate can be obtained with at least 20% down. (A down payment of less than 20% will require private mortgage insurance.) If you are a first-time buyer, which is defined as someone who hasn't owned property within the past three years, you may qualify for state-backed programs that feature lower down-payment requirements and below-market interest rates.

MAKING AN OFFER

The longer a home has been on the market, the more likely you can negotiate a discount on the purchase price. The most anxious sellers are those who have already purchased another home. Given LA's current housing market, like much of the nation, it's not unusual to find a house lingering on the market. When the market was tight, buyers had to be prepared to make an offer and a deposit (typically 3% of the home's asking price) immediately upon viewing a house—or risk missing out. Now that sales have cooled to a twenty-year low, it's safe to say you have time to think about buying that house. When making the offer, mini-mally, you should protect yourself by making your purchase offer contingent on financing (if applicable) and on the approval of a professional inspector, keeping in mind that sellers and their agents dislike contingencies and in a competitive market, a contingency-free offer is the most attractive bid to the seller. Offers, which should be submitted in writing to the seller, may mention the following:

- Address and legal description of the property
- Price you will pay for the home
- Terms (how you will pay)
- Seller's promise to provide clear title
- Target date for closing (when the property is actually transferred to you, and the funds are transferred to the seller)
- Down payment accompanying the offer—how much and in what form
- Plan for prorating utilities, taxes, etc., between buyer and seller
- Provisions: who will pay what extra costs (e.g., insurance, survey)
- Type of deed
- Contingencies

To get your offer seriously considered in a tight market, the strategy would be to offer fair market price, include a statement of the source of your down payment, your pre-approval letter, and even a note to the seller about why/how much you want the house. Buyers offering cash, or with a pre-approval in hand, will be more attractive to the seller, and conversely, an offer made contingent upon the sale of the buyer's home will not be appealing. Should you still find yourself in a soft market when you're ready to make an offer, your agent can provide the best advice for how to get the most bang for your buck.

CONTINGENCIES, PURCHASE AND SALE (P&S) AGREEMENT

Common **contingencies** include an appraisal of the house that is satisfactory to the bank, financing (in cases where the buyer has not been pre-approved), a free and clear title, selling a current residence, and receiving a satisfactory inspection report of the property. Some buyers put into their offer "on terms to be approved by the buyer's attorney." In the competitive Los Angeles housing market, making the offer is the most important part of the buying process, not the closing. The closing is just signing the paperwork that finalizes what you agreed to in your offer. If the seller agrees to your written offer, it becomes a binding sales contract, called a **purchase and sale (P&S) agreement.** If you default on this contract, you can lose your deposit money. If the seller defaults, you can sue him to force the sale to which he agreed in writing.

That said, after you make an offer, the buyer will accept it, reject it, or make a counteroffer, at which point you may accept, reject, or change the counteroffer, and so on. When both parties agree, it becomes a binding purchase agreement.

INSPECTION

As mentioned above, **inspections** are crucial, particularly for older homes. Because many Los Angeles residences were built decades ago, hiring an inspector to perform a thorough check of the property you are considering is recommended. You can ask your realtor for a reference or try one of the following:

- **California Real Estate Inspection Association** certified inspector, 800-848-7342, www.creia.org
- **American Society of Home Inspectors**, 800-743-2744, www.ashi.com
- **National Association of Certified Home Inspectors**, 877-FIND-INS, www. nachi.org

All of the above should be able to make referrals for more specialized testing of home environmental toxins such as mold, lead, asbestos, radon and the like, which are *not* covered in a standard home inspection.

CLOSING

Assuming the inspection goes well and/or all issues are resolved to your satisfaction, it is time for closing. At the closing, also known as "settlement" or "escrow," costs, such as transfer taxes, closing costs, legal fees, and adjustments are paid. (Closing costs for a $400,000 home will run about $10,000.) This is a brief process in which the title to the property is transferred from seller to buyer; the seller gets his payment and you get the keys, and the closing agent officially records your loan.

FIRST-TIME HOMEBUYERS

Buying a home for the first time can be a financially overwhelming experience. **First-time** buyers can turn to home-buying assistance programs through local **Neighborhood Housing Services:**

- **Inglewood,** 310-674-3756, www.cityofinglewood.org
- **LA County,** 888-895-2647, www.lanhs.org
- **Long Beach,** 562-570-6855, www.longbeach.gov
- **Pasadena,** 626-744-8316, www.cityofpasadena.net/housing/homebuyer.asp
- **Pacoima Homeownership Center,** 818-834-7858, www.lanhs.org
- **South Bay Homeownership Center,** 310-514-9444, www.lanhs.org

Services include down-payment and closing-cost assistance, arranging home-rehabilitation loans, and home-maintenance classes.

Another source of assistance is the **LA County Housing Department's Home Ownership Assistance Program,** designed specifically to help low- to moderate-income households and first-time homebuyers purchase a home. Call 213-381-2862 or visit the county's web site, www.lacdc.org, for more information. The **California Association of Realtors'** web site, www.car.org, also lists home-buyer-assistance programs.

ONLINE RESOURCES—HOUSE HUNTING

Web sites for would-be homeowners include the following:

- **FISBO Registry for Homebuyers,** www.fisbos.com
- **Move.com,** www.move.com; comprehensive site where you can find apartments, homes, and roommates; sales and rentals.
- **HomeGain,** www.homegain.com
- **Homes.com,** www.homes.com
- **MSN Real Estate,** http://realestate.msn.com
- **The National Association of Realtors,** www.realtor.com
- **Real Estate Book,** http://realestate.citysearch.com
- **ZipRealty,** www.ziprealty.com, a national real estate site.

If you want to investigate homes **for sale by owner,** try:

- **For Sale By Owner:** www.forsalebyowner.com
- **IsoldMyHouse.com:** www.isoldmyhouse.com
- **For Sale By Owner Network:** www.fsbopublishers.org
- **LosAngelesFSBO.com:** www.losangelesfsbo.com
- **OCHomeList.com:** www.ochomelist.com
- **Owners.com,** www.owners.com
- **HomesByOwner.com:** www.homesbyowner.com

ONLINE RESOURCES—MORTGAGES

In addition to the information included in the text of this chapter, the following sites might help you on your quest to finance a home:

- **Bankrate.com**, www.bankrate.com; everything about mortgages and lending.
- **Dirs.com**, www.dirs.com; links and information on mortgages and home equity loans.
- **Fannie Mae**, www.fanniemae.com; loans for real estate purchases; dedicated to helping Americans achieve the dream of homeownership.
- **Freddie Mac**, www.freddiemac.com; provides information on low-cost loans, a home-inspection kit, and tips to help avoid unfair lending practices.
- **Interest.com**, www.interest.com; shop for mortgages and rates.
- *Los Angeles Times*, http://latimes.interest.com/calculators.asp; link to research daily mortgage rates. Also offers a mortgage calculator.
- **The Mortgage Professor**, www.mtgprofessor.com; demystifies and clarifies the confusing and often expensive world of mortgage brokers, helpfully written by an emeritus Wharton professor who answers questions (!); useful calculators.
- **Quicken Home**, www.quickenloans.com

ADDITIONAL RESOURCES—BUYING A HOME

Finally, aside from the selection of books you can pick up at your local bookstore or at an online bookseller, consider the following resources and publications:

- *10 Steps to Homeownership: A Workbook for First Time Home Buyers* (Three Rivers Press) by Ilyce R. Glink
- *The 106 Common Mistakes Homebuyers Make (and How to Avoid Them)*, 4th edition (Wiley) by Gary W. Eldred
- *Everything You Need to Know Before Buying a Co-Op, Condo, or Townhouse* (AMACOM) by Ken Roth
- "**Opening the Door to a Home of Your Own**": a pamphlet by Fannie Mae for first-time homebuyers. Call 800-834-3377 or visit www.fanniemaefoundation. org for a copy.
- **Score Card**; if you're particularly concerned about environmental toxins at your new property, check out www.scorecard.org, a site sponsored by the Environmental Defense Fund.
- *The National Association of Realtors Guide to Home Buying* (Wiley) by National Association of Realtors

HAVING FOUND AND SECURED A PLACE TO LIVE, YOU HAVE NOW THE task of getting your stuff here and perhaps finding storage. The how-tos follow, as well as a section detailing which agency to contact regarding consumer complaints against moving companies, information about moving with children, and specifics regarding tax-deductible moving expenses.

TRUCK RENTALS

First determine if you are going to move yourself or hire someone else to do it for you. If you prefer doing it all yourself, you can rent a vehicle, load it up, and hit the road. Look in the Yellow Pages under "Truck Rental" and call around and compare; also ask about any specials. Below is a list of four national truck rental companies and their toll-free numbers and web sites. For the best information, you should call a local office. Note: most truck rental companies offer "one-way" rentals as well as packing accessories and storage facilities. Of course, these extras are not free. If you're cost conscious you may want to scavenge boxes in advance of your move or buy some directly from a box company. (Those moving locally should check Smart and Final stores, which frequently offer empty boxes in a bin by the entrance of the store.)

If you're planning to move during the peak moving months (May through September), call well in advance, at least a month ahead of when you think you'll need the vehicle. Remember that Saturday is a popular moving day; you may be able to get cheaper rates if you book a different day.

Once you're on the road, keep in mind that your rental truck may be a tempting target for thieves. If you must park it overnight or for an extended period (more than a couple of hours), try to find a safe place, preferably somewhere well-lit and easily observable by you, and do your best not to leave anything of particular value in the cab. Make sure you lock the back door and, if possible, use a steering wheel lock or other easy-to-purchase safety device.

Four national self-moving companies to consider:

- **Budget**, 800-428-7825, www.budget.com
- **Penske**, 800-222-0277, www.penske.com
- **Ryder**, 800-297-9337, www.ryder.com (now a Budget company, still operating under the Ryder name)
- **U-Haul**, 800-468-4285, www.uhaul.com

COMMERCIAL FREIGHT CARRIERS AND CONTAINER-BASED MOVERS

A little wary of driving a big truck yourself? Commercial freight carriers, such as **ABF U-Pack**, 800-355-1696, www.upack.com, offer an in-between service; they deliver a 28-foot trailer to your home, you pack and load as much of it as you need, and they drive the vehicle to your destination (often with some other freight filling the remaining space). ABF charges by the linear foot, so you pay only for the linear feet you use (a minimum charge applies). However, if you have to share truck space with another customer you may arrive far ahead of your boxes—and bed. Try to estimate your needs beforehand and ask for your load's expected arrival date. You can get an online estimate from some shippers, so you can compare rates.

If you aren't moving an entire house and can't estimate how much truck space you will need, keep in mind this general guideline: two to three furnished rooms equal a 15-foot truck; four to five rooms, a 20-foot truck.

Another transportation option is the container-based move. Large, closet-shaped containers that you load and pack are delivered to your home. The company retrieves the containers and transfers them to trucks that deliver them to your new home. ABF, **PODS** (877-776-PODS, www.pods.com), **Door-to-Door Storage and Moving** (888-505-3667, www.doortodoor.com), and several other companies offer container-based moves. You pay by the container. Keep in mind these containers may not work for transporting large furniture. Inquire about the containers' *interior* dimensions beforehand to make sure they'll meet your needs.

MOVERS

INTERSTATE

Probably the best way to find a mover is by **personal recommendation**. Absent a friend or relative who can recommend a trusted moving company, you can turn to what surveys show is the most popular method of finding a mover: the **Yellow Pages**. Then there's the **internet**: just type in "movers" on a search engine and you'll be directed to hundreds of more or less helpful moving-related sites.

In the past, *Consumer Reports*, www.consumerreports.org, has published useful information on moving. You might ask a local realtor, who may be able to steer you towards a good mover, or at least tell you which ones to avoid. A valuable resource is **Consumers Relocation Services**, 800-839-MOVE, www. consumersrelocation.com, which will assign the member a personal consultant to handle every detail of the move and offers savings from discounts arranged with premier moving companies for a service fee. Members of the American Automobile Association can get the service fee waived.

But beware! Since 1995, when the federal government eliminated the Interstate Commerce Commission, the interstate moving business has degenerated into a wild and mostly unregulated industry with thousands of unhappy, ripped-off customers annually. (There are so many reports of unscrupulous carriers that we no longer list movers in this book.) Since states do not have the authority to regulate interstate movers and the federal government has been slow to respond, you are pretty much on your own when it comes to finding an honest, hassle-free mover. That's why we can't emphasize enough the importance of carefully researching and choosing who will move you.

Watch out for shakedown schemes that begin with a lowball bid off the Internet and end with the mover holding your belongings hostage for a high cash ransom. Despite the fact that federal law says that movers cannot charge more than 10% over any written estimate, it is not unusual for unscrupulous movers to charge you several times their written estimates—and with your possessions in their possession, you may find yourself paying anyway, since companies that operate this way also won't tell you where they're holding your stuff.

To get informed about moving cons, check out the **MovingScam** web site (www.movingscam.com). MovingScam.com strives to educate consumers and better consumer protections in the moving industry. The site features articles, moving news, and maintains a "Blacklist." It has lively message boards for those with moving-related questions. The FMCSA, 888-368-7238 or 202-358-7028, www.protectyourmove.gov, offers similar information. The web site lets you check that an interstate mover is properly registered and insured. Criminal investigations and convictions are kept up to date on the site. Also, you'll find links to local Better Business Bureaus, consumer protection agencies, state attorneys general, and state moving associations. Consumer advocates and attorneys general around the country urge you to take precautions before hiring a mover by doing the following things:

- Make sure the mover is licensed and insured. If the company appears to be federally licensed, check for complaints with the Better Business Bureau (www. bbb.org).
- Get several written estimates from companies. Only deal with those that send a sales representative to your home to do a visual inspection of the goods to be moved. Cost is not the concern here; estimates should always be free. If not,

don't use them. Make sure each company is giving you an estimate for approximately the same poundage of items to be moved, and for the same services so that you can have an accurate comparison. Finally, accept only estimates that are written on a document that contains the company's name, address, phone number, and signature of the salesperson. Be aware that an estimate can be either binding or non-binding. A binding estimate guarantees the total cost of the move based upon quantities and services listed. A non-binding estimate is what your mover believes the cost will be, with the final charges based upon the services provided and the actual weight of your shipment. With a non-binding estimate, you should be prepared to pay up to 10% more than the estimated charges upon delivery.

- Remember that you get what you pay for. Who would you trust your worldly possessions with more? Poorly paid strangers or well-paid ones?
- Ask for references and check them.
- Read and understand the terms of your moving contract. It's not fun but it's for your protection. If there's something you don't understand, ask for an explanation. Get everything in writing, including the mover's liability to you for breakage or loss. Consider purchasing additional replacement insurance to cover loss or damage. Check your homeowner's or renter's insurance policy to see what, if any, coverage you may already have for your belongings while they are in transit. If the answer is "none," ask your insurer if you can add coverage for your move. You can purchase coverage through your mover, but coverage is normally based on the weight of the items being insured, not on their value. To cover the actual value of your belongings, you need to purchase "full value" or "full replacement" insurance.
- Consider packing and moving irreplaceable, fragile or sentimental items, documents, and jewelry personally. This is the only way to guard against loss or breakage.
- Ask your mover what is not permitted in the truck: usually anything flammable or combustible, as well as certain types of valuables.
- Consider keeping a log of every expense you incur for your move, i.e., phone calls, trips to LA, etc. In many instances, the IRS allows you to claim these types of expenses on your income taxes. (See **Taxes** below.)
- Be aware that during the busy season (May through September), demand can exceed supply and moving may be more difficult and more expensive than during the rest of the year. If you must relocate during the peak moving months, call and book service well in advance of when you plan on moving. A month at least. If you can reserve service way in advance, say four to six months early, you may be able to lock in a lower winter rate for your summer move.
- Although movers will put numbered labels on your possessions, you should make a numbered list of every box and item that is going in the truck. Detail box contents and photograph anything of particular value. Once the truck ar-

rives on the other end, you can check off every piece and know for sure what did (or did not) make it. In case of claims, this list can be invaluable. Even after the move, keep the list; it can be surprisingly useful.

- Oversee the loading and unloading of your things. Write "subject to further inspection for concealed loss or damage" on the moving contract to allow for damage you may discover as you unpack.

- Get specifics on how to pay the full moving bill upon delivery. Cash or bank/cashier's check may be required. Some carriers will take VISA and MasterCard but it is a good idea to get it in writing that you will be permitted to pay with a credit card since the delivering driver may not be aware of this and may demand cash. Unless you routinely keep thousands in greenbacks on you, you could have a problem getting your stuff off the truck.

- File a written claim with the mover immediately if any loss or damage occurs—and keep a copy of your claim, as well as all the other paperwork related to your move. If your claim is not resolved within a reasonable time, file complaints with the Better Business Bureau and appropriate authorities, as well. (See **Consumer Complaints—Movers,** below.)

To aid your search for an **interstate mover**, we offer a few general recommendations:

First, get the names of a half-dozen movers and check to make sure they are licensed by the US. With the **Department of Transportation's Federal Motor Carrier Safety Administration** (**FMCSA**) movers' Motor Carrier (MC) numbers in hand, call 800-832-5660 or go to www.fmcsa.dot.gov to see if the carriers are licensed and insured. If the companies you're considering are federally licensed, your next step should be to check with the **Better Business Bureau**, www.bbb.org, in the state where the moving companies are licensed as well as with the states' consumer protection boards (in Los Angeles call 800-952-5210 or go to www.dca.ca.gov), or attorneys general. Also check FMCSA's **Household Goods Consumer Complaint** web site, http://nccdb.fmcsa.dot.gov, where they maintain complaints that have been filed on interstate movers. Assuming there is no negative information, you can move on to the next step: asking for references. Particularly important are references from customers who did moves similar to yours. If a moving company is unable or unwilling to provide references, eliminate it from your list. Unscrupulous movers have even been known to give phony references who will falsely sing the mover's praises—so talk to more than one reference and ask questions. If something feels fishy, it probably is. One way to learn more about a prospective mover: Ask them if they have a local office (they should) and then walk in and check it out.

Once you have at least three movers you feel reasonably comfortable with, it's time to ask for price quotes (always free). Best is a binding "not-to-exceed" quote, of course in writing. This will require an on-site visual inspection of what you are shipping. If you have *any* doubts about a prospective mover, drop it from your list before you invite a stranger into your home to catalog your belongings.

Recent regulations by FMCSA require movers to supply several documents to consumers before executing a contract. These include two booklets: *Important Information for Persons Moving Household Goods (within California)*, which must be provided at the first-person contact between the consumer and the mover, and *Your Rights and Responsibilities When You Move*. You should also receive a concise and accurate written estimate of charges, a summary of the mover's arbitration program, the mover's customer complaint and inquiry handling procedure, and the mover's tariff containing rates, rules, regulations, classifications, etc. For more about FMCSA's role in handling household goods, you can go to its consumer page at www.protectyourmove.gov.

INTRASTATE AND LOCAL MOVERS

The **California Public Utilities Commission** (**CPUC**), www.cpuc.ca.gov, regulates the licensing, rates, and rules of the Household Goods moving industry in California. All companies involved in the moving business must be insured and hold a license that permits them to provide moving services within or from/to California. To verify certification of your chosen mover, call the CPUC at 800-877-8867 or the **California Moving and Storage Association** (**CMSA**) at 800-672-1415 and have the mover's CAL T number (listed on the mover's literature) ready. The CMSA, http://thecmsa.org, is a nonprofit trade organization that offers references to legitimate movers and provides information to help consumers avoid "bandit movers" (movers that engage in unlawful practices and/or bully the customer into paying outrageous prices once the move has started). According to the CMSA, 80% of the calls to them involve complaints about bandit movers. They recommend against booking online or over the phone without investigating the company's physical address first and confirming it's licensed (with a CAL T number) with the CPUC. For moves within California, the CPUC regulations require all movers to provide each client with a written "not to exceed price" before the move commences. This price should be clearly disclosed on your Agreement for Service form. The mover will have you sign this form before the move begins.

CONSUMER COMPLAINTS—MOVERS

If a **move goes badly** and you blame the moving company, you should first file a written claim with the mover for loss or damage. If this doesn't work and it's an **intrastate move**, call 800-366-4782 to file a complaint with the CPUC. If the mover is a CMSA member, the CMSA will intervene on the consumer's behalf if there is a problem.

If your grievance is with an **interstate carrier**, your choices are limited. Interstate moves are regulated by the Federal Motor Carriers Safety Administration (FMCSA), 888-368-7238, www.dot.fmcsa.gov, an agency under the Department of Transportation, with whom you can file a complaint against a carrier. While its role in the regulation of interstate carriers historically has been concerned with safety issues rather than consumer issues, in response to the upsurge in unscrupulous movers and unhappy consumers, it has issued a recent set of rules "specifying how interstate household goods (HHG) carriers (movers) and brokers must assist their individual customers shipping household goods." According to its consumer page, carriers in violation of said rules can be fined, and repeat offenders may be barred from doing business. In terms of loss, however, "FMCSA does not have statutory authority to resolve loss and damage of consumer complaints, settle disputes against a mover, or obtain reimbursement for consumers seeking payment for specific charges. Consumers are responsible for resolving disputes involving these household goods matters." It is not able to represent you in an arbitration dispute to recover damages for lost or destroyed property, nor enforce a court judgment. If you have a grievance, your best bet is to file a complaint against a mover with FMCSA and with the Better Business Bureau, www.bbb.org, in the state where the moving company is licensed, as well as with that state's attorney general or consumer protection office. To seek redress, hire an attorney.

PACKING AND ORGANIZING

Don't wait until the last minute to think about packing. You'll need plenty of boxes, tape, and packing material—probably more than you think. Moving and truck rental companies sell boxes, as do most office supply stores, but most grocery stores or liquor stores will let you scrounge some empty boxes. For foam "peanuts," bubble wrap, and other materials to protect fragile items, look in the Yellow Pages under "Packaging Materials"; if you have some especially fragile and valuable items, you might also want to look under "Packaging Service."

LOADING AND UNLOADING

If you are driving a rental truck or using a freight carrier, but you are disinclined to load and unload the truck yourself, many moving companies and independent businesses offer "pack and load" services. Companies that provide these services generally charge by the person/hour, with a minimum charge. (Call around, as hourly rates and minimums vary tremendously.) The same cautions that apply to hiring full-service movers apply equally to pack-and-loaders: try to get a recommendation from a trusted source, make sure the company is insured, and always check references. Beware of companies that use inexperienced temporary workers who may not be especially careful with either your belongings or your walls, and who may not pack your items securely in the truck—a fact which you may not discover until you unpack your crushed possessions at the end of your journey.

Because packing and loading do not involve the actual transport of goods, the businesses that provide these services are often unregulated. One way to protect yourself is to see if the business is a member of the National Association of Professional Organizers (www.napola.org).

Whatever moving method you plan to use, make sure you'll have a spot at both ends of your move to park the truck or to place the trailer or containers. Some cities require a permit to park a truck or place containers on a public street; others don't require a permit, but will issue one so that you can reserve a parking place for your moving truck. If you are moving to or from a large apartment building, check with the manager to see if you need to reserve a time to load or unload.

STORAGE WAREHOUSES

Storage facilities may be required when you have to ship your furniture without an apartment to receive it or if your apartment is too small for all your belongings. The CPUC regulates short-term storage (under 90 days), but not long-term or self-storage. If your mover maintains storage warehouse facilities in the city, as many do, you'll probably want to store with them. Some even offer one month's free storage. Look in the Yellow Pages under "Storage," and shop around for the best and most convenient deal. Below are a couple of major moving/storage companies. Listing here does *not* imply endorsement by First Books.

- **Door to Door Storage**, 888-366-7222, www.doortodoor.com, has warehousing for cargo containers, which it delivers to you for packing, and then its trucks transport the container back to its facilities (several throughout Los Angeles).
- **Public Storage**, 800-447-8673, www.publicstorage.com, offers locations throughout the county for self-service storage, pick-up service and storage, full-service moving, and/or truck rentals.

SELF-STORAGE

The ability to rent anything from 5' x 5' rooms to storage rooms large enough to accommodate a car is a great boon to urban dwellers. Collectors, people with old clothes they can't bear to give away, and those with possessions that won't fit in a sublet or shared apartment all find mini-warehouses a solution to too-small living spaces.

Rates for space in Los Angeles self-storage facilities are competitive: Expect to pay at least $95 a month for a 5' x 5' (25 sq ft), $135 a month for a 5' x 10' space (50 sq ft), and so on. Some offer free pick-up, otherwise you or your mover delivers the goods. If you're looking for lower rates, inquire with the storage facility for move-in specials or other locations.

As you shop around, you may want to check the facility for cleanliness and security. Does the building have sprinklers in case of fire? Does it have carts and hand trucks for moving in and out? Does it bill monthly, or will it automatically charge the bill to your credit card? Access should be 24-hour or nearly so, and some are air conditioned, an asset if you plan to visit your locker in the summer. Is the rental month to month or is there a minimum lease?

Finally, a word of warning: Unless you no longer want your stored belongings, pay your storage bill and pay it on time. Storage companies may auction the contents of delinquent customers' lockers.

Here are a few area self-storage companies. For more options, check the Yellow Pages under "Storage."

- **Price Self Storage**, www.priceselfstorage.com, two locations in West LA: 3430 South La Brea Ave, 323-299-2699 or 10151 National Blvd, 310-837-7700; with individually alarmed units that range in size from 5' x 5' to 12' x 30'. It also offers truck and driver services.
- **Extra Space Storage**, 800-895-5921, www.extraspace.com, has facilities all over Los Angeles.
- **Mobile Mini, Inc.,** 866-344-4092, www.mobileminiinc.com; delivers storage containers from 5' x 8' to 40' x 10' that you fill and it will transport to a location you specify or to its own secured facilities.
- **Public Storage**, 877-788-2028, www.publicstorage.com; also offers pick-up and delivery services at certain locations: 866-836-4838, www.pspickup.com.
- **Los Angeles Security Storage**, 323-469-1402, 6372 Santa Monica Blvd., LA; has been in business at this location since 1923.
- **Linkletter Self Storage**, 2318 E South St, Long Beach, 562-634-4084, www.linkletterselfstorage.com
- **U-Haul Self-Storage**, 800-GO-U-HAUL, www.uhaul.com, multiple warehouses. Prices for rooms vary by their location and availability.

CHILDREN AND MOVING

Studies show that moving, especially frequent moving, can be hard on children. According to an American Medical Association study, children who move often are more likely to suffer from such problems as depression, low self-esteem, and aggression. Often their academic performance suffers as well. Aside from not moving more than is necessary, there are a few things you can do to help your children through this stressful time:

- Talk about the move with your kids. Be honest but positive. Listen to their concerns. To the extent possible, involve them in the process.

- Make sure children have their favorite possessions with them on the trip; don't pack "blankey" in the moving van.
- Make sure you have some social life planned on the other end. Your children may feel lonely in your new home, and such activities can ease the transition. If you move during the summer you might find a local camp (check with the YWCA or YMCA) at which they can sign up for a couple of weeks in August to make new friends.
- Keep in touch with family and loved ones as much as possible. Photos and phone calls are important ways of maintaining links to the important people you have left behind.
- If your children are school age, take the time to involve yourself in their new school and in their academic life. Don't let them fall through the cracks.
- Try to schedule a move during the summer so they can start the new school year at the beginning of the term.
- If possible, spend some time in the area prior to the move doing fun things in the area to which you are moving, such visiting a local playground or playing ball in a local park or checking out the neighborhood stores with teenagers. With any luck they will meet some other kids their own age.

For children ages 9–12, try *The Moving Book: A Kids' Survival Guide* by Gabriel Davis or *My Moving Activity Journal: Activities, Games, Crafts, Puzzles, Scrapbooking, Journaling, and Poems for Kids on the Move* by Nicole LV Jaeger. For general guidance, read *How to Survive a Move* by Kazz Regelman. And for younger kids, *Max's Moving Adventure: A Coloring Book for Kids on the Move* by Danelle Till, illustrated by Joe Spooner, is a perfect gift.

PETS

Moving our four-legged or feathered friends across the country is stressful for everyone involved, whether animal or human. The **Pet-Moving Handbook** by Carrie Straub, available from First Books (www.firstbooks.com), provides practical answers for all your pet-moving questions and covers domestic and international moves via car, airplane, ferry, etc.

In general, driving your pets thousands of miles comes with its own set of challenges, including dealing with extreme weather (which could prevent you from leaving your pet in the car while you eat, for example) and finding pet-friendly overnight accommodation. If your pets fly, you'll have to navigate the maze of regulations, services, and prices that each airline has devised for animal transport; some airlines will not transport pets at all, others allow them only in the cabin as carry-on luggage, and still others will only transport animals when outdoor temperatures are moderate. A few airlines have special climate-controlled pet care facilities at their hub airports, and will place pets in a climate-controlled cargo bay on the plane. At a minimum, you'll need to get a health certificate from your veterinarian.

Before moving pets, attach a tag to your pet's collar with your new address and phone number in case your furry friend accidentally wanders off in the confusion of moving. Your pet should travel with you and you should never plan on moving a pet inside a moving van.

Given the complications of moving animals over long distances, you might want to leave the task to professionals. **Jet Set 'N Pets** will make all the arrangements with airports, airlines, and the licensing authorities at your destination—and, of course, they'll move your pet in accordance with the Animal Welfare Act and USDA specifications. Call 877-PETS FLY or 323-256-9930, or visit www.jetsetnpets.com. If moving a pet within Los Angeles, one option is A Pet Taxi (310-575-1985, www.lapettaxi.com), which can transport your pet for you.

A word of warning, the following animals are illegal to keep as pets in California: gerbils, ferrets, skunks, hedgehogs, snapping turtles, and wolf-dog hybrids. See the California Department of Fish & Game's website for the complete list: http://www.dfg.ca.gov/wildlife/species/nuis_exo/ferret/ferret_issues_table6. html.

TAXES AND MOVING

If your move is work-related, some or all of your moving expenses may be tax-deductible—so you may want to keep those receipts. Though eligibility varies, depending, for example, on whether you have a job or are self-employed, generally, the cost of moving yourself, your family, and your belongings is tax deductible, even if you don't itemize. The criteria: In order to take the deduction your move must be employment-related, your new job must be more than 50 miles away from your current residence, and you must be here for at least 39 weeks during the first 12 months after your arrival. If you take the deduction and then fail to meet the requirements, you will have to pay the IRS back, unless you were laid off through no fault of your own or transferred again by your employer. IRS publication 521 (available from the IRS web site at www.irs.gov or by phone at 800-829-3676) provides full details of the moving expenses deduction. It's a good idea to consult a tax expert if you are unsure whether, or to what extent, your move qualifies for the deduction. However, if you're a confident soul, get a copy of IRS Form 3903 (www.irs.gov) and do it yourself!

In general, you can deduct:

- The cost of moving household goods from your old residence to your new one
- The cost of storing household goods in your new city for up to 30 consecutive days
- The cost of shipping your car
- The cost of moving your household pets
- The cost of your family's trip to your new residence (including transportation and lodging, but not meals)

Keep your receipts for these expenses.

ADDITIONAL RELOCATION AND MOVING INFORMATION

- **www.firstbooks.com**, relocation resources and information on moving to Atlanta, Boston, Chicago, Minneapolis–St. Paul, New York, Portland, San Francisco, Seattle, Texas, Washington, D.C., as well as London, England, and China. Also publisher of the *Newcomer's Handbook® for Moving to and Living in the USA*; *The Moving Book: A Kids' Survival Guide*; *Max's Moving Adventure: A Coloring Book for Kids on the Move*; and the *Pet-Moving Handbook*.
- **BestPlaces**, www.bestplaces.net; compares quality-of-life and cost-of-living data of US cities.
- **DataMasters**, www.datamasters.com; for basic community statistics by zip code
- **Employee Relocation Council**, www.erc.org; if your employer is a member of this professional organization, you may have access to special services, including specialized reports on the relocation and moving industries. Non-members can use the online database of real estate agents and related services.
- *How to Move Handbook* by Clyde and Shari Steiner, an excellent general guidebook
- **http://houseandhome.msn.com**; online quotes
- **The Riley Guide**, www.rileyguide.com/relocate.html; online moving and relocation clearinghouse. Lists moving and relocation guides and web sites, offers links to sites that cover cost of living/demographics as well as real estate links and school and health care directories.
- **www.allamericanmovers.com**, 800-989-6683; online quotes
- **www.move.com**, provides realty listings, moving tips, cost-of-living calculators, and more.
- **www.moving.org**, American Moving & Storage Association offers referrals to interstate movers, local movers, storage companies, and packing and moving consultants.
- **www.american-car-transport.com**; if you need help moving your car
- **www.erc.org**, see Employee Relocation Council above
- **www.homestore.com**; relocation resources, including a handy salary calculator that will compare the cost of living in US cities
- **www.usps.com**, relocation information from the United States Postal Service

FTER FINDING YOUR NEW PLACE OF RESIDENCE, THE NEWCOMER'S first order of business probably will be opening a bank account. The following information about personal savings, checking accounts, and credit unions should make the task less daunting. (Keep in mind, however, that some landlords may be reluctant to accept a temporary check from a freshly opened bank account as a deposit; in this situation, your old bank account—from your former place of residence—will still be useful.)

Most major national and some international financial institutions have branches in Los Angeles, so shop around for what suits your needs. A section on credit cards and credit reports follows, and, for your edification come April 15, we've included information about federal and state income tax procedures, as well as details for those wanting to start or move a business.

BANKING

Bank of America (800-792-0808, www.bankamerica.com), **Washington Mutual** (800-788-7000, www.wamu.com), and **Wells Fargo** (800-869-3557, www.wells-fargo.com) are the three largest banks on the West Coast, and the numerous branches each bank offers can be convenient. Online banking has become the most popular way to check your balance and track transactions (in fact some banks charge you to walk in and conduct your banking in person); in addition, most banks offer direct deposit, ATM service, and automated telephone system service.

Additional banks serving LA and its environs include (check the Yellow Pages for a complete listing):

- **Bank of the West**, 800-488-2265, www.bankofthewest.com
- **California National Bank**, 866-373-7838, www.calnationalbank.com
- **CitiBank**, 800-374-9700, www.citibank.com

- **East West Bank**, 888-895-5650, www.eastwestbank.com
- **First Bank of Beverly Hills**, 800-515-1616, www.fbbh.com
- **Ing Direct**, 888-464-0727, www.ingdirect.com
- **Pacific Western Bank**, www.pacificwesternbank.com
- **Security Pacific Bank**, 877-772-2761, www.securitypacificbank.com
- **Union Bank of California**, 323-720-2000, www.uboc.com
- **Wachovia**, 800-922-4684, www.wachovia.com

Larger banks entice customers with low or no service fees. However, smaller banks offer more personalized service. Other trade-offs with a smaller bank: fewer branches, a limited number of ATMs, and your chosen bank may end up merging with the very bank you were trying to avoid.

CREDIT UNIONS

According to the **National Credit Union Administration** (**NCUA**), "A federal credit union is a nonprofit, cooperative financial institution owned and run by its members." Organized to serve and democratically controlled, credit unions provide their members with a safe place to save and borrow at reasonable rates. Most who qualify for membership to a credit union elect to join. Credit unions offer nearly the same services as regular banks, but they typically offer lower fees and higher interest rates. Perks, such as discount coupons for movies, theme parks, and other entertainment options, are sometimes part of the package as well. Membership generally is limited to a specific group or employee association; the **LA Federal Credit Union** (818-242-8640), for example, is limited to Los Angeles city employees and their families and the **First Entertainment Credit Union** (888-800-3328, www.firstent.org) is limited to employees of the entertainment industry in LA.

For a complete list of local credit unions or for more information about them, you can visit the **National Association of Credit Union Service Organizations** (www.nacuso.org, or the **NCUA**, http://ncua.gov).

CHECKING AND SAVINGS ACCOUNTS

Many establishments will not take your check unless it is local and imprinted with your name, address, and telephone number. There are exceptions, such as when you're moving into a new apartment. Needless to say, it helps to get your checking (and savings) accounts set up as soon as possible. If you have moved to Los Angeles from another US city and previously banked with a large national institution with offices in LA, chances are you can simply transfer your account. Otherwise, a minimum deposit (amounts vary by bank) is required to open an account, and you'll need to bring a photo ID and your new address. For fee-free checking, you may need to maintain a certain monthly balance (fee-free accounts typically are not interest-bearing accounts). Some opt to connect checking with savings for overdraft protection. Other products and services to inquire about: online or telephone banking, certificates of deposit, safe deposit boxes, hours, and fees. You can expect a debit card to be issued with your checking account.

ONLINE BANKING

Today, it is rare when a bank does not offer online banking. Generally this includes balance and other account information inquiries, making transfers, paying bills, and even applying for loans. Security should be a chief concern when accessing your private financial information over the internet. While banks should encrypt your personal information and password, the user should also take standard precautions as well: Don't share your password with anyone, and change it often; don't send confidential information through e-mail or over unsecured web space; and restrict your banking interactions to private computers—not a work computer with a shared network or at an internet café.

Online access services and fees vary from bank to bank, so check with individual institutions for information.

CONSUMER COMPLAINTS—BANKING

Federal and state government regulates bank policies on discrimination, credit, anti-redlining, truth-in-lending, etc. If you have a problem with your financial institution, you should first attempt to resolve the issue directly with the bank. Should you need to **file a formal complaint**, you can do so through the Board of Governors of **Federal Reserve Consumer Help**. For specifics, call 888-851-1920 or go to www.federalreserveconsumerhelp.gov. You can also pursue the issue with the following agencies:

- Nationally chartered commercial banks go through the **US Comptroller of the Currency**, Customer Assistance Group, 1301 McKinney St, Ste 3450, Houston, TX 77010; 800-613-6743; www.occ.treas.gov.
- **US Office of Thrift Supervision**, 1700 G St NW, Washington, D.C. 20552, 202-906-6000, www.ots.treas.gov; for thrift institutions insured by the Savings Association Insurance Fund and/or federally chartered (i.e., members of the Federal Home Loan Bank System).
- Federally chartered credit unions; state chartered credit unions with federal insurance: **National Credit Union Administration**, 1775 Duke St, Alexandria, VA 22314-3428, 800-755-1030, www.ncua.gov.

CREDIT CARDS

A list of low-rate card issuers can be found on the internet at **CardWeb** (www.cardweb.com, 800-874-8999), **Consumer Action** (www.consumer-action.org), and **BankRate.com** (www.bankrate.com, 561-630-2400). For consumer information regarding credit cards, check with these web sites, or with the **Consumer Action Federal Citizen Information Center** (www.consumeraction.gov). In addition, you might want to investigate reward cards. Some cards are offering rebates on certain types of purchases (groceries, gasoline, restaurant meals, etc.) for an indefinite period; such cards could be worth your while.

To request a credit card application you can contact one of the following:

- **American Express**, 800-THE-CARD, www.americanexpress.com
- **Diners Club**, 800-2-DINERS, www.dinersclub.com
- **Discover Card**, 800-347-2683, www.discovercard.com
- **VISA** and **MasterCard** can be obtained through banks and other financial service associations. Check first with your bank, and shop around for the lowest interest rate, annual fees, and frequent flyer–miles deals.
- **Department stores in Los Angeles** also offer their own store credit cards, although most department stores will take local personal checks with proper identification or major credit cards. The advantages of having a store credit card include advance notice of sales and often no annual fee.

CREDIT REPORTS

Those interested in seeing a personal credit report can go to www.annualcreditreport.com, where you can obtain a free copy of your credit report from the three main credit bureaus, Equifax, Experian, and TransUnion. It's best to get a copy from each service because each company's report may be different. If you discover any inaccuracies, you should contact the service immediately and request that it be corrected. By law they must respond to your request within 30 days. Under federal law, these reports can be ordered without charge by consumers. Credit FICO **scores**, however, still cost a fee. Note: Checking your credit report frequently can adversely affect your credit rating.

You can also visit or call each bureau individually:

- **Equifax**, P.O. Box 740241, Atlanta, GA 30374, 800-685-1111, www.equifax.com
- **Experian**, 888-397-3742, www.experian.com
- **TransUnion**, P.O. Box 6790, Fullerton, CA 92834, 877-322-8228, www.transunion.com

INCOME TAXES

There is no city income tax for residents of Los Angeles, Beverly Hills, Burbank, Culver City, Glendale, West Hollywood, Malibu, or Santa Monica. The City of Los

Angeles has a business license tax for those who run a business (that includes independent contractors) within the city confines. You are exempt from paying the tax if your business grossed less than $100,000 in one year or you work as a "creative artist" and earned less than $300,000. Keep in mind, the city still expects you to file the application for business tax registration/renewal even if you qualify for the exemption. The California Franchise Tax Board shares its information with the city so that it can locate businesses that haven't registered with the city. The city has been quite proactive about sending tax enforcement notices. Visit the city's **Office of Finance** web site to download the form and for more information: www.lacity.org/finance.

FEDERAL INCOME TAX

Resources for federal income tax information and forms:

- **Federal income tax forms** can be obtained by calling 800-829-FORM or visiting www.irs.gov/formspubs/index.html. Or visit your local post office or library (the Beverly Hills Library frequently has the most complete selection of forms).
- **IRS Tax Help Line**, 800-829-1040, www.irs.gov; for consumers with questions and/or in need of forms.
- **Federal Teletax Information Line**, 800-829-4477

STATE INCOME TAX

State income tax forms can be obtained from the **State Franchise Tax Board Office**, 300 South Spring Street, downtown LA, or by calling 800-852-5711, www.ftb.ca.gov. The Franchise Tax Board office is open from 8 a.m. to 5 p.m., Monday–Friday. As with federal forms, your local post office or library may have state forms, as well.

The Franchise Tax Board is the department that administers state personal income taxes and corporation taxes for the State of California. Their web site has a taxpayer advocate link that provides information on taxpayers' rights and how to request the assistance of an advocate: www.ftb.ca.gov.

STATE SALES TAX

In California, a sales tax is imposed on retail sales or consumption of personal property (fast food, snacks, etc.). Statewide, the sales tax is 7.25%, but LA County tacks on an additional 1% for the Metropolitan Transportation Authority. The breakdown of the tax follows:

State General Fund: 4.75%
State Fiscal Recovery Fund: .25%
State Local Revenue Fund: .5%
State General Fund: .25%
State Local Public Safety Fund: .5%
Local County & City transportation, operations funds: 1%
MTA: 1%
Total: 8.25%

Within Orange County, with the exception of Laguna Beach, the sales tax totals 7.75%, because the OC Local Transportation Authority (OCTA) only takes .5%. In Laguna Beach, the local transportation tax ups their total sales tax to that of LA.

MOVING OR STARTING A BUSINESS

In order to do business in Los Angeles, you'll need to file your Fictitious Business Name (FBN) statement with the County Recorder's office (fee $23) and renew it every 5 years (fee: $18). First and most importantly, you must come up with a fictitious business name that isn't already in use. You may conduct a search via their web site or in person in their office. Within 30 days of filing, you must publish the FBN statement for four weeks in a newspaper of general circulation in the county in which the principal place of business is located. You can download the FBN form and view said newspapers at www.lavote.net, or write the **Registrar, Recorder/County Clerk, Business Filing and Registration**, P.O. Box 53592, Los Angeles, CA 90053-0592, to request the form. You may also call 562-462-2177 with any questions. A word of warning for the home-based business owner, the address you publish becomes public information. To maintain your privacy, consider leasing a private mail box for purposes of registration and conducting business.

To obtain a business license, contact the **city hall** of the municipality where your business will be conducted. For a business to be conducted in an unincorporated area of the county, contact the **LA County Business License** office at 213-974-2011, http://ttc.lacounty.gov. As stated in the beginning of this chapter, anyone conducting business within the city of LA must pay business tax. The amount varies depending on your industry, and small businesses qualify for exemptions. See http://lacity.org/finance for a tax registration application, or contact the **City of LA Office of Finance** at 213-473-5901. If your business operates outside the City of LA but you do business within the city, you still have a tax liability. Both this web site and www.lacity.org list a wealth of information including business incentives and necessary permits for doing business in Los Angeles. If your business involves sales of tangible personal property, you'll have to apply for a seller's permit from the **State of California Board of Equalization** (800-400-7115, www.boe.ca.gov). This web site provides information about doing business in California, including employer tax forms and the *California Employer's Guide*. The Board of Equalization's information center can also answer your tax questions.

Additional resources for those wanting to start or move a business to LA include:

- **LA County Bar Association**, 213-627-2727, www.lacba.org, 261 S Figueroa, Ste 300, LA, CA 90012
- **Internal Revenue Service**, 800-829-1040, www.irs.gov, for a tax ID number.
- **US Small Business Administration**, 800-827-5722, www.sba.gov
- **California State's** web site, www.ca.gov, has all sorts of information about starting a business in the state. Tax, license, and permit forms are available online.

O KAY. YOU'VE FOUND A PLACE TO LIVE, ESTABLISHED A CHECKING account, and now you are ready to unpack and truly get settled in. The following covers most of the services you will need: electric, water, gas, and telephone, and those modern almost-necessities of cable television and internet service providers. There is also automobile-related information, including registering your car with the DMV and parking details, as well as specifics on getting a library card, registering to vote, finding a physician, subscribing to local newspapers and magazines, information about owning a pet, and finally some hints about personal safety.

UTILITIES

Upon moving into your Los Angeles apartment or home, your landlord/building manager or real estate agent will be able to provide you with a list of numbers for setting up utilities. For those establishing these accounts from afar, you'll need to have your new address handy when dialing these numbers. If you don't mind paying a service to set up the utilities for you, **Connect Utilities**, aka **White Fence** (www.ConnectUtilities.com, 866-298-1514), offers such a service. Their web site also serves as a one-stop site that lets you compare service plans, and links you to your cable, phone, and power provider for free.

Note: For those of you needing to dig in your yard—say for a garden—call **Under Ground Service Alert** (811, www.digalert.com or www.call811.com) at least two days before. This non-profit organization will notify the water, phone, cable, and electric companies, which will then send representatives to your place to mark their lines.

GAS

Gas service in greater LA and Orange County is provided by **So Cal Gas** (800-427-2200, www.socalgas.com). A service establishment fee of $25 is required to set up an account. A credit check will be run when setting up service to determine what the amount of your deposit will be (which can range from $20 to $200). The deposit will be refunded after one year of timely payments. If you have only a gas cooking range, you can expect your monthly bill to be minimal. If you have gas heat, your bills will be slightly higher during the winter, but remember, temperatures seldom drop below 45 degrees here, so your heating bills will not be a major part of your budget.

In Long Beach, the provider is **Long Beach Gas & Oil** (562-570-2000, www.longbeach.gov/lbgo). The service establishment fee is $35.

ELECTRICITY AND WATER

Commonly called the DWP, the **Los Angeles Department of Water and Power** is the municipal service that provides electricity and water to the majority of Los Angeles. There is a one-time set-up fee of $13. Those with credit issues (and they'll be able to tell who you are), or with no identification, will have to put down a $205 deposit, which will be refunded after a year of timely payments. For most apartment rentals, water is covered by the landlord. Questions regarding LA's water quality (see below) should be directed to the DWP, by calling 800 DIAL-DWP. Tap water is fluoridated.

The DWP's conservation efforts benefit homeowners and include a shade tree program (attend a free workshop and get up to seven free trees to plant around your home) and the RETIRE program where you can exchange your old, energy-guzzling refrigerator for $35's worth of compact fluorescent bulbs (and they will even come to pick up your old fridge and recycle it for you, too).

(For an interesting fictionalized account of the history of this powerful government office, view Roman Polanski's *Chinatown* (1974), starring Jack Nicholson. It tells the story of how early Los Angeles officials secured water rights for the city during its boom years. The main character, Hollis Mulwray, is a thinly veiled reference to William Mulholland, a turn-of-the-20th-century water engineer who is now immortalized by the 22-mile skyline Mulholland Highway on the crest of the Santa Monica Mountains.)

- **Los Angeles Department of Water and Power**, www.ladwp.com
  Metropolitan LA: 213-481-5411
  San Fernando Valley: 818-342-5397
  Other areas: 800-342-5397

Additional utility providers include (if yours is not listed, check with your municipality):

- **Southern California Edison**, 800-655-4555, www.sce.com, provides electricity to areas not covered by the DWP, including Orange County, and within LA County, the communities of Santa Clarita, Culver City, Santa Monica, South Pasadena, Inglewood, and portions of Marina del Rey and Manhattan Beach.
- **The Municipal Water District of Orange County**, 714-963-3058, www.mw doc.com, provides water to most of the OC, leaving Anaheim, Fullerton, and Santa Ana to the **Metropolitan Water District**, 213-217-6000, www.mwd.dst. ca.us.
- **Southern California Water Company**, 310-838-2143, www.aswater.com/ Organization/Company_Links/SCWC/scwc.html, services other parts of Los Angeles not covered by the DWP, including Culver City, El Segundo, Hawthorne, Redondo Beach, and Inglewood.
- **Burbank** has its own water and power company, **Public Service, City of Burbank**, 818-238-3700, www.burbankwaterandpower.com. A $40 deposit is required to set up service, which is refunded after one year of timely payments.
- **Glendale** residents should call **Public Service, City of Glendale**, 818-548-3300, www.glendalewaterandpower.com.
- **Long Beach** has its own water and power companies, the **Long Beach Water Department**, 562-570-2300, www.lbwater.org, and the **Long Beach Gas & Electric Department**, 562-570-2000, www.longbeach.gov/lbgo.
- **Malibu** is served by the **Las Virgenes Municipal Water Company**, 818-251-2200, www.lvmwd.dst.ca.us, and the Los Angeles County Water District #29, 310-456-6621 or 626-458-4357.
- **Pasadena** has its own water and power company, **Pasadena Water and Power**; call 626-744-4409 for general information, or 626-744-4005 to set up service, or visit www.ci.pasadena.ca.us.
- **South Pasadena** residents should contact the **City of South Pasadena Public Works Department**, 626-403-7240.
- **Santa Clarita** has a number of water companies, by county: **Castaic Lake Water Agency**, 661-259-2737, www.clwa.org; **Valencia Water Company**, 661-294-0828, www.valenciawater.com; **Newhall County Water District**, 661-259-3610, www.ncwd.org; **LA County Waterworks District #36**, 661-942-1157.
- **Santa Monica** has its own water department, the **City of Santa Monica Water Division**, 310-458-8224, www.smgov.net.

WATER QUALITY

In California, chemical additives are mixed in with gasoline to make it burn cleaner for better air quality. However, scientists have discovered that one of these additives, MTBE, a carcinogen, can contaminate groundwater, and is not as readily removable as other contaminates. The City of Santa Monica, West Los Angeles, and Culver City had their water fields shut down as a result of the contamination. Clean-up of the wells is still ongoing, and MTBE-contaminated wells have been suspended from service indefinitely. The California Department of Health Services requires all water systems in the state to monitor for MTBE and has established a limit for MTBE within tap water at 13 micrograms per liter. In 2000, Governor Gray Davis requested a ban on MTBE, but proposals to phase out MTBE have been repeatedly delayed. The future of a total phase-out is questionable. Visit the **California Department of Public Health** web site at www.cdph.ca.gov to read about MTBE in drinking water. For additional information about LA-area water quality, there are a number of departments to contact: **City of Santa Monica Water Department**, 310-458-8235; **Los Angeles County Department of Health Care Services**, **Environmental Health Department**, 626-430-5200, www.dhcs.ca.gov; or the **LA Regional Water Quality Control Board**, 213-576-6600, www.swrcb.ca.gov/rwqcb4.

TELEPHONE

AT&T (formerly **SBC**, **Southwest Bell Company**, 800-288-2020, www.att.com) is the primary telephone provider in Los Angeles, except for the Westside. In Orange County, service is provided by SBC or **Verizon** (800-483-4000, www.verizon.com). The western portions of Los Angeles—Malibu, Mar Vista, Marina del Rey, Pacific Palisades, Playa del Rey, Santa Monica, Venice, portions of Brentwood, Culver City, and Topanga—are also covered by Verizon. Both SBC and Verizon offer local as well as long-distance service. Assuming you have an established credit history with a telephone company, and if you have not had your service temporarily or completely disconnected in the last year for non-payment, and you have paid all previous "final" bills older than 45 days, you will not be required to put down a deposit for service. There is a one-time charge of $36 to activate your service. Both companies offer additional services, including voice mail, call waiting, call blocking, repeat dialing, and number referral services. For a complete list of the services available, check their web site or call for details.

If you find yourself doing a lot of business with companies outside your immediate calling territory and you don't have easy internet access, it's a good idea to collect phone books from the different sections of Los Angeles: Beverly Hills & Santa Monica make up one directory, as does Greater Los Angeles, the San Fernando Valley East, the San Fernando Valley West, and Burbank and Glendale. You may order from AT&T by calling 800-288-2020—the price varies depending upon which directory you need—or simply ask friends and/or co-workers if they have any extras.

LONG-DISTANCE SERVICE PROVIDERS

At the time you install your telephone service, you will be asked to name a long-distance carrier. Unless you bundle your long-distance service with your local carriers, you will receive two separate telephone bills. Currently some of the lowest per-minute rates can be found through calling cards offered at gas stations and grocery stores. If you want to compare long-distance pricing, go to **SmartPrice** at www.smartprice.com or call 888-865-6760. You will be asked questions regarding your phone usage, your area code, and the first three digits of your phone number. They will then provide a free instant analysis of the carriers available in your area. You can also contact **Telecommunications Research and Action Center** (**TRAC**), a consumer organization that publishes charts comparing plans and prices at 202-263-2950, www.trac.org.

Major long-distance service providers in LA include:

- **GTC Telecom**, 800-486-0082, www.gtctelecom.com
- **IDT**, 800-982-0593, www.idt.net
- **MCI WorldCom**, 800-444-3333, www.mci.com
- **Qwest Communications**, 800-475-7526, www.qwest.com
- **Sprint**, 800-877-4646, www.sprint.com
- **Verizon**, 800-483-4000, www.verizon.com

CELL PHONES

For many Angelenos, especially actors waiting for a call back, a cellular phone is an absolute must—and their only phone, having completely skipped the land line. Many cell phone providers operate out of strip mall storefronts, kiosks in local malls, or outside on campus squares (see phone numbers below to call for locations). When you buy a cellular phone, you will need to set up service, typically a minimum two-year contract. Depending on the service contract you select, the cost of your cell phone may be refunded to you, making the cell phone itself free. The largest cellular service operators in the area are **AT&T Wireless** (formerly **Cingular Wireless**, 800-888-7600, www.wireless.att.com); **NexTel** (800-639-8359, www.nextel.com); **Sprint PCS** (888-253-1315, www.sprintpcs.com); **T-Mobile** (800-866-2453, www.t-mobile.com); and **Verizon** (800-256-4646, www.verizonwireless.com).

Note: In 2003, the California Public Utilities Commission granted local number portability to cell phone users. This means that you can keep your same phone number if you change telephone providers within the same local area and, in limited cases, move a phone number from a land line to a wireless phone. And in another victory for consumers, California adopted the Telecommunications Bill of Rights in 2004, which provides some protections, such as requiring companies to bill customers only for services they request and allowing customers 30 days to drop a service without penalty.

DIRECTORY ASSISTANCE

For local directory assistance calls, the first three of which are free each month (after that they cost $1.50), dial 411 (for national listings, the charge is $1.99 per request); repair service is 611. For the correct time, dial 853-1212 and any four digits—there is no charge.

INTERNET SERVICE PROVIDERS

Many are cruising the virtual highway (when not sitting on a freeway). Standard dial-up service and DSL (Digital Subscriber Line) plans are available from **America Online** (800-827-6364, www.aol.com); **Earthlink** (800-511-2041, www. earthlink.net); and **AT&T** (800-288-2020, www.att.com). Request internet access software by phoning the provider. Availability of DSL service is determined by your proximity to a central switching office; contact the provider you're considering for availability. For cable modem, order through your cable provider (see the cable section).

Internet services that are advertiser-supported cost less, though you must be willing to provide some demographic information about yourself upon signing up (this is for directed advertising) and give up a small portion of your computer-screen space for ad banners while online. **Net Zero** (www.netzero.net) is one such advertiser-supported internet service provider (ISP).

While you're waiting for your internet connection to start up, some places you can go to hook up via WiFi are coffeeshops like Starbucks and public libraries. Libraries also offer internet access via their public computers. Internet cafés are rare birds in LA since many hotels have a business center that provides internet access for their customers, but the Yellow Pages might point you toward a handful.

CONSUMER PROTECTION—UTILITY COMPLAINTS

There are a number of agencies available to report problems with your utilities. The **State of California Public Utilities Commission**, which has an office in LA (320 West 4th Street, Suite 500, 213-576-7000, www.cpuc.ca.gov), is the place to go with inquiries and complaints about electric, gas, water, and telephone services. The **Consumer Affairs Department of California** (800-952-5210, www.dca. ca.gov) is another source for help, as is the **LA County Department of Consumer Affairs** (213-974-1452 or 800-593-8222, http://consumer-affairs.co.la.ca.us).

Additionally, if you look at your phone bill and think you've been **slammed** (your long-distance provider or established services were changed without your approval) or **crammed** (calls you didn't make were added to your bill), and you can't get help from your local service provider or from the State of California's **Attorney General's Office** (916-322-3360 or 800-952-5225, http://caag.state. ca.us), you can file a complaint with the **Federal Communication Commission's**

Consumer Center (888-225-5322, www.fcc.gov; or the Federal Trade Commission, 877-382-4357, www.ftc.gov).

GARBAGE AND RECYCLING

Apartment dwellers should ask their landlord or building manager about trash pickup and recycling. Homeowners will need to make arrangements for refuse collection by contacting the **Sanitation District of Los Angeles County** at 562-699-7411 or 562-908-4288, www.lacsd.org. In Santa Clarita, contact the **Environmental Services** division at 661-295-6300 or 661-222-7222, www.santa-clarita.com/cityhall/cmo/environment. In Orange County, talk to **Integrated Waste Management** at 714-834-4000, www.oclandfills.com.

Recycling is a way of life in Southern California. Some neighborhoods have curbside pickup along with regular refuse collection, others have drop-off points. For recycling, contact the **LA County Department of Public Works, Recycling and Household Hazardous Waste Program,** at 888-253-2652, www.ladpw.org or www.888cleanla.com, or the **County of Orange Integrated Waste Management Department** (see above) to locate the recycling center nearest you. Since old computers, their peripherals, cell phones, and compact fluorescent light bulbs are considered hazardous waste in California, the City of Los Angeles created regular Household Hazardous/Electronic Waste collection events and permanent collection centers. Contact them via the **Bureau of Sanitation** (800-988-6942, www.lacity.org/san/solid_resources/special/hhw/safe_centers/index.htm) for a complete listing of locations.

PRINT AND BROADCAST MEDIA

TELEVISION

Heaven forbid you should miss an episode of your favorite TV show! The major television network affiliates in Los Angeles and Orange County, plus the large local station, are as follows:

ABC – 7
CBS – 2
FOX – 11
KCAL – 9
NBC – 4
PBS – 28
CW – 13

Starting on February 17, 2009, all TV broadcasts will be in digital format nationwide (analog format will stop airing as mandated by Congress). Those of you who do not subscribe to cable (that is, receive only free over-the-air TV) will need a digital TV with a built-in digital tuner, or a digital-ready monitor that has a separate digital tuner set-top box, or an analog TV with digital-to-analog set-top converter box to view digital broadcasts. This converter box can be purchased at any electronics retail store. Once you have the right equipment, you just need to attach antennae ("rabbit ears" that can receive UHF signals) to receive over-the-air programming. All TVs sold after May 2007 should contain a digital tuner or give notice that they do not contain one. The Federal Communications Commission has set up a phone number and web site devoted to answering questions about this transition: 888-225-5322 (TTY: 1-888-835-5322), www.dtv.gov.

CABLE TELEVISION

Aside from offering nearly 100 stations, cable also provides better reception in some areas. Since there are several cable companies in Los Angeles, the City of Los Angeles has an **Information Technology Agency**, 213-485-4636, http://ita. lacity.org, that will help direct you to your cable company. The monthly fee for basic cable can start as low as $11, but most companies bundle their services, the total for which can easily approach $100 a month.

Many cable companies now offer digital telephone and high-speed internet service too, all of which can be bundled together with your cable service. It's easy and you get the benefit of a single bill and discounts for subscribing to multiple services from one provider. Obviously, plans and pricing vary widely; contact the cable provider for the most up-to-date information:

- **Cox Communications**, 949-240-1212, www.cox.com: Orange County
- **Comcast**, 888-255-5789, www.comcast.com: covers a large section of LA County, from West Los Angeles to East Los Angeles, in addition to portions of Orange County
- **Charter Communications**, 888-438-2427, www.charter.com: Burbank, Glendale, Norwalk, West Covina, Alhambra, Pasadena, Altadena, Monterey Park, Artesia, Cerritos, Covina, Arcadia, Long Beach, Thousand Oaks, Calabasas, Topanga Canyon, and Malibu
- **Time Warner Communications**, 888-TW-CABLE, www.accesstimewarner. com: covers Northridge, Encino, Woodland Hills, and Van Nuys, South Pasadena, parts of Santa Clarita, and areas within Orange County

RADIO

Maddening daily commutes have many tuning in for up-to-the-minute traffic reports. AM stations 980 and 1070 give frequent and regular traffic reports (every 5 minutes for 1070 and "on the ones," 9:01, 9:11, etc., for 980).

Most of the following stations can be received in both Los Angeles and Orange counties.

AM

- **KABC** 790 Talk Radio
- **KFI** 640 Talk/Sports
- **KSPN** 710 Sports
- **KFWB** 980 News
- **KHJ** 930 Spanish
- **KLAC** 570 Sports
- **KNX** 1070 News
- **KDIS** 1110 Radio Disney
- **KTLK** 1150 Progressive Talk
- **KYPA** 1230 Korean
- **KXTA** 1150 Sports/Talk
- **KMPC** 1540 Sports

FM

- **KBIG** 104.3 Adult Contemporary
- **KCBS** 93.1 Rock
- **KHHT** 92.3 Urban Contemporary
- **KIIS** 102.7 Top 40
- **KLOS** 95.5 Rock
- **KKBT** 100.3 Hip Hop
- **KKGO** 105.1 Country
- **KKLA** 99.5 Christian
- **KLVE** 107.5 Spanish
- **KPWR** 105.9 Hip Hop
- **KOST** 103.5 Adult Contemporary
- **KROQ** 106.7 Alternative
- **KSCA** 101.1 Spanish
- **KTWV** 94.7 Smooth Jazz
- **KYSR** 98.7 Adult Contemporary
- **KMVN** 93.9 Dance

NEWSPAPERS AND MAGAZINES

Neighborhood publications that focus on community issues include:

- ***Arcadia Weekly***, 626-294-1090
- ***Argonaut***, 310-822-1629, www.argonautnewspaper.com

- *Beverly Hills Courier*, 310-278-1322, www.todaysplanet.com/pg/beta/bh courier1
- *Burbank Leader*, 818-843-8700, www.burbankleader.com
- *Culver City News*, 310-313-6727
- *Daily Breeze*, 310-540-5511, www.dailybreeze.com (Torrance)
- *Downtown Gazette*, 562-433-2000, www.gazettes.com (Long Beach)
- *Glendale News Press*, 818-241-4141, www.glendalenewspress.com
- *Long Beach Press Telegram*, 562-435-1161, www.presstelegram.com
- *Los Angeles Downtown News*, 213-481-1448, www.losangelesdowntown.com
- *Los Angeles CityBeat*, 323-938-1700, www.lacitybeat.com
- *Los Angeles Independent*, 323-556-5720, www.laindependent.com
- *Los Angeles Jewish Times*, 323-933-0131, www.etta.org/jewishtimes.htm
- *Malibu Times*, 310-456-5507, www.malibutimes.com
- *Mid Valley News*, 626-443-1753, www.midvalleynews.com
- *Pasadena Weekly*, 626-795-0149, www.pasadenaweekly.com
- *Random Lengths/Harbor Independent News*, 310-519-1442, www.random lengthsnews.com (San Pedro)
- *Santa Monica Mirror*, 310-577-6507, www.smmirror.com
- *Santa Monica Observer*, 310-260-2199, www.smobserver.com
- *Signal*, 661-259-1000, www.the-signal.com (Santa Clarita)
- *The Tidings*, 213-637-7360, www.the-tidings.com (Catholic)
- *Tolucan Times*, 818-762-2171, www.tolucantimes.com (Toluca Lake)
- *Vanguard News*, 800-773-5228, www.vanguardnews.com (Acton)
- *Venice Paper*, 310-581-5575, www.venicepaper.net
- *Westside Weekly*, 310-314-1297
    Citywide publications include:
- *Los Angeles Times*, 213-237-5000 or 800-252-9141, www.latimes.com; primary newspaper in LA, it publishes a separate but similar edition for the Valley. Its Sunday edition (available as early as Saturday morning at convenience stores and newsstands) makes for hefty weekend reading.
- *Daily News*, 818-713-3000, www.dailynews.com; based in the Valley and competitor to the *Times*.
- *LA Weekly*, 323-465-9909, www.laweekly.com; this alternative paper is what many Angelenos turn to for information on movies, clubs, and fun (wholesome and not-so-wholesome) in LA. Their provocative personal ads are a hoot. The paper is free for the taking at newsstands, supermarkets, coffeehouses, convenience stores, etc. If you want a home-delivered subscription, you'll have to pay.
- *Los Angeles Magazine*, 800-876-5222, www.lamag.com; nice glossy spread covering the hip and happening in the LA scene, some fashion and food as well.
- *Orange County Register*, 877-469-7344, www.ocregister.com; the major daily in Orange County.

- **OC Weekly**, 714-550-5900, www.ocweekly.com; the Orange County counterpart to the *LA Weekly*.

AUTOMOBILES

DRIVER'S LICENSES

California drivers must have a valid California driver's license; upon arrival, you have 10 days to get the task done. A California driver's license is valid for up to five years and expires on the birthday of the license holder. You will be sent a renewal notice approximately two months before the expiration date. The renewal fee for a standard Class C and/or M1/M2 license is $28. Bring the notice and your license with you when you renew. You may be eligible to renew your license by mail without taking a test, if you have a good driving record.

If you have an out-of-state or out-of-country license, you must be at least 18 years of age, complete all the steps required for a permit (see below), and surrender your valid out-of-state driver's license. A driving test for license renewals or holders of out-of-state or US territory licenses is normally waived. However, driving tests are required for out-of-country license holders.

To get a permit, you must:

- Be at least 18 years of age (those under 18 who are licensed to drive outside of California should check with the DMV for specifics on how to acquire a California driver's license)
- Fill out the DMV application form (DL 44)
- Provide your full legal name
- Present an acceptable birth-date/legal-presence document
- Provide your social security number
- Pay the required $28 application fee
- Pass an eye exam (by law, any person with a corrected-vision score of 20/200 will not be issued a driver's license)
- Have your picture taken
- Give a thumbprint
- Pass a traffic laws and road-signs test

The DMV may cancel your license or refuse to issue you a license if you:

- Have a history of alcohol or drug abuse
- Have used the license illegally
- Have lied on your application
- Do not understand traffic laws or signs
- Do not have the skill to drive
- Have a health problem that makes your driving unsafe

- Have an outstanding traffic citation because you failed to appear or failed to pay
- Have not complied with a judgment or order for family support payments
- Cheated on any license examination
- Impersonated an applicant or allowed someone else to impersonate you to fraudulently qualify for a license
- Refuse to give a thumbprint
- Refuse to sign the certification on the application (form DL 44)
- Submit a fraudulent birth-date/legal-presence document or social security document

STATE IDs

If you don't drive, California IDs are available at the Department of Motor Vehicles. Contact the department at 800-777-0133, or go to www.dmv.ca.gov for locations. You will need to provide your social security number and documents (such as a U.S. birth certificate or U.S. passport) to verify your birth date and legal presence. There is a $20 application fee for a state ID and it is valid for six years.

AUTOMOBILE REGISTRATION

In California, cars need to be registered and insured, and they must pass emissions inspection (smog check). As with licenses, the **Department of Motor Vehicles** (**DMV**) web site is a good resource for those with questions about automobile registration.

Residents who come from out of state need to register their vehicles in California within 20 days. Take your most recently issued auto registration, smog certificate, and purchase information to your nearest DMV office. (A smog certificate is required by the state, the certificate itself is $8.25, but a smog test must be performed to get the certificate, and that price will vary from shop to shop. See your Yellow Pages under "Automobile Repairing & Service" for ones that conduct smog checks or look for repair garages in your neighborhood that hang a sign with a red check mark, indicating smog check service.) Various fees are due upon registering your vehicle. Amounts vary by vehicle; they include a registration fee of $31 and CHP (California Highway Patrol) fee of $10, a $1 reflectorized license plate fee, and a vehicle license fee (VLF). The formula for VLF assessment is based upon the purchase price of the vehicle or the value of the vehicle when acquired. The VLF decreases with each renewal for the first 11 years and is tax deductible.

Unfortunately, DMVs are notorious for their long lines. If you are applying for a license or identification card or registering your vehicle, you can reduce your wait time by making an appointment via the phone or their web site. (Or, if you have AAA membership, you can walk into your AAA office to renew your registration once you have a California registration and driver's license.) Following are the **DMV offices** in the Los Angeles area; every office now uses the central number, 800-777-0133:

- **Culver City**, 11400 Washington Blvd.
- **Glendale**, 1335 W Glenoaks Blvd
- **Hollywood**, 803 N Cole Ave
- **Inglewood**, 621 N La Brea Ave
- **Long Beach**, 3700 E Willow St
- **Newhall**, 24427 Newhall Ave
- **Northridge**, 14920 Vanowen
- **Pasadena**, 49 S Rosemead Blvd
- **Santa Monica**, 2235 Colorado Ave
- **Van Nuys**, 14920 Vanowen St
- **West Hollywood**, 936 N Formosa Ave
- **Winnetka**, 20725 Sherman Way

Following are some **DMV offices** in the Orange County area:

- **Costa Mesa**, 650 W 19th St
- **Laguna Hills**, 23535 Moulton Pkwy
- **Santa Ana**, 1330 E 1st St
- **Westminster**, 13700 Hoover St

AUTOMOBILE INSURANCE

California's Compulsory Financial Responsibility Law requires every driver and every owner of a motor vehicle to have liability coverage.

The minimum amount your insurance must cover per accident is: $15,000 for a single death or injury, $30,000 for death or injury to more than one person, and $5,000 for property damage.

If you recently moved here from out of state, you should know that many out-of-state insurance companies are not authorized to do business in California. Before you drive here you should ask your insurance company if you are covered in case of an accident. Should you become involved in an accident in California, the DMV requires all three of the following conditions be met to avoid suspension of your license: You must have insured the vehicle before you came to California (you cannot renew the out-of-state policy once the vehicle is registered in California); your insurance company must file a power of attorney, allowing the DMV to act as its agent for legal service in California; and your liability policy must provide bodily injury and property damage coverage that equals or exceeds the limits stated above.

Be aware, Los Angeles has some of the highest automobile insurance rates in the country. In fact, according to a survey conducted in 2007 by a cost-of-living analysis service (Runzheimer International, www.runzheimer.com), LA ranked as the third most expensive metropolitan area in the USA in which to own and operate a car, with LA's insurance rates being the largest contributing factor. To make bare-bones coverage affordable to low-income households, in 2000, the state started a pilot program for Los Angeles residents called the **California Automobile Assigned Risk Plan**; call 866-602-8861 or go to www.aipso.com/lc for more information. The **State of California Department of Insurance** annually surveys auto and homeowner insurance providers in Los Angeles; go to the web site and click Consumers Overview to see a general side-by-side premium comparison or call 213-897-8921 or 800-927-HELP.

If you're tempted by a too-good-to-be-true rate by a small insurance company, call the State of California Department of Insurance to verify that the broker or company is licensed by the California Department of Insurance.

For most auto-related information, including insurance, emergency road service, DMV registration renewal, and travel services (including great free maps), you may find it worth the $47 annual membership fee (plus a one-time $20 initiation fee) to join the **Automobile Club of Southern California**, the regional branch of AAA, 800-222-8794, www.aaa-calif.com.

AUTOMOBILE SAFETY

Driving under the influence of drugs or alcohol is illegal in California. The legal blood alcohol limit is .08. If you are pulled over for driving under the influence, you will likely be arrested, have your car towed, and be given a Breathalyzer test. (A first-time refusal of a breath or blood test in California will result in an automatic license suspension for one year; if this is your second refusal, your license will be revoked for two years.) If you fail the chemical test, a first offense will result in a four-month driving suspension. A second or subsequent offense within seven years will result in a one-year suspension. For more information, go to www.dmv.ca.gov/dl/driversafety/dsalcohol.htm.

California has a mandatory **seatbelt law**. All occupants of a vehicle—be it a car, truck, or van—must be properly buckled in, including children in safety seats. The law is very specific with regard to children. Infants under one or who weigh less than 20 pounds are required to ride in rear-facing, reclined (45 degrees) car seats. Toddlers ride in upright, forward-facing seats, with a harness, until 40 pounds. Children who are over 40 pounds must use a lap and shoulder belt-positioning booster seat until they are at least six years old or weigh 60 pounds. Children may not ride (secured) in the front seat until they are at least 6 years old or weigh at least 60 pounds, but it is highly preferred that they be secured in the back seat. Visit the California Highway Patrol's web site for further information: www.chp.ca.gov/community/child_safetyseat_faqs.html.

Two new laws of which you should be aware came into effect in 2008. Smoking is banned when a person under 18 is present in the car. California is the third state to implement this smoke-free car rule. Drivers 18 years of age and over may not use a cell phone unless a hands-free device is being used. Drivers under the age of 18 may not use a cell phone at all, even with a hands-free device.

PURCHASING AN AUTOMOBILE

The experience of purchasing a car is both exciting and a hassle, and always a big expense. It pays to conduct research beforehand to determine the worth of the car you're thinking of purchasing. For used cars, check out the Kelley Blue Book site at www.kbb.com. To research dealer invoice prices for new cars, check www.edmunds.com or www.intellichoice.com. AAA offers a walk-in vehicle pricing report service to members and non-members for a nominal fee. Also, *Consumer Reports* offers a low-cost auto pricing information service, available via their web site: www.consumerreports.org.

Many local automobile dealers publish advertised specials of new and used vehicles in the automotive classifieds of the *Los Angeles Times* and run internet specials on their web pages. Used cars also can be purchased through the classified advertisements in local newspapers. Or visit your local newsstand for a free copy of the *Auto Trader* (800-395-7355, www.traderonline.com), or *Recycler Auto Buys* (800-300-2777, www.recycler.com). It's a good idea to pay to have an auto mechanic inspect and evaluate any used vehicle you are considering buying.

CONSUMER PROTECTION—AUTOMOBILES

When you buy a new car in California, it's good to know about the state's Motor Vehicle Warranty and Lemon Law for new and leased vehicles. The Lemon Law is applicable during the first 18 months or within the first 18,000 miles, whichever occurs first. A new or leased car is a "lemon" if it has a defect that "substantially impairs the use, value, or safety of the vehicle" and cannot be fixed after a "reasonable" number of repair attempts, i.e., four or more times for the same problem or 30 days out of service for any combination of problems.

If it is determined in court or arbitration that your car is indeed a lemon, you are entitled to either a refund or a replacement vehicle. Keep in mind that a car manufacturer can argue that it has not had "reasonable" opportunity to repair your car, or that the defect is the result of abuse or does not substantially affect the vehicle's use, value or safety to you, to negate its Lemon Law obligations, so be sure to keep a record of all repair attempts, number of days in the shop, and any comments from the mechanics who worked on your vehicle, to build your case.

The **California Department of Consumer Affairs** offers detailed information on this law at www.dca.ca.gov or 800-952-5210. You may apply for the state-certified arbitration program via the Better Business Bureau's Auto Line: 800-955-5100, www.bbb.org.

PARKING

Parking regulations vary from neighborhood to neighborhood. Some areas require residents to display a permit to park on the street in front of their apartment building; others—particularly ones that are close to shopping and business districts—allow only two-hour parking, unless you have a residential parking permit. Parts of Beverly Hills and Burbank allow no overnight parking on the street. Certain parts of the Westside, particularly Santa Monica and Westwood, have some of the fastest meter maids in the county.

Once each week, most residential streets are cleaned by sweepers; during this time there is usually a two-hour block of time when cars may not park—look for signs posting the day and hours. If you forget about your car on street-sweeping day, you're likely to find a ticket on it afterwards. Be especially aware of restricted parking on high-traffic streets, effective during certain parts of the day, usually at rush hour. Tow truck operators are known to lie in wait for the minute they can begin towing offending cars.

Do not be lax about paying parking tickets. After five unpaid tickets, a meter maid will boot your car. This immobilizes the vehicle and if your booted car is parked in restricted parking, your car will be ticketed for continued parking violations where it sits. A large sticker on your vehicle will give you the parking violation division's phone number as well as the place you'll need to contact to pay off all unpaid tickets plus an additional $125 for the boot removal.

The best advice is to read carefully the signs in your neighborhood. If permits are required for on-street parking, contact the permit department in your local city hall. The following are direct numbers for obtaining **residential parking permits** where they are required:

- **Beverly Hills**, 310-285-2548, www.beverlyhills.org
- **Los Angeles**, 866-561-9742, www.lacity-parking.org
- **Santa Monica**, 310-458-8291, www.smgov.net/planning/transportation/pref erentialparking.html
- **West Hollywood**, 323-848-6375, www.weho.org

TOWED OR STOLEN AUTOMOBILES

When an automobile is impounded, the lot will release the car only after collecting storage and tow fees. If you find yourself chasing after a tow truck that's taking your car off into the sunset, don't panic. First call the traffic division of the police department for the area where your car was originally parked (see the **neighborhood profiles** for contact information). They will then direct you to the impound lot where your car is being held. An impounded car will be released only to the car's registered owner or to the person bearing a notarized letter of authorization from the car's registered owner. Expect to pay approximately $144 in tow fees and $33 (or more) per day for storage fees. Many impound lots are in unsavory parts of town—best to bring a friend along. The process is not a fun one. After a local news story ran about predatory tow truck drivers who illegally tow vehicles, the governor signed a bill regulating towing that went into effect in 2007. The law specifies that a car be illegally parked over one hour before it can be towed and tows cannot be farther than 10 miles. Additional requirements can be viewed here: http://dca.lacounty.gov/law07TowComp.html.

If your car has been stolen, contact the police department as soon as possible. The police will need your driver's license, the car's year, make, model, and color as well as the vehicle identification number. Once you file a report, the police department will notify you as soon as your car has been located. If you have engraved a unique identification number on your car stereo or other accessories, the police can better identify those items should they be recovered.

ANTI-THEFT DEVICES

The Automobile Club of Southern California recommends anti-theft devices on cars. The general feeling is that although few mechanisms will stop a professional car thief determined to take your car, devices do thwart amateurs. If you decide to buy an anti-theft device, be sure to tell your automobile insurer, as they often offer discounts for car owners who have them on their vehicles.

Steering wheel locks, like the Club, are one of the cheapest ways to go. While a pro can break through them with ease (in about 15 seconds), they may still be enough of a deterrent for the thief to move on to the next target. Ditto for audible **car alarms**. Be aware, however, the California Vehicle Code allows police to tow and impound an unattended vehicle after its alarm has blared for 45 minutes, so be careful not to set it too sensitively, and park it where you will be able to hear it. **Kill switches** can be installed to shut down your car's starter, fuel pump, or ignition, unless the switch is first disengaged by the motorist. Those truly serious about anti-theft devices should consider having a tracking transmitter installed, offered by **Lojack** (www.lojack.com) and **Teletrac** (www.teletrac. net). Lojack systems are tracked by police cars with homing devices, while Teletrac does the tracking itself and then tells police where to look for your vehicle. Both systems have excellent recovery rates (about 90%).

VOTER REGISTRATION

Before you can vote, or sign a petition for that matter, you must be registered to vote. For those wanting to take part in an upcoming election, registration must occur 29 days prior to Election Day. Voter registration forms can be obtained at post offices and through the **LA County Registrar of Voters** (562-466-1323, www.lavote.net), or the **Orange County Registrar of Voters** (714-567-7600, www.ocvote.com). As an election approaches, you will see volunteers from Democratic and Republican parties registering voters at public places like shopping malls and grocery stores.

After the registrar processes your registration, you will be mailed a voting guide, which lists the candidates and propositions on the ballot. Every guide also contains an application to request an absentee ballot by mail. A request for an absentee ballot must be filed with the Registrar at least seven days prior to the election. You do have the option to register as a permanent absentee voter. If you do not turn in a ballot for two consecutive statewide general elections, you will be deleted from the absentee list and you will have to register again to get back on the list.

If you elect to vote in person, look in the back of your voting guide for the address of the polling location assigned to your mailing address—the location may change from election to election or may even fall outside your precinct, depending on volunteers and redrawing of precincts. Or call the Registrar for assistance with locating your polling location. It is important to vote at the poll set up for your precinct because ballots usually carry candidates for local elections specific to your area. The county is in constant need of volunteer precinct officers (bilingual, especially) and locations for polling. If you want to help or volunteer your place of residence or business for polling to make voting more convenient for your neighbors, call your respective Registrar.

The **State of California Voter's Assistance Hotline**, 800-345-8683, www.sos.ca.gov, is a good resource; call it to report voter fraud, receive an absentee ballot, find out who your elected representatives are, and locate your polling center.

Area parties and voter information groups include:

- **LA County Democratic Party**, 213-382-0063, lacdp.org
- **Republican Party of Los Angeles County**, 323-215-4471, www.lagop.com
- **American Independent Party** (headquartered in Torrance), 619-460-4484, www.aipca.org
- **League of Women Voters**, 213-368-1616 (LA, San Fernando Valley), 818-247-2407 (Glendale, Burbank); www.lwvlosangeles.org

- **Project Vote Smart**, 888-VOTE-SMART, www.votesmart.org, provides information on state and national candidates and voting issues
- **State Secretary's Voting Site**: www.sos.ca.gov/elections/elections.htm

PASSPORTS

Many passport renewals can be handled by mail or at one of the city's Passport Application Acceptance Facility locations (usually a post office). For detailed information and to download the proper mail-in forms, you can visit the **US Department of State Bureau of Consular Affairs National Passport Information Service**, http://travel.state.gov, or call them at 877-487-2778, TDD 888-874-7793, Monday–Friday 8 a.m. to 8 p.m. Eastern Time. (General travel information and advisories are available at the Bureau of Consular Affairs' home page.)

If you are applying for a passport for the first time, you must have (1) proof of citizenship: an original or copy of your birth certificate with a raised seal, or naturalization papers, and (2) proof of your identity: a driver's license or other ID with a photograph and signature. (If you don't have these papers, call the number above for alternatives.) Your social security number is required. You will need two passport photos (which can be made while you wait in most neighborhood photo shops) and $100 if you are age 16 or older, $85 for those under age 16, and $75 for renewals. Allow six weeks for your completed passport to be processed. For expedited service, add $60; you can expect to receive your passport in three weeks. Normal processing time is four to six weeks. New applications for passports use form DS-11, and for minors under age 14, an additional consent form, DS-3053, is required. You will find the necessary forms at many post offices and libraries, at county court offices, or online at the State Bureau of Consular Affairs. You must appear in person to get your first passport; this includes minors.

The **Los Angeles Passport Agency** serves only customers who are traveling within 14 days or are submitting their passports for foreign visas. Their office is at the Federal Building, 11000 Wilshire Boulevard, Suite 1000, in Westwood. For information, call 310-575-5700 or visit http://travel.state.gov/passport/about/agencies/agencies_909.html. Office hours are from 8 a.m. to 3 p.m. Since Los Angeles is a port of immigration, lines for the passport room typically start forming hours beforehand.

Those in need of emergency passports should contact the Bureau of Consular Affairs for assistance. You can also try **Travisa Passport and Visa Services** at 800-421-5468, www.travisa.com, a private service that promises to process an emergency passport application with a one- to two-day turnaround.

LIBRARY CARDS

You can apply for a library card at any local library (check the neighborhood profiles for the one nearest you). Los Angeles County's Central Library is located downtown at 630 West Fifth Street, 213-228-7000, www.lapl.org. Hours are 10 a.m. to 8 p.m., Monday–Thursday, 10 a.m. to 6 p.m. Friday–Saturday, and 1 p.m. to 5 p.m. on Sunday. To renew a book by phone, call 888-577-5275. In Orange County, check with the Orange County Public Library at www.ocpl.org for a list of branches. (See **Literary Life** in the **Cultural Life** chapter for more information about area public libraries and for a list of specialty libraries.)

FINDING A PHYSICIAN

Choosing a personal physician is more like choosing a mate than buying a car. You're looking for a doctor who has graduated from an excellent medical school, done residency in a good teaching hospital, is board certified, has practiced long enough to know what he or she is doing but not so long as to be out of touch with the latest research and technology, and has just the right professional manner—concerned, straightforward, a listener with, perhaps, a good sense of humor. In short, you want a doctor you can rely on. If you put it off until you need one, you're apt to wind up sitting miserably in the nearest emergency room, followed by a big bill.

If you are enrolled in an HMO or PPO through your employer or independently, you are probably limited in your choice of physicians to those listed by that HMO or PPO. This makes choosing somewhat easier, but the criteria for choosing remain the same.

You may choose a physician as many do, on the basis of the recommendation of friends, which can be a good start. Or, if you had physicians you liked before moving, they may be able to recommend a colleague here who will suit you. The Yellow Pages contains a list of docs in its "Physicians & Surgeons, MD" section, or try a **physician referral line**:

- **Cedars-Sinai Physician Referral Line**, 800-CEDARS-1, www.csmc.edu
- **Children's Hospital Los Angeles**, 323-361-2323
- **Doctor Finder—Glendale Memorial Hospital**, 818-502-2378
- **UCLA Medical Group**, 800-UCLA-MD1
- **USC University Hospital Physician Referral**, 800-USC-CARE

For those wanting to know if their doctor is board certified in a specialty area, check with the **American Board of Medical Specialists**, 866-275-2267, www.abms.org.

PET LAWS AND SERVICES

As a renter, can you bring your Portuguese water dog and your Burmese cat to Los Angeles? Will that pose a problem? Yes and maybe. The biggest hurdle to clear will be the first: finding an apartment that will accept pets (fish don't count). As a general rule, you can expect landlords to prohibit pets, particularly dogs, which means you may have to choose between the perfect apartment and the perfect pet. Be sure to inquire as you search for a pet-friendly home, and don't plan to sneak one in where they are prohibited. As well, California law prohibits ownership of certain animals (although there are groups working to change some of these laws). Currently, prohibited pets include gerbils, ferrets, skunks, and sugar gliders. If you have an unusual animal as a pet, you might want to check on the legality of owning it in California. Dogs and cats being the most common city pets, we'll address their needs here.

Resident dogs (not cats) of the City of Los Angeles are required to be licensed; licenses are available from shelters, through veterinarians, or by mail: write to the **Department of Animal Regulation**, 419 South Spring Street, Room 1400, Los Angeles, CA 90013, or call 888-452-7381, or download an application from www.laanimalservices.com. Allow six to eight weeks for processing. If the application is submitted in person to any departmental office (see below), processing takes only minutes. The annual fee for dogs (four months or older) is $15 if spayed or neutered and $100 otherwise. Free licenses for spayed or neutered dogs are available to seniors (62 years or older) who meet financial requirements and to disabled persons who own a guide dog or service dog. LA also has a spay/neuter program called **The Big Fix** that provides free spaying and neutering for dogs and cats owned by qualified persons living within the City of Los Angeles—basically, the same persons meeting the criteria for free dog licenses may have their pets altered at no cost. The centers listed below offer spaying and neutering services. All dogs over the age of four months must be vaccinated against rabies. A dog license is issued only when the required rabies vaccination certificate, from a licensed veterinarian, is provided, and only as long as the rabies vaccination is current.

Here is a list of LA County Animal Care and Control Centers:

- **Burbank Animal Control**, 818-238-3340, 1150 N Victory Pl, Burbank
- **East Valley Animal Care and Control Center**, 14409 Vanowen St, Van Nuys, 888-452-7381
- **Harbor Animal Care and Control Center**, 735 Battery St, San Pedro, 888-452-7381
- **Hermosa Beach Animal Control**, 1035 Valley Dr, Hermosa Beach, 310-318-0360
- **Long Beach Animal Control**, 3001 E Willow, Long Beach, 562-570-7387
- **Manhattan Beach Animal Control**, 1400 Highland Ave, Manhattan Beach, 310-545-5621
- **Monterey Park Animal Control**, 320 W Newmark Ave, Monterey Park, 626-307-1201
- **North Central Animal Care and Control Center**, 3201 Lacy St, Los Angeles, 888-452-7381
- **Orange County Animal Control**, 561 City Dr S, Orange, 714-935-6848, www.ocpetinfo.com

- **Santa Monica Animal Shelter**, 1640 9th St, Santa Monica, 310-458-8594
- **South LA Animal Care and Control Center**, 3612 11th Ave, Los Angeles, 888-452-7381
- **Southeast Area Animal Control Center**, 9777 Seaaca St, Downey, 562-803-3301, www.seaaca.org
- **West LA Animal Care and Control Center**, 11361 W Pico Blvd, Los Angeles, 888-452-7381
- **West Valley Animal Care and Control Center**, 20655 Plummer St, Chatsworth, 888-452-7381

In Orange County, **Animal Care Services** can be reached at 714-935-6942, http://ocpetinfo.com. It costs $95 to license an unsterilized dog, $23 for a sterilized one. Cat licensing is optional; it is $5 to license a cat.

OFF-LEASH PARKS

Off-leash canine parks are popular in this dog-loving city, which otherwise has a zero tolerance policy for off-leash dogs. Some of the dog parks listed below are outfitted with doggie drinking fountains and free scoop-the-poop baggies. While obviously popular with Fido, dog parks have also become a hot spot for meeting friends or even a significant other.

- **Calabasas**: Calabasas Bark Park, 4232 Las Virgines Rd, across from A.E. Wright Middle School
- **Encino**: Sepulveda Basin Off-Leash Dog Park, White Oak and Victory Blvd
- **Hollywood**: Laurel Canyon Park, Mulholland Dr just off Laurel Canyon; open after 3 p.m.; Runyon Canyon Park, 2000 N Fuller Ave
- **Long Beach**: Long Beach Dog Park, 7th St and Park
- **Los Angeles**: Silverlake Dog Park, 1850 W Silverlake Dr; Griffth Park Dog Park, north end of the John Ferraro Soccer Field on N Zoo Dr; Hermon Park, 5566 Via Marisol; Whitnall Off-Leash Dog Park, 5801 1/2 Whitnall Hwy, N Hollywood
- **Pasadena**: Brookside Park, 360 N Arroyo Blvd
- **West Los Angeles**: Westminster Park, 1234 Pacific Ave (on east side of the park)

In Orange County try:

- **Costa Mesa**: Costa Mesa Bark Park, Arlington Ave and Newport Blvd, www.cmbarkpark.org
- **Huntington Beach**: Huntington Central Park Dog Park, 1800 Goldwest St
- **Irvine**: Central Bark, 6405 Oak Canyon
- **Laguna Beach**: Laguna Canyon Rd, south of El Toro Rd.
- **Laguna Niguel**: Pooch Park, Golden Lantern near Chapparosa Park

SAFETY AND CRIME

Every city has its high- and low-crime areas, and Los Angeles is certainly no exception. Check out prospective communities to try and determine how comfortable and secure you might feel living there. Observe. Is there a lot of graffiti? Litter? Loiterers? Security bars? All these are indicators that should not be ignored.

Big city rules apply here in LA. Use common sense and be cautious when it comes to your safety:

- Keep your doors and windows locked. If you like fresh air and want to keep your windows open a crack, take extra precautions and buy a window lock (available at hardware stores) that prevents the window from being slid further open, or wedge it with a stick. Bear in mind that upper-level apartments are less easy targets than lower ones.
- Walk with a purpose, trust your instincts, and keep clear of abandoned areas, especially at night. Be particularly cautious in South Central.
- When taking public transportation, ride toward the front of the bus, next to the driver. On the Metro, sit in a populated car; make note of where the emergency bell is.
- Be extra aware of your surroundings in unfamiliar areas. Once you get a feel for your personal comfort level in the neighborhoods you frequent, you'll fall right in with the pace of the city and, like most Angelenos, go about your days without incident.

To investigate the safety of a neighborhood, you'll want to inquire with the LAPD, LA Sheriff, or whichever police department patrols your neighborhood(s) of interest. The California Department of Justice maintains a map of registered sex offenders residing in Los Angeles County (available on the internet at http://gismap.co.la.ca.us/sols/default.htm or in person through a community officer). Megan's Law, which passed in 1996, gives residents the right to know the general whereabouts of registered sex offenders who are classified as either "Serious" or "High Risk." You may view areas of the map by zip code, city/community, or specific address.

You can also be proactive in keeping your new home's community safe by starting a **Neighborhood Watch Program** if one doesn't exist already. The LAPD (213-485-3134 or 877-ASK-LAPD, www.lapdonline.org) or your Sheriff substation (323-267-3435, www.lasd.org) can provide this information as well as personal safety, identity theft, ATM safety, and car theft prevention information.

AUTO SAFETY

Safety experts say that with the advent of car alarms and other anti-theft devices, autos are getting more difficult to steal. Unfortunately, thieves who formerly would steal unattended parked cars have learned that violent confrontation, i.e., car-jacking, may be the only way to get the cars they want. Here are some guidelines for auto safety:

- Know how to get to where you are going. Study your route ahead of time to eliminate the need to look at a map while driving.
- Keep your car doors locked while driving, and keep windows up in unfamiliar areas. If it is hot and you have no air conditioning, roll down the window enough to get air in the car, but not enough for an arm to get in.
- Keep your wallet or purse hidden, either under the seat or in the trunk. When parking your car, do not leave anything tempting, like a cell phone, iPod, backpack, etc., in plain view—hide it in the trunk or take it with you.
- Park in well-lit areas. If you are in a questionable area and need to use a pay phone or purchase gasoline, stop where the attendants can see you. While more costly, having someone pump gas for you is safer than getting out of your car and paying yourself. Avoid parking in alleys; their low visibility makes them a favorite for thieves.
- Do not be tricked into getting out of your car. If you are rear-ended in a remote or dark area and feel uneasy about getting out of your car to exchange insurance information, motion to the other driver to follow you to a police or fire station, or a 24-hour store.
- Do not stop for flashing white lights. Law enforcement vehicles use red flashers or blue and white ones.
- Drive in the middle lane if you feel insecure in a certain area. Try not to get into a lane where you can easily be cut off. When pulling up to a car at a light, leave room so that you can maneuver around the car if needed. If a car blocks you intentionally, honk repeatedly for help, but do not get out of your car.
- Most importantly, if you are confronted, give up your car, your jewelry, your wallet or purse. Often violence occurs when citizens resist a car-jacking or mugging. No possession is more valuable than your life.

And one word about valet parking. Give only your car key to the valet; keep it on a separate key chain for easy removal. Do not provide any identifying information about yourself. You wouldn't give a total stranger the keys to your home, would you?

POLICE COMPLAINTS

The police have a separate unit to handle complaints about their officers. If an incident occurs between you and an officer, file a complaint with the appropriate officer/sheriff's department. The LAPD has a special number; call 800-339-6868 or file online at www.lapdonline.org.

S ETTING UP YOUR HOME MAY REQUIRE HIRING OUT FOR ASSIS-tance. Some of the services you'll find in this chapter are those designed to make your life easier, like house cleaning and pest control; other sections, such as **Services for People with Disabilities**, **Immigrant Newcomers**, and **Gay and Lesbian Life**, detail services relevant to specific communities.

RENTAL SERVICES

Just about anything you need can be rented in Los Angeles. Unless otherwise noted, the following listings are in the City of LA.

APPLIANCE RENTAL

In LA, it is common to find apartments that are not equipped with major appliances, particularly refrigerators. While most opt to buy what they need, there are a few rental outfits you can go to. Consider the following or look in the Yellow Pages under "Appliances–Major–Renting" for more listings:

- **Aim Rental**, 3562 Rodeo Pl, 323-293-2000
- **Anthony Rents**, 11012 Ventura Blvd, Studio City, 818-980-1001, www.anthony rents.com
- **Azuma Leasing**, 800-707-1188, www.azuma.com
- **Rent-A-Center**, multiple locations, 800-665-5510, www.rentacenter.com
- **J&R Appliances**, 7137 Owensmouth Ave, Canoga Park, 818-716-5737

DOMESTIC SERVICES

For those who could use some help around the house, the following services may be of interest.

DRY CLEANING DELIVERY

There seems to be a dry cleaner on every other street corner in LA, with many offering a drive-thru window for pick-up and drop-off—this must explain why so few offer delivery service. Nonetheless, here are some that will pick-up and deliver:

- **Beverly Crest Cleaners**, 10301 Santa Monica Blvd, 310-277-5165; www.merry goroundcleaners.com
- **Bowers and Sons Cleaners**, 2509 S Central Ave, 213-749-3237
- **Effrey's**, 8917 Melrose Ave, Beverly Hills, 310-858-7400
- **Encino Dry Cleaners**, 16946 Ventura Blvd, Encino, 818-986-8464, www.ven turablvd.com/drycleaners
- **Fazio Cleaners**, six locations, 800-553-2680, http://faziocleaners.com
- **Merry Go Round & Burton Way Cleaners**, 9038 Burton Way, 310-277-5165, www.merrygoroundcleaners.com
- **Pico Cleaners**, 9150 W Pico Blvd, 310-274-2431, www.picocleaners.com
- **Sterling Cleaners**, 1600 Westwood Blvd, Westwood; 3405 Overland Ave, West LA, 800-278-3754, http://sterlingcleaners.com
- **Value Village Cleaners**, 912 W Glenoaks Blvd, Glendale, 818-243-1811, http://valuevillagecleaners.com
- **Wetherly Cleaners**, 8764 Beverly Blvd, West Hollywood, 310-360-0854

HOUSE CLEANING SERVICES

For those needing maid service there are plenty of options. Check the telephone directory under "House Cleaning" for a complete listing of agencies near you. If you choose a service, make sure it's bonded and insured.

- **AMAIDzing! Inc.**, 323-460-6232, 310-278-7812, 818-902-1935, www.amaid zing.com
- **Betty's Maid Service**, 800-877-6243, www.bettysmaidservice.com
- **Dana's Housekeeping Personnel Service**, 310-781-9201, 818-342-3930, 626-821-8626, 562-425-5554, www.danashousekeeping.com
- **Golden Maid Agency**, 818-783-7777
- **Merry Maids**, 818-508-7411, 818-609-8570, 310-973-5030, 626-564-8724, 310-837-6243, 562-929-6177, www.merrymaids.com
- **Mission Maids**, 323-957-0344, 310-355-0344, 818-764-0344, www.mission -maids.com
- **You've Got It Maid**, 310-694-5375, 818-897-6782, www.youvegotitmaid.net

MAIL AND SHIPPING SERVICES

Renting a post box at a mail receiving center is a good option for those still on the hunt for a house, for those who are frequently out of town, or for those who work from home but don't want to use their residence address for business. Aside from mailbox companies, boxes can also be rented at your local post office—however, these typically have a waiting list of three months or more. Check with your local post office or try one of the following:

- **Beverly Hills Mailbox**, Beverly Hills, 310-286-0675 or 310-286-0005, www. beverlyhillsmailbox.com
- **Mail Services Etc.** in Long Beach, 562-377-1212, www.msetc.com
- **Mail Service Center** in LA, 310-365-6921, www.mailservicecenter.com
- **The Mail Shoppe** in LA, 323-466-9050
- **The UPS Store** (formerly Mail Boxes Etc.) has multiple locations in Los Angeles; hours and days of operation vary. Call 888-346-3623 or visit www.mbe.com for a complete list of locations.
- **Beverly Hills United Mail Boxes**, Beverly Hills, 310-652-7522, www.bhumb. com

JUNK MAIL

Junk mail will surely follow you to your new locale. In order to curtail this kind of unwanted mail we suggest you send a written note, including name and address, asking to be purged from the **Direct Marketing Association's** list (Direct Marketing Association's Mail Preference Service, Box 643, Carmel, NY 15012-0643, or visit their web site: www.the-dma.org). Some catalogue companies will need to be contacted directly with a purge request. You can also check the *JunkBusters Guide to Reducing Junk Mail* at www.junkbusters.com. For **junk e-mail**, you can go to the **DMA**'s consumer information web site, www.dmaconsumers.org, and request an opt-out service for your e-mail address. The service will accept three non-business e-mail addresses at a time. This should reduce the amount of e-mail you receive from national e-mail lists. Another option is to call the "opt-out" line at 888-567-8688, and request that the main credit bureaus not release your name and address to interested marketing companies. (**Curb phone solicitations** by going to the government's Do Not Call Registry, www.donotcall.gov, and registering your phone number.)

US POSTAL SERVICE

Mail delivery within the city is fast and efficient. Generally, the only time you have to worry about your mail is once it hits your mailbox, where theft may be a problem. If you are experiencing stolen or missing mail, speak to someone at your local post office or contact the US Post Office's Consumer Affairs at 800-275-8777, www.usps.com.

Most post offices in the county close by 5 p.m., although a few close a little later (there are no 24-hour post offices in LA):

- **Dockweiler Station**, 3585 S Vermont Ave, accepts mail until 7 p.m.
- **Farmers' Market Station**, 110 S Fairfax Ave, Ste A11, accepts mail until 8:30 p.m.
- **Greenmead Station**, 900 E Gage Ave, accepts mail until 8 p.m.
- **Hollywood Station**, 1615 Wilcox Ave, accepts mail until 7 p.m.
- **LAX Airport Station**, 9029 Airport Blvd, accepts mail until 11 p.m.
- **Los Angeles Main Office**, 7101 S Central Ave, accepts mail until 7 p.m.
- **Los Feliz Station**, 1825 N Vermont Ave, accepts mail until 7 p.m.
- **Oakwood Station**, 265 S Western Ave, accepts mail until 7 p.m.
- **Van Nuys Main Office**, 15701 Sherman Way, Van Nuys, accepts mail until 8 p.m.

SHIPPING SERVICES

Couldn't get everything to fit in the moving truck? You can always ship it via one of these services:

- **DHL Worldwide Express**, 800-225-5345, www.dhl-usa.com
- **FedEx**, 800-463-3339, www.fedex.com
- **Roadway Express**, 800-313-4089, www.roadway.com
- **UPS**, 800-742-5877, www.ups.com
- **US Postal Service Express Mail**, 800-222-1811, www.usps.com

CONSUMER PROTECTION

"Buyer beware" may be a cliché, but it is the best line of defense against fraud and consumer victimization. Sometimes, an unscrupulous business operator can hoodwink even the most cautious of us. Here are some agencies that, depending on your concern, may be able to help you on your quest for justice:

- **Automotive Repair Bureau**, Department of Consumer Affairs, 310-410-0024, 866-272-9642, www.smogcheck.ca.gov
- **California Attorney General's Office**, 800-952-5225, http://ag.ca.gov
- **California Department of Consumer Affairs**, 800-952-5210, www.dca.ca.gov
- **California Department of Insurance**, 800-927-HELP, www.insurance.ca.gov
- **LA County Bar Association**, 213-243-1525, www.lacba.org; operates an attorney referral line and the Smart Law information line, 213-243-1500, which has

several prerecorded messages providing basic information about many areas of law.

- **LA County Department of Consumer Affairs**, 213-974-1452, http://dca.lacounty.gov
- **Los Angeles Better Business Bureau**, 818-401-1480, 310-945-3166, 562-216-9242, www.labbb.org
- **US Consumer Product Safety Commission**, 800-638-2772, www.cpsc.gov

SERVICES FOR PEOPLE WITH DISABILITIES

Los Angeles has a variety of resources for people with special needs. Many public, private, and commercial facilities provide for sight-, hearing-, and/or mobility-impaired people. Public transit provides various types of assistance to the elderly and disabled. Major crosswalks equipped with audio signals and ramps are most common in neighborhoods where colleges and universities are located. Here is a list of some available services and agencies that can offer referrals and assistance:

- **Assistive Technology Network**, 800-390-2699, TTY 800-900-0706, www.atnet.org; provides information on obtaining assistive devices and services.
- **Braille Institute**, 800-272-4553, www.brailleinstitute.org; serves anyone with reading difficulties due to visual impairment or physical disability. Their Books on Tape program, 800-808-2555, www.braillelibrary.org, is popular.
- **California Telephone Access Program**, 800-806-1191, TTY 800-806-4474; provides information on obtaining assistive devices and services.
- **California Department of Rehabilitation**, 916-324-1313, TDD 916-558-5807, www.dor.ca.gov; they also offer emergency preparedness tips for those with disabilities.
- **Center for the Partially Sighted**, 310-458-3501, www.low-vision.org; counseling, equipment, and rehabilitative programs for independent living
- **Computer Access Center**, 310-338-1597, www.cac.org; information on assistive technology for people with disabilities.
- **Crisis Line for the Handicapped**, 800-426-4263; a 24-hour support and information line.
- **Driving Systems, Inc.**, 818-782-6793, www.drivingsystems.com; develops customized adaptive driving devices.
- **Easter Seals Southern California**, 714-834-1111, http://southerncal.easterseals.com or www.easterseals.com; gives infant-care education, adult day programs, and referrals to rehabilitation services.
- **Greater Los Angeles Agency on Deafness** (**GLAD**), 323-478-8000, TTY 323-550-4226, www.gladinc.org; counseling, job development, translation, and information for the hearing-impaired
- **Goodwill Industries of Southern California**, 323-223-1211, www.goodwillsocal.org; counseling, job placement, and educational services.

- **Independent Living Center of Southern California**, 800-524-5272, TTY 818-785-7097, http://ilcsc.org
- **Jay Nolan Community Services**, 818-361-6400, www.jaynolan.org; serves people with developmental disabilities, including autism.
- **Link2Care**, www.link2care.net, offers an online resource for California caregivers.
- **Los Angeles Caregiver Resource Center**, 800-540-4442, www.usc.edu/lacrc or www.losangelescrc.org; resource for caregivers of brain-impaired adults.
- **Los Angeles County Adult Protective Services**, 213-351-5401, Elder Abuse Hotline: 877-477-3636, www.ladcss.org; report abuse of dependent adults to this number.
- **Los Angeles County Commission on Disabilities**, 213-974-1053, TTY 213-974-1707, http://laccod.org
- **Los Angeles County Deaf Information**, TDD 800-660-4026
- **Los Angeles City Department on Disability**, 213-485-6334, TTY 213-485-6655, www.lacity.org/dod
- **LA Unified School District Parent Resource Network**, 800-933-8133, www.lausd.k12.ca.us; information and referrals to special education programs.
- **North Los Angeles County Regional Center**, 818-778-1900, www.nlacrc.org; services for people with developmental disabilities.
- **Recording for the Blind and Dyslexic**, 866-732-3585, www.rfbd.org; records over 3,000 new books each year on audio cassettes for loan to students and adults who cannot read standard print because of a visual, perceptual, or physical disability: Los Angeles, 323-664-5525.
- **Social Security and Medicare Eligibility Information**, 800-772-1213, TTY 800-288-7185, www.ssa.gov
- **Spinal Cord Injury Network International**, 800-548-2673, www.spinalcordinjury.org; information network and video library for people with spinal cord injuries.
- **Venice Skills Center**, 310-664-5889, http://www.lausd.net/Venice_Skills_Center; offers free rehabilitation services for people with disabilities, such as sign language interpreters for the hearing impaired, job skills training, and job placement assistance and counseling.
- **Westside Regional Center**, 310-258-4000, www.westsiderc.org; offers a variety of services, from counseling to living skills, for seniors and people with developmental disabilities.
- **Westview Services**, 562-428-1626, www.westviewservices.org; offers many enrichment programs for the disabled.

COMMUNICATION

Telephone relay service for the hearing/speech impaired is available free of charge via the **California Relay Service** (**CRS**). They will relay phone calls between TTY and voice callers. There is no charge for the service itself; however, regular toll and long-distance fees apply. For TTY to voice call 800-735-2929; voice to TTY, 800-735-2922. You can also dial 711 anywhere in the US to reach the relay service. Their web site, www.ddtp.org/california_relay_service, provides detailed information on how to complete such calls.

Special adaptive telecommunications equipment can be obtained free of charge by qualified California residents via the **California Telephone Access Program**, 800-806-1191, TTY 800-806-4474, www.ddtp.org/CTAP.

GETTING AROUND

Contact your local **DMV** for handicapped licenses: In LA, call 800-777-0133, TTY 800-368-4327, or visit www.dmv.ca.gov. If you need a blue curb painted at your residence, contact the city's **Department of Disability** at 213-485-6334, www. lacity.org/dod, for information only, as all requests have to be submitted in writing. You need to submit a copy of your disabled-person parking placard and a copy of your DMV placard identification card in addition to your contact information and the location you wish to have blue curb zoning. For those who need other forms of special transportation, these are some options:

- **Access Paratransit/Services** provides curb-to-curb transportation for disabled residents of LA County, and is a clearinghouse of transportation services for seniors and mobility-impaired residents of LA County, 800-827-0829, TTY 800-827-1359, www.asila.org.
- **Cityride** provides curb-to-curb transportation for seniors and mobility-impaired residents of the San Fernando Valley and Los Angeles, 213- or 323- or 310- or 818-808-RIDE, www.ladottransit.com.
- **Culver City Bus**, 310-253-6510, TTY 310-253-6548, www.culvercity.org
- **Lift Van Program**, 323-761-8810, www.ladottransit.com, provides inexpensive lift van transportation for wheelchair-bound residents to a destination up to 20 miles within one of three zones in the county.
- **Health Link Medi-van**, 888-633-4826, www.hlmv.com, provides non-emergency medical transportation service for Valley and Los Angeles residents.
- **Metrolink**, 800-371-5465, TTY 800-698-4833, www.metrolinktrains.com
- **Metro**, 800-266-6883, TTY 800-252-9040, www.mta.net; **Disabled Riders Emergency Hotline**, 800-621-7828; **Wheelchair Lift Hotline**, 800-621-7828
- **Santa Monica Municipal Bus Lines**, 310-451-5444, TTY 310-395-6024, www. bigbluebus.com

- **Taxi Coupons**, 323-761-8810, www.ladottransit.com; program allows persons age 65 and older, and residents of any age who are wheelchair-users or blind, to purchase one book of discounted taxi coupons per month.

ADDITIONAL RESOURCES—PEOPLE WITH DISABILITIES

- The Los Angeles Housing Department sponsors a **Handyworker** program, providing minor repairs to low- and moderate-income homeowners who are physically disabled, or to senior citizens 62 years and older, free of charge. Repairs can take place anywhere from two weeks to nine months after a request, depending upon the required repair and the demand for services in your area. There is currently a waiting list for service in some communities. Call 213-808-8803, 866-557-7368, or go to http://lahd.lacity.org for more information.
- **Disabled People & Disaster Planning** has a web site with detailed information on handling a disaster geared toward the disabled: www.citycent.com/dp2.
- The **American Red Cross** has a downloadable booklet titled "Preparing for Disaster for People with Disabilities and other Special Needs" on their web site: www.redcross.org
- **Bet Tzedek Legal Services**, 323-939-0506, www.bettzedek.org, provides free legal services to low- and moderate-income residents, the disabled, and the frail elderly in the areas of nursing home law, power of attorney, and other health issues.
- The **Disability Rights Legal Center** (formerly the **Western Law Center for the Handicapped** at Loyola Law School), 213-736-1031, www.disabilityrights legalcenter.org, offers legal advocacy on disability rights issues.
- The **Partners Adult Day Healthcare Center**, 323-883-0330, sponsored by the city of West Hollywood, is for the frail elderly, younger disabled adults, and persons with AIDS.

IMMIGRANT NEWCOMERS

Those new to the USA may find the following information useful.

CONSULATES

There are over 30 consulates in Los Angeles. Here are a few:

- **Consulate General of Australia**, Century Plaza Towers, 19th Fl, 2049 Century Park East, LA, CA 90067, 310-229-4800, www.losangeles.consulate.gov.au/losa/home.html
- **Consulate General of Austria**, 11859 Wilshire Blvd, Ste 501, LA, CA 90025, 310-444-9310, www.austria.org

- **Consulate General of Brazil**, 8484 Wilshire Blvd, Ste 730, LA, CA 90211, 323-651-2664, www.brazilian-consulate.org
- **Consulate General of Canada**, 550 S Hope St, 9th Fl, LA, CA 90071, 213-346-2700, www.canadianembassy.org
- **Consulate General of China**, 443 Shatto Pl, LA, CA 90020, 213-807-8088, http://losangeles.china-consulate.org
- **Consulate General of Colombia**, 8383 Wilshire Blvd, Ste 420, LA, CA 90211, 323-653-4299, http://consuladocolombiala.org
- **Consulate General of Costa Rica**, 1605 W Olympic Blvd, Ste 400, LA, CA 90015, 213-380-7915, http://costarica-embassy.org
- **Consulate General of Finland**, 1801 Century Park East, Ste 2100, LA, CA 90067, 310-203-9903, www.finlandla.org
- **Consulate General of France**, 10990 Wilshire Blvd, Ste 300, LA, CA 90024, 310-235-3200, www.consulfrance-losangeles.org
- **Consulate General of Germany**, 6222 Wilshire Blvd, Ste 500, LA, CA 90048, 323-930-2703, www.germany-info.org
- **Consulate General of Greece**, 12424 Wilshire Blvd, Ste 800, LA, CA 90025, 310-826-5555, www.greekembassy.org
- **Consulate General of Guatemala**, 1605 W Olympic Blvd, 422, LA, CA 90015, 213-365-9251, www.guatemalaembassy.org
- **Consulate General of Honduras**, 3550 Wilshire Blvd, Ste 410, LA, CA 90010, 213-383-9244
- **Consulate General of Indonesia**, 3457 Wilshire Blvd, LA, CA 90010, 213-383-5126, www.kjri-la.net
- **Consulate General of Israel**, 6380 Wilshire Blvd, Ste 1700, LA, CA 90048, 323-852-5500, http://israelemb.org/la
- **Consulate General of Italy**, 12400 Wilshire Blvd, Ste 300, LA, CA 90025, 310-820-0622, www.conslosangeles.esteri.it
- **Consulate General of Japan**, 2350 S Grand Ave, Ste 1700, LA, CA 90071, 213-617-6700, www.la.us.emb-japan.go.jp
- **Consulate General of Malaysia**, 550 S Hope St, Ste 400, LA, CA 90071-1203, 213-892-1238, www.malaysianconsulatela.com
- **Consulate General of Mexico**, 2401 W 6th St, LA, CA 90057, 213-351-6800, www.sre.gob.mx/losangeles
- **Consulate General of The Netherlands**, 11766 Wilshire Blvd, Ste 1150, LA, CA 90025, 310-268-1598, www.ncla.org
- **Consulate General of Nicaragua**, 3550 Wilshire Blvd, Ste 200, LA, CA 90010, 213-252-1170, www.consuladodenicaragua.com
- **Consulate General of New Zealand**, 12400 Wilshire Blvd, Ste 1150, LA, CA 90025, 310-207-1605, http://nzcgla.com
- **Consulate General of Peru**, 3450 Wilshire Blvd, Ste 800, LA, CA 90036, 213-252-5910, no web site.

- **Consulate General of the Philippines**, 3600 Wilshire Blvd, Ste 500, LA, CA 90010, 213-639-0980, www.philcongenla.org
- **Consulate General of Poland**, 12400 Wilshire Blvd, Ste 555, LA, CA 90025, 310-442-8500, www.losangeleskg.polemb.net
- **Consulate General of Portugal**, 1801 Ave of the Stars, Ste 400, LA, CA 90067, 310-277-1491, www.portugal.org
- **Consulate General of Romania**, 11766 Wilshire Blvd, Ste 560, LA, CA 90025, 310-444-0043, www.consulateromania.org
- **Consulate General of Saudi Arabia**, 2045 Sawtelle Blvd, LA, CA 90025, 310-479-6000, www.saudiembassy.net
- **Consulate General of South Korea**, 3243 Wilshire Blvd, LA, CA 90010, 213-385-9300, www.koreanconsulatela.org
- **Consulate General of Spain**, 5055 Wilshire Blvd, Ste 960, LA, CA 90036, 323-938-0158, www.spainemb.org
- **Consulate General of Sweden**, 10940 Wilshire Blvd, Ste 700, LA, CA 90024, 310-445-4008, www.swedenabroad.com
- **Consulate General of China** (**Taiwan**), 3731 Wilshire Blvd, Ste 700, LA, CA 90010, 213-389-1215, www.taiwanembassy.org
- **Consulate General of Thailand**, 611 N Larchmont Blvd, 2nd Fl, LA, CA 90004, 323-962-9574, www.thai-la.net
- **Consulate General of Britain and Northern Ireland**, 11766 Wilshire Blvd, Ste 1200, LA, CA 90025-6540, 310-481-0031, www.britainusa.com/la

IMMIGRATION AND NATURALIZATION SERVICE

The Los Angeles District Office for the **US Citizenship and Immigration Services** (**CIS**) is at 300 North Los Angeles Street, Room 1001, Los Angeles, CA 90012, 213-830-5122. However, this is a community services office only and it does not process applications. Call 800-375-5283 or visit http://uscis.gov for immigration information.

IMMIGRATION RESOURCES

- **Bureau of Immigration and Customs Enforcement**, www.bice.immigration.gov
- **Customs & Border Protection**, www.cbp.gov
- **Department of Homeland Security**, www.dhs.gov, www.whitehouse.gov/deptofhomeland
- **General Government Questions**, 800-688-9889, www.firstgov.gov
- **Social Security Administration**, 800-772-1213, www.ssa.gov
- **US Bureau of Consular Affairs**, www.travel.state.gov

- **US Department of State, Visa Services**, http://travel.state.gov/visa_services
- **US Immigration Online—Green Cards, Visas, Government Forms—USA Immigration Services**, www.usaimmigrationservice.org

IMMIGRATION PUBLICATIONS

- *Newcomer's Handbook for Moving to and Living in the USA*, by Mike Livingston (First Books)

MOVING PETS TO THE USA

Pacific Pet Transport, with an office in LAX, 310-318-5702, www.pacpet.com, has been shipping dogs and cats all over the world. Contact them with questions or concerns regarding air transportation arrangements, vaccinations, and quarantine times.

GAY AND LESBIAN LIFE

When you're in Los Angeles, especially around West Hollywood and Los Feliz, the joke about that cute single man probably being gay is often true. In fact, the City of West Hollywood is *the* openly gay and lesbian enclave, offering a Domestic Partnership Ordinance to its residents. This ordinance officially recognizes domestic partnerships between two adults (regardless of sexual orientation) if they are each other's sole partner and are responsible for each other's welfare. Contact **Domestic Partnerships registration** at 323-848-6400, www.weho.org for information on how to apply for a Domestic Partnership registration (a $25 fee applies).

Much of the night scene is focused on a long stretch of Santa Monica Boulevard in West Hollywood, from La Brea Avenue to La Cienega Boulevard, where bars, restaurants, and clubs are packed shoulder to shoulder on weekend nights. Every June the Gay Pride Parade (www.lapride.org), also known as the GLBT Pride Parade, is held on this same street. On Halloween night, those of every persuasion converge on the Boulevard in costume. The main event at this free, wild street party is the show by the drag queens, who pull out all the stops.

In the summer, head to Silverlake for the annual Sunset Junction Street Festival (323-661-7771, www.sunsetjunction.org). Originally held in 1980 to ease tensions between the established working class Latino families and the then newer gay residents, today this block party is a well-established and well-received annual event. A donation is requested for entry.

Following is a list of some **local organizations** that specialize in gay and lesbian issues:

- **AIDS Project Los Angeles**, 213-201-1600, www.apla.org; provides comprehensive assistance to persons living with HIV/AIDS, and an AIDS information hotline
- **American Civil Liberties Union** (**ACLU**), 213-235-0420, www.aclu-sc.org; provides civil liberties litigation and legal referrals
- **Anti-Gay-Bashing Resources**, 323-848-6414
- **GLAAD**, Los Angeles chapter, 323-933-2240, www.glaad.org
- **Gay & Lesbian Association of Santa Clarita**, 661-288-2814, www.glasc.com
- **Gay & Lesbian Adolescent Social Services**, 310-358-8727, www.glassla.org
- **Gay and Lesbian Sports Alliance of Greater Los Angeles**, 310-515-3337, www.glsportsalliance.homestead.com or www.lasportsalliance.com; promotes recreational and competitive sports within the community
- **Los Angeles Gay & Lesbian Center**, 323-993-7400, www.laglc.org; provides a variety of social and health services
- **West Hollywood Cares**, 310-659-4840, www.weholife.org

LOCAL GAY PUBLICATIONS

- *The Advocate*, 800-827-0561, www.advocate.com
- *Frontiers Magazines*, 323-848-2222, www.frontierspublishing.com
- *The Lesbian News*, 800-458-9888, www.lesbiannews.com

A S IN MOST MAJOR US CITIES, FINDING AND AFFORDING A GOOD education from daycare to college can be difficult. This chapter introduces the educational opportunities that abound for those of any age here.

Waiting lists abound for highly recommended daycare centers. Los Angeles has over 2,700 licensed childcare centers and over 3,700 licensed family childcare providers, the quality of which varies, so screen carefully. California requires a license for any childcare provider who cares for the children of more than one family. To check if your childcare provider's license is up to date, or to investigate any filed complaints against the provider, call the **Department of Social Services Community Care Licensing Offices**, 310-337-4333 or 323-981-3350, or go to www.ccld.ca.gov to conduct a search. If a provider is exempt from licensing, you can contact the **Trust Line**, 800-822-8490, http://trustline.org, to see if she is registered. All providers registered on Trust Line's site have passed a background check. The provider pays a listing fee that subsidizes the cost of the check so there's no charge for the inquiry.

Other resources for parents include the **National Resource Center for Health and Safety and Child Care**, 800-598-KIDS, http://nrc.uchsc.edu. Los Angeles parents might want to visit LA Parent's web site, www.LAparent.com, for its community discussion boards on topics from the going rate for a babysitter to determining when your youngster is ready for kindergarten.

Please note: Listing in this book is merely informational and is **not** an endorsement. When entrusting your child to strangers, always err on the side of safety and caution.

CHILDCARE

DAYCARE

When looking for the right daycare, begin with referrals from friends, family, and co-workers or try the **California Child Care Resource & Referral Network**, 800-543-7793, www.rrnetwork.org, a state resource and referral agency. Additional organizations that offer resources and referrals for daycare providers, and in some cases parenting advice or other services, include:

- **Cedars-Sinai WARM Line**, West Hollywood, 310-423-3500; a 24-hour information hotline, sponsored by Cedars-Sinai Hospital, for a variety of questions on rearing children from birth to age six.
- **Center for Community and Family Services**, 310-217-2935 or 888-421-4247, provides referrals for the county.
- **Child Care Resource Center**, San Fernando Valley, 818-256-1020; refers parents to child daycare and family daycare centers.
- **Crystal Stairs**, South Los Angeles, 323-299-8998, www.crystalstairs.org; childcare resource and referral service.
- **Pathways**, 213-427-2700, www.pathwaysla.org; provides referrals for Central Los Angeles, Hollywood, Silverlake, and Beverly Hills.
- **Connections for Children**: Santa Monica, 310-452-3202, www.cfc-ca.org
- **The Help Company**, Santa Monica, 888-HELP-880, www.thehelpcompany.com; a childcare referral service.
- **LA County Child Care Information and Resources Directory**, http://www.ladpss.org/dpss/child_care/default.cfm, has an exhaustive directory of licensed childcare centers. Their web site also provides links to local childcare referrals, a childcare provider checklist, and after-school enrichment programs.
- **YWCA** of Los Angeles, 213-365-2991, www.ywcagla.org; provides childcare and support services for parents.

List of prospective childcare providers in hand, your next step should be to make sure a facility is licensed by checking out www.ladpss.org, and then investigate the centers, visiting each at least a couple times, preferably unannounced. Consider the following:

- Is the center conscientious about how it handles check-ins and check-outs?
- Examine the kitchen, play area, bathroom, and grounds for safety and cleanliness: Is disinfectant used in the kitchen and bathroom? Are toys age-appropriate and in good condition? Are there any potential hazards lying around?
- Check for indoor and outdoor play areas.
- Watch the children at the center: Do they seem happy, well-behaved, and well-supervised? Do they respond well to the attendants? Observe the caregivers with the children.

- Review the daily schedule to make sure the kids have what you think is an appropriate balance of active time and quiet time, and age-appropriate activities.
- You should also determine qualifications of the employees and ask about the staff turnover rate. Also, ask for references—names and phone numbers of parents whose children are enrolled, whom you can contact.

BABYSITTERS

The best source for babysitting is to ask around—friends, neighbors, co-workers; if you're lucky they may give up a name from their list. Membership in a church or synagogue can be a good source for referrals. In the Yellow Pages, check out the "Baby-Sitters" and "Nurses & Nurses Registries" sections. The **LA Baby Sitters Guild**, 310-837-1800 and the **Glendale, Burbank, Pasadena Baby Sitters Guild**, 818-552-2229, offer referrals. These on-call services (with a four-hour minimum) may be able to point you to someone who will provide regular service.

NANNIES

Need a sitter on a more permanent basis? Tired of toting the kids off to daycare? A nanny may be the right choice for you. If the cost is prohibitive and you aren't in need of a full-time nanny, consider doing a nanny-share with another family and thereby splitting the cost. To find a good match, nanny referral agencies are available and offer the benefit of prescreening applicants for you, but they will cost more than if you locate one yourself. If you are hiring a nanny without the help of an agency (see below), you'll want to do a background check, which can be done online. Go to any search engine and type in "employment screening." A host of companies is available to research criminal records, driving records, and credit information for you. Check local parent magazines or the "Help Wanted" section in the *Los Angeles Times*, or see the resources above under **Babysitters** for more ideas. The following companies offer a range of domestic care providers. For a full listing check the Yellow Pages under "Nannies" (inclusion here does not imply endorsement by First Books):

- **Buckingham Nannies**, 310-247-1877, 818-784-6504, www.buckinghamnannies.com
- **Elite Domestic Agency**, 310-424-5068, www.elitedomesticagency.com
- **Family Care Agency**, 818-345-2950, www.monitorvisitations.com
- **Golden Maid Agency**, 818-981-4444
- **Huntington Nannies**, 626-799-1300, www.huntingtonnannies.com
- **Nannies Etc.**, 310-696-0707, 818-342-5454, 661-222-9186, www.nanniesetc.com
- **Neverland Nannies & Domestics**, 818-888-9397, www.neverlandnannies.com

- **The Nanny Exchange,** 310-440-1088
- **TeacherCare,** 888-TEACH-07, www.teachercare.com
- **VIP Nanny Agency,** 818-907-1017, www.vipnannyagency.com

NANNY TAXES

For those hiring a nanny directly (not using a nanny agency) there are certain taxes you will be responsible for calculating, specifically social security and Medicare, and possibly unemployment. For help with such issues, check the **Nanitax** web site, www.4nannytaxes.com, or call 800-626-4829. Nanitax provides household payroll and employment tax preparation services. You can also check with the **Nanny Tax Company,** 800-747-9826, www.nannytaxprep.com, or the **IRS's household employer tax guide,** which discusses taxes for household employees (publication 926), and can be downloaded at www.irs.gov.

AU PAIRS

If you land the right applicant, an au pair (typically, a young woman—18 to 25—from abroad who will take care of your child and do light housekeeping in exchange for room, board, and a weekly stipend) may be a better alternative than a nanny. However, an au pair will likely not have the extended experience of a professional nanny, usually works for only one year, and is required to enroll in an accredited post-secondary institution for not less than six semester hours of academic credit. The **US Department of State's Bureau of Educational and Cultural Affairs,** 202-647-4000, http://exchanges.state.gov, oversees and approves the organizations that offer this service in the US. The national agencies below can match your family with an au pair:

- **Au Pair in America,** 800-928-7247, www.aupairinamerica.com
- **Au Pair USA/Interchange,** 212-924-0446 www.interexchange.org
- **AuPairCare,** 888-AUPAIR1, www.aupaircare.com
- **Cultural Care Au Pair,** 800-333-6056, www.culturalcare.com
- **EurAupair Intercultural Child Care Programs,** 949-494-2002, www.eurau pair.com
- **Go Au Pair,** 888-AUPAIR1, www.goaupair.com
- **GreatAuPair.com,** 775-215-5770, www.greataupair.com

SCHOOLS

The following covers elementary and secondary schools; colleges and universities are discussed at the end of this chapter.

PARENT RESOURCES

Newcomers with school-aged children may find it helpful to obtain a listing of schools in LA County when beginning their search for a school. The **LA County Office of Education's (LACOE)** web site, www.lacoe.edu, offers a listing of its school districts. For more information, call or write: 562-922-6111, 9300 Imperial Highway, Downey, CA 90242. For a listing of all the public and private schools in Los Angeles County, visit the **California Department of Education's** school directory at www.cde.ca.gov/re/sd. You may purchase a hard copy of its "Public Schools Directory" or "Private Schools Directory" by calling 916-319-0800.

Parents researching an appropriate school for their children have a number of resources at their disposal. Comprehensive web sites to investigate public and private school scores and standings include the **California Department of Education's** web site, www.cde.ca.gov, and the **Ed-Data Education Partnership**, www.ed-data.k12.ca.us, which posts the latest fiscal, demographic, and performance data on public schools. Some opt to use **Instant SchoolMatch**, www.schoolmatch.com, 904-230-3001, to research public school districts based on selected criteria for free. There is a fee for their detailed "report card." The **School Report** provides free information consisting mainly of statistics (total enrollment, student to teacher ratio, etc.) for any school district of your choice at www.homefair.com. Another site widely used by real estate agents, which "helps parents get smart about schools," is **School Wise Press**, www.schoolwisepress. com. The site offers school rankings and profiles, as well as school-related news articles. In-depth reports are available for a fee.

Often, parents' involvement in their children's education does not end once the kids are enrolled. Parent groups include the **California State Parent Teacher Association (PTA)**, 213-620-1100, www.capta.org, a united forum of parents, teachers, and school administrators that meet to address education issues; **Parents for Unity (PFU)**, 323-734-9353, which provides assistance with grievance resolution within LA Unified School District; and the **California Association for the Gifted**, 916-441-3999, www.cagifted.org, which provides support for the academically advanced child.

PUBLIC SCHOOLS

The **Los Angeles Unified School District (LAUSD)**, www.lausd.net, has the second largest student population in the nation, serving over 694,000 students. And, as with most metropolitan areas in the USA, student test scores tend to be higher in the wealthier communities. Within LA Unified, the Westside and the San Fernando Valley are home to some of the more highly regarded schools, and Beverly Hills Unified School District is lauded as one of the best school districts in LA County. Keep in mind, however, that student achievement scores don't tell the whole story. A school's overall test scores may be affected by immigrant students who have yet to achieve English proficiency, and parental involvement and dedicated teachers have more to do with student performance than income levels.

Individual neighborhood districts within LA Unified are broken into "clusters." When considering a prospective neighborhood, call LA Unified to find out which cluster/district your child would be attending, and whether students are bused in (done to ease overcrowding in certain schools). LA Unified's school locator information line is 213-241-KIDS, or go online to www.lausd.net. To register your child in LA Unified, you must show proof of the child's age, residency, and immunization for polio, diphtheria, tetanus, hepatitis B, whooping cough, rubeola (measles), rubella, and mumps. Call 800-933-8133 for enrollment information or the School Nursing Services at 213-763-8374 for more information about immunizations. About one-third of the schools within LA Unified are "multi-track" (also called year-around), which is where a student enrolls in one of three to four possible schedules or "tracks"), but most follow traditional "single-track" September-to-June schedules.

LA Unified offers a straightforward open enrollment program: A student who resides in one cluster can petition to attend a school outside of his or her cluster—on a space-available basis; the number of seats available to students who want to take advantage of this program is limited. State law requires that a school accommodate students from its neighborhoods first before offering open enrollments. Factors involved in the scarcity of seats at some schools include the rise in immigration to Los Angeles and the ambitious class-size reduction program (mandating a maximum of 20 students to one teacher in kindergarten through third grades and in some ninth grade classes). Priority is given to current open-enrollment students who wish to continue attending schools in the same feeder-school pattern, which follows the district's general student transfer policies. Parents may apply for open enrollment transfers to as many schools as they wish. If parents are applying to send several children to the same school, a separate application must be filled out for each child. Applications are typically accepted during May for the following school year. The list of schools with open enrollment seats is usually available in the main office of every school beginning in late April or early May. Once the application period ends in late May, schools with more applicants than seats available will hold random drawings to determine who will be invited to enroll.

Within Los Angeles there are over 130 **magnet schools** and **magnet centers** that emphasize specialty areas, such as mathematics and science, and performing arts. Contact your prospective district for specific information on its magnet programs and to request an application form. Applicants do not have to meet any criteria (grades, test scores, auditions, etc.) to be admitted to a magnet school, the only exception being the highly gifted magnets (applicants must meet intellectual assessment criteria set by the LAUSD). The application deadline is typically late January for enrollment for the following fall. Parents are notified in April or May as to whether their children are accepted or wait-listed. Most children accepted for a magnet are provided with transportation.

Some of LA Unified's magnet schools are:

- The **Brentwood Science Magnet School**, 740 Gretna Green Way, West LA, 310-826-5631, www.lausd.k12.ca.us, is the largest magnet elementary school in the LA Unified School District. Over 1,000 students make up the kindergarten through fifth grades. Studies emphasize one of four areas: Biological Science, Physical Science, Earth Science, and Computer Literacy.

- The **32nd Street/USC Magnet School**, 822 W 32nd St, LA, 213-748-0126; its inner-city campus comprises two distinct schools, a visual and performing arts magnet school of K–8th grades and a math/science magnet for high school. It is one of only five campuses in the Los Angeles Unified School District to have all grade-school ages. The magnet is a member of the University of Southern California's "Family of Five Schools" program (www.usc.edu/ext-relations/ccr/programs/fos/) where USC students perform outreach work and share university resources with young students.

- **Fairfax High School**, 7850 Melrose Ave, 323-370-1200, www.fairfaxhs.org; the only visual arts magnet in LA.

- **Portola Middle School**, 18720 Linnet St, Tarzana, 818-342-6173, www.lausd.net/Portola_Gifted_MS; offers "enriched and accelerated academic opportunities" among a multicultural student body. Students must meet the LA Unified's intellectual assessment criteria to apply for enrollment in a highly gifted magnet.

- The **North Hollywood High School**, 5231 Colfax Ave, North Hollywood, 818-753-6200, www.lausd.k12.ca.us or www.nhhs.net, is a year-round school that is the base for two magnet programs, the Biological Sciences Zoo Magnet and the Highly Gifted Magnet. Of special note is that the biological sciences magnet classes are held at the Los Angeles Zoo.

- **Los Angeles High School**, 4650 W Olympic Blvd, 323-900-2700, www.lahigh.org; math and science magnet. Their highly touted Academic Decathlon teams frequently advance to the state and national level competitions.

- **Downtown Magnets High School**, 1081 W Temple St, 213-481-0371, www.downtownmagnets.org; business and fashion careers magnet.

- **Holmes International Middle School**, 9351 Paso Robles, Northridge, 818-678-4100, http://holmesms.org; international humanities magnet.

- **Venice High School**, 13000 Venice Blvd, 310-577-4200, www.venicehigh.net; foreign language and international studies magnet.

LOS ANGELES COUNTY SCHOOL DISTRICTS

- **Acton-Agua Dulce Unified School District**, 32248 N Crown Valley Rd, Acton, CA 93510, 661-269-0750, www.aadusd.k12.ca.us

- **Antelope Valley Union High School District,** 44811 Sierra Hwy, Lancaster, CA 93534, 661-948-7655, www.avdistrict.org
- **Bellflower Unified School District**, 16703 Clark Ave, Bellflower, CA 90706, 562-866-9011, www.busd.k12.ca.us
- **Beverly Hills Unified School District,** 255 S Lasky Dr, Beverly Hills, CA 90212, 310-551-5100, www.beverlyhills.k12.ca.us
- **Burbank Unified School District**, 1900 W Olive Ave, Burbank, CA 91506, 818-729-4400, www.burbank.k12.ca.us
- **Culver City Unified School District,** 4034 Irving Pl, Culver City, CA 90232, 310-842-4220, www.ccusd.k12.ca.us
- **Downey Unified School District**, 11627 Brookshire Ave, Downey, CA 90241, 562-469-6500, www.dusd.net
- **El Segundo Unified School District**, 641 Sheldon St, El Segundo, CA 90245, 310-615-2650, www.elsegundousd.com
- **Glendale Unified School District,** 223 N Jackson St, Glendale, CA 91206, 818-241-3111, http://gusd.net
- **Inglewood Unified School District**, 401 S Inglewood Ave, Inglewood, CA 90301, 310-419-2700, www.inglewood.k12.ca.us
- **La Canada Unified School District,** 5039 Palm Dr, La Canada, CA 91011, 818-952-8300, www.lcusd.net
- **Lancaster School District**, 44711 N Cedar Ave, Lancaster, CA 93534, 661-948-4661, www.lancaster.k12.ca.us
- **LA County Office of Education**, 9300 Imperial Hwy, Ste 109, Downey, CA 90242, 562-922-6111, www.lacoe.edu
- **LA Unified School District**, 333 S Beaudry Ave, LA, CA 90017, 213-241-1000; www.lausd.net
- **Long Beach Unified School District**, 1515 Hughes Way, Long Beach, CA 90810, 562-997-8000, www.lbusd.k12.ca.us
- **Manhattan Beach Unified School District,** 325 S Peck Ave, Manhattan Beach, CA 90266, 310-318-7345, www.manhattan.k12.ca.us
- **Newhall School District**, 25375 Orchard Village Rd, Valencia, CA 91355, 661-291-4000, www.newhallschooldistrict.net
- **Norwalk-La Mirada Unified School District,** 12820 Pioneer Blvd, Norwalk, CA 90650, 562-868-0431, www.nlmusd.k12.ca.us
- **Palmdale School District,** 39139 N 10th St East, Palmdale, CA 93550, 661-947-7191, www.psd.k12.ca.us
- **Paramount Unified School District**, 15110 California Ave, Paramount, CA 90723, 562-602-6000, www.paramount.k12.ca.us
- **Pasadena Unified School District**, 351 S Hudson Ave, Pasadena, CA 91109, 626-795-6981, www.pasadena.k12.ca.us or www.pusd.us
- **Redondo Beach Unified School District**, 1401 Inglewood Ave, Redondo Beach, CA 90278, 310-379-5449, www.rbusd.org

- **San Marino Unified School District**, 1665 West Dr, San Marino, CA 91108, 626-299-7000, www.san-marino.k12.ca.us
- **Santa Monica–Malibu Unified School District**, 1651 16th St, Santa Monica, CA 90405, 310-450-8338, www.smmusd.org
- **Saugus Union School District**, 24930 Ave Stanford, Santa Clarita, CA 91355, 661-294-5300, www.saugus.k12.ca.us
- **South Pasadena Unified School District**, 1020 El Centro St, South Pasadena, CA 91030, 626-441-5810, www.spusd.net
- **Torrance Unified School District**, 2335 Plaza Del Amo, Torrance, CA 90501, 310-972-6500, www.tusd.k12.ca.us or www.tusd.org
- **William S. Hart Union High School District**, 21515 Centre Point Pkwy, Santa Clarita, CA 91350, 661-259-0033, www.hart.k12.ca.us

SURROUNDING COUNTY SCHOOL DISTRICTS

- **Anaheim City School District**, 1001 S East St, Anaheim, CA 92805, 714-517-7500, www.acsd.k12.ca.us
- **Buena Park School District**, 6885 Orangethorpe Ave, Buena Park, CA 90620, 714-522-8412, www.bpsd.k12.ca.us
- **Huntington Beach City School District**, 20451 Craimer Ln, Huntington Beach, CA 92646, 714-964-8888, www.hbcsd.k12.ca.us
- **Irvine Unified School District**, 5050 Barranca Pkwy, Irvine, CA 92604; 949-936-5000, www.iusd.org
- **Laguna Beach Unified School District**, 550 Blumont St, Laguna Beach, CA 92651, 949-497-7700, www.lbusd.org
- **Newport-Mesa Unified School District**, 2985-A Bear St, Costa Mesa, CA 92626, 714-424-5000, www.nmusd.k12.ca.us
- **Orange County Department of Education**, 200 Kalmus Dr, Costa Mesa, CA, 92626, 714-966-4000, www.ocde.k12.ca.us
- **Riverside County Office of Education**, 3939 Thirteenth St (P.O. Box 868), Riverside, CA, 92502-0868, 951-826-6530, www.rcoe.k12.ca.us
- **San Diego County Office of Education**, 6401 Linda Vista Rd, San Diego, CA, 91111-7399, 858-292-3500, www.sdcoe.k12.ca.us
- **Santa Ana Unified School District**, 1601 E Chestnut Ave, Santa Ana, CA 92701, 714-558-5501, www.sausd.k12.ca.us
- **Tustin Unified School District**, 300 South C St, Tustin, CA 92780, 714-730-7301, www.tustin.k12.ca.us
- **Ventura County Superintendent of Schools Office**, 5189 Verdugo Way, Camarillo, CA 93012, 805-383-1900, www.vcss.k12.ca.us

PRIVATE SCHOOLS

If you are considering private schooling for your child, there are a lot of options. Many parents choose private schooling because of the lower student-to-teacher ratio and its reputation for higher quality education. However, it doesn't come cheap. Entrance requirements vary from school to school, so get details when you contact them. For a list of all the private schools within LA, check the **California Department of Education's School Directory** at www.cde.ca.gov/re/sd, or call 916-319-0800. As well, the city's **Human Relations Commission**, 213-978-1660, may be able to provide information. The following list is a sample of private schools. Check **Parent Resources** (see above) for tips on researching schools:

- **Academy of Princeton College Preparatory** (6–12), 14615 Sherman Way, Van Nuys, 818-766-9346, www.princetoncollegeprep.com
- **Bethel Lutheran Elementary** (K–6), 17500 Burbank Blvd, Encino, 818-788-2663, www.bethells.org
- **Beverly Hills Prep** (7–12), 9250 Olympic Blvd, Beverly Hills, 310-276-0151
- **Beverly Hills Montessori School** (pre-school–K), 1105 N Laurel Ave, West Hollywood, 323-650-2922, www.bhms.org
- **Burbank Montessori Academy** (pre-school–3), 217 N Hollywood Way, Burbank, 818-848-8226, www.burbankmontessoriacademy.com
- **Fairfield School** (K–8), 16945 Sherman Way, Lake Balboa, 818-996-4560
- **Glendale Adventist Academy** (K–12), 700 Kimlin Dr, Glendale, 818-244-8671, www.glendaleacademy.org
- **Harvard-Westlake School** (7–12), 3700 Coldwater Canyon, Studio City, 818-980-6692, www.hw.com
- **Hillel Hebrew Academy** (K–8), 9120 W Olympic Blvd, Beverly Hills, 310-276-6135, www.hillelhebrew.org
- **Laurel Hall** (K–8), 11919 Oxnard St, North Hollywood, 818-763-5434, www.laurelhall.com
- **Los Angeles Lutheran Junior-Senior High School** (7–12), 13570 Eldridge Ave, Sylmar, 818-362-5861, www.lalhs.org
- **Mirman School** (5–14), 16180 Mulholland Dr, 310-476-2868, www.mirman.org
- **Montessori Academy of Culver City** (2–6), 5881 Green Valley Circle, Culver City, 310-215-3388, www.montessoriacademyofculvercity.com
- **Montessori School Santa Monica** (K–9), 1909 Colorado Ave, Santa Monica, 310-829-3551, www.montessorischoollosangeles.org
- **New World Montessori School** (K–6), 10520 Regent St, West LA, 310-838-4044, www.newworldmontessori.com
- **Oakwood Academy** (K–6), 2951 Long Beach Blvd, Long Beach, 562-424-4816, www.acceleratededucation.com
- **Sage Academy** (K–6), 5901 Lindley Ave, Tarzana, 818-343-4600, www.sageacademy.net

- **Saint Monica's Catholic High School** (9–12), 1030 Lincoln Blvd, Santa Monica, 310-394-3701, www.stmonicahs.org
- **Southbay Junior Academy** (K–10), 4400 Del Amo Blvd, Torrance, 310-370-6215, www.sbja.com
- **Summit View School** (K–12), 6455 Coldwater Canyon Ave, Valley Glen, 818-623-6300, www.summitview.org
- **Venture School** (9–12), 11477 Jefferson Blvd, Culver City, 310-559-2678, www.ventureschool.com
- **West LA Baptist School** (7–12), 1609 S Barrington Ave, West LA, 310-826-2050, www.westlabaptist.com
- **Westerly School** (K–8), 2950 E 29th St, Long Beach, 562-981-3151, www.westerlyschool.com

HOME SCHOOLING RESOURCES

California's Department of Education currently requires a parent to file a Private School Affidavit with the state that establishes the filer as a small private school. A child may be home schooled in California as long as the child is taught by a credentialed tutor(s) or the student is enrolled in an independent study program run by a charter or private or public school district while being taught at home. This affidavit is available at the agency's website: www.cde.ca.gov/sp/ps, or call 916-319-0800 for more information. Enforcement of the filing requirement and checking for credentials has traditionally been very lax. An early 2008 ruling by the state appellate court reinforces the requirement that the person teaching the home school student (such as the parent) must have teaching credentials. The Home School Legal Defense Association's website, www.hslda.org, is useful for reading up on the most up-to-date legal options for home schoolers by state.

Those who educate their children at home can turn to the **Home School Association of California**, www.hsc.org, for assistance with starting a school at home. The **Alternative Schools of California**, 818-846-8990, and **HomeSchool-LA.org**'s website, http://homeschoolla.org, are additional resources.

COLLEGES AND UNIVERSITIES

Los Angeles has a number of first-rate institutions providing a wide range of higher education options. In addition to their degree programs, local colleges and universities offer concerts, plays, lectures, and many other cultural opportunities to the public. The *US News & World Report* recently ranked USC and UCLA among the top 30 American colleges. CalTech came in #5 on the latest rankings. Call the campus in which you are interested or visit its web site for more information.

Here are just a few local colleges and universities:

- **Art Center College of Design**, 1700 Lida St, Pasadena, 626-396-2200, www.artcenter.edu; a four-year college known for its classes in both fine and applied arts.
- **Biola University**, 13800 Biola Ave, La Mirada, CA 90639, 562-903-6000, www.biola.edu; Protestant university with a wide range of undergraduate and graduate programs, and host to cultural events.
- **California Institute of Technology**, 1201 E California Blvd, Pasadena, 626-395-6811, www.caltech.edu; a small, highly regarded school devoted to the study of science and mathematics, and the place where news cameras turn for information after local earthquakes.
- **California Institute of the Arts**, 24700 W McBean Pkwy, Valencia, 661-255-1050, www.calarts.edu; referred to as Cal Arts, this avant-garde school focuses on visual, theatrical, and written arts. Funded in part by the family of founder Walt Disney.
- **California State University Long Beach (CSULB)**, 1250 Bellflower Blvd, Long Beach, 562-985-4111, www.csulb.edu; offers degrees in business, education, engineering, health, and liberal arts. The CSULB Blue Pyramid is a popular venue for concerts and events.
- **Loyola Marymount University**, 1 LMU Dr, 310-338-2700, www.lmu.edu; renowned Catholic University.
- **Mount Saint Mary's College**, 12001 Chalon Rd, West LA, 310-954-4000, www.msmc.la.edu; located in the scenic hills above Brentwood with views of the city below, this Catholic school hosts art gallery shows and other cultural events.
- **Pepperdine University**, 24255 W Pacific Coast Hwy, Malibu, 310-506-4000, www.pepperdine.edu; a marquee name and a magnificent ocean view.
- **University of California, Irvine**, intersection of Campus and University drives, Irvine, 949-824-5011, www.uci.edu, currently enrolls more than 23,000 students, and is consistently ranked by *U.S. News and World Report* among the country's best public universities. A major research university, with undergraduate and graduate programs as well as a medical school, UCI sponsors numerous plays, concerts, and lectures that are open to the public.
- **University of California, Los Angeles**, 405 Hilgard Ave, Westwood, 310-825-4321, www.ucla.edu, has the largest enrollment of all nine campuses in the UC system, with more than 35,000 students, and is one of the more difficult UC schools to get into. Walking tours of the pretty, 419-acre campus are available. Don't miss the Franklin D. Murphy Sculpture Garden.
- **University of Southern California**, Exposition Blvd, between Vermont Ave and Figueroa St, 213-740-2311, www.usc.edu; this private school has a number of galleries and museums open to the public, as well as displays of scripts and movie memorabilia at the Cinema Special Collections Library. Its cinema, law, and dentistry schools are considered top-notch.

COMMUNITY COLLEGES

The California Community Colleges System (916-445-8752, www.cccco.edu) oversees community colleges here. Listed below is a sampling of area community colleges that offer two-year Associate degree and/or vocational certificate programs. Many offer online or flexible class schedules; check with the specific school.

- **El Camino College**, 16007 Crenshaw Blvd, Torrance, 310-532-3670, www.elcamino.edu
- **Glendale Community College**, 1500 N Verdugo Blvd, Glendale, 818-240-1000, www.glendale.edu
- **Los Angeles City College**, 855 N Vermont Ave, 323-953-4000, www.lacc.cc.ca.us, is a large, two-year community college with an ethnically mixed student body in an urban environment.
- **Los Angeles Community College District**, 770 Wilshire Blvd, 213-891-2000, www.laccd.edu
- **Long Beach City College**, 4901 E Carson St, Long Beach, 562-938-4353, www.lbcc.edu
- **Pasadena City College**, 1570 E Colorado Blvd, Pasadena, 626-585-7123, www.pasadena.edu; this two-year community college hosts cultural events, as well as special programs for part-time students.
- **Santa Monica College**, 1900 Pico Blvd, Santa Monica, 310-434-4000, www.smc.edu, is a well-respected, two-year community college with a high transfer rate to UCLA.
- **West LA College**, 9000 W Overland Ave, Culver City, 310-287-4200, www.wlac.edu

T WOULD BE AN UNDERSTATEMENT TO SAY THAT SHOPPING IS A POPULAR pastime in Los Angeles. From chi-chi shopping on Rodeo Drive in Beverly Hills to Pasadena's Rose Bowl Flea Market, LA is a slice of heaven for shopping mavens, some of whom liken it to an indoor sport.

Below is a list of full-service department stores where you can do a good portion of your shopping, followed by specialty stores, a list of secondhand shopping districts, and finally, food…shopping requires so much energy. (Bookstores are discussed separately in the **Cultural Life** chapter.)

Unless otherwise noted, listings are in Los Angeles.

SHOPPING MALLS AND DISTRICTS

MALLS

The Grove and Hollywood & Highland are the two newest malls within the city and have been wildly successful at revitalizing their neighborhood environs. Most of the full-service department stores like Macy's can be found in the larger malls. Here are the major malls, and the big department stores that anchor them

- **Baldwin Hills Crenshaw Blvd**, 3650 W Martin Luther King Blvd, 323-290-6636; Macy's, Sears, and Wal-Mart anchor the 100+ stores here.
- **The Beverly Center**, 8500 Beverly Blvd, 310-854-0070, www.beverlycenter. com; this mall includes Macy's and Bed, Bath & Beyond.
- **Burbank Town Cente**r, 201 E Magnolia Blvd, Burbank, 818-566-8556, www. burbanktowncenter.com; anchored by Macy's, Sears, and AMC Theaters.
- **Del Amo Fashion Mall**, 3525 W Carson St, Torrance, 310-542-8525, http://del-amo-mall.com; Macy's and Sears anchor the 300+ shops here.

- **Glendale Galleria**, 2148 Glendale Galleria, Glendale, 818-240-9481, www. glendalegalleria.com; anchored by Nordstrom and Macy's.
- **The Grove**, 189 The Grove Dr, 323-900-8080, www.thegrovela.com; European-inspired open-air mall with a trolley that runs through the middle of its cobblestoned street, next door to the year-round Farmers' Market.
- **Hollywood & Highland**, 6201 Hollywood Blvd, Hollywood, 323-467-6412, www.hollywoodandhighland.com; home of the Kodak Theater, upscale restaurants, retail stores, a nightclub, and Renaissance Hollywood Hotel.
- **Northridge Fashion Center**, 9301 Tampa Ave, Northridge, 818-701-7051, www.northridgefashioncenter.com; features Macy's and Sears.
- **Paseo Colorado**, 280 E Colorado Blvd, Pasadena, 626-795-8891, www.paseo coloradopasadena.com.
- **The Promenade at Howard Hughes Center**, 6081 Center Dr, 310-641-8073, www.hhpromenade.com.
- **Puente Hills Mall**, 1600 S Azusa Ave, City of Industry, 626-912-8777, www.pu entehills-mall.com; anchored by Macy's and Sears.
- **Santa Monica Place**, 395 Santa Monica Pl, Santa Monica, 310-394-1049, www. santamonicaplace.com; closed for renovation in 2008.
- **South Coast Plaza**, 3333 Bristol St, Costa Mesa, 800-782-8888, www.south coastplaza.com; with over 300 shops, it's not an indoor mall—it's an indoor city.
- **Sunset Plaza**, 8623 W Sunset Blvd, West Hollywood, 310-652-2622; chic outdoor strip lined with designer clothiers and trendy sidewalk cafés.
- **Two Rodeo**, 9480 Dayton Way, Beverly Hills, 310-247-7040, www.tworodeo. com; beautiful cobblestone street lined with upscale stores, anchored by Tiffany's.
- **Westfield Shoppingtown Century City**, 10250 Santa Monica Blvd, Century City, 310-277-3898, www.westfield.com; anchored by Macy's and Bloomingdale's.
- **Westfield Shoppingtown Fashion Square**, 14006 Riverside Dr, Sherman Oaks, 818-783-0550, www.westfield.com; anchored by Macy's and Bloomingdale's.
- **Westfield Shoppingtown Fox Hills**, 924 Foxhills Mall, Culver City, 310-390-5073, www.westfield.com; major department stores include Macy's and JC Penney.
- **Westfield Shoppingtown Promenade at Woodland Hills**, 6100 Topanga Canyon Blvd, Woodland Hills, 818-594-8740, www.westfield.com
- **Westfield Shoppingtown Topanga**, 6600 Topanga Canyon Blvd, Canoga Park, 818-594-8732, www.westfield.com; featuring Nordstrom and Macy's.
- **Westfield Valencia Town Center**, 24201 W Valencia Blvd, Valencia, 661-287-9050, www.valenciatowncenter.com; anchored by Robinsons-May and Sears.
- **Westside Pavilion**, 10800 W Pico Blvd, W LA, 310-474-6255, www.westside pavilion.com; anchored by Nordstrom and Macy's.

SHOPPING DISTRICTS

- For the area's choicest department stores head to, where else, **Beverly Hills**, 800-345-2210, www.beverlyhillsbehere.com. Along Wilshire Boulevard, west of Rodeo Drive, are Tiffany's, Neiman-Marcus, Saks Fifth Ave, Barney's, and Bloomingdale's. Go north on Rodeo Drive and you can check out the likes of Cartier, Salvador Ferragamo, and Prada.

- **Downtown** is *the* place to go when you want to buy directly from the wholesaler, often at a significant discount. The flower, produce, toy, textiles and fabrics, and jewelry districts are clustered here. These are wholesalers, some of whom will sell to the public, so don't expect much in the way of presentation: Fresh **flowers** are available at Wall and 7th streets; the **fashion district**, 213-488-1153, www.fashiondistrict.org, is centered at East Olympic Boulevard and Los Angeles Street (Santee Alley, between Santee and Maple, is crammed with stalls that hawk cheap trendy clothing and knock-offs; trendy designers at The Mart, 127 East 9th Street, www.newmart.net, offer sample sales once a month to the public, it is open only to the wholesale trade the rest of the year); **produce** dominates along Central Avenue between 8th and 9th streets; **textiles and fabrics** are at Wall and 8th streets; **toys** can be found along 3rd Street between South San Pedro and Los Angeles streets; and finally, **jewelry** is located on Hill Street between 6th and 7th streets. Expect a lot of walking and bring quarters to feed the meter.

- **Melrose Ave,** between La Brea Ave and La Cienega Blvd, is the old standby for funky fashions and food.

- **Old Pasadena**, 626-356-9725, www.oldpasadena.org, is a lovely shopping district where contemporary favorites like Sur La Table, Gap, and Restoration Hardware are housed in well-preserved, historical buildings. It is a 20-block area stretching along Colorado Boulevard, between Pasadena Avenue on the west, and Arroyo Parkway on the east, Walnut Street on the north, and Del Mar on the south. Upscale shopping district **South Lake Ave**, 626-792-1259, www.southlakeavenue.com, offers 10 blocks of shopping between Colorado and California boulevards, just outside of Old Town Pasadena.

- Santa Monica's **Third Street Promenade**, 310-393-8355, http://hirdstreetpromenade.org; permanently closed to cars between Broadway and Wilshire Boulevard, offers three city blocks of shops, cafés, and the interspersed visual delights of street performers. The Promenade also hosts a farmers' market twice a week. If this isn't enough, there's more: **Montana Avenue,** between 9th and 17th streets, and **Main Street** between Hill Street and Marine Street. Montana Avenue is densely packed with stores, while Main Street has more restaurants interspersed with unique stores.

- **San Vicente Boulevard** at Barrington Avenue in Brentwood consists of four blocks lined with trees and fashionable stores. On the same street is a small three-story strip mall, Brentwood Gardens, at 11677 San Vicente Blvd, 310-820-2300, with additional chic shops and restaurants.
- **Abbot Kinney Boulevard** in Venice offers some one-of-a-kind boutiques between Westminster Avenue and Venice Boulevard.

DEPARTMENT STORES

Check the malls (above) for the locations of your favorite department store. The most popular department stores in Los Angeles include the following:

- **Bloomingdale's**, www.bloomingdales.com; high-end, good selection of clothing, jewelry, and make-up.
- **JC Penney**, www.jcpenney.com; affordable chain with your standard department store selections, good variety of children's clothing.
- **Macy's**, www.macys.com; a solid, all-around department store that won't break the bank; very respectable household goods and bedding department.
- **Nordstrom**, www.nordstrom.com; upscale store with a reputation for outstanding, you-gotta-hear-what-they-did-for-me customer service, clothing, shoes, jewelry, make-up, and home decorations.
- **Sears**, www.sears.com; carries just about anything you'd need for your home: clothing, furniture, household goods, and electronics.

DISCOUNT DEPARTMENT STORES

- **Kmart or Big K**, www.kmart.com; budget chain with numerous locations throughout LA.
- **Loehmann's**, www.loehmanns.com; discounted designer clothing.
- **Marshall's**, www.marshallsonline.com; discontinued housewares and clothing.
- **Ross Dress for Less**, www.rossstores.com, offers discontinued or slightly blemished designer clothing and housewares at discount prices.
- **Target**, 800-800-8800, www.target.com; all-around chain for reasonably priced clothing, household goods, food, and furniture. Numerous locations throughout LA.
- **T.J. Maxx**, www.tjmaxx.com; similar to Ross Dress for Less, limited number of locations.
- **Wal-Mart**, www.walmart.com; limited locations, more expected in the suburbs.

HOUSEHOLD SHOPPING

COMPUTERS, ELECTRONICS, AND APPLIANCES

In addition to the following chains, many department, office supply, and wholesale stores also sell computers and household electronics and appliances.

- **Apple Store**, 800-MY-APPLE, www.apple.com
- **Best Buy**, 11301 W Pico Blvd, West LA, 310-268-9190; 21601 Victory Blvd, Woodland Hills, 818-713-1007; 888-237-8289, www.bestbuy.com
- **Circuit City**, 401 N First St, Burbank, 818-558-1172; 5660 Sepulveda Blvd, Culver City, 310-313-6002; 200 E Broadway St, Glendale, 818-247-0410; 4400 Sunset Blvd, Hollywood, 213-663-6033; 1839 La Cienega Blvd, 310-280-0700; 3115 Sepulveda Blvd, West LA, 310-391-3144; 1145 Gayle Ave, Westwood, 310-208-6885; 25610 N The Old Road, Valencia, 661-260-3751; 13630 Victory Blvd, Van Nuys, 818-782-3355; 6401 Canoga Ave, Woodland Hills, 818-888-3233; 800-843-2489, www.circuitcity.com
- **Fry's Electronics**, 2311 N Hollywood Way, Burbank, 818-526-8100; 3600 Sepulveda Blvd, Manhattan Beach, 310-364-FRYS; 6100 Canoga Ave, Woodland Hills, 818-227-1000; 877-688-7678, www.outpost.com
- **Radio Shack**, 800-843-7422, www.radioshack.com
- **Sony Style Store**, 877-865-7669, www.sonystyle.com

BEDS, BEDDING, AND BATH

MATTRESSES

A good selection of mattresses and bedding can be found at most major department stores or you can try one of the following:

- **Leeds Mattress Stores**, 877-905-3337, www.leedsmattress.com
- **The Mattress Store**, www.themattressstoreonline.com, various locations.
- **Ortho Mattress**, 800-734-6784, www.orthomattress.com; 8161 Beverly Blvd; 8413 Beverly Blvd; 1563 N Victory Pl, Burbank; 2202 S Garfield Ave, Commerce; 111 N Central Ave, Glendale; 2153 Bellflower Blvd, Long Beach; 1315 Sepulveda Blvd, Manhattan Beach; 2570 S Lincoln Blvd, Marina del Rey; 6205 Wilshire Blvd; 3130 E Colorado Blvd, Pasadena; 1423 Wilshire Blvd, Santa Monica; 12205 Ventura Blvd, Studio City; 8500 Melrose Ave, West Hollywood; 20051 Ventura Blvd, Woodland Hills
- **Simmons-Beautyrest Mattress**, call 877-399-9397, www.simmons.com; numerous locations.

- **Sit'n Sleep**, 800-675-3536, www.sitnsleep.com; 3824 Culver Center, Culver City; 18833 Hawthorne Blvd, Torrance; 130 N Central Ave, Glendale; 25017 The Old Road, Santa Clarita; 310 S Lake Ave, Pasadena
- **Sweet Dream USA**, 909 S Vermont Ave, 323-588-7277, www.sweetdreamusa. com

BEDDING

For one-stop shopping for bedding, towels and other linens, try one of these chains:

- **Anna's Linens**, 6340 W 3rd St, 323-939-7201; 12201 Victory Blvd, North Hollywood, 818-763-3006; 6735 Van Nuys Blvd, Van Nuys, 818-785-6234; 928 N San Fernando Rd, Burbank, 818-729-0790; 866-ANNAS-2-U, www.annaslinens.com
- **Bed, Bath & Beyond**, 11801 W Olympic Blvd, 310-478-5767; 142 S San Vicente Blvd, 310-652-1380; 1255 Ventura Blvd, Studio City, 818-980-0260; 19836 Ventura Blvd, Woodland Hills, 818-702-9301; 800-GO BEYOND, www.bed bathandbeyond.com
- **The Great Indoors**, 1301 N Victory Pl, Burbank, 818-260-8000, 13000 Peyton Dr, Chino Hills, 909-972-6000, 71 Technology Dr, Irvine, 949-340-6000, www. thegreatindoors.com
- **Linens 'N Things**, 11250 Olympic Blvd, 310-479-6655; 19500 Plummer, Northridge, 818-882-3377; 13730 Riverside Dr, Sherman Oaks, 818-461-0770; 1601 N Victory Pl, Burbank, 818-260-9110; 866-568-7378, www.lnt.com

CARPETS AND RUGS

In addition to the listings below, don't forget to look into the flooring departments of home improvement chains like Lowe's and Home Depot.

- **Carpet Depot**, 13451 Sherman Way, North Hollywood, 818-765-3622
- **Carpet Factory**, 5836 Sepulveda Blvd, Sherman Oaks, 818-780-4044
- **Carpet Manufacturers Warehouse**, 6111 E Randolph St, Commerce, 323-888-2424, www.carpetmfgwhse.net
- **Carpet Market Outlet**, 5900 Kester Ave, Van Nuys, 818-989-0940, http://carpet2001.com
- **The Carpet Showcase**, 1430 Lincoln Blvd, Santa Monica, 310-395-4575, www.thecarpetshowcase.com
- **Close Out Carpets**, 1446 S Robertson Blvd, West LA, 310-273-1464
- **Culver Carpet Center**, 4026 S Sepulveda Blvd, Culver City, 310-391-5286, 323-870-5797
- **Fairfax Carpet Company**, 657 S LaBrea Ave, 323-932-8881, www.fairfaxcarpetco.com

- **IKEA**, 600 N San Fernando Blvd, Burbank, 818-842-4532; 20700 S Avalon Blvd, Carson, 310-527-4532, 848 S Barranca Ave, Covina, 626-732-4532, www.ikea. com
  - **Pier 1 Imports**, locations throughout the city, go to www.pier1.com or call 800-245-4595 for a store locator.

FURNITURE/HOUSEWARES

Upscale houseware and furniture stores are scattered throughout LA. Style-conscious shoppers with big budgets head to Robertson Boulevard and surrounding areas in West Hollywood, the interior design mecca of greater Los Angeles. Here are some of the more popular furniture and housewares establishments:

- **Cost Plus World Market**, 877-967-5362, www.worldmarket.com; locations throughout the city.
- **Crate & Barrel**, 800-967-6696, www.crateandbarrel.com; locations throughout the city.
- **Ethan Allen Home Interiors**, 888-EAHELP1, www.ethanallen.com; locations throughout the city.
- **HD Buttercup Furniture Mart**, 3225 Helms Ave, 310-558-8900, www.hdbuttercup.com; housed in the historic Helms Bakery building, manufacturers sell their furniture direct to the consumer over 100,000 square feet of display space.
- **Home Depot Expo Design Center**, www.expo.com; 10861 Weyburn Ave, 310-824-8400; 407 W Huntington Dr, Monrovia, 626-599-3400; 1519 Hawthorne Blvd, Redondo Beach, 310-921-1400
- **Identity Craft**, 2830 E Foothill Blvd, Pasadena, 626-568-8100; wood-crafted furniture.
- **IKEA**, 600 N San Fernando Blvd, Burbank, 818-842-4532; 20700 S Avalon Blvd, Carson, 310-527-4532, 848 S Barranca Ave, Covina, 626-732-4532, www.ikea. com
- **Just Like the Model**, 18429 Pacific St, Fountain Valley, 714-968-9888, www.justlikethemodel.com; this 24,000-square-foot Orange County warehouse sells the furniture used to decorate model homes from housing tracts at 30% to 70% below retail prices.
- **Pier 1 Imports**, 800-245-4595, www.pier1.com; locations throughout the city.
- **Pottery Barn**, 888-779-5176, www.potterybarn.com; locations throughout the city.
- **Plummers Home and Office Interiors**, 12240 Sherman Way, North Hollywood, 818-765-0401; 8876 Venice Blvd, West LA, 310-837-0138; 21725 Erwin St, Woodland Hills, 818-888-9474, 3635 E Colorado Blvd, Pasadena, 626-744-0211, 8881 Warner Ave, Huntington Beach, www.plummers.com

- **Rapport International Furniture**, 401 N La Brea Ave, 323-930-1500, www.rapportusa.com
- **Restoration Hardware**, www.restorationhardware.com; locations throughout the city.
- **The Sofa Company**, 100 W Green St, Pasadena, 2316 Lincoln Blvd, Santa Monica, 888-778-7632, www.thesofaco.com
- **Target**, 800-800-8800, www.target.com; locations throughout the city.
- **Williams-Sonoma**, 877-812-6235, www.williams-sonoma.com; locations throughout the city.
- **Z Gallerie**, 800-358-8288, www.zgallerie.com; locations throughout the city.

LAMPS AND LIGHTING

In addition to the listings below, also check the Yellow Pages under "Lamps."

- **The Great Indoors**, 1301 N Victory Pl, Burbank, 818-260-8000; 13000 Peyton Dr, Chino Hills, 909-972-6000; 71 Technology Dr, Irvine, 949-340-6000, www.thegreatindoors.com
- **IKEA**, 600 N San Fernando Blvd, Burbank, 818-842-4532; 20700 S Avalon Blvd, Carson, 310-527-4532; 848 S Barranca Ave, Covina, 626-732-4532, www.ikea.com
- **Lamps Plus**, 200 S Brand Blvd, Glendale, 818-247-3005; 200 S La Brea Ave, 323-931-1438; 12206 Sherman Way, North Hollywood, 818-764-2666; 2012 S Bundy Dr, West LA, 310-820-7567; 800-782-1967, www.lampsplus.com
- **Light Bulbs Unlimited**, 8383 Beverly Blvd, 323-651-0330; 2309 Wilshire Blvd, Santa Monica, 310-829-7400; 14446 Ventura Blvd, Sherman Oaks, 818-501-3492, www.light-bulbs-unlimited.net
- **Lightwave Lighting**, 8211 Melrose Ave, 323-658-6888
- **Pottery Barn**, 888-779-5176, www.potterybarn.com; locations throughout the city.
- **Restoration Hardware**, www.restorationhardware.com; locations throughout the city.
- **Target**, 800-800-8800, www.target.com; locations throughout the city.

HARDWARE, PAINTS, WALLPAPER, AND GARDEN CENTERS

Most homeowners, do-it-yourselfers especially, come to know their local hardware stores quickly. At the mom-and-pops in particular, seasoned associates can be extremely helpful when you're trying to decide exactly which widget you need. Check out the stores mentioned in the **Green Living** chapter for environmentally friendly products. In addition to the many **Ace Hardware** (www.

acehardware.com) and **True Value Hardware** (www.truevalue. com) stores, you can look for the following:

- **Armstrong Garden Centers**, 800-55-PLANT, www.armstronggarden. com; 5816 San Fernando Rd, Glendale, 818-243-4227; 3232 Wilshire Blvd, Santa Monica, 310-829-6766; 12920 Magnolia Blvd, Sherman Oaks, 818-761-1522; 352 E Glenarm St, Pasadena, 626-799-7139, 3226 Wilshire Blvd, Santa Monica, 310-829-6766; 3842 E 10 St, Long Beach, 562-433-7413
- **Burkard Nurseries**, 690 N Orange Grove Blvd, Pasadena, 626-796-4355, www. burkardnurseries.com
- **Frazee Paint**, www.frazee.com; 1404 S La Cienega Blvd, 310-289-0461 is one of several locations.
- **Do-It Center**, www.doitcenter.com; 3221 W Magnolia Blvd, Burbank, 818-845-8301; 23314 W Valencia Blvd, Valencia, 661-255-7355
- **Dunn Edwards**, www.dunnedwards.com, multiple locations.
- **Hashimoto Nursery**, 1935 Sawtelle Blvd, 310- 473-6232
- **Home Depot**, 800-553-3199, www.homedepot.com; 12975 W Jefferson Blvd is one of several locations.
- **International Garden Center**, 155 N Sepulveda Blvd, El Segundo, 310-615-0353, www.intlgardencenter.com
- **Koontz Hardware**, 8914 Santa Monica Blvd, West Hollywood, 310-652-0123, www.koontzhardware.com
- **LivingGreen**, 10000 Culver Blvd, Culver City, 310-838-8442, www1.livingreen. com
- **Lowe's Home Improvement**, 800-445-6937, www.lowes.com; 2000 Empire Ave, Burbank, 818-557-2300, one of several locations.
- **Marina del Rey Garden Center**, 13198 Mindanao Way, Marina del Rey, 310-823-5956, www.marinagardencenter.com
- **Orchard Supply Hardware**, 888-746-7674, www.osh.com
- **Sherwin-Williams**, www.sherwin.com, multiple locations.
- **Target**, 800-440-0680, www.target.com, multiple locations.
- **Theodore Payne Foundation Nursery**, 10459 Tuxford St, Sun Valley, 818-768-1802, www.theodorepayne.org, a nonprofit retail nursery specializing in California native plants and seeds.

SECONDHAND SHOPPING

A popular and inexpensive way to shop for furniture, clothing, and vintage housewares is in secondhand stores. Merchandise runs the gamut from trendy to tacky to vintage to designer cast-offs from the costume departments of the local film and TV industries. The web site www.bargainsla.com is another good source of thrift stores. Check the Yellow Pages under "Clothing–Used" for listings in your area or try one of the following:

- **Aardvark's Odd Ark**, 7579 Melrose Ave, 323-655-6769; 1253 E Colorado Blvd, Pasadena, 626-583-9109; 85 Market St, Venice, 310-392-2996; 21434 Sherman Way, Canoga Park, 818-999-3211
- **ACS (American Cancer Society) Discovery Shop**; 9300 W Pico Blvd, Beverly Hills, 310-276-6812, is one of several locations; www.cancer.org.
- **All American Hero**, 314 Santa Monica Blvd, Santa Monica, 310-395-4452
- **B&B Hardware**, 12450 W Washington Blvd, 310-390-9413; 929 Wardlow Rd, Long Beach, 562-490-2669; 387 Redondo Ave, Long Beach, 562-438-2669, http://bnbhardware.com; specializes in Craftsman and other period hardware.
- **Buffalo Exchange**, www.buffaloexchange.com, 131 N La Brea Ave, 323-938-8604; 4608 E 2nd St, Long Beach, 562-433-1991; see web site for additional locations.
- **Couture Exchange**, 12402 Ventura Blvd, Studio City, 818-752-6040
- **Fashion Institute of Design & Merchandising (FIDM) Scholarship Store**, 919 S Grand Ave, 213-624-1200, www.fidm.com; manufacturers and retailers donate clothing for public sale to benefit students of FIDM.
- **Goodwill Retail Store**, multiple locations, http://www.shopgoodwill.org or http://locator.goodwill.org
- **Habitat for Humanity's Home Improvement Store**, 17700 S Figueroa St, Gardena, 310-323-5665, www.shophabit.org
- **It's a Wrap**, 3315 W Magnolia Blvd, Burbank, 818-567-7366; 1164 S Robertson Blvd, 310-246-9727, www.itsawraphollywood.com; selection includes clothing used for film or television tapings, brought in by studio costuming departments. Most of the clothing sizes run small, but stock rotates frequently.
- **Jetlag**, 825 N La Brea Ave, 323-939-0528; best bargains are on Sundays where everything placed in the parking lot is a buck.
- **Junk for Joy**, 3314 W Magnolia Blvd, Burbank, 818-569-4903, www.junkforjoy.com
- **Out of the Closet Thrift Store**. All donations made to this thrift store are tax deductible at their fair market value; the money benefits the AIDS Healthcare Foundation, 877-274-2548, www.outofthecloset.org: 360 N Fairfax Ave, Fairfax District, 323-934-1956; 1408 N Vine St, Hollywood, 323-466-0747; 4136 Beverly Blvd, 213-380-8955; 6241 Laurel Canyon Blvd, North Hollywood, 818-769-0503; 1908 Lincoln Blvd, Santa Monica, 310-664-9036; 8224 Santa Monica Blvd, West Hollywood, 310-473-7787; 1608 Sawtelle Blvd, West LA, 310-473-7787; 21703 Sherman Way, Woodland Hills, 818-676-0105; additional locations on web site.
- **The Paperbag Princess**, 8818 Olympic Blvd, Beverly Hills, 310-360-1343, www.thepaperbagprincess.com
- **Polkadots & Moonbeams**, 8367 W Third St, 323-651-1746, www.polkadotsandmoonbeams.com
- **Reel Clothes and Props**, 818-951-7692, www.reelclothes.com; similar to It's a Wrap, but online sales only.

- **Scavengers Paradise**, 5453 Satsuma Ave, North Hollywood, 323-877-7945, 818-761-5257, www.scavengersparadise.com
- **Supply Sergeant**, 6664 Hollywood Blvd, 323-463-4730; 1431 Lincoln Blvd, Santa Monica, 310-458-4166; 503 N Victory Blvd, Burbank, 818-845-9433; http://supplysergeant.com

One of the largest flea markets in the Los Angeles area, the **Rose Bowl Flea Market** (323-560-7469, www.rgcshows.com), brings in 2,000 vendors to the Rose Bowl Stadium parking lot. It is held on the second Sunday of every month from 9 a.m. to 3 p.m. Admission is charged; for an additional fee, special advance admission can be had. Some of the hip Los Angeles furniture retailers shop here, and after some touch-up work on their swap-meet purchases, resell them in their stores. The **Valley Indoor Swap Meet** (6701 Variel Ave, Woodland Hills, 818-340-9120, www.indoorswap.com) runs every Friday, Saturday, and Sunday, 10 a.m. to 6 p.m. Another smart source for used goods is *The Recycler* (www.recycler.com), published each Thursday and available at most convenience stores.

FOOD

GROCERIES

The major supermarket chains that operate here—**Ralphs** (www.ralphs.com), the biggest and most successful chain in Southern California, **Vons** (www.vons. com), the oldest chain in Southern California, and the relative newcomer, **Albertsons** (www.albertsons.com)—are your everyday neighborhood grocery stores that also offer member discounts. Many Ralphs and Vons stores have remodeled, making the shopping experience markedly more pleasant. **Pavilions** (www.pavilions.com) is an upscale version of Vons, and **Fresh Faire** is an upscale version of Ralphs. **Gelson's** (www.gelsons.com) and **Bristol Farms** (www.bristolfarms.com) are gourmet market chains with premium prices but first-rate service. **Trader Joe's** (www.traderjoes.com) is known for its specialty foods and wine sections at bargain prices. **Whole Foods** (www.wholefoods.com) is an upscale health-food grocery chain with a large selection of fresh and prepared foods. The latest grocery chains to reach LA are **Hows Markets** (www.howsmarkets.com), an arm of Hughes Family Grocers, and **Fresh & Easy** (www.freshandeasy.com), billed as a British version of Trader Joe's.

Grocery-delivery service options are limited in LA. Vons.com and Albertsons.com are the largest providers at the moment—you simply make your grocery selections at their web site, and you pay a convenience fee. People who use these services tend to stay away from ordering produce because ripeness selection is subjective and cannot be specified. **Yummy.com** is another option for those in West Hollywood and Santa Monica. And there are **Pink Dots** (www. pinkdot.com) currently in West Hollywood, Century City, and Venice.

WAREHOUSE STORES

Food 4 Less (www.food4less1.com) is a bulk-item grocery store with no-frills presentation, no membership required.

- Hollywood, 5420 W Sunset Blvd, 323-871-8011
- Los Angeles, 1717 S Western Ave, 323-731-0164
- Los Angeles, 1091 S Hoover St, 213-386-1680
- Los Angeles, 1700 W 6th St, 213-353-0920
- Los Angeles, 1748 S Jefferson Blvd, 323-735-8317
- Santa Clarita, 18649 Via Princessa, 661-250-2818
- South Pasadena, 4910 Huntington Dr, 626-222-2659
- Torrance, 2751 Sky Park Dr, 310-891-1020
- Woodland Hills, 20155 Saticoy, 818-998-8074
- Van Nuys, 16530 Sherman Way, 818-997-0170

Costco (www.costco.com) is a members-only warehouse-sized store that sells bulk food, as well as cleaning supplies, health and beauty aids, clothing, appliances, and furniture.

- Burbank, 1051 Burbank Blvd, 818-557-3780
- Inglewood, 3560 W Century Blvd, 310-672-1296
- Los Angeles, 2901 Los Feliz Blvd, 323-644-5201
- Marina Del Rey, 13463 Washington Blvd, 310-754-2003
- Northridge, 8810 Tampa Ave, 818-775-1322
- Norwalk, 12324 Hoxie Ave, 562-029-0826
- Woodland Hills, 21300 Roscoe Blvd, 818-884-8982
- Van Nuys, 6100 N Sepulveda Blvd, 818-989-5256

Smart and Final (www.smartandfinal.com) is a warehouse-sized store that sells groceries and office products in bulk, no membership required. Below is just a partial listing; additional locations can be found throughout LA.

- Burbank, 3708 W Burbank Blvd, 818-562-3234
- Encino, 16847 Ventura Blvd, 818-789-0242
- Glendale, 6850 San Fernando Rd, 818-238-0223
- Hollywood, 939 N Western Ave, 323-466-9289
- Los Angeles, 12210 Santa Monica Blvd, 310-207-8688; 7720 Melrose Ave, 323-655-2211
- North Hollywood, 6601 Laurel Canyon Blvd, 818-769-2292
- Pasadena, 1382 Locust St, 626-793-2195
- West Hollywood, 1041 Fuller Ave, 323-876-0421
- West LA, 12210 Santa Monica Blvd, 310-207-8688
- Woodland Hills, 19718 Sherman Way, 818-996-1331
- Van Nuys, 7817 Van Nuys Blvd, 818-780-7222
- Venice, 604 Lincoln Blvd, 310-392-4954

HEALTH FOOD STORES

Local health food outlets (and there are a lot in LA) include the following:

- **Erewhon Natural Foods**, 7660 Beverly Blvd, 323-937-0777, www.erewhon market.com; well stocked and has a busy juice bar/deli.
- **Full O'Life Natural Foods Market & Restaurant**, 2515 W Magnolia Blvd, Burbank, 818-845-8343, www.fullolife.com
- **Lassen's Natural Foods & Vitamins**, 26861 Bouquet Canyon Rd, Santa Clarita, 661-263-6935
- **One Life Natural Foods**, 3001 Main St, Santa Monica, 310-392-4501; established as a commune, it also has a juice bar, herb room, and deli.
- **VP Discount**, an organic grocery that features a great selection of vitamins; 8001 Beverly Blvd, 323-658-6506; 12740 Culver Blvd, Marina Del Rey, 310-448-2715 are two of many locations.
- **Whole Foods**, top-quality selection and presentation. Multiple locations: call 866-WFM-CALL or go to www.wholefoods.com for a location near you.
- **Wild Oats Natural Marketplace**, www.wildoats.com; well-stocked, picture-perfect presentation; becoming part of Whole Foods. In: Pasadena, 603 S Lake Ave, 626-792-1778; Santa Monica, 1425 Montana Ave, 310-576-4707; and Santa Monica, 500 Wilshire Blvd, 310-395-4510
- **Windward Farms**, 105 Windward Ave, Venice, 310-392-3566; organic market.

MAKE-AND-TAKE MEAL ASSEMBLY

The time-crunched who want to go a step above Lean Cuisine may want to consider make-and-take meal assembly. The company does the shopping, chopping, saucing, and menu planning for you. You pay a fee, go to their kitchen's assembly stations to put together your meals, then take them home to freeze and heat at your convenience. This option is at its most economical when stocking your freezer with a large quantity of meals for the entire family. The **Easy Meal Prep Association**'s web site (www.easymealprep.com) has updated lists and locations.

- **Dream Dinners**, www.dreamdinners.com
- **My Girlfriend's Kitchen**, www.mygirlfriendskitchen.com
- **Super Suppers**, www.supersuppers.com
- **Supper Thyme USA**, www.supperthymeusa.com
- **Your Dinner Secret**, www.yourdinnersecret.com

COMMUNITY GARDENS

In some parts of Los Angeles, neighborhoods are provided with plots of vacant land where neighbors come together to grow fruits, vegetables, and herbs. These gardens are self-maintained and self-policed by its members. In addition to providing food, the process develops a sense of community pride, helping to revitalize urban centers. Contact the **City of LA Department of Recreation and Parks** (888-LA-PARKS; "horticultural centers" at www.laparks.org) to find out about obtaining gardening space at one of the following community gardens, or contact the coordinator of the specific garden you're interested in. Below is just a sample of what's available; the **LA Community Garden Council** has a complete list at their web site, http://lagardencouncil.org. The Council can also help you organize a community garden if you don't have one near you.

- **Eagle Rockdale Community Garden & Art Park**, 1003–11000 Rockdale Ave, Eagle Rock, 323-344-8425
- **Howard Finn Park Community Garden**, 7747 Foothill Blvd, Sunland, 818-756-8188
- **Orcutt Ranch Horticultural,** 23600 Roscoe Blvd, West Hills, 818-883-6641; one weekend a year in July, the public is allowed to pick oranges and grapefruit from the ranch for a nominal fee.
- **Sepulveda Garden Center**, 16633 Magnolia Blvd, Encino, 818-784-5180

The **LA County Common Ground**, an urban gardening program that operates with the assistance of UC Davis, has a help line for would-be green thumbs wanting to grow their own food garden. Contact them at 323-260-3348, or go to http://celosangeles.ucdavis.edu/Common%5FGround%5FGarden%5FProgram.

FARMERS' MARKETS

There are numerous farmers' markets throughout the city, including the famous year-round market at **Third and Fairfax** (323-933-9211, www.farmersmarketla. com) which offers the adventurous shopper gorgeous seasonal produce stalls, butchers, and tourist-oriented shops. Below are some of the many neighborhood outdoor farmers' markets that sell fruits, eggs, fish, vegetables, honey, nuts, cut flowers, plants, and more—usually for less than you would find at supermarkets. (Go to www.cafarmersmarkets.com or www.farmernet.com/events/cfms for a complete listing.) Many stalls feature organically grown produce, but be sure to ask, or look for the "certified organic" sign, if that's important to you.

- **Beverly Hills**, N Canon Dr between Clifton and Dayton ways, Sundays, 9 a.m. to 1 p.m., 310-285-1048

- **Brentwood**, 11600 block of Chayote St, between Barrington Pl and Sunset Blvd, Wednesdays, 3:30 to 7 p.m. during daylight saving time, 3:30 to 6 p.m. standard time.
- **Burbank**, Orange Grove Ave and 3rd St, Saturdays, 8 a.m. to 12:30 p.m.
- **Calabasas**, 23504 Calabasas Rd at El Canon Ave, Saturdays, 8 a.m. to 1 p.m.
- **Culver City**, Media Park, Culver Blvd and Canfield Ave, Tuesdays, 3 p.m. to 7 p.m., 310-253-5775
- **El Segundo**, Main St between Grand and Holly avenues, Thursdays, 3 p.m. to 7 p.m.
- **Encino**, 17400 Victory Blvd between Balboa Blvd and White Oak Ave, Sundays, 8 a.m. to 1 p.m.
- **Glendale**, Brand Blvd between Broadway and Wilson Ave, Thursdays, 9:30 a.m. to 1 p.m.
- **Hollywood**, Ivar Ave and Selma Ave, Sundays, 8 a.m. to 1 p.m., 323-463-3171
- **Los Angeles**, W Adams Blvd and Vermont Ave, Wednesdays, June–August, 1 p.m. to 6 p.m.; September–May, 2 p.m. to 5 p.m.; Seventh Market Pl, 735 S Figueroa St, Thursdays, 10am to 4 p.m.
- **Long Beach**, CityPlace Center at Promenade North and E 4th St, Fridays, 10 a.m. to 4 p.m.; Alamitos Bay Marina, E Marina Dr south of E 2nd St, Sundays, 9 a.m. to 2 p.m.; 46th St and Atlantic Ave, Thursdays, 3 p.m. to 6:30 p.m.
- **Norwalk**, Alondra Blvd, west of Pioneer Blvd, Tuesdays, 9 a.m. to 1 p.m.
- **Pasadena**, Villa Park, 363 E Villa St at Garfield Ave, Tuesdays, 9 a.m. to 1 p.m.; Victory Park, 2800 block of N Sierra Madre Blvd, between Paloma and Washington avenues, Saturdays, 8:30 a.m. to 1 p.m.
- **Santa Clarita**, College of the Canyons lot 8, Valencia Blvd and Rockwell Canyon Rd, Sundays, 8:30 a.m. to noon
- **Santa Monica**, Arizona Ave between 2nd and 3rd streets, Wednesdays, 9 a.m. to 2 p.m., Saturdays, 8:30 a.m. to 1 p.m.; Pico Blvd. at Cloverfield Ave, Saturdays, 8 a.m. to 1 p.m.; 2640 Main St at Ocean Park Blvd, Sundays, 9:30 a.m. to 1 p.m.
- **Studio City**, Ventura Pl between Ventura and Laurel Canyon boulevards, Sundays, 8 a.m. to 1 p.m.
- **South Pasadena**, Meridian Ave at Mission St, Thursdays, 4 p.m. to 8 p.m.
- **Venice**, Venice Blvd at Venice Way, Fridays, 7 a.m. to 11 a.m.
- **West Hollywood**, Plummer Park, 7377 Santa Monica Blvd, Mondays, 9 a.m. to 2 p.m.
- **Westwood**, Weyburn Ave at Westwood Blvd, Thursdays, 2 p.m. to 7 p.m.; Broxton Ave and Le Conte Ave, Sundays 10 a.m. to 3 p.m.

PRODUCE HOME DELIVERY

If you love a wide variety of locally produced, in-season vegetables and fruits, but just don't have the time to shop for them, you can arrange to have produce delivered to your home or office—typically on a recurring basis. Some options include:

- **The Farmer's Cart**, 213-509-9821, www.thefarmerscart.org
- **Los Angeles Organic Vegetable Express**, 310-821-LOVE, http://lovedelivery. com
- **Organic Express**, 310-674-2642, www.organicexpress.com
- **Paradise O**, www.paradiseo.com

ETHNIC FOOD

As one of the biggest melting pots in the nation, LA's substantial Middle Eastern, Hispanic, Jewish, and Asian populations mean plenty of stores to go to if you need to stock up on ghee, kreplach, or kimchi. Many of the markets listed below are located within their respective ethnic communities.

Los Angeles' Chinatown still has an authentic air to it with a smattering of dim sum restaurants and grocery stores, but it has experienced a decline lately, at least perhaps in its hustle and bustle. Much of its thunder has been stolen by the community of **Monterey Park**, nicknamed "Little Hong Kong" because of its burgeoning population of recent **Chinese** immigrants; Chinese groceries, restaurants, and goods can be found in this lively neighborhood. One of the largest Chinese grocery chains is **99 Ranch Market** (800-600-TAWA, www.99ranch. com; in Monterey Park at 771 West Garvey Ave, 626-458-3399, and in Van Nuys at 6450 North Sepulveda Boulevard, 818-988-7899). The **Shun Fat Supermarket** (626-280-9998, www.shunfatmkt.com) operates a very competitive rival, the **San Gabriel Superstore** (1635 South San Gabriel, in San Gabriel).

To stock up on **English** pantry items, try **Tudor House** (1403-1409 Second Street, Santa Monica, 310-451-4101, www.thetudorhouse.com), or the little grocery store attached to the **Buchanan Arms** restaurant (2013 West Burbank Blvd, Burbank, 818-845-0692). Indian grocery stores, mentioned later in this section, are another go-to source for British foodstuffs. For sturdy **German** fare, visit **Van Nuys German Deli** (16155 Roscoe Boulevard, 818-892-2212). Another option for great German sausage is the **Alpine Village Market** (833 West Torrance Boulevard, Torrance, 310-327-4384, www.alpinevillage.net).

Those in need of a knish should head down to the Fairfax District on North Fairfax Avenue between Melrose Avenue and Beverly Boulevard for mom-and-pop stores that carry kosher food and other supplies. **Jewish** delis like **Jerry's Deli** are dotted throughout LA, so you'll never be far from some good matzo ball soup.

Many know about Koreatown in Los Angeles, located along Western Avenue between Olympic and Beverly boulevards. The **Hannam Chain** (2740 West Olympic Boulevard, 213-382-2922, www.hannamchain.com) is a popular grocery store there, but there is also a large **Korean** population in Northridge—just look for the Korean script on signage. **HK Korean Supermarket** (in Los Angeles at 124 North Western Ave, 213-469-8934, and in Van Nuys at 17634 Sherman Way, 818-708-7396) is a favorite. **Koreatown Plaza Market** is another grocer closer to Koreatown (928 South Western Ave, 213-385-1100). The **Koreatown Galleria** (at 3250 West Olympic Blvd, 323-733-6000, www.koreatowngalleria.com) contains a popular market as well.

Meticulously clean **Little Tokyo**, between First, 4th, San Pedro and Alameda streets, in LA, is popular for a sushi fix. **Mitsuwa Marketplace** (333 South Alameda Street, 213-613-0573—go to www.mitsuwa.com for additional locations) can supply all of your ingredients for the perfect California roll. Outside of Little Tokyo, Sawtelle Boulevard north of Olympic Boulevard in West LA contains a stretch of Japanese stores, including the **Nijiya Market** (2130 Sawtelle Boulevard, #105, 310-575-3300—go to www.nijiya.com for additional locations).

Need some spice in your life?—say, a bite of vindaloo? For this and other **Indian** favorites, try the **Bharat Bazaar** (1510 West Washington Boulevard in Culver City, 310-398-6766) or **India Sweets and Spices** (in Los Angeles at 3126 Los Feliz Boulevard, 323-345-0860, www.indiasweetsandspices.net; those in the Valley should head to its sister store at 18110 Parthenia Street, in Northridge, 818-407-1498).

Pasta aficionados looking for the perfect **Italian** ingredients will want to go to **Bay Cities Italian Deli** (1517 Lincoln Boulevard, Santa Monica, 310-395-8279, www.baycitiesitaliandeli.com) or **Claro's Italian Markets** (1003 East Valley Boulevard, San Gabriel, 800-507-0450, http://store.claros.com).

With strong ties to its neighbor to the south, LA is renowned for its fine selection of authentic **Mexican** cuisine and food markets. In particular, Boyle Heights (along First Street and Cesar E. Chavez Avenue), Los Feliz, and East LA are largely Mexican. The best place for a taste of Mexico City is said to be **El Gallo Giro**, a combination restaurant, bakery, meat market, and juice bar. (In East Los Angeles they can be found at 5686 East Whittier Boulevard, 213-726-1246; in El Monte at 11912 Valley Boulevard, 626-575-1244; and in Huntington Park at 7148 Pacific Avenue, 213-585-4433; visit www.gallogiro.com for additional locations.) Another popular place for Mexican foodstuffs is at the **Grand Central Public Market** (317 South Broadway, downtown, 213-624-2378, www.grandcentralsquare.com). For shelves of Mexican foods, try the growing **Vallarta Supermarkets** chains (www.vallartasupermarket.com for locations). Cubans know the best place for a pressed sandwich is **Porto's Bakery** (Glendale: 314 North Brand Boulevard, 818-956-5996; Burbank: 3614 West Magnolia Boulevard, 818-846-9100); the Cuban bakery is wildly popular for its cakes and pastries too.

A mix of Armenian, Persian, Israeli, and Greek populations resides along the western border of Los Angeles. In addition, the city of Glendale has a large **Middle Eastern** population; drive through the neighborhood to browse the restaurants, bakeries, and grocers. If you're in Pasadena, check out Allen and Washington boulevards for Middle Eastern goods. Or try these Middle Eastern favorites: **Elat**

Market (8730 West Pico Boulevard, 310-659-7070, www.elatmarket.com); **Good Food Market** (1864 East Washington Boulevard, Pasadena, 626-794-5367). For **Greek** foods, **Papa Cristo's** (2771 West Pico Boulevard, 800-732-3212, www.papacristo.com) can't be beat. Opa!

Borscht anyone? **Russian** groceries can be found at **Royal Gourmet Deli** (8151 Santa Monica Boulevard, West Hollywood, 213-650-5001) and **Tatiana** (8205 Santa Monica Boulevard, West Hollywood, 323-656-7500).

To satisfy your injera craving—or, at least, to find out what this savory crepe/bread tastes like—head to **Little Ethiopia**, along a small segment of Fairfax Avenue, south of Olympic Boulevard. There's an excellent selection of buffet restaurants and tiny immigrant-owned shops featuring **East African** culture to discover.

WINE, BEER, AND LIQUOR

Libations can be purchased at grocery stores, convenience stores, gas stations, and liquor stores between 6 a.m. and 2 a.m., seven days a week. Here is a partial list of popular LA wine stores.

- **Bottle Rock**, 3847 Main St, Culver City, 310-836-9463, www.bottlerock.net
- **Colorado Wine Company**, 2114 Colorado Blvd, Eagle Rock, 323-478-1985, www.cowineco.com
- **John & Pete's Fine Wines & Spirits**, 621 N La Cienega Blvd, 310-657-3080, www.johnandpetes.com
- **K&L Wine Merchants**, 1400 Vine St, Hollywood, 323-464-9463, www.klwines. com
- **Rosso Wine Shop**, 3459½ N Verdugo Rd, Glendale, 818-330-9130, www.rosso wineshop.com
- **Silver Lake Wine**, 2395 Glendale Blvd, 323-662-9024, www.silverlakewine. com
- **Wally's Wine and Spirits**, 2107 Westwood Blvd, 310-475-0606, www.wally wine.com
- **Wine House**, 2311 Cotner Ave, 310-479-3731, www.winehouse.com

EATING OUT

In Philly it's cheesesteaks, Chicago, deep-dish pizza—ask an Angeleno about Los Angeles's equivalent fast-food fame and they'll rave to you about LA chili-cheeseburgers. Perhaps it is the exquisite meeting of the Southwest flavors of the chili with the red-white-and-blue standard hamburger; whatever the reason, the chili-cheeseburgers here are justifiably famous, and everyone swears by their favorite burger joint. Dine around for your favorite—just don't forget the antacid!

- **The Apple Pan**, 10801 Pico Blvd, Westwood, 310-475-3585; a Westwood institution, known for its burgers and for its pies.
- **Carney's**, 12601 Ventura Blvd, Studio City, 818-761-8300, www.carneytrain. com; housed in an old train car, Carney's aficionados swear by the chili-burgers and chili-fries.
- **Clifton's Cafeteria**, 648 S Broadway, 213-627-1673, www.cliftonscafeteria. com; this downtown cafeteria has been serving comfort food cafeteria-style at very affordable prices since the '30s. The 20-foot waterfall in their dining room is a refreshing surprise while dining in "old Los Angeles" style.
- **Fatburger**, www.fatburger.com, various locations citywide. These spots stay open late, perfect for those midnight cravings.
- **In-N-Out Burger**, www.in-n-out.com, various locations citywide. For the one nearest you, call 800-786-1000.
- **Marty's Hamburger Stand**, 10558 W Pico Blvd, West LA, 310-836-6944; this is the original Marty's. Also at 1255 La Cienega Blvd, 310-652-8047; the brave here go for "the combo," a chili-cheeseburger with a sliced hot-dog on top.
- **Philippe, The Original**, 1001 N Alameda St, 213-628-3781, www.philippes. com; one of LA's oldest restaurants, it claims to be the birthplace of the famous French Dip sandwich.
- **Pink's**, 709 N La Brea Blvd, 213-931-4223, www.pinkshollywood.com; a favorite late-night chili-dog stop with constant lines, open till 2 a.m. during the week and 3 a.m. on weekends.
- **Tito's Tacos**, 11222 Washington Pl, Culver City, 310-391-5780, www.titostacos. com; don't be daunted by the line out front, it moves fast.
- **Tommy's**, www.originaltommys.com; various locations citywide. A popular chili-burger joint with imitators all over the city.

OTHER SHOPPING

ART SUPPLIES

This being an entertainment-industry town, the artists here require specialized material that can only be obtained from well-stocked art supply stores. A sampling of such stores is below.

- **Aaron Brothers**, multiple locations, www.aaronbrothers.com
- **Blick Art Materials**, multiple locations, 800-828-4548, www.dickblick.com
- **Michael's, The Arts & Crafts Store**, multiple locations, www.michaels.com
- **Pearl Art & Craft Supplies**, 1250 S La Cienega Blvd, 310-854-4900, www.pearl paint.com

- **Swain's Art Supplies**, 537 N Glendale Ave, Glendale, 818-243-3129, www. swainsart.com
- **Utrecht Arts Supplies**, 11677 Santa Monica Blvd, 310-478-5775, www.utrecht. com
- **World Supply Inc**, 3425 Cahuenga Blvd West, 323-851-1350

CIGARS

In LA, the **Cenzia Cigar Lounge**, 260 East Colorado Boulevard, Pasadena, 626-795-4664, boasts a 2500-square-foot lounge for enjoying a stogie, wireless internet, and coffee. An even more luxurious lounge can be found at the **Buena Vista Cigar Club**, 9715 Santa Monica Boulevard, Beverly Hills, 310-273-8100, www. buenavistacigarclub.com, which boasts a full bar in addition to a great selection in their humidor. Other cigar shops, more down-to-earth but full of character, are downtown: **La Planta Cigar Company**, 124 West Second Street, 213-452-4427, www.2ndstreetcigarandgallery.com, and **Diplomat Cigars**, 806 West Seventh Street, 213-627-6434, www.diplomatcigars.com. Many fine wine stores also carry cigars.

FOR CHILDREN

Everything you need to outfit your child's room can be found at just about any children's or discount store. The chains such as **Toys 'R' Us**, **Baby Gap**, and **Target** have well-stocked children's sections. Local "baby lifestyle stores" gain fame when a celebrity pops in to shop for their progeny, so these boutiques tend toward trendy clothing and top-of-the-line toys and furniture.

- **Entertaining Elephants**, 12053 Ventura Pl, Studio City, 818-766-9177, www. entertainingelephants.com
- **Fred Segal**, 420 Broadway, Santa Monica, 310-458-9940, www.fredsegal.com
- **Flicka**, 204 N Larchmont Blvd, 323-466-5822
- **Harper Lane**, 2665 Main St, Santa Monica, 310-314-2233
- **Kitson Kids**, 115 S Robertson Blvd, West Hollywood, 310-246-3829, www. shopkitson.com
- **Naked Baby Boutique**, 12334 Ventura Blvd, Studio City, 818-760-8851, www. nakedbabyboutique.com
- **Tough Cookies Children's Boutique**, 13638 Ventura Blvd, Sherman Oaks, 818-990-0972, www.shoptoughcookies.com
- **Wonderland, A Child's Place,** 11726 Barrington Ct, Brentwood, 310-440-9970, www.childrenswonderland.com

MUSIC

While increasing numbers of people are opting to download their music online rather than making their purchase at a brick-and-mortar store, independent music sellers are still managing to thrive. **Amoeba Music**, 6400 West Sunset Boulevard, 323-245-6400, www.amoeba.com, is tops on the list for new and used music and movies, along with the **Virgin Megastore**, 8000 West Sunset Boulevard, 323-650-8666, www.virgin.com/megastores. Both Amoeba and Virgin host musical-artist signing events and promotional concerts at their stores. **SecondSpin**, specializing in secondhand music, operates two stores here: 1332 Wilshire Boulevard, Santa Monica, 310-395-4334, and 14564 Ventura Boulevard, Sherman Oaks, 818-986-6866, www.secondspin.com. If you prefer your music new and from a neighborhood chain, Borders, Sam Goody, and FYE are just some of the choices, in addition to the department and electronics stores previously mentioned.

PARTY SUPPLIES

In a town known for glamorous parties and elaborately decorated houses during various holidays (we have a city full of set decorators and designers, you know), the hard part for any LA party planner is not finding supplies, it's staying on budget. **Party America** and **Party City** are some of the chains with stores here. For warehouse-sized selections of celebratory supplies and themed decorations, local retailers include the **Vine American Party Store**, 5969 Melrose Avenue, 323-467-7124, www.vineamericanparty.com, and **Stats Floral Supply**, 120 South Raymond Avenue, Pasadena, 626-795-9308, www.statsfloral.com. Boutique party stores are as plentiful as palm trees: **Party on La Cienega**, 350 South La Cienega Boulevard, 310-659-8717, www.partypaperlife.com, is one of the popular ones. Floral supply stores like **Moskatel's** and **Floral Supply Syndicate** on Wall Street in the downtown Flower Market are also poorly kept secrets for party stuff. Check the yellow pages for additional party supply stores.

A S HOME TO THE ENTERTAINMENT INDUSTRY, AS WELL AS TO thousands of artists, musicians, and writers, LA seems to offer an infinite number of things to do to occupy your leisure time. Whatever your interests, from music to theater to the visual arts, Los Angeles has not only a wide variety of cultural offerings, but some of the finest in the world as well.

If you want to find out what's going on this day, week or month, check out the following publications and web sites:

- **City Search Los Angeles**, http://LosAngeles.CitySearch.com, has an exhaustive entertainment section.
- **Daily Candy Los Angeles**, www.dailycandy.com/los_angeles; their weekend guide details unique happenings from gourmet mushroom–hunting trips to couture-fashion sales.
- *The Daily News Los Angeles* offers www.LA.com, a site devoted entirely to entertainment offerings around the county.
- **Experience LA**, www.experienceLA.com, is devoted to cultural offerings in LA.
- **LA Convention and Visitors Bureau**, 213-624-7300 or 800-228-2452, www.discoverlosangeles.com; geared toward visitors, but still a useful resource for local entertainment suggestions and cultural guides.
- The **LA Department of Cultural Affairs**, 213-202-5500, www.culturela.org, is a great resource for events. For round-the-clock access to the latest information about music, art, dance, theater, special events, festivals, and community events going on throughout Los Angeles, go to www.artscenecal.com or www.lacountyarts.org.
- *LA Parent*, www.laparent.com, is a free monthly magazine with a calendar section listing activities and workshops for kids and their parents.
- *LA Weekly*, www.laweekly.com; most-read free weekly newspaper in Los Angeles. Editorial coverage includes social and political issues as well as extensive

film, art, music, and restaurant critiques. Each week, the "Calendar" section lists some 50 pages of events—everything from coffeehouse folk performances to Latin dance clubs to political symposiums. (And don't forget the personal ads; they offer entertainment unto themselves!) Distributed on Thursdays.

• **Los Angeles Times** publishes an event guide, www.theguide.latimes.com, that covers a variety of cultural and entertainment options throughout LA; check the paper on Thursdays for The Guide, a detailed pull-out of upcoming weekend events.

• **Los Angeles**, www.lamag.com, is a monthly city magazine; check the back section for entertainment listings.

Tickets to many events can be purchased through each venue's web site or box office, or through **Ticketmaster** (213-480-3232, www.ticketmaster.com), **Telecharge** (800-432-7250, www.telecharge.com), or **Stub Hub** (866-STUB-HUB, www.StubHub.com).

If you have the energy and enthusiasm to take in a lot of attractions within a short span of time, look into the Go Los Angeles Card at www.golosangelescard. com. They sell 1- to 7-day multi-attraction passes (starting at $55 for adults and $39 for children 3 to 12) that allow you to enter attractions and museums such as the Queen Mary, Huntington Library, and LA Zoo for free. This is a great bargain if you pack in a lot of visits. You do not have to use your pass on consecutive days, but you do have to use it up within two weeks of first use. Each pass comes with a guidebook that lists all participating venues.

Unless otherwise noted, addresses listed are in Los Angeles.

PERFORMING ARTS

MUSIC

For a complete listing of the week's musical offerings, refer to *LA Weekly*, which offers the most comprehensive guide to the vast Los Angeles music scene. Here is a glimpse of classical musical offerings in and around LA.

CLASSICAL

• **Los Angeles Philharmonic Orchestra**, 213-972-7300, www.laphil.com, presents a variety of concerts, recitals, and special programs. In October 2003, it moved into its new home at the Walt Disney Concert Hall—a steely architectural marvel designed by Frank Gehry; in the summer, however, it continues to hold performances at the Hollywood Bowl (renovated in 2004). For more information, call The Music Center, 135 N Grand Ave, downtown, 213-202-2200 or 213-972-7211, or go to www.musiccenter.org.

- **Beverly Hills Symphony**, 310-276-8385, www.beverlyhills.org, has been in existence since 1993, and is led by conductor Bogidar Avramov. Its summer series is held outdoors at Greystone Park on the grounds of the historic Doheny mansion, built in 1928. The winter series is held at various civic sites in Beverly Hills.
- **Santa Monica Symphony Orchestra**, 310-395-6330, www.smsymphony. org, has performed for over half a century, and is now led by conductor Allen Robert Gross. All their performances of classical and contemporary music are free to the public at the Santa Monica Civic Auditorium. Most of its musicians are nonprofessionals drawn from the community and area colleges and universities.

Other Los Angeles area orchestral groups include:

- **Burbank Philharmonic Orchestra**, 818-771-7888, www.burbankphilharmonic.com
- **Glendale Symphony**, 818-500-8720, www.glendalesymphony.org
- **Hollywood Bowl Orchestra**, 323-850-2000, www.hollywoodbowl.com (summer only)
- **Long Beach Symphony Orchestra**, 562-436-3203, www.lbso.org
- **Pasadena Symphony**, 626-793-7172, www.pasadenasymphony.org
- **Santa Clarita Symphony**, 661-857-0867, www.scsymphony.com
- **San Fernando Valley Symphony**, 818-347-4807, www.sfvsymphony.com
- **Symphony in the Glen**, 213-955-6976, www.symphonyintheglen.org (summer only)

CHORUSES

- **Angeles Chorale**, 818-591-1735, www.angeleschorale.org; as large as the LA Master Chorale, but entirely composed of volunteer community members, the chorus primarily performs at Royce Hall on the UCLA campus. Its conductor, Donald Neuen, is also chair of Choral Music at UCLA.
- **Gay Men's Chorus of Los Angeles**, 800-MEN-SING, www.gmcla.org; directed by Jon Bailey, tickets for this popular and talented group may be purchased through Telecharge at 800-233-3123. It performs primarily in the Alex Theatre in Glendale.
- **Los Angeles Master Chorale**, 213-972-7282, www.lamc.org; this 100+-voice professional symphonic chorus, directed by Grant Gershon, performs its subscription series at the Walt Disney Concert Hall.
- **Los Angeles Children's Chorus**, 626-793-4231, www.lachildrenschorus.org; made up of 250 children from throughout LA County, its mission is to provide advanced musical training for children regardless of financial constraints. It presents two major concerts a year, one each in the spring and winter; consult its calendar for additional smaller concerts.

- **South Coast Chorale**, 562-439-6919, www.southcoastchorale.org, is a community group that performs at various venues from The Queen Mary to the Long Beach Performing Arts Center.

OPERA

The world-class **Los Angeles Opera** performs September through June at The Music Center in the Dorothy Chandler Pavilion, 135 North Grand Avenue, 213-972-8001, www.losangelesopera.com. Tickets may be purchased in person at The Music Center box office, via its web site, or by calling Ticketmaster, 213-480-3232. Also check out the **Santa Monica Civic Light Opera**, 310-458-5939, www.smclo.org. Recent performances include "Who's Afraid of Virginia Woolf" and "The Sound of Music." Performances are in the restored 1938 art deco Barnum Hall Theater. For a more contemporary take on the medium, the **Long Beach Opera**, 562-439-2580, www.longbeachopera.org, fits the bill. It stages performances of new works and reinvents the classics, emphasizing striking visual drama. Recent performances of a commissioned work were performed at the Belmont Plaza Olympic Pool.

CONTEMPORARY MUSIC

CONCERT FACILITIES

Tickets can be obtained by standing in line at the venue itself or through Ticketmaster, 213-480-3232, www.ticketmaster.com.

- **Gibson Amphitheatre**, 100 Universal City Plaza, Universal City, 818-622-4440, www.hob.com
- **Greek Theatre**, 2700 N Vermont Ave, Los Feliz, 323-665-5857, www.greektheatrela.com
- **Hollywood Bowl**, 2301 N Highland Ave, Hollywood, 323-850-2000, www.hollywoodbowl.org
- **John Anson Ford Amphitheatre**, 2580 E Cahuenga Blvd, 323-461-3673, www.fordamphitheatre.org
- **Kodak Theatre**, 6801 Hollywood Blvd, Ste 180, Hollywood, 323-308-6363, www.kodaktheatre.com
- **LA Forum**, 3900 W Manchester Blvd, Inglewood, 310-330-7300, www.thelaforum.com
- **Los Angeles Sports Arena**, 3939 S Figueroa St, 213-747-7111, www.lacoliseum.com
- **Nokia Center LA Live**, 777 Chick Hearn Ct, 213-763-6030, www.nokiatheatrelalive.com

- **Shrine Auditorium**, 665 W Jefferson Blvd, 213-748-5116, www.shrineaudito
rium.com
- **Staples Center**, 1111 S Figueroa St, 213-742-7340, www.staplescenter.com
- **UCLA's Royce Hall**, 405 Hilgard Ave, Westwood, 310-825-4401, www.uclalive.
com
- **Walt Disney Concert Hall**, 111 S Grand Ave, 213-972-7211, www.wdch.com
- **Wiltern LG Theatre**, 3790 Wilshire Blvd, 213-388-1400

COFFEEHOUSE PERFORMANCES

This relaxing, semi-Bohemian alternative to clubs and restaurants offers aficionados food, music, socializing and, of course, coffee and tea. Here are a few local
coffeehouses that offer music and other performances on a regular basis, as well
as an alternative to the omnipresent Starbucks and Coffee Bean & Tea Leaf.

- **Buzz Coffee**, 800 W Sunset Blvd, 323-656-7460
- **Cobalt Café**, 22047 Sherman Way, Woodland Hills, 818-348-3789
- **Coffee Gallery**, 2029 Lake Ave, Altadena, 626-398-7917
- **Cow's End**, 34 Washington Blvd, Venice, 310-574-1080
- **Creama**, 440 Pine Ave, Long Beach, 562-435-8435, www.creamacafe.com
- **Gourmet Coffee Warehouse**, 671 Rose Ave, Venice, 310-392-6479
- **Groundwork Coffee Community**, 1501 Cahuenga Blvd, Hollywood, 323-871-
0107, www.lacoffee.com
- **The Healthy Bean**, 8470 Santa Monica Blvd, West Hollywood, www.the
healthybean.com
- **Highland Grounds**, 742 N Highland Ave, Hollywood, 323-466-1507
- **Insomnia Café**, 7286 Beverly Blvd, Fairfax District, 323-931-4943
- **Karma Coffeehouse**, 1544 N Cahuenga Blvd, 323-460-4188, www.karma
coffeehouse.com
- **Kings Road Café**, 8361 Beverly Blvd, Fairfax District, 323-655-9044
- **LA Mill Coffee Boutique**, 1636 Silver Lake Blvd, Silverlake, 323-663-4441,
www.lamillcoffee.com; the only coffeehouse in LA that has a Clover coffee
machine.
- **Literati Café**, 12081 Wilshire Blvd, 310-231-7484
- **Lulu's Beehive**, 13203 Ventura Blvd, Studio City, 818-986-2233
- **Novel Café**, 212 Pier Ave, Santa Monica, 310-396-8566, www.novelcafe.com
- **Romancing the Bean**, 150 S San Fernando Blvd, Burbank, 818-524-2326
- **Un-urban Café**, 3301 Pico Blvd, Santa Monica, 310-315-0056

NIGHTCLUBS

There are many, many, many nightclubs in LA. Cover charge varies by venue and
day. Here is a sampling of the most well known; refer to other music genres in this
chapter for more choices, or check out the *LA Weekly* for a complete guide:

- **Air Conditioned Supper Club**, 625 Lincoln Blvd, Venice, 310-230-5343, www. airconditionedbar.com
- **The Avalon**, 1735 Vine St, 323-462-8900, www.avalonhollywood.com
- **The Derby**, 4500 Los Feliz Blvd, 323-663-8979, www.clubderby.com
- **The Highlands Hollywood**, Hollywood & Highland, 6801 Hollywood Blvd, 323-461-9800, www.thehighlandshollywood.com; dance to a panoramic view of Hollywood.
- **House of Blues**, 8430 Sunset Blvd, West Hollywood, 323-848-5100, www.hob. com; the dance floor is close enough to the stage that your favorite blues singer might even climb down to boogie with you. Excellent sight lines and sound system for live bands despite also being a restaurant.
- **The Joint**, 8771 W Pico Blvd, West LA, 310-275-2619; an eclectic venue for local bands.
- **Key Club**, 9039 Sunset Blvd, West Hollywood, 310-274-5800, www.keyclub. com; two-level showcase featuring a variety of acts. Three full bars feature a "tequila library."
- **Mayan Theatre**, 1038 S Hill St, 213-746-4674; normally an LA nightclub, its cool, gothic building makes it irresistible as a concert venue.
- **The Troubadour**, 9081 Santa Monica Blvd, West Hollywood, 310-276-6168, www.troubadour.com; considered the granddaddy since it's been in operation for more than 40 years.

ACOUSTIC PERFORMANCES

- **Coffee Gallery Backstage**, 2029 N Lake Ave, Altadena, 626-398-7917, www. coffeegallery.com; small showroom dedicated to acoustic performance.
- **Genghis Cohen**, 740 N Fairfax Ave, Fairfax District, 323-653-0640, www.geng hiscohen.com; half–Chinese restaurant, half–music den.
- **The Hotel Café**, 1623 1/2 N Cahuenga Blvd, 323-461-2040; it's all about the music here.
- **Luna Park**, 665 Robertson Blvd, West Hollywood, 310-652-0611, http://luna parkla.com; this restaurant/music hangout plays host to a variety of acts, from folk to Brazilian pop.
- **McCabe's Guitar Shop**, 3101 Pico Blvd, Santa Monica, 310-828-4497, www. mccabes.com; yes it's a guitar store, but there's a back room that features fine acoustic performances.

ALTERNATIVE, ROCK, HIP-HOP, AND POP

A good web site to look up independent bands is at the Los Angeles Indie-Music Project: http://la.indiemusicproject.com.

- **Al's Bar**, 305 S Newitt St, downtown, 213-625-9703; a gritty, trendy downtown standard.

- **Alligator Lounge**, 3321 Pico Blvd, Santa Monica, 310-449-1844; this Westside club is a popular place with the alternative music scene.
- **Dragonfly**, 6510 Santa Monica Blvd, Hollywood, www.thedragonfly.com; no-attitude club for rock and pop, often featuring local bands.
- **14 Below**, 1348 14th St, Santa Monica, 310-451-5040, www.14below.com; live music and dancing every night, plus pool, darts, and lots of beer on tap.
- **Knitting Factory**, 7021 Hollywood Blvd, Hollywood, 323-463-0204, www.knit tingfactory.com; their mainstage hosts popular bands, their AlterKnit Lounge hosts cutting edge bands.
- **The Mint**, 6010 W Pico Blvd, 323-954-9400, www.themintla.com; indie rock nights alternate with blues nights.
- **Molly Malone's Irish Pub**, 575 S Fairfax Ave, Fairfax District, 323-935-1577, www.mollymalonesla.com; for Irish, folk, rock, and R&B.
- **Roxy Theatre**, 9009 Sunset Blvd, West Hollywood, 310-276-2222, www.theroxyonsunset.com; this venue often serves as a showcase for the music industry's newest signs.
- **The Scene Bar**, 806 E Colorado Blvd, Glendale, www.thescenebar.com; short on atmosphere, long on indie pop and bluesy rock.
- **Spaceland**, 1717 Silver Lake Blvd, 323-662-7728, www.clubspaceland; the place to go to take in the underground music scene.
- **The Troubadour**, 9081 Santa Monica Blvd, West Hollywood, 310-276-6168, www.troubadour.com; a tried and true venue for nightly live performances.
- **The Viper Room**, 8852 Sunset Blvd, West Hollywood, 310-358-1880, www.vi perroom.com.
- **Whiskey-a-Go-Go**, 8901 Sunset Blvd, West Hollywood, 310-652-4202, www.whiskeyagogo.com; a popular club to rock out at.

COUNTRY

- **Cowboy Country**, 3321 E South St, Long Beach, 562-630-3007, www.cowboy country.mu.
- **The Cowboy Palace Saloon**, 21635 Devonshire St, Chatsworth, 818-341-0166, www.cowboypalace.com; live country music and dancing seven nights a week.
- **Culver Saloon**, 11513 Washington Blvd, Culver City, 310-391-1519; a country nightclub featuring local acts.
- **Saddle Ranch Chop House**, 8371 Sunset Blvd, West Hollywood, 323-656-2007, and 1000 Universal Studios Blvd, Universal City, 818-760-9680, www.srrestau rants.com; one of the few places cowboys and cowgirls can ride a mechanical bull to their favorite tunes.
- **Oil Can Harry's**, 11502 Ventura Blvd, Studio City, 818-760-9749, www.oil canharrysla.com ; enjoyed by cowboy hat–clad gay and straight clientele.

JAZZ, R&B

- **Atlas Supper Club**, 3760 Wilshire Blvd, 213-380-8400, www.clubatlas.com; a 1940s-style jazz supper club.
- **Babe & Ricky's Inn**, 4339 Leimert Park, 323-295-9112, www.bluesbar.com; LA's longest-running blues club, located in Leimert Park, which in the 1950s was the heart of the city's African-American music community.
- **The Baked Potato**, 3787 Cahuenga Blvd, Studio City, 818-980-1615, www.the bakedpotato.com; a small, well-known jazz spot that serves 21 kinds of baked potatoes. Cover charge. Also at 26 E Colorado Blvd, Pasadena, 626-564-1122.
- **B.B. King's Blues Club**, 1000 Universal Center Dr, Universal City, 818-622-5464, www.bbkingblues.com; sister to the flagship club in Memphis, this large dinner club features a variety of live blues performances.
- **Catalina Bar & Grill**, 1640 N Cahuenga Blvd, 323-466-2210, www.catalinajazz club.com; an upscale jazz supper club, often with big-name acts on the bill.
- **Golden Gopher**, 417 W 8th St, 213-614-8001, http://goldengopher.la; take in some soul at this former speakeasy with the oldest liquor license in LA.
- **Harvelle's**, 1432 Fourth St, Santa Monica, 310-395-1676, www.harvelles.com; funky, small blues spot that gets very crowded.
- **House of Blues**, 430 Sunset Blvd, West Hollywood, 323-848-5100, www.hob. com; the restaurant's second floor overlooks the homey club below.
- **Jazz Bakery**, 3233 Helms Ave, Culver City, 310-271-9039, www.jazzbakery.org; a popular place to hear local and touring jazz acts.
- **The Room SM**, 1323 Santa Monica Blvd, Santa Monica, 310-458-0707; good R&B in a difficult-to-find spot.
- **Spazio Jazz Supper Club**, 14755 Ventura Blvd , Sherman Oaks, www.spazio.la; great food rivals the great music during their jazz brunch.
- **Vibrato Grill Jazz**, 2930 Beverly Glen Cir, Bel Air, 310-474-9400; upscale restaurant and bar lets you enjoy jazz artists by candlelight.
- **Zanzibar**, 1301 5th St, Santa Monica, 310-451-2221, www.zanzibarlive.com; Moroccan themed setting for Afro-Funke.

LATIN, BRAZILIAN, AND SPANISH CLUBS

- **El Floridita**, 1253 Vine St, Hollywood, 323-871-8612, www.elfloridita.com; Cuban music and food.
- **Café Sevilla & Nightclub**, 140 Pine Ave, Long Beach, 562-495-1111, www.cafe sevilla.com; regular flamenco and tango dinner shows.
- **Cha, Cha, Cha**, 7953 Santa Monica Blvd, West Hollywood, 323-848-7700, and 656 N Virgil Ave, Silverlake, 323-664-7723, www.theoriginalchachacha.com; Caribbean restaurant with a Latin beat.
- **Club Bahia**, 1130 W Sunset Blvd, 213-250-4313; crowds love to get sweaty to sultry Latin tunes here.

- **La Chavela**, 7230 Topanga Canyon Blvd, Canoga Park, 818-226-9911
- **La Masia**, 9077 Santa Monica Blvd, West Hollywood, 310-273-7066, a supper club featuring the cuisine of northeastern Spain, plus live salsa and merengue music.
- **Los Globos Nightclub**, 3040 W Sunset Blvd, 323-663-6517; get your salsa and reggeaton fix on weekends.
- **Rumba Room**, CityWalk, 1000 Universal Studios Blvd #208, Universal City, 818-622-1227, www.rumbaroom.com.
- **Sangria**, 68 Pier Ave, Hermosa Beach, 310-376-4412, www.sangriahermosa.com; flamenco and Latin jazz are regular offerings.
- **Temple Bar**, 1026 Wilshire Blvd, Santa Monica, 310-393-6611, www.temple barlive.com; hip Latin music scene on most Wednesdays.
- **Zabumba**, 10717 Venice Blvd, West LA, 310-841-6525, www.zabumba.com; for Brazilian food, music, and fun.

FREE CONCERTS

In addition to all of the above, there are often free concerts throughout the city, especially during the summer months. The city of Santa Monica sponsors the **Twilight Dance Series** on Thursday nights from 7:30 p.m. to 9:30 p.m., located at the Santa Monica Pier. Featured musicians include jazz, rock, blues, salsa, gospel, and international artists. For more information, call 310-458-8900 or go to www.twilightdance.org. Another seaside community, Long Beach, holds free **Sea Festival Twilight Concerts in the Park** during its annual Sea Festival, 562-434-1542, www.longbeachseafestival.com. The Valley Cultural Center offers **Summer Concerts in the Park** in Warner Park at Woodland Hills. Past performers include Air Supply, the LAPD Concert Band, and the San Fernando Valley Symphony. Go to www.valleycultural.org or call 818-704-1358 for details. Pasadena also offers annual summer concerts at the Levitt Pavilion; visit www.levittpavilionpasadena.org, or call 626-683-3230.

For a free concert series experience within an urban setting, head downtown to the California Plaza (at Grand Avenue and 4th Street). In between two high-rise towers is the Watercourt Stage, which is ringed by a water fountain. This is where free noon and evening concerts are staged by **Grand Performances** in the summer. This city-sponsored event brings in a wide range of musical entertainment, from jazz to big band to world music; consult their schedule for details at 213-687-2159 or go to www.grandperformances.org. Also, the **Pershing Square Summer Concert Series** runs one Sunday a month, from June to September. For more information, call 888-527-2757 or go to www.laparks.org. The **Los Angeles County Museum of Art** features a variety of free concerts, including Sundays Live, a chamber music series that performs 50 times a year, from 6 p.m. to 7 p.m., in a museum auditorium (and also simultaneously streamed live on LACMA's web site or delayed broadcast on 88.5 FM). For more information, call

323-857-6000 or visit www.sundayslive.org. If you're craving wine and jazz, you'll want to do the Hollywood & Highland Center's **Wine & Jazz Series**, in the central courtyard on Tuesday evenings from 7 p.m. to 9 p.m. starting in June, 323-467-6412, www.hollywoodandhighland.com. The music is free, and they offer wine tastings for a fee.

DANCE

One area of the arts that's a tad underrepresented in Los Angeles is the world of dance. Visiting companies like the Joffrey Ballet have largely overshadowed the smaller productions here. As young dancers make their way through local schools, the artistic directors are ever hopeful that a new rising star will help Los Angeles carve its own niche in the national dance scene.

Local **dance companies** include:

- **Festival Ballet Theater of Southern California**, 9527 Garfield Ave, Fountain Valley, 714.962.5440, http://festivalballet.org; performs a mix of classical and contemporary programs.
- **City Ballet of Los Angeles & School**, 1532 W 11th St, 323-292-1932, www.cityballetofla.org; just opened in 2000, this newcomer performs in different venues. Check their web site or the arts and entertainments guides listed above for upcoming performance information.
- **Joffrey Ballet**, 312-386-8905, www.joffrey.com; founded by Robert Joffrey and Gerald Arpino, the famous Chicago-based touring company makes annual, well-received stops in Los Angeles.
- **Lula Washington Dance Theater**, 3773 S Crenshaw Blvd, 323-292-5852, www.lulawashington.com; when the company moved to its new home in 2004 it became one of the few nonprofit modern dance companies to own and operate its own facility—just in time to celebrate its 25th anniversary in 2005. Founded by the internationally known choreographer Lula Washington and still run by her, the group has toured around the country. Performances include a variety of contemporary works.
- **Long Beach Ballet Arts Center**, 1122 E Wardlow Rd, Long Beach, 562-426-4112, www.longbeachballet.com; established in 1956, this institution has remained grounded in classical productions. Graduating students produce and perform a commencement program each summer; tickets are available to the public.
- **Pasadena Civic Ballet** (PCB), 253 N Vinedo Ave, Pasadena, 626-792-0873, www.pcballet.com; formed in 1980, the PCB is an organization of pre-professional dancers from ages 10 and up (its members start training as young as 3½ years of age). Every summer, the students put on a large-scale production; "It's a Small World" was a recent show.
- **Pasadena Dance Theatre Conservatory of Performing Arts**, 626-683-3459, www.pasadenadance.org; organizes modern and classical performances.

- **California Dance Theatre**, 5863 Kanan Rd, Agoura Hills, 818-707-3267, www. californiadancetheatre.com; home to three regional performing companies: Pacific Festival Ballet Company; Dazzle, a professional tap/jazz group; and The Dance Connection, a competition team.
- **Masterpiece Dance Theater**, 1365 Westwood Blvd, Westwood, 310-477-6414, www.balletla.com; base of the Vaganova Ballet Academy in Los Angeles, the only officially endorsed ballet school in North America authorized to instruct the Vaganova ballet curriculum. It produces "The Nutcracker" annually.

THEATER

Each week there are dozens of fine theatrical productions going on in Los Angeles. Check one of the weekly newspapers for a full listing.

PROFESSIONAL THEATER

Below are some of the larger and/or better-known theaters in the area.

- **Beverly Hills Playhouse**, 254 S Robertson Blvd, Beverly Hills, 310-855-1556, www.bhplayhouse.com
- **Carpenter Performing Arts Center**, 6200 Atherton St, Long Beach, 562-985-4274, www.carpenterarts.org
- **Falcon Theater**, 4252 Riverside Dr, Burbank, 818-955-8101, www.falconthe atre.com
- **Geffen Playhouse**, 10886 Le Conte Ave, Westwood, 310-208-5454, www.gef fenplayhouse.com; formerly the Westwood Playhouse, it was renamed after receiving a generous donation from entertainment mogul David Geffen.
- **Glendale Centre Theatre**, 324 N Orange St, Glendale, 818-244-8481, www. glendalecentretheatre.com
- **International City Theatre**, 300 E Ocean Blvd, Long Beach, 562-436-4610, www.ictlongbeach.org
- **Musical Theatre West**, 4350 E 7th St, Long Beach, 562-856-1999, www.musi cal.org
- **The Music Center** (Dorothy Chandler Pavilion, Mark Taper Forum, and Ahmanson Theatre), 135 N Grand Ave, 213-972-7211, www.musiccenter.org
- **Odyssey Theatre Ensemble**, 2055 S Sepulveda Blvd, West LA, 310-477-2055, www.odysseytheatre.com
- **Pantages Theatre**, 6233 Hollywood Blvd, Hollywood, 323-468-1700, www. broadwayla.org
- **The Pasadena Playhouse**, 39 S El Molino Ave, Pasadena, 626-356-7529, www. pasadenaplayhouse.org
- **Ricardo Montalbán Theatre**, 1615 N Vine St, Hollywood, 323-463-0089, www. ricardomontalbantheatre.org

- **Santa Monica Playhouse**, 1211 4th St, 310-394-9779, www.santamonicaplayhouse.com
- **Theatre/Theater**, 5041 Pico Blvd, 323-422-6361, www.theatretheater.net
- **East West Players David Henry Hwang Theater**, 120 N Judge John Aiso St, 213-625-7000, www.eastwestplayers.org
- **Long Beach Playhouse**, 5021 E Anaheim St, Long Beach, 562-494-1014, www.lbph.com
- **Will Geer Theatricum Botanicum**, 1419 N Topanga Canyon Blvd, Topanga Canyon, 310-455-2322, www.theatricum.com; features Shakespeare and more in a rustic, outdoor amphitheater.

COMMUNITY THEATER

In this city of actors, community theaters are everywhere, and often are quite good. Many theaters are clustered in Hollywood. Check out the LA Stage Alliance's web site, www.theatrela.org, or browse through one of the weekly newspapers for a complete list.

- **Actors' Gang at The Ivy Substation**, 9070 Venice Blvd, Culver City, 310-838-4264, www.theactorsgang.com
- **Actor's Forum Theatre**, 10655 Magnolia Blvd, North Hollywood, 818-506-0600, www.nohoartsdistrict.com
- **Celebration Theatre**, 7051 Santa Monica Blvd, 323-957-1884, www.celebrationtheatre.com
- **The Colony Theatre Company**, Burbank Town Center Mall, 501 N 3rd St, Burbank, 818-558-7000, www.colonytheatre.org
- **Downtown Playhouse**, 929 E 2nd St, Ste 105, 213-626-6906
- **Eclectic Theatre Company**, 5312 Laurel Canyon Blvd, North Hollywood, 818-508-3003, www.eclecticcompanytheatre.org
- **Hollywood Court Theater** in the Hollywood Methodist Church, 6817 Franklin Ave, Hollywood, 323-874-2104, www.hollywoodumc.org
- **Open Fist Theater Company**, 6209 Santa Monica Blvd, 323-882-6912, www.openfist.org
- **68 Cent Crew Theatre Company**, 5419 Sunset Blvd, Hollywood, 323-960-7827, http://68centcrew.com
- **Theatre of NOTE**, 1517 Cahuenga Blvd, Hollywood, 323-856-8611, www.theatreofnote.com

COMEDY

Famous comedians often "drop by" various clubs around LA to try out new material, so you never know when you might be in for a special treat. There are several popular comedy clubs in and around Los Angeles, including:

- **Acme Comedy Theater**, 135 N La Brea Blvd, 323-525-0202, www.acmecomedy.com
- **The Comedy & Magic Club**, 1018 Hermosa Ave, Hermosa Beach, 310-372-1193, www.comedyandmagicclub.com; Jay Leno is a frequent guest here.
- **Comedy Store**, 8433 Sunset Blvd, West Hollywood, 323-650-6268, www.thecomedystore.com
- **Conga Room**, www.congaroom.com; reopening in fall of 2008 by the Staples Center.
- **The Found Theatre**, 599 Long Beach Blvd, Long Beach, 562-433-3363, www.foundtheatre.org; bills itself as an alternative theatre.
- **Groundlings Theatre**, 7307 Melrose Ave, 323-934-4747, www.groundlings.com; this improvisational comedy troupe was the training ground for several "Saturday Night Live" veterans, such as Phil Hartman and Julia Sweeney.
- **Ice House**, 24 N Mentor Ave, Pasadena, 626-577-1894, www.icehousecomedy.com
- **The Improv**, 8162 Melrose Ave, 323-651-2583, http://improv2.com
- **iO West**, 6366 Hollywood Blvd, 323-962-7560, www.iowest.com
- **LA Connection Comedy Theatre**, 13442 Ventura Blvd, Sherman Oaks, 818-710-1320, www.laconnectioncomedy.com
- **Laugh Factory**, 8001 Sunset Blvd, Hollywood, 323-656-1336; www.laughfactory.com
- **Mixed Nuts Comedy Club**, 4000 W Washington Blvd, 323-735-6622, www.mixednutscomedy.com
- **Second City Studio Theater**, 6560 Hollywood Blvd, 323-464-8542, www.secondcity.com

MOVIE THEATERS

As one might expect, movies are a big deal in Los Angeles. Most feature flicks open here and in New York ahead of the rest of the country. You may be approached in front of theaters to attend market survey screenings, where you can watch a free movie in exchange for filling out a questionnaire at the end of the show. While the large multi-screen theaters are everywhere (the biggies are AMC, Mann, Loews, and Edwards/Regal/UA)—check the telephone directory or newspaper for the one nearest you—here are a few alternative theaters that feature foreign, classic, budget and/or art films.

- **American Cinematheque**, 6712 Hollywood Blvd, Hollywood, 323-466-3456, www.americancinematheque.com; screens alternative, classic, foreign, and art house movies at the Egyptian Theatre ($15 million was spent on renovating the Egyptian-themed 1920s landmark) and Aero Theatre, 1328 Montana Ave, Santa Monica.
- **ArcLight Cinema**, 6360 W Sunset Blvd, 323-464-1478, www.arclightcinemas.com; features 14 auditoriums and the Cinerama Dome (a unique, geodesic-

shaped theater that's the ultimate in giant movie screens), and all-reserved seating for a premium movie-going experience. They have a second location at 15301 Ventura Blvd, Sherman Oaks, 818-501-7033.

- **The Bridge Cinema De Luxe**, 6081 Center Dr, 310-568-3375, www.thebridge cinema.com; located inside the Promenade at Howard Hughes Center, this 16-screen complex houses a full-service restaurant, plus an IMAX screen, concierge services, and reserved seating (for an additional charge).
- **The CineFamily at the Silent Movie Theater**, 611 N Fairfax, Fairfax District, 323-655-2510, www.silentmovietheatre.com; the only movie house in the nation that features only "pre-talkies," accompanied by a live band.
- **Cinespia at the Hollywood Forever Cemetery**; 6000 Santa Monica Blvd, Hollywood, www.cemeteryscreenings.com; every summer starting in May, this group hosts creepy movie screenings on the cemetery grounds.
- **Fine Arts Theatre**, 8556 Wilshire Blvd, Beverly Hills, 310-360-0455, www.stu dioscreenings.com/FAT.html
- **Laemmle Theatres**: www.laemmle.com; Grande 4-Plex, 345 S Figueroa St, 213-617-0268; Regent Showcase, 614 La Brea Ave, Hollywood, 323-934-1770; Music Hall 3, 9036 Wilshire Blvd, Beverly Hills, 310-274-6869; Town Center 5, 17200 Ventura Blvd, Encino, 818-981-9811; Playhouse 7, 673 E Colorado Blvd, Pasadena, 626-844-6500; One Colorado, 42 Miller Alley, Pasadena, 626-744-1224; Monica 4, 1332 2nd St, Santa Monica, 310-394-9741; Sunset 5, 8000 Sunset Blvd, West Hollywood, 323-848-3500; Royal, 11523 Santa Monica Blvd, West LA, 310-477-5581
- **Landmark Theaters**: www.landmarktheaters.com; Rialto, 1023 S Fair Oaks, South Pasadena, 626-388-2122; Regent, 1045 Broxton Ave, 310-281-8223; Nuart, 11272 Santa Monica Blvd, West LA, 310-281-8223; Royal, 11523 Santa Monica Blvd, West LA, 310-477-5581; Westside Pavilion, 10850 W Pico Blvd, West LA, 310-470-0492
- **Levitt Pavilion at Memorial Park**, 85 E Holly St in Old Pasadena, 626-683-3230, www.levittpavilionpasadena.org or www.oldpasadena.org; the Old Pasadena Management District presents "Cinema in the Park," a free movie series that screens a classic every Saturday in May under the stars beginning at sunset (pick up your free ticket one week prior).

TELEVISION TAPINGS

Live-audience TV shows are mostly filmed during the week. Watching a sitcom taping is a guaranteed way to see a celebrity. Mementos from shows, such as T-shirts and autographed scripts, are sometimes given away to audience members. Be prepared to devote several hours to the taping and to clap on demand. If you would like to be an audience member at a live taping, write to the **LA Convention and Visitors Bureau**, 333 South Hope Street, LA, CA 90071, and enclose a self-addressed, stamped envelope. (For more information, contact them at 213-

624-7300 or go to www.discoverlosangeles.com.) Popular shows in particular are booked months in advance. Or you can go straight to the source: **Audiences Unlimited** is hired directly by the production companies to provide free tickets to people to attend tapings of their TV show, special, or game show, anything that requires a live audience. For listings, call 818-753-3470 or visit www.tvtickets. com. (They also have a seat-filler registration service for those who are interested in filling seats at various awards shows or special events.) A similar service is available through **Audience Associates**, 323-653-4105, www.tvtix.com, which does a lot of game show tapings. Or, contact the network studio that carries your favorite live-taped show directly: **CBS**, 323-575-2345, www.cbs.com; **NBC**, 818-840-3537, www.nbc.com; and for ABC shows, contact **Paramount Studios Guest Relations**, 323-956-1777. Tickets are free, but more tickets than seats are always issued, so arrive early.

MUSEUMS

If it can be exhibited, it's on display somewhere in the LA area. Many museums offer free admission once a month; contact the museum for the specific day. If you're up for a full day of exhibit-hopping you might want to head for what is known as "Museum Row," along Wilshire Boulevard running east from Fairfax. In these few blocks you'll find the Los Angeles County Museum of Art, Craft and Folk Art Museum, Petersen Automotive Museum, and the Page Museum at the La Brea Tar Pits. It could make for quite an interesting outing!

ART

- **Craft and Folk Art Museum**, 5814 Wilshire Blvd, Fairfax District, 323-937-4230, www.cafam.org; international and American folk art is featured here in the heart of "Museum Row." Free admission every first Wednesday of the month.
- **Geffen Contemporary at MOCA**, 152 N Central Ave, 213-626-6222, www.moca-la.org; this is one of three exhibit locations for MOCA..
- **Huntington Library**, **Art Collections**, **and Gardens**, 1151 Oxford Rd, Pasadena, 626-405-2141, www.huntington.org, features an extensive European art collection, a scholarly library, plus notable botanical gardens. Free admission the first Thursday of every month, but you must request free tickets from 800-838-3006 or via their web site.
- **J. Paul Getty Center**, 1200 Getty Center Dr, 310-440-7300, www.getty.edu; this $1 billion, 110-acre museum "campus" opened in 1997 and houses a vast and impressive collection of art and antiquities. European paintings and sculptures, drawings, decorative arts, and photographs are free to view, but parking is $8. Its sister property, **The Getty Villa,** 17985 Pacific Coast Hwy, Pacific Palisades, is located on the Malibu cliffs overlooking the Pacific Ocean,

the original site of the Getty Museum. After a nine-year closure and renovation, the Villa reopened in 2006; its focus is ancient Grecian and Roman art housed in a recreation of a Roman villa. Admission to both locations is free, but the Villa requires advance reservations.

- **Los Angeles Contemporary Exhibition (LACE)**, 6522 Hollywood Blvd, Hollywood, 323-957-1777, www.artleak.org, presents contemporary and experimental art in a variety of media.
- **Los Angeles County Museum of Art (LACMA)**, 5905 Wilshire Blvd, Fairfax District, 323-857-6000, www.lacma.org; houses everything from American and European art to photography to Southeast Asian art. It also has a fine film department featuring lectures and screenings. If a major traveling exhibition is coming to Los Angeles it will usually mount the show at LACMA. The **Broad Contemporary Art Museum (BCAM)**—just opened in early 2008 on the LACMA campus—features modern art. Free admission on the second Tuesday of each month, and after 5 p.m. on any day, you can pay what you wish.
- **Long Beach Museum of Art**, 2300 E Ocean Blvd, Long Beach, 562-439-2119, www.lbma.org; every Friday, admission is free.
- **Museum of African-American Art**, 4005 S Crenshaw Blvd, 3rd Fl, 323-294-7071; permanent and rotating exhibits by African-American artists, as well as seasonal events, performances, and lectures. Admission is free.
- **Museum of Contemporary Art (MOCA)**, 250 S Grand Ave, 213-621-2766, www.moca-la.org; permanent collection features painting, sculpture, live performances, and environmental work, all in a landmark building designed by Arata Isozaki. Free admission Thursdays from 5 p.m. to 8 p.m.
- **MOCA Pacific Design Center**, 8687 Melrose Ave, West Hollywood, 310-289-5223, www.moca-la.org; rotating architectural exhibits and other selections from MOCA's permanent collection.
- **Norton Simon Museum of Art**, 411 W Colorado Blvd, Pasadena, 626-449-6840, www.nortonsimon.org; recently renovated, houses a permanent collection of European art from the Renaissance to the mid-20th century.
- **Santa Monica Museum of Art**, Bergamot Station G1, 2525 Michigan Ave, 310-586-6488, www.smmoa.org; this small museum features changing contemporary exhibitions. An admission donation of $5 is encouraged.
- **Skirball Cultural Center**, 2701 N Sepulveda Blvd, 310-440-4500, www.skirball.org; features Jewish fine arts, archaeological artifacts, ceremonial and religious objects, photographs, and folk arts.
- **UCLA/Armand Hammer Museum of Art**, 10899 Wilshire Blvd, Westwood, 310-443-7000, www.hammer.ucla.edu; the permanent collection features more than five centuries' worth of Western European art.
- **Watts Towers**, 1727 E 107th St, Watts, 323-860-9964, www.wattstowers.org; though not a museum in the traditional sense, this monumental piece of folk art took artist Sam Rodia 33 years to complete. The towers are built of salvaged steel rods, dismantled pipes, bed frames and cement, and are covered with

bottle fragments, ceramic tiles, china plates, and more than 70,000 seashells. The adjacent Watts Towers Art Center hosts visual and performing art exhibits, poetry readings, and other events.

HISTORICAL, CULTURAL, AND SCIENCE MUSEUMS

- **Academy of Motion Picture Arts & Sciences**, 8949 Wilshire Blvd, Beverly Hills, 310-247-3600, www.oscars.org; film industry–related displays in their lobby and fourth floor gallery. Free admission.
- **Autry Museum of Western Heritage**, 4700 Western Heritage Way, Griffith Park, 323-667-2000, www.autry-museum.org; founded by famed movie cowboy Gene Autry, this museum houses a permanent collection of art and artifacts depicting the history of the American West. Admission is free on the second Tuesday of every month.
- **California African-American Museum**, 600 State Dr, 213-744-7432, www. caam.ca.gov; focuses on African-American achievements in science, politics, religion, athletics, and the arts. Admission is free.
- **California Heritage Museum**, 2612 Main St, Santa Monica, 310-392-8537, www.californiaheritagemuseum.org.
- **California Science Center**, 700 State Dr, 323-SCI-ENCE, www.casciencectr.org (formerly the California Museum of Science and Industry); free admission to over 100 interactive exhibits within four themed worlds that demonstrate real-life examples of science at work—the largest of its kind on the West Coast.
- **The Erotic Museum**, 6741 Hollywood Blvd. Hollywood, 323-463-7684, www. theeroticmuseum.com; new in 2003, this museum specializes in human sexuality as interpreted through history and art. The first of its kind on the West Coast. Only 18 and over admitted.
- **Fashion Institute of Design & Merchandising Gallery and Annette Green Perfume Museum**, 919 S Grand Ave, 213-236-1397, www.fashionmuseum.org; the perfume museum is the only one of its kind dedicated to olfactory science and culture; the FIDM gallery often showcases elaborate costumes from film and television. Free admission.
- **Fowler Museum at UCLA**, UCLA, Westwood, 310-825-4361, www.fowler.ucla. edu; admission is free, though UCLA campus-parking fees do apply.
- **Griffith Park Observatory**, 2800 E Observatory Road, Griffith Park, 213-473-0800, www.griffithobs.org; a $93-million-dollar renovation and expansion doubled the observatory's size—and there's also the Leonard Nimoy Event Horizon Theater and a café. Be sure to catch the planetarium show accompanied by live narration. Free admission, but there is a fee to see the planetarium show.
- **Heritage Square Museum**, 3800 Homer St, 323-225-2700, www.heritage square.org; eight Victorian-era homes let you see life at the end of the 19th

century. Open to the public on Friday, Saturday, and Sunday, and on most holiday Mondays; guided tours on weekends.

- **Hollywood Guinness World Records Museum**, 6764 Hollywood Blvd, 323-463-6433, www.guinnessattractions.com; showcases record-breaking achievements in entertainment and sports, plus historic human endeavors.
- **Hollywood Wax Museum**, 6767 Hollywood Blvd, Hollywood, 323-462-5991, www.hollywoodwax.com.
- **Japanese American National Museum**, 369 E First St, downtown, 213-625-0414, www.janm.org; this cultural center illustrates the history of Japanese immigration to the United States.
- **Los Angeles Natural History Museum**, 900 Exposition Blvd, 213-763-DINO, www.nhm.org. Free admission the first Tuesday of every month.
- **Los Angeles Fire Department Museum & Memorial**, 1355 N Cahuenga Blvd, Hollywood, 323-464-2727, www.lafdhs.com; 20,000 square feet of firefighting history is open on Saturdays to the public.
- **Museum of Flying**, 2772 Donald Douglas Loop, Santa Monica, 310-392-8822, www.museumofflying.com; new site under construction, scheduled to open in 2008.
- **Museum of Jurassic Technology**, 9341 Venice Blvd, Culver City, 310-836-6131, www.mjt.org; features "exhibits of idiosyncratic and curious things throughout the world."
- **Museum of Tolerance**, 9786 W Pico Blvd, Beverly Hills, 310-553-8043, www.museumoftolerance.com; features high-tech exhibits dedicated to the examination of racism and prejudice, with an exhibit devoted to reenacting the events leading up to the Holocaust. Some exhibits are not recommended for those under twelve. Advance reservations and a photo ID are needed for admission.
- **Pacific Asia Museum**, 46 N Los Robles Ave, Pasadena, 626-449-2742, www.pacificasiamuseum.org; the only museum in the Southwest dedicated to Asian and Pacific Islands art and culture. Free admission every fourth Friday of the month.
- **Page Museum at the La Brea Tar Pits**, 5801 Wilshire Blvd, Fairfax District, 323-934-PAGE, www.tarpits.org; features fossils from La Brea Tar Pits, and other paleontology exhibits. Admission is free the first Tuesday of every month.
- **The Paley Center for Media**, 465 N Beverly Dr, Beverly Hills, 310-786-1000, www.mtr.org. Ever wanted to hear Welles' infamous 1938 "War of the Worlds" broadcast? Or would you be tickled at viewing an old episode of "The Brady Bunch"? Then look no further—make a reservation at the front desk to utilize its screening/listening consoles. There are also daily screenings and radio presentations usually grouped around themes such as American Pop and Black History month. Free admission, but donations are accepted.

- **Petersen Automotive Museum**, 6060 Wilshire Blvd, Fairfax District, 323-930-CARS, www.petersen.org; where else, besides Detroit, would you expect to find a museum devoted to the automobile?
- **South Pasadena Historical Museum at the Meridian Iron Works**, 913 Meridian St, South Pasadena, 626-799-9089, www.sppreservation.org/museum-home.htm; South Pas history housed in a restored iron works building. Free admission.
- **Southwest Museum of the American Indian**, 234 Museum Dr, 323-221-2164, http://autrynationalcenter.org/southwest or www.swmfuture.org; Los Angeles' first museum, founded in 1907, it contains an important collection of Native American art and artifacts. Closed for renovation and scheduled to reopen in 2010.

LITERARY LIFE

The *LA Times* **Festival of Books** is the largest book festival in the country. Hundreds of publishers, specialty booksellers, and authors come to the UCLA campus for one weekend each April to speak, sell books, give readings and demonstrations, and offer to autograph copies of recent best sellers. For details about this free festival, go to www.latimes.com or call 213-237-6552.

BOOKSTORES

Chain bookstores, such as Barnes & Noble and Borders, and specialty stores such as Book Soup, host weekly readings and author signings, and organize book clubs to satisfy any bibliophile. Inquire with the stores or look at the Book Review section in the Sunday *LA Times* for listings.

CHAIN BOOKSTORES

- **Barnes & Noble** superstores, www.bn.com, offer vast selections of literary, reference, trade, and children's books, plus large selections of magazines and newspapers from around the world. They also host author readings and events—including an annual wine tasting—plus reading groups and workshops. Most locations have in-store cafés. A few Barnes & Noble stores are identified as Bookstar. Locations throughout the county; see the Yellow Pages or www.bn.com.
- **Borders Books & Music**; www.bordersstores.com; this national bookseller has many locations throughout LA as well. Offers a wide range of events from author readings to book groups to live music, all of which are free and open to the public. Check the Yellow Pages or www.borders.com for a location near you.

INDEPENDENT/SPECIAL INTEREST BOOKSTORES

If you're seeking a non-chain or specialty bookstore, try the following:

- **A Different Light Bookstore**, 8853 Santa Monica Blvd, 310-854-6601, www. adlbooks.com; specializes in gay and lesbian literature.
- **Autobooks/Aerobooks**, 3524 W Magnolia, Burbank, 818-845-0707, www.au tobooks-aerobooks.com; features aviation and automotive literature.
- **Berj Armenian Bookstore**, 422 S Central Ave, Glendale, 818-244-3830
- **Builders Book Inc. & Bookstore**, 8001 Canoga Ave, Woodland Hills, 818-887-7828, www.buildersbook.com
- **Book'Em Mysteries**, 1118 Mission, South Pasadena, 626-799-9600, www. bookem.com
- **Book Castle's Movie World**, 212 N San Fernando Blvd, Burbank, 818-845-1563, www.bookcastlesmovieworld.com
- **Book Soup**, 8818 Sunset Blvd, West Hollywood, 310-659-3110, www.book soup.com; boasts an unusual collection of fiction and nonfiction titles not normally found in mainstream stores, plus a large number of author readings and signings.
- **Children's Book World**, 10580 3/4 W Pico Blvd, West LA, 310-559-BOOK, www. childrensbookworld.com
- **China Modern Bookstore LA**, 8450 E Valley Blvd, #104, Rosemead, 626-288-3274, www.chinamodernbooks.com
- **Chevalier's Books**, 126 N Larchmont Blvd, 323-465-1334
- **Cook's Library**, 8373 W Third St, 323-655-3141, www.cookslibrary.com
- **Cook Books Janet Jarvits**, 1388 E Washington Blvd, Pasadena, 626-296-1638, www.cookbookjj.com
- **Distant Lands**, 56 S Raymond Ave, Pasadena, 626-449-3220, http://distant lands.com
- **Hennessey & Ingalls Art & Architecture Books**, 214 Wilshire Blvd, Santa Monica, 310-458-9074, www.hennesseyingalls.com
- **Medical Tech Book Center**, 8001 Canoga Ave, Woodland Hills, 818-347-7438, www.medicaltechbooks.com
- **The Mysterious Bookshop**, 8763 Beverly Blvd, 310-659-2959
- **Opamp Technical Books**, 1033 N Sycamore Ave, 800-468-4322, http://opamp. com
- **Russian Books**, 13757 Victory Blvd, Van Nuys, 818-781-7533
- **Samuel French's Theatre & Film Bookshops**, www.samuelfrench.com; 7623 Sunset Blvd, 323-876-0570; 11963 Ventura Blvd, Studio City, 818-762-0535
- **Shalom House Jewish Store**, 19740 Ventura Blvd, Woodland Hills, 818-704-7100, www.shalomhouse.com
- **Storyopolis Children's Bookstore**, 116 N Robertson Blvd, 310-358-2500, www.storyopolis.com

- **Taschen,** 354 N Beverly Dr, Beverly Hills, 310 274 4300, www.taschen.com; the US flagship store of the German publisher of the same name peddles its eclectic art and culture titles in this super-glossy store.
- **Traveler's Bookcase,** 8375 W Third St, 323-655-0575, www.travelbooks.com
- **Valley Book & Bible Stores,** 20936 Roscoe Blvd, Woodland Hills, 818-709-5610; 6502 Van Nuys Blvd, Van Nuys, 818-782-6101, www.vbb.com
- **Vroman's Bookstore,** 695 E Colorado Blvd, Pasadena, 626-449-5320, http://vromansbookstore.com; oldest and largest independent bookstore in Southern California.

USED BOOKS

The internet has made it possible for book collectors to conduct their own search for hard-to-find titles without ever leaving home. However, your local network of used and rare booksellers may have just what you need (and there is nothing quite like browsing through the old and rare titles of a used bookstore, often with a resident cat snoozing nearby in a sunlit corner). Check your Yellow Pages under "Books–Used & Rare" for a complete listing of local stores. Here are just a few:

- **Acres of Books,** 240 Long Beach Blvd, Long Beach, 562-437-6980, www.acresofbooks.com
- **Angel City Books,** 218 Pier Ave, Santa Monica, 310-399-8767, www.angelcitybooks.com
- **Bargain Books,** 14426 Friar, Van Nuys, 818-782-2782, www.bargainbooks-online.com
- **Bodhi Tree Bookstore,** 8585 Melrose Ave, West Hollywood, 310-659-1733, www.bodhitree.com
- **Books on the Boulevard,** 13551 Ventura Blvd, Sherman Oaks, 818-905-0988, www.booksontheblvd.com
- **Book Alley Fine & Old Books,** 1252 E. Colorado Blvd, Pasadena, 626-683-8083, www.bookalley.com
- **Book Castle's Movie World,** 212 N San Fernando Blvd, Burbank, 818-845-1563, www.bookcastlesmovieworld.com
- **Book City,** 818-731-9565, www.hollywoodbookcity.com; this internet-only store is dedicated to screenplays of your favorite movies.
- **Brand Bookshop,** 231 N Brand Blvd, Glendale, 818-243-4907, www.abebooks.com
- **Cliff's Books,** 630 E Colorado Blvd, Pasadena, 626-449-9541
- **Counterpoint Records & Books,** 5911 Franklin Ave, 323-957-7965, http://counterpointrecordsandbooks.com

- **Dave's Old Bookshop**, 350 N Sepulveda Blvd, Manhattan Beach, 310-376-0879
- **Heritage Book Shop**, 8540 Melrose Ave, West Hollywood, 310-659-3674
- **Iliad Bookshop**, 5400 Cahuenga Blvd, North Hollywood, 818-509-2665, http://iliadbooks.com
- **William Dailey Rare Books Ltd**, 8216 Melrose Ave, 323-658-8515, www.daileyrarebooks.com

UNIVERSITY BOOKSTORES/LIBRARIES

College bookstores, such as UCLA's and USC's, are another resource for general and specialized publications that are open to the public. As well, non-students can access libraries at many colleges and universities in the Los Angeles area. If you want to be able to check out books, but are not a student or alumnus, you may have to pay a fee. For more information, contact the following schools:

- **California State University Los Angeles**, 323-343-3000, http://calstate-la.bncollege.com
- **California State University Northridge**, 818-885-1200, www.csun.edu
- **Los Angeles City College**, 323-953-4000, www.lacitycollege.edu
- **Santa Monica College**, 310-450-5150, www.smc.edu
- **University of California Los Angeles**, 310-825-4321, www.uclastore.com
- **University of Southern California**, 213-740-0066, www.uscbookstore.com
- **West Los Angeles College**, 310-287-4200, www.wlac.edu

LIBRARIES

There are numerous **specialty libraries** in LA; some of those open to the public include:

- **Margaret Herrick Library at the Academy of Motion Pictures Arts & Sciences**, 310-247-3020, www.oscars.org/mhl
- **Frances-Henry Library of Hebrew Union College**, 213-749-3424, www.huc.edu
- **LA County Law Library**, 310-288-1269, http://lalaw.lib.ca.us
- **Norris Medical Library**, 323-442-1111, www.usc.edu/hsc/nml
- **University of Southern California**, 213-740-2311, www.usc.edu; houses several specialized subject libraries including architecture, education, philosophy, music, science, social work, and East Asian collections.

PUBLIC LIBRARIES

City and county libraries offer a wealth of free to low-cost community services such as lectures, health and wellness programs, crafts workshops for adults or children, teen activities, computer and internet access and classes, movie rentals, book sales and clubs, storytelling, readings, and, of course, books. Los Angeles County and the City of Los Angeles operate separately, although a resident of the City of LA may use both systems; an application will need to be filled out for each library card.

Call 213-228-7272 or visit the **City of LA Public Library's** web site, www.lapl.org, to investigate the locations of more than 60 branch libraries and to find out about upcoming community events. Their catalog is viewable directly from their web site.

The **LA County Public Library** system can be reached via www.colapublib.org, or call 562-940-8415 for assistance with locating a community branch near you. To view the entire catalog of library holdings of LA County Library, go to http://catalog.colapl.org.

Orange County's library system, which consists of 34 branches, can be contacted by phone by calling 714-566-3000, or go to www.ocpl.org; to search its database, go to http://orca.ocpl.org.

You can also check the listings at the end of the **Neighborhood Profiles** for a branch library near you. Or visit one of these main libraries:

- **Los Angeles Central Library**, 630 W 5th St, 213-228-7000, www.lapl.org/central; at the heart of this towering, multistoried library (and old, built in 1926) is a vast collection of books, magazines, audio/video tapes, and databases. Populated with unique architecture, murals, statues, fountains, and an eight-story atrium, the library offers hour-long public tours throughout the year. The Los Angeles Public Library is accessed by local residents, as well as by libraries and other organizations from across the USA. Their public computer center has 63 stations.

Flagship libraries in Orange County include:

- **Anaheim Central Library**, 500 W Broadway, Anaheim; 714-765-1880, www.anaheim.net
- **Huntington Beach Central Library**, 7111 Talbert Ave, Huntington Beach; 714-842-4481, www.hbpl.org

CULTURE FOR KIDS

Children can keep busy year round in Los Angeles. Options range from visiting a working farm to participation in a youth chorus to viewing a children's theater production. In addition to the museums below, most of the "adult" museums listed in this chapter organize workshops and activities geared for kids. Contact the museums for more information.

MUSEUMS

- **The Bunny Museum**, 1933 Jefferson Dr, Pasadena, 626-798-8848, www. thebunnymuseum.com; view a collection of over 23,000 plush bunnies in a private home—by appointment only. Free admission, but they accept plush bunny donations and cash donations to their selected charity.
- **California Science Center**, 700 State Dr, 323-SCI-ENCE, www.casciencectr.org; see description above.
- **Discovery Science Center**, 2500 N Main St, Santa Ana, 714.542.2823, www.dis coverycube.org; science demonstrations and a 4-D theater in a cube-shaped building.
- **Kidspace Museum**, 480 N Arroyo Blvd, Pasadena, 626-449-9144, www.kid spacemuseum.org; participatory museum with exhibits scaled for kids 12 and under.
- **LA Children's Museum**, Administrative Offices, 205 S Broadway, Ste 608, 213-687-8800, www.childrensmuseumla.org; the downtown museum closed in 2000 and is moving to the Hansen Dam Recreation Area, where a new facility is being built. Construction has been completed, and when this 60,000-square-foot building opens, it will include indoor and outdoor exhibit space, a café, playground, and a performing arts theater. Visit its web site for updates.
- **Museum of Flying**, www.museumofflying.com; new site under construction, scheduled to open in mid to late 2009 at the Santa Monica Airport..
- **Travel Town Museum** in Griffith Park, 5200 Zoo Dr, 323-662-5874, www. laparks.org; the "railroad petting zoo" has free admission but a nominal fee for the popular miniature train ride.
- **Zimmer Children's Museum**, 6505 Wilshire Blvd, Ste 100, 323-761-8989, www. zimmermuseum.org; a 10,000-square-foot museum located in The Goldsmith Jewish Federation Center. Open to the public

PLAY/DISCOVERY FACILITIES

- **AdventurePlex**, Manhattan Beach, 310-546-7708, www.AdventurePlex.org; a health and fitness center designed especially for kids, with an outdoor climbing wall, gymnasium and fitness center, challenging mazes, tunnels, and slides.
- **Creative Kids**, West LA, 310-473-6090, www.mycreativekids.com; offers classes in cooking, dancing, music, and art to keep kids 14 and under busy year round. Free trial classes offered. Also hosts birthday and slumber parties.
- **Creative Leap**, Northridge, 818-366-3036, www.creativeleap.biz; in addition to the expected play structures, there are yoga classes, a video game arcade, and a dinosaur room equipped with a fossilized climbing wall in a prehistoric setting.
- **Gymboree Play and Music Center**, www.gymboreeclasses.com, 310-338-8030; Sherman Oaks, 818-905-6225; Northridge, 818-349-8814; South Pasadena,

626-445-1122; Burbank, 818-955-8964; padded, colorful playgrounds for youngsters, and music classes for kids 4 and younger. Sessions run 10 weeks.

- **Joey's Gym for Children**, Beverly Hills, 310-855-0146, www.joeysgym. com, is popular for birthday bookings; in addition to its fantastic play space, it will provide balloons, banners, streamers, tables, benches, and music for parties.
- **Kid Concepts, USA**, Torrance, 310-465-0075, www.kidconceptsusa.com; giant play structures, arts and crafts classes, toddler area, rock climbing, and a restaurant. Memberships available.
- **The Playroom**, 14392 Ventura Blvd, Sherman Oaks, 818-784-7529, www.the playroomvalley.com; indoor playground and event venue.
- **Under the Sea Indoor Playground**, www.undertheseaindoorplayground. com; Altadena, 323-782-3852; Culver City, 310-915-1133; Beverly Hills, 323-782-3852; Burbank, 818-567-4944; Manhattan Beach, 310-379-2600; Northridge, 818-772-7003; Woodland Hills, 818-999-1533; popular for theme parties for 14-year-olds and younger.
- **Wondernation**, 3625 N Sepulveda Blvd, Manhattan Beach, 310-545-4550; music and dance classes in a "discovery and enrichment studio."

OUTDOOR

- **Cirque du Soleil**, 800-678-5440, www.cirquedusoleil.com; this funky Montreal circus-like-no-other pitches its colorful tents at the Staples Center parking lot when in town.
- **The Farm**, 8101 Tampa Ave, Reseda, 818-341-6805; an animal farm with pony rides. Open weekends.
- **Forneris Farms**, 15200 Rinaldi St, Mission Hills, 818-730-7709, www.forneris farms.com; the farm is open year round, with an annual harvest festival and corn maze in the fall.
- **Family Fun Days**, Theatricum Botanicum, 1419 N Topanga Canyon Blvd, Topanga, 310-455-3723, www.theatricum.com; summer series featuring popular, kid-friendly musical guests and plays.
- **Griffith Park** offers pony and wagon rides, a miniature train, and an old-fashioned carousel—enough to take up a full day.
- **Long Beach Aquarium of the Pacific**, Shoreline Drive and Aquarium Way, Long Beach, 562-590-3100, www.aquariumofthepacific.org; situated across from the Queen Mary, the aquarium shows off over 10,000 fish in 17 habitat tanks.
- **Los Angeles Zoo**, Griffith Park, 323-644-4200, www.lazoo.org, is a modest-sized zoo with a petting area that recently received a bond for expansion.
- **Moorpark College Teaching Zoo**, 7075 Campus Rd, Moorpark, http://www. moorparkcollege.edu; open on weekends.

- **Summer Sounds: Music for Kids at the Hollywood Bowl**, Hollywood Bowl Plaza, Highland Ave, Hollywood, 323-850-2000, www.hollywoodbowl.org; a summer series of arts and crafts workshops for kids. Fees vary.
- **Pierce College Animal Farm**, 6201 Winnetka Ave, Woodland Hills, 818-710-4253, www.lapc.cc.ca.us; a working farm that hosts a FarmWalk once a year.
- **Ringling Bros Barnum & Bailey Circus**, www.ringling.com; the famous traveling circus makes the rounds from the LA Sports Arena to the Great Western Forum during select weekends in the summer. Visit its web site for specific dates.
- **San Diego Wild Animal Park**, 15500 San Pasqual Valley Rd, Escondido, 760-747-8702, www.sandiegozoo.org, is a little like going on a safari, over 400 species roam together on 1,800 acres that visitors can see primarily by monorail.
- **San Diego Zoo**, 2920 Zoo Dr, San Diego, 619-234-3153, www.sandiegozoo.org; over 100 acres are devoted to the care and exhibition of animals for conservation, research, and education at this world-class zoo.
- **Santa Monica Pier Aquarium**, 1600 Ocean Front Walk, Santa Monica, www.healthebay.org/smpa; small educational exhibits tucked under the Carousel building.
- **Star Eco Station Environmental Science Museum & Exotic Wildlife Rescue Facility**, 10101 W Jefferson Blvd, Culver City, 310-842-8060, www.ecostation.org; open to the public year round on weekends.
- **Underwood Family Farms**, 3370 Sunset Valley Rd, Moorpark, 805-529-3690; animal farm with pony rides and pick-your-own vegetables.
- **Universal City Walk**, 1000 Universal Center Dr, 818-622-3801, www.citywalkhollywood.com; while this outdoor mall is popular with adults, it's the pulsing, interactive water fountain that kids can't resist. Free admission, but there is a fee for parking.
- **William S. Hart Park**, 24151 N San Fernando Rd, Newhall, 661-259-0855, www.hartmuseum.org; in addition to a Western-themed museum, inside the park is a barnyard animal-feeding area for kids. Don't miss the herd of American bison.

THEATER FOR KIDS

The following theaters perform regularly to the delight of young audiences:

- **Bob Baker Marionette Theater**, 1345 W First St, 213-250-9995, www.bobbakermarionettes.com; the oldest of its kind in the USA, with an impressive collection of over 3,000 puppets.
- **Burbank Little Theater**, 1100 Clark Ave, Burbank, 818-238-9998; performs children's stories and fairy tales such as "Treasure Island" and "Peter Pan"; the audience is encouraged to supply the sound effects.

- **Comedy Pups**, 4397 Tujunga Ave, Studio City, 818-769-3622; stand-up comedians as young as six perform their funny antics for free at Jennifer's Coffee Connection.
- **Comedy Sportz Los Angeles**, 733 N Seward St, 323-871-1193, www.comedy sportzla.com; their Comedy Sportz Kidz interactive shows are performed the first Saturday of every month.
- **LA Connection Comedy Theatre**, 13442 Ventura Blvd, Sherman Oaks, 818-710-1320, www.laconnectioncomedy.com; offers a "Comedy Improv for Kids" program, call for more information.
- **Limecat Family Theatre @ ZJU**, 4850 Lankershim Blvd, North Hollywood, 818-202-4120, http://limecat.homestead.com; high-energy children's performances.
- **Occidental Children's Theater**, 1600 Campus Rd, Eagle Rock, 323-259-2771, www.oxy.edu
- **Puppet & Magic Center**, 1014 Broadway, Santa Monica, 310 656-0483, www.puppetmagic.com; musical variety shows and home to a museum of more than 400 puppets, marionettes and ventriloquist figures.
- **Santa Monica Playhouse**, 1211 Fourth St, 310-394-9779, www.santamonica playhouse.com; regular family-oriented performances by the Playhouse Actors' Repertory Theater Company and the Young Professionals' Company.

OTHER

- **American Youth Symphony**, 310-451-3400, www.aysymphony.org
- **Los Angeles Children's Chorus**, 626-793-4231, www.lachildrenschorus.org
- **San Fernando Valley Youth Chorus**, 818-895-7071, www.valleyyouthchorus.org
- **Toyota Symphonies for Youth**, 213-972-0704, www.laphil.org

AMUSEMENT PARKS

The Los Angeles area is home to several amusement parks, including the granddaddy of them all, Disneyland. To avoid sticker-shock, you might want to call ahead to find out the various parks' admission and parking prices, which can be steep. The biggies include:

- **Disneyland and Disneyland's California Adventure**, 714-781-4565, www.disneyland.com
- **Hurricane Harbor**, 661-255-4100, www.sixflags.com
- **Knott's Berry Farm**, 714-220-5200, www.knotts.com
- **Legoland**, 760-918-5346, www.legoland.com
- **Raging Waters**, 909-802-2200, www.ragingwaters.com
- **Santa Monica Pier**, 310-458-8900, www.santamonicapier.org
- **Six Flags Magic Mountain**, 661-255-4111, www.sixflags.com
- **Universal Studios Tour**, 818-508-9600, www.universalstudios.com

THE EXCELLENT YEAR-ROUND WEATHER IN LOS ANGELES MAKES IT A great place for those interested in watching or playing professional athletics. With professional teams that include an indoor football team, two baseball teams, two basketball teams, and an ice hockey team, and a powerhouse of college athletics, sports fans can keep very busy here. LA teams have bragging rights to the World Series, NBA Championships (three in a row), and the Rose Bowl, to name a few. The venues in which champs are made are equally top-notch. The slick and glossy Staples Center boasts a $1.5-million-dollar sound system, two floors of luxury box suites, and excellent sight lines, making it the best and most popular sports venue in LA. The Home Depot Center in Carson, opened in 2003, sprawls over 85 acres. This complex of Olympian proportions features two world-class stadiums (one dedicated to soccer and tennis only) and track and cycling fields.

Fans keep tabs on their favorite teams through the extensive sports sections of the *LA Times* or *Daily News*. Radio stations KSPN 710AM, KLAC 570AM, and KAVL 610AM are devoted to sports and more sports. All local television news broadcasts regularly set aside the last five to ten minutes of airtime for sports reporting. Fox Sports Net's Southern California Sports Report broadcasts every night from its studio in the Staples Center. The **LA Sports Council**, www.lasports. org, responsible for wooing major sporting events to town, has information about local sports venues and most importantly a detailed calendar of sporting events.

Possibilities for the fitness minded are vast, including a good selection of public tennis courts, soccer fields, city-run recreation centers, and loads of membership gyms. Also notable here is the world's largest public golf course system, the world's first disc golf course, and, for dedicated runners, Los Angeles hosts one of the largest marathons.

Clubs or leagues revolving around a particular sport are often the best place to start when seeking information about events, tournaments, and opportunities to join in. Sometimes the local sporting goods store will have a bulletin board that you can check for postings by sports leagues or even informal pick-up games. And for kids, parents of sporty tykes often refer to *Los Angeles Family*, www.familymagazinegroup.com, a free monthly magazine that lists child-friendly venues for baseball, swimming, summer camps, even yoga.

PROFESSIONAL SPORTS

Several ticket agencies handle professional games and venues in the Los Angeles area. Ticketmaster is the standard and official vendor, but if price is no object, other agencies may be worth checking into, after the box office and Ticketmaster are sold out. (Sometimes tickets are auctioned off at eBay, www.ebay.com or StubHub, www.stubhub.com.) When purchasing from a ticket agency or online at the venue's box office, expect to pay a convenience charge.

- **Ticketmaster**, 213-480-3232 or 866-448-7849, www.ticketmaster.com
- **Barry's Tickets**, 888-749-8499, www.barrystickets.com
- **VIP Tickets**, 888-474-9490, www.viptickets.com

BASEBALL

Baseball season runs from April through October.

- **The Los Angeles Angels of Anaheim** play at **Angel Stadium of Anaheim** (lovingly called "The Big A") in Orange County. Once under Disney ownership, the Angels had only sporadic success. Then they shocked the world with their game seven win in the 2002 World Series. Fans today wave the rally monkey to cheer on manager Mike Scioscia and rightfielder Vladimir Guerrero as they attempt to repeat the Angels miracle. For ticket information, call 888-796-4256 or go to http://losangeles.angels.mlb.com.
- The **Los Angeles Dodgers** play at **Dodger Stadium** in Chavez Ravine. The Dodgers last won the World Series in 1988 under the leadership of famous manager, eater, and dieter Tommy Lasorda. Just as Fernando Valenzuela's pitching success in the early 1980s drew a new crowd of fans to the park, pitching sensation Hideo Nomo from Japan produced what was locally known as "Nomomania" in the early 1990s. Fans today have high hopes for their boys in blue, led by new-for-2008 manager Joe Torre. Game day tickets for adults range from $11 to $130, giving Dodger games the moniker of "the cheapest ticket in town." For ticket information, call 866-DODGERS or go to http://los angeles.dodgers.mlb.com.

- For minor league baseball, the nearest teams are the **Lancaster Jethawks**, 661-726-5400, www.jethawks.com, at Clear Channel Stadium; the **Lake Elsinore Storm**, 909-245-4487, www.stormbaseball.com, at The Diamond in Lake Elsinore; the **Inland Empire 66'ers** (formerly the San Bernardino Stampede), 909-888-9922, www.ie66ers.com, at the Arrowhead Credit Union Park; and the **Rancho Cucamonga Quakes**, 909-481-5252, www.rcquakes.com, at The Epicenter.

BASKETBALL

Basketball season picks up after baseball, and runs from October through April.

- Since 1999, the **Los Angeles Clippers** (season seats, 888-895-8662, www.nba.com/clippers) have called the **Staples Center** home. In this town, used to the Lakers glory days of Magic Johnson, Kareem Abdul Jabbar, and Shaquille O'Neal, the Clippers are often treated like poor second cousins. A 2004 increase in ticket prices to fund stronger free agents paid off in the 2004–05 season when they had a better record than the Lakers for the first time since1993. For ticket information, call www.ticketmaster.com, or the Staples Center, 213-742-7340, www.staplescenter.com.
- The **Los Angeles Lakers** (season seats, 800-4-NBA-TIXS, www.nba.com/lakers) have likewise nested in the Staples Center. After their failed bid to win a fourth NBA Championship in 2004 under head coach Phil Jackson, the team underwent a rapid and major exodus of players, including veteran players Shaquille O'Neal and Gary Payton; even coach Jackson packed his bags. Since coach Jackson's return in 2005, high hopes have also returned to fans for the team, still led by star Kobe Bryant, culminating in their second place finish in the 2008 season. For ticket information call Ticketmaster, 213-480-3232, www.ticketmaster.com, or the Staples Center, 213-742-7340, www.staplescenter.com.
- The local WNBA team, the **Los Angeles Sparks** (tickets, 877-44-SPARKS, www.wnba.com/sparks) also plays in the Staples Center, feasible because the women's season coincides with the men's off-season. Founded in 1997, the Sparks excited fans by becoming back-to-back WNBA champions in 2001 and 2002. Although they haven't gained a league championship since 2002, they do feature the amazing Lisa Leslie, who in 2004 received both the WNBA's Defensive Player of the Year and Most Valuable Player awards.

FOOTBALL

Purists have been pining for an NFL team franchise since the Los Angeles Rams played their last professional NFL game here in 1994, and many football fans turn to local college football to satisfy their football fix. But in 2000 the **Arena**

Football League's Los Angeles Avengers kicked off their inaugural season. While not exactly what NFL fans were hoping for, some football fans were placated, especially when the Avengers won a division title in 2005. A fast-moving alternative to regulation football, arena football is played on an indoor field that is half the size of what NFL teams play on, resulting in a higher scoring game. The Avengers (for season tickets, call 888-AVENGERS or go to www.laavengers. com) play at the Staples Center from April to July. For ticket information, call Ticketmaster, 213-480-3232, www.ticketmaster.com, or the Staples Center, 213-742-7340, www.staplescenter.com.

HOCKEY

- The **Los Angeles Kings** (season seats, 888-KINGS-LA, http://kings.nhl.com) also play at the Staples Center. Ice hockey season begins in November and ends in March but playoffs can extend the season for several months. Indeed, in 1993, the Kings made it to the Stanley Cup finals in June. "The Great One," Wayne Gretzky, popularized hockey here in a city that only sees ice or snow on television. For ticket information, call Ticketmaster, 213-480-3232, www.ticket master.com, or the Staples Center, 213-742-7340, www.staplescenter.com.

HORSE RACING

There are three racetracks in the Los Angeles area:

- **Hollywood Park**, Inglewood, 310-419-1574, www.hollywoodpark.com; races are run April through July, and November through December.
- **Los Angeles County Fairgrounds**, 909-623-3111, www.fairplex.com; races are held at the fair each September.
- **Santa Anita Park**, Arcadia, 626-574-RACE, www.santaanita.com; races are run October through November, and then December through April.

SOCCER

- Major League Soccer's (MLS) **LA Galaxy** is one of ten US Division One franchise start-up teams that date back to 1996. Over five seasons, head coach Sigi Schmid guided his team to three titles, winning the 2002 MLS Cup Championship, the 2001 US Open Cup Championship, and the 2000 CONCACAF Champions' Cup. Retired Galaxy player Paul Caligiuri was inducted into the Hall of Fame in 2004. Shake-ups in 2007 saw the arrival of super hot David Beckham and replacement of Schmid with Ruud Gullit, and even more trades for 2008 are expected to shore up this perennial contender. The LA Galaxy play at the **Home Depot Center** in Carson (www.homedepotcenter.com). Call 877-3-GALAXY, http://la.galaxy.mlsnet.com, for tickets. The season runs April through September.

- **Club Deportivo Chivas USA** was founded in 2004 and coached by Preki. The Chivas share the Home Depot Center (www.homedepotcenter.com) with the Galaxy. Since this young team won the 2007 MLS western conference champion title, many eyes are trained on this club. Call 877-CHIVAS-1 or visit http://chivas.usa.mlsnet.com for tickets.

TENNIS

The local major men's tennis event is the **Countrywide Classic** (www.country wideclassic.com) which is played in July at the Los Angeles Tennis Center at UCLA. For professional women's tennis, at this point you might want to travel to Indian Wells, near Palm Springs, for the Pacific Life Open Tennis Tournament (men and women) in March. For more information on either of the tournaments, contact the local **United States Tennis Association** office at 310-208-3838, www.usta. com.

X-GAMES

Los Angeles has been the host to the Summer X-Games every August since 2003. Extreme athlete stars perform skateboarding tricks, Big Air BMX, and freestyle Moto X riding…to put it simply for the uninitiated, incredible daredevil type stunts. Venues vary from the Home Depot Center to Staples Center. Los Angeles will remain the host of the Summer X-Games through 2009. For more information, visit www.expn.com

COLLEGE SPORTS

In Los Angeles, college games are plentiful and dependable. Many college sports enthusiasts find living here a heavenly experience, as the local schools consistently boast some of the nation's finest athletes and teams.

UCLA's basketball program is legendary, producing such stars as Kareem Abdul-Jabbar (then Lou Alcindor), Gail Goodrich, Jamaal (then Keith) Wilkes, Bill Walton, Marcus Johnson, Ann Meyers (sister of Dave), Reggie Miller, and Ed O'Bannon. The football program is no slouch either, with former players Troy Aikman and Ken Norton on the roster, and the home field being none other than the Rose Bowl.

Likewise **USC** football can usually be described as nothing short of a powerhouse, energized in the past by the likes of Mike Garrett, Charles White, Marcus

Allen, Ricky Bell, Ronnie Lott, Junior Seau, and yes, O.J. Simpson. Cheryl Miller, one of the greatest female basketball players ever, also was a Trojan.

Other local college sports programs of note are baseball at **Cal State Fullerton, Pepperdine's** tennis and water polo, **Loyola Marymount** for basketball, **Long Beach State's** basketball, UCLA's volleyball, gymnastics, softball, and water polo, and USC's water polo.

For **athletic ticket information,** call the following numbers:

- **Cal State Fullerton,** 714-278-2783, www.fullerton.edu
- **Loyola Marymount,** 310-338-LION, www.lmu.edu
- **Long Beach State,** 562-985-4949, www.csulb.edu
- **Pepperdine,** 866-WAVE-TIX, www.pepperdine.edu
- **UCLA,** 310-UCLA-WIN, www.ucla.edu
- **USC,** 213-740-4672, www.usc.edu

PARTICIPANT SPORTS AND ACTIVITIES

PARKS AND RECREATION DEPARTMENTS

The **County of Los Angeles Department of Parks and Recreation,** 213-738-2961 or www.lacountyparks.org, oversees an incredible 63,000 acres of parks, gardens, lakes, trails, natural areas, and the world's largest public golf course system. In addition, the City of LA runs many recreation programs and supervises the use of its city pools, greenspaces, and urban forests. Contact the **City of LA Department of Recreation and Parks** at 888-LAPARKS, www.laparks.org. Both organizations offer extensive information on park facilities, leagues, clubs, and lessons on their web sites. Additional city park departments include:

- **Azusa Recreation and Parks Department**, 626-812-5215, www.ci.azusa. ca.us
- **Beverly Hills Recreation and Parks Department**, 310-285-2537, www.bev erlyhills.org
- **Burbank Parks and Recreation Department**, 818-238-5300, www.ci.burbank. ca.us
- **Calabasas Recreation and Parks Department**, 818-878-4225, www.cityof calabasas.com
- **Carson Recreation and Parks Department**, 310-847-3570, www.ci.carson. ca.us
- **Cerritos Recreation and Parks Department**, 562-916-1254, www.ci.cerritos. ca.us
- **Culver City Recreation Department**, 310-253-6470, www.culvercity.org
- **El Segundo Recreation and Parks Department**, 310-524-2700, www.else gundo.org

- **Glendale Parks Recreation Department**, 818-548-2000, www.ci.glendale.ca.us
- **Long Beach Department of Parks, Recreation and Marine**, 562-570-3100, www.ci.long-beach.ca.us
- **Malibu Parks and Recreation Department**, 310-317-1364, www.ci.malibu.ca.us
- **Manhattan Beach Recreation Department**, 310-802-5448, www.ci.manhattan-beach.ca.us
- **Monterey Park Recreation and Parks Department**, 626-307-1388, www.ci.monterey-park.ca.us
- **Pasadena Parks and Recreation Department**, 626-744-7275, www.ci.pasadena.ca.us
- **Santa Monica Recreation Division**, 310-458-8311, www.ci.santa-monica.ca.us
- **Santa Clarita Parks and Recreation Department**, 661-255-4910, www.santa-clarita.com
- **West Hollywood Recreation Department**, 310-848-6308, www.weho.org

BASEBALL/SOFTBALL

Many of the numerous baseball and softball leagues throughout Los Angeles are organized through the workplace. There is, for instance, an advertising league and a law league. For more information, ask your colleagues, call your department of parks and recreation, or contact the **US Amateur Baseball Association**, 425-776-7130, www.usaba.com. If you've got money to burn and a dream to fulfill, sign up for the **Dodgers Adult Baseball Camp**, 800-334-7529, www.ladabc.com. The month-long camp provides pro-level baseball practice and coaching by the LA Dodgers staff and ex-players like Steve Garvey to anyone...with $4,595.

BASKETBALL

Pick-up basketball games are available all over the city, with competition ranging from friendly to fierce. Particularly renowned is the busy pick-up basketball scene at Venice's Boardwalk. While it may seem like this is the spot with the best and flashiest players in town, there are good games to be found all over, from schoolyards to city parks. The John Wooden Center's indoor courts at UCLA, 310-206-8308, www.recreation.ucla.edu, are where the "big names" show up, and it's not uncommon for hot college players, former professionals, or even a current pro to drop by for a game of pick-up. Check out www.socalhoops.com for the latest leads. Here is a sampling of neighborhood parks and recreation centers with basketball courts:

- **Balboa Sports Center**, Burbank and Balboa blvds, Encino, 818-756-9642
- **Roxbury Park**, S Roxbury Dr and Olympic Blvd, Beverly Hills, 310-550-4761
- **Reed Park**, Wilshire and Lincoln blvds, Santa Monica, 310-458-8974
- **Santa Clarita Sports Complex**, 20870 Centre Pointe Pkwy, Santa Clarita, 661-250-3710
- **Victory-Vineland Recreation Center**, Victory Blvd and Vineland Ave, North Hollywood, 818-985-9516
- **Venice Beach Recreation Center**, Ocean Front Walk and Winward Ave, Venice, 310-399-2775
- **West Hollywood Park**, N San Vicente and Santa Monica blvds, West Hollywood, 323-848-6534
- **Westwood Recreation Center**, S Sepulveda and Wilshire blvds, Westwood, 310-473-3610

BICYCLING

Both tour bicycling and mountain biking are popular in Los Angeles. The most traveled bike path is the **coastal bike path** from **Pacific Palisades** in the north to **Torrance** in the south. On weekends, the path resembles a bicycling and skating freeway. If you don't own a bike, rentals are available at several shacks on the beach in Marina del Rey, Venice, and Santa Monica. Other popular trails include the **Ballona Creek Trail** and the **Pasadena bike trail**. Mountain bikers enjoy the challenging trails in the **Santa Monica Mountains**, including Sullivan Canyon along (and through) the creek bed, the **Malibu Canyon trails**, **Topanga State Park**, 310-455-2465, and **Sycamore Canyon**. For more information about area routes, call **Bike Metro** at 858-486-3015; their web site www.bikemetro.com can suggest a bike route if you enter your starting and ending destination. The site www.labikepaths.com is an excellent resource for bike enthusiasts, and includes an extensive list of trails and paths.

A detailed list of local **bicycling groups** can be found at www.bikecal.com, they include:

- **The Los Angeles Wheelmen**, 310-556-7967, www.lawheelmen.org
- **The Los Angeles County Bicycle Coalition** (LACBC), 213-629-2142, www.la bike.org; a membership-based advocacy organization that works to improve the bicycling environment and quality of life in Los Angeles County. They also organize the annual Los Angeles River Ride in June.

For bicycling equipment and other information, check with the following cycling retailers and local bike tour operator:

- **Bikecology**: 9006 W Pico Blvd, Beverly Hills, 310-278-0915; 29211 Heathercliff Rd, Malibu, 310-589-2048, www.cycledesignbike.com

- **Helen's Cycles:** 1570 Rosecrans Ave, Manhattan Beach, 310-643-9140; 2472 Lincoln Blvd, Marina del Rey, 310-306-7843; 2501 Broadway, Santa Monica, 310-829-1836; 1071 Gayley Ave, Westwood, 310-208-8988; 142 East Huntington Dr, Arcadia, 626-447-3181; www.helenscycles.com
- **Hollywood Pro Bicycles**, 6733 Hollywood Blvd, Hollywood, 323-466-5890, www.hollywoodprobicycles.com

BILLIARDS/POOL

Pool possibilities, though somewhat limited in Los Angeles, run the gamut from lone tables in the middle of seedy bars, to old-fashioned billiard halls, to the trendy pool halls where pagers are handed out to those waiting for a pool table. You may be able to find a table or two at many bowling places. But here are a few dedicated venues for you to sample:

- **Fantasia Billiards**, 133 N San Fernando Blvd, Burbank, 818-848-6718
- **House of Billiards**, 1901 Wilshire Blvd, Santa Monica, 310-828-2120
- **Hollywood Billiards**, 5750 Hollywood Blvd, 323-465-0115, www.hollywood billiards.com
- **Jillian's Billiards**, Universal City Walk, 1000 Universal Studios Blvd, Universal City, 818-985-8234, www.jilliansbilliards.com
- **Mr. Pockets Sports Bar**, 516 N Sepulveda Blvd, Manhattan Beach, 310-372-4343, www.mrpockets.com
- **Q's Billiard Club & Restaurant**, 11835 Wilshire Blvd, Brentwood, 310-477-7550; 99 East Colorado Blvd, Pasadena, 626-405-9777; www.qsbilliards.com
- **Stick & Stein Eatery and Sports Parlor**, 707 Sepulveda Blvd, El Segundo, 310-414-9283
- **Yankee Doodles**, 1410 Third Street Promenade, Santa Monica, 310-394-4632; 21870 Victory Blvd, Woodland Hills, 818-883-3030, www.yankeedoodles.com; 4100 Ocean Blvd, Long Beach, 562-439-9777, www.yankeedoodleslongbeach. com

BOATING/SAILING/WINDSURFING

Marina del Rey is the spot for most boating and water sport activity in the Santa Monica Bay. The **United States Sailing Center**, once dedicated to training sailors for the Olympics but now open to all enthusiasts, is at 5489 East Ocean Boulevard, Long Beach, 562-433-7939, www.ussclb.org. They host regular youth and teen sailing camps as well as adult clinics and large regattas.

The **South Bay Yacht Racing Club**, also in Marina del Rey at 310-822-0776, www.sbyrc.org, and the **Women's Sailing Association of Santa Monica Bay**, 310-397-8585, www.wsasmb.org, are some clubs you can get involved in. The

Marina del Rey's Convention and Visitors Bureau web site, www.visitthemarina.com, has a list of boating/sailing clubs. **Redondo Beach's** King Harbor, and **Long Beach's** downtown marina, 562-570-1815, are also busy with private sailboats, speedboats, jet-craft, and plain old yachts. In addition, many companies offer sailing lessons and rentals out of the marinas. Novices seeking basic sailing lessons should inquire with the City of Los Angeles, Recreation and Parks Department's **Aquatics Division**, 323-906-7953, www.laparks.org/dos/aquatic/aquatic.htm.

Not all water sports companies are located near a marina, so check your Yellow Pages under "Boat Renting & Leasing" for a complete list. Here are just a few:

- **Blue Pacific Boating**, 14000 Palawan Way, Suite C, Marina del Rey, 310-398-8830, www.bluepacificboating.com
- **Bluewater Sailing**, 13505 Bali Way, Marina del Rey, 310-823-5545, www.bluewatersailing.com
- **FantaSea Yachts & Yacht Club**, 4215 Admiralty Way, Marina del Rey, 310-827-2220, www.fantaseayachts.com
- **Gondola D'Amore**, slip D-3713 (Basin D and Panay Way), Marina del Rey, 310-736-7301, www.gondoladamore.com
- **Marina Boat Rentals**, 13719 Fiji Way, Fisherman's Village, 310-574-2822
- **Offshore Water Sports**, 128 E Shoreline Village Dr, Long Beach, 562-436-1996, www.owsrentals.com
- **Pacific Sailing**, 419 Shoreline Village, Long Beach, 562-590-0323, www.pacificsailing.net
- **Rent-A-Sail**, 13719 Fiji Way, Marina del Rey, 310-822-1868
- **UCLA Marina Aquatic Center (MAC)**, 14001 Fiji Way, Fisherman's Village, 310-305-1587, http://marinaaquaticcenter.org

BOWLING

AMF operates a chain of bowling facilities in Southern California. Call 800-BOWL-AMF or go to www.amf.com to locate the one nearest you. Contact the **Los Angeles Bowling Association**, 818-784-3352, or the **North Los Angeles County Bowling Association**, 818-718-0193, www.nlacbowling.com, for more information about leagues. Area bowling lanes include:

- **Allstar Lanes**, 4459 Eagle Rock Blvd, 323-254-2579, www.allstarlanes.net
- **Bahama Lanes**, 3545 E Foothill Blvd, Pasadena, 626-351-8858, www.amf.com
- **Bay Shore Bowl**, 234 Pico Blvd, Santa Monica, 310-399-7731, www.amf.com
- **Canoga Park Bowl**, 20122 Vanowen St, Woodland Hills, 818-340-5190, www.canogaparkbowl.com
- **Jewel City Bowl**, 135 S Glendale Ave, Glendale, 818-243-1188, http://jewelcitybowl.com

- **Jillian's High Life Lanes Universal City Walk**, 1000 Universal Way, Universal City, 818-985-8234, www.jilliansbilliards.com
- **Lucky Strike Lanes**, 6801 Hollywood Blvd, Hollywood, 323-467-7776, www.bowlluckystrike.com
- **Mar Vista Bowl**, 12125 Venice Blvd, West LA, 310-391-5288, www.amf.com
- **Pickwick Bowling Center**, 1001 Riverside Dr, Burbank, 818-846-0035, www.pickwickgardens.com
- **Pinz Bowling Center**, 12655 Ventura Blvd, Studio City, 818-769-7600, www.pinzbowlingcenter.com
- **Santa Clarita Lanes**, 21615 Soledad Canyon Rd, Saugus, 661-254-0540, www.santaclaritalanes.com
- **Woodlake Bowl**, 23130 Ventura Blvd, Woodland Hills, 818-225-7181, www.amf.com

CHESS

The **Southern California Chess Federation** (**SCCF**) is the affiliate organization recognized by the US Chess Federation, www.uschess.org. Inquire about membership, local tournaments, and club activities at www.scchess.com. The **Los Angeles Chess Club** is another chess resource: www.lachessclub.com.

It is not uncommon to find informal groups that meet for casual play. Chess tables are available daily from sunup to sundown at the **Santa Monica International Chess Park**, which is on the promenade just south of the Santa Monica pier. Players gather for casual chess, blitz, and occasional summer tournaments.

Some "pick-up games" require a little sleuthing to locate. Many Starbucks serve as informal hosts to players on weekends. The unspoken rule is that players buy a cup or two of coffee while playing to compensate the establishment for the use of its tables. Here's a listing of just some local establishments that are known to welcome chess players. Call for specific dates and times and bring your own equipment.

- **Glendale**: Java City Café, 134 N Brand Ave, 818-956-3925; Glendale Chess Park, 227 N Brand Blvd, www.ci.glendale.ca.us
- **Long Beach:** the chess room in Bixby Park Community Center, 130 Cherry Ave, 562-570-1601; when this room closes, players gather for casual play at Golden Burger, 2301 E 4th St, 562-434-2625.
- **Los Angeles:** The Exposition Park Public Library, 3665 S Vermont Ave, 323-732-0169, is the Exposition Park Chess Club's turf. Go to http://chess.expoparkla.com to find out more. The Baldwin Hills Public Library at 2906 S La Brea Ave (323-733-1196) hosts another group. Tang's Donuts, 4341 W Sunset Blvd, 323-662-4085, hosts casual and speed chess players, mostly on weekends.

- **North Hollywood**: North Hollywood Public Library, 5211 Tujunga Ave, 818-766-7185; mainly for students in grades K–12, but all ages are welcome. Sundays.
- **Pasadena**: Pasadena Senior Center, 85 E Holly St, 626-795-4331, hosts the Pasadena Chess Club on Friday nights. This is one of the oldest So Cal clubs.
- **Santa Clarita**: the California Youth Chess League, 661-288-1705, www.cycl. org; call for open play locations.
- **Santa Monica**: St. Andrew's Lutheran Church, Nolte Hall, 11555 National Blvd, 310-827-2789; where the Santa Monica Bay Chess Club meets Monday evenings.
- **West Hills**: the West Valley Jewish Community Center at 22622 Vanowen St, 818-464-3300, hosts the West Valley Chess Club on Thursdays. It is one of the largest local clubs. All are welcome.

FISHING

If you are over 16 years of age, you must purchase a fishing license ($32.80 for freshwater, and an additional $2.65 for saltwater) good through December 31. Fishing licenses may be purchased from any bait and tackle shop; see your Yellow Pages under "Fishing Tackle Dealers" for locations. Sport fishing enthusiasts should inquire at such shops for information on fishing charters. The **California State Fish and Game Department**, located in Long Beach, 562-590-5187, www. dfg.ca.gov, can provide more information on local fishing laws. A reduced fee and free fishing licenses are available to those who meet age and income or disability criteria. There are also two free fishing dates a year where a license is not required to fish; dates are announced on their web site, but they usually occur in June and September. They've also implemented a Fishing in the City program to teach urban dwellers the joy of fishing; go to www.dfg.ca.gov/fishinginthecity/la or call 562-342-7148 for more information and for details about annual fishing events.

Popular saltwater fishing spots are off the many piers in the Westside, particularly the Santa Monica Pier. For freshwater fishing, Castaic Lake is one of the most popular spots. It is just north of Santa Clarita at 32100 North Ridge Route Road in Castaic. Call 661-257-4050 or visit www.castaiclake.com for more information.

FRISBEE

An impromptu game of Frisbee can be had in any open field, especially the larger parks like Will Rogers State Park in the Pacific Palisades or Sepulveda Basin Recreation Area in Van Nuys. Contact area parks and recreation departments for information about Frisbee clubs or groups. Ultimate Frisbee is popular at many area colleges; the **Los Angeles Organization of Ultimate Teams**, www.laout. org, also provides information about pick-up games as well as team and league play. The **Southern California Disc Golf Association**, www.socaldiscgolf.org, organizes many tournaments in the area. For disc golf, many head to Pasadena to the challenging Oak Grove Park Disc Golf Course, the world's first. Call 626-797-1114 or visit www.ogdgc.org for specifics. Another good course can be found in Long Beach's El Dorado Park, 562-570-1773, www.longbeach.gov.

GOLF

There are more than 100 **public golf courses** in the greater Los Angeles area. The City of Los Angeles operates seven 18-hole courses, five 9-hole courses, and a junior golf learning center called the Tregnan Golf Academy. For information, call the golf reservation office 818-291-9980, or visit www.laparks.org/dos/sports/golf.htm. Los Angeles County operates 17 courses; for information, call 213-738-2961, or visit www.lacountyparks.org.

Other popular spots include, but are not limited to:

- **Eaton Canyon Golf Course**, 1150 N Sierra Madre Villa Ave, Pasadena, 626-794-6773; 30-year-old, 2,900-yard, nine-hole layout featuring two par fives
- **Wilson (Griffith Park) Golf Course**, 4730 Crystal Springs Dr, Los Angeles, 323-664-2555; two 18-hole courses, practice bunker, and lit driving range
- **Armand Hammer Pitch and Putt Golf Course**, 601 Club View Dr, Westwood, 310-276-1604; 18-hole pony golf course, three-par
- **Malibu Country Club Golf Course**, 901 Encinal Canyon Rd, Malibu, 818-889-6680, www.malibucountryclub.net; 18-hole course
- **Penmar Municipal Golf Course**, 1233 Rose Ave, Venice, 310-396-6228; nine-hole course
- **Rancho Park 18-Hole Golf Course**, 10460 Pico Blvd, West LA, 310-838-7373; billed as one of the busiest golf courses in the country; features an 18-hole course plus a par three nine-hole pitch-n-putt
- **Roosevelt Golf Course**, 2650 N Vermont Ave in LA, 323-665-2011; nine-hole course
- **Scholl Canyon Golf and Tennis Club**, 3800 East Glenoaks Blvd, Glendale, 818-243-4100
- **Sepulveda Basin Recreational Area**, Burbank and Balboa blvds, Encino, 310-989-8060; there are two 18-hole golf courses at this 60-acre wildlife refuge

HIKING

The **Santa Monica** and **San Gabriel mountains** provide miles of varied hiking trails. The Santa Monica Mountains Conservatory operates a web site that contains a hiking event calendar, www.lamountains.com. The following are local state parks offering **hiking trails**:

- **Coldwater Canyon Park**, 818-766-8445, www.laparks.org; located along the southern slope of the Santa Monica Mountains, five-plus miles of hiking trails
- **Elysian Park**, 213-485-5054, www.laparks.org; located in Echo Park; over 10 miles of hiking trails, winding through forested hills and lush valleys
- **Griffith Park**, 323-913-4688, www.lacity.org/RAP/dos/parks/griffithPK/index. htm; located above Hollywood, vast park with 35 miles of trails
- **Malibu Creek State Park**, 310-880-0350, www.parks.ca.gov; more than 15 miles of hiking trails weaving through a mostly undeveloped area—a true retreat to unspoiled nature
- **Santa Monica Mountains National Recreation Area**, 818-597-1036, http:// smmc.ca.gov; the Santa Monica Mountains stretch almost 50 miles across Los Angeles. The range is host to the **Will Rogers State Historic Park**, 310-454-8212, www.parks.ca.gov (includes the 31-room former ranch home of actor, humorist, and columnist Will Rogers and the miles of trails behind his house). Most of the trails in the Santa Monica Mountains are part of, or hook up to, the Backbone Trail (so named for its knobby resemblance to the human spine). Spanning 70 miles from Point Mugu State Park to Will Rogers State Historic Park, the Backbone Trail runs along the crest of the Santa Monica Mountains.
- **Temescal Gateway Park**, 310-454-1395, http://smmc.ca.gov, 20-acre park in Pacific Palisades includes a trail that travels north over 12 miles to the Backbone Trail
- **Topanga State Park**, 310-455-2465, www.parks.ca.gov; 10,000-acre park that offers 32 miles of hiking

Use of city, state, and federal trails is free, although there may be a parking fee. Also, be aware that state budget cuts may result in some park closures, so call before planning your trip. There are about 330 miles of country-side trails in Los Angeles (see www.parks.ca.gov, www.lacountyparks.org, and www.laparks.org for more information), including **Frank G. Bonnell Regional Park Trail** in San Dimas; **Schabarum Trail**, from Whittier to Rowland Heights; **Colby Dalton Trail** in Glendora; **Altadena Crest Trail**, Altadena; **La Canada Open Space Trail**, La Canada Flintridge; **Los Angeles River Trail**, from Downey to Long Beach; **Devil's Punchbowl Nature Trail** in Antelope Valley; **Los Pinetos Trail**, Sylmar; **Coastal Slope Trail**, Malibu; and **Eaton Canyon Park Trail** in Pasadena. (For an informative guide to local hiking and biking trails, check the **Los Angeles Reading List** at the end of this book.)

HIKING/WALKING CLUBS AND PROGRAMS

Local hiking resources include:

- **William O. Douglas Outdoor Classroom,** Sooky Goldman Nature Center, Beverly Hills, 310-858-7272; organizes hiking and picnics
- **Desert & Mountain Conservation Authority**, Santa Clarita, 661-945-2604, http://dmca.ca.gov
- **Children's Nature Institute**, Santa Monica, 310-860-9484; offers walks throughout LA geared to parents and children
- **Placerita Canyon Nature Center**, Newhall, 661-259-7721, www.placerita.org; organizes Saturday hikes
- **Santa Monica Mountains Recreational Area,** Thousand Oaks, 805-370-2301, www.nps.gov/samo; numerous outdoor programs
- **Sierra Club**, Los Angeles headquarters, 213-387-4287, http://angeles.sierra club.org; many join their organized evening hikes through Griffith Park and other locales
- **Trail Runners Club,** Pacific Palisades, www.trailrunnersclub.com
- **Will Rogers State Historical Park,** Pacific Palisades, 310-454-8212, www.parks. ca.gov; nature walks for adults and families on weekends

HORSEBACK RIDING

There are no city- or county-sponsored programs for horse riding and lessons. Several private stables that offer horseback riding rentals, lessons, and/or boarding include:

- **Altadena Stables,** Altadena, 626-797-2012
- **Griffith Park Horse Rentals,** Burbank, 818-840-8401, www.griffithparkhorses. com
- **Circle K Riding Stables**, Glendale, 818-843-9890/818-242-8443; trails in Griffith Park
- **Los Angeles Equestrian Center,** Burbank, 818-840-9063, http://la-equestrian center.com
- **Los Angeles Horseback Riding**, Topanga Canyon, 818-591-2032, www.los angeleshorsebackriding.com
- **Malibu Riding and Tennis Club,** Malibu, 310-457-9783
- **Mill Creek Equestrian Center,** Topanga, 310-455-1116, www.millcreekequest riancenter.com
- **Sunset Ranch Hollywood Stables**, Hollywood, 323-469-5450, www.sun setranchhollywood.com; offers moonlight rides through Hollywood Hills and Griffith Park

ICE SKATING

If ice skating is your sport, try one of the following rinks for public skating or lessons:

- **Culver City Ice Arena**, 4545 Sepulveda Blvd, 310-398-5718, www.culverice arena.com
- **Ice'O Plex**, 8345 Hayvenhurst Pl, North Hills, 818-893-1784, www.iceoplex. com
- **Iceland Ice Skating Rink**, 14318 Calvert St, Van Nuys, 818-785-2171, www.van nuysiceland.com
- **Paramount Iceland Skating Rink**, 8041 Jackson St, Paramount, 562-633-1171, www.paramounticeland.com
- **Pasadena Ice Skating Center**, 310 E Green St, 626-578-0800, www.skatepasa dena.com
- **Pickwick Ice Arena**, 1001 Riverside Dr, Burbank, 818-845-5300, www.pick wickgardens.com

IN-LINE/ROLLER SKATING

The parks and beaches of Los Angeles are bustling with in-line and roller skaters. Rentals can be found at several shacks along the coastal path of Marina del Rey, Venice, and Santa Monica. (Pedestrians beware, bicyclists and skaters turn the bike path into a fast-moving freeway on weekends.) Santa Clarita operates a **Skate & Bike Park**, 20850 Center Pointe Parkway, 661-250-3710, that offers challenging paved runs for skateboarders, skaters, and bicyclists. For a unique experience, join the **Friday Night Skate**, 310-57-SKATE, www.fridaynightskate. org, a loosely knit group of bladers who get together Friday of every month. The effect is a roving 10-mile, traffic-stopping, three-hour-long, noisy party on wheels in Santa Monica (and Hollywood once a month).

Pleasant year-round weather keeps the offering of **indoor skating rinks** to a minimum. The ones that remain are listed below:

- **World on Wheels**, 4645 1/2 Venice Blvd, 323-933-5170, http://wowsk8.com
- **Moonlight Rollerway**, 5110 San Fernando Rd, Glendale, 818-241-3630, www. moonlightrollerway.com
- **Northridge Skateland**, 18140 Parthenia St, Northridge, 818-885-7655, www. skateland.net
- **Robinson Park**, 1081 N Fair Oaks Ave, Pasadena, 626-744-7330, www.ci. pasadena.ca.us

PADDLE TENNIS

Those aren't kiddie-sized tennis courts you see dotting the beaches along the bike path, they're paddle tennis courts. Similar to tennis, paddle tennis is played on a smaller court with deadened tennis balls and with paddles rather than rackets. You can try your talent for this unique game at one of the following spots:

- **Culver City Paddle Tennis Park**, 310-202-5689; three courts at the corner of Culver Blvd and Elenda Ave, and two courts at Culver West Park, 4162 Wade St
- **Marina Del Rey's Glen-Alla Park**, 310-305-9550; three paddle tennis courts at 4601 Alla Rd
- **Santa Monica**, 310-294-6011; two paddle tennis courts located just off the beach in Ocean View Park
- **Venice Recreational Center**, 310-399-2775; eleven paddle tennis courts located on the beach
- **Wilson Park Sports Center**, 310-328-4964, two courts at 2400 Jefferson St, Torrance, www.ci.torrance.ca.us

ROCK CLIMBING

Climbing enthusiasts head out of the city for the big rocks of **Stoney Point** in Chatsworth's Stoney Point Park, www.laparks.org. Being such a quick drive from LA, Stoney Point is particularly crowded on summer weekends. **Vasquez Rocks Natural Area Park**, in Agua Dulce, 805-268-0840, www.lacountyparks.org, and Joshua Tree Rock Climbing School in **Joshua Tree National Park**, 800-890-4745, www.nps.gov/jotr, are also popular. The **California State University Northridge** (CSUN) Leisure Studies Department, 818 677-3202, offers mountain climbing training information. For alternatives, check with your local health club to see if they offer a rock-climbing wall or try one of the following indoor climbing centers:

- **Beach City Rocks**, 4926 W Rosecrans Ave, Hawthorne, 310-973-3388, www.beachcityrocks.com
- **Rockreation Sport Climbing Center**, 11866 La Grange Ave, 310-207-7199, www.rockreation.com
- **Rock Gym**, 2599 E Willow St, Long Beach, 562-981-3200, www.therockgym.com

RUNNING

The miles-long beaches of the Pacific coast provide beautiful settings for runners. Another popular Westside running spot is the median park strip on **San Vicente Boulevard**, starting in Brentwood and continuing through Santa Monica to the cliffs above the ocean. In the Hollywood area, the path around the **Hollywood Reservoir** (also known as Lake Hollywood) is popular with runners.

Some Santa Monica runners like to include in their loop a strenuous staircase that runs from the end of 4th Street, north of San Vicente Boulevard, and leads into Santa Monica Canyon. In fact, many people bike or drive over to this spot, just to tread up and down these 200 steep steps, known as the **4th Street Stairs**. Aside from a beautiful ocean vista and a good workout, the stairs also provide an active social scene, particularly on weekends when it gets downright crowded. But if you want to give the steps a try, watch your manners; climbers don't appreciate perfume or cologne wearing, which interferes with their huffing and puffing, and be sure not to mess with the stones and other markers at the top and bottom of the steps, which help exercisers keep track of how many flights they have completed.

Each March, the **Los Angeles Marathon** gathers more than 24,000 competitors. The course route, reworked most recently in 2007 to include more of the city, starts in Universal City and finishes downtown. For more information, call 310-444-5544 or go to www.lamarathon.com. For novice runners who have never accomplished a marathon or active runners who want to train with a group, consider the official training group for the marathon, the **LA Roadrunners**, 909-364-8533, www.laroadrunners.com. They schedule training runs and guest speakers; registration fees start at $155. The **LA Leggers**, 310-577-8000, www.laleggers.org, has a one-year membership training/preparation program for the marathon that starts at $55, fees increase the later in the season you join.

Another popular running club (for gays, lesbians, and friends of) is the **Los Angeles Frontrunners**, 323-460-2554, www.lafrontrunners.com.

SCUBA DIVING

Many private scuba schools as well as local parks departments offer scuba instruction. While the diving in the **Santa Monica Bay** doesn't provide the greatest visibility, day trips to **Catalina Island** and the **Channel Islands** near Santa Barbara offer clear waters and exhilarating outings. For those particularly interested in diving with marine mammals like seals and sea lions, the California coast is the place.

LA County's Parks and Recreation Department **Underwater Unit**, 310-965-8258, www.lascuba.com, offers scuba certification and classes in scuba air snorkeling classes, basic and advanced scuba diving, and underwater instructor certification. Started in 1954, it was the first in the country to create a recreational scuba diving certification course.

Here are a few of the many private dive shops/schools in the area; check your telephone directory under "Diving Instruction" for others:

- **Action Water Sports**, 4144 Lincoln Blvd, Marina Del Rey, 310-827-2233, www.actionwatersports.com
- **Aqua Adventures Unlimited**, 2120 W Magnolia Blvd. Burbank, 818-848-2163, http://aquaadventuresunlimited.com
- **Eco Dive Center**, 4027 Sepulveda Blvd, Culver City, 310-398-5759, www.ecodivecenter.com
- **Hollywood Divers**, 3575 Cahuenga Blvd W #104, Hollywood, 323-969-9800, www.hollywoodivers.com
- **Malibu Divers**, 21231 Pacific Coast Hwy, Malibu, 310-456-2396, www.malibudivers.com
- **Reef Seekers**, 8612 Wilshire Blvd, Beverly Hills, 310-652-4990, www.reefseekers.com
- **Sea d Sea**, 1911 S Catalina Ave, Redondo Beach, 310-373-6355, www.seadsea.com

SKATEBOARDING

One of the joys for skateboarders is that Los Angeles is often host to the annual X Games, a professional competition for extreme sports of which skateboarding is one of the biggest draws. When not admiring their skateboarding heroes, many looking to perfect their ollie or bluntside grind head to the following:

- **Glendale-Verdugo Skateboard Park**, 21 Canada Blvd, Glendale, 818-548-6420, www.glendaleskatepark.com
- **Hollenbeck Skate Park** at 415 S St Louis St, Boyle Heights, 323-261-0113, www.laparks.org
- **Santa Clarita Skate & Bike Park**, 20850 Center Pointe Pkwy, 661-250-3710; offers a 75-foot snake run, a double bowl and other challenging runs
- **Torrance Skate Board Park**, 2200 Crenshaw Blvd, Torrance, 310-328-6069
- **Whittier Skateboard Park** at 7630 Washington Ave, 562-464-3430, www.whittierch.org

Inquire at these skate parks about monthly competitions. For more information about skateboarding in LA, go to www.socalskateparks.com.

SOCCER

Soccer is a popular sport in Los Angeles. The City of LA organizes a multitude of adult soccer leagues for men and women of varying skill levels, for more information call 818-246-5613 or visit www.laparks.org. **Balboa Park Soccer Field** at 17015 Burbank Boulevard in Encino is a busy site for organized matches between multi-ethnic club teams, as is the **John Ferraro Soccer Complex** on Zoo Drive in Griffith Park. Check your phone directory under "Soccer Clubs" for more information. For youth soccer, check with your local parks and recreation program or contact the **American Youth Soccer Organization**, 800-USA-AYSO, http://soccer.org, for a soccer league in your area or check with Major League Soccer's LA Galaxy, which offers many programs for LA youth (see above under **Professional Sports**).

SURFING

Beach culture and surfing go hand in hand in Southern California. All along the southern Pacific coastline there are beaches and coves where surfing reigns supreme. For information on where to surf, contact LA County's **Department of Beaches and Harbors** at 310-305-9503, http://beaches.co.la.ca.us; in Orange County, contact the **Department of Harbors, Beaches, and Parks** at 866-OCPARKS, www.ocparks.com. To learn how to surf, one option is trial by fire; head to Malibu for an afternoon to watch the veterans, then grab a board and give it a try. (Keep in mind that the locals can be territorial, and newcomers aren't always welcome.) If you have a buddy who already surfs, you might be better off letting him or her show you the ropes.

Before you head out, here are the numbers to call for **surfing conditions**, or visit www.surfline.com or www.watchthewater.org for surf reports, live beach cams, and more:

- **Central Section**, 310-485-0478
- **Northern Section**, 310-457-9701
- **San Pedro-Cabrillo Beach Section**, 310-832-1130
- **Southern Section**, 310-379-8471

SWIMMING—POOLS

Aside from that big outdoor pool called the Pacific Ocean, there are several places you can go to swim in Los Angeles. Contact the **LA Aquatics Division**: 323-906-7953 or visit www.laparks.org for a complete listing of county pools and links to local clubs. Many **YMCAs** offer use of their pool for a fee, as do several city-run parks and recreation facilities, including those listed below. All are open year round.

- **Amateur Athletic Foundation (AAF) Rose Bowl Aquatics Center** (outdoor pool and heated therapy pool), 360 N Arroyo Blvd, Pasadena, 626-564-0330, www.rosebowlaquatics.com
- **Echo Park Indoor Pool** (one indoor Olympic sized, one outdoor shallow), 1419 Colton St, Echo Park, 213-481-2640
- **Fremont Pool** (indoor), 7630 Towne Ave, 213-847-3401

- **Glassell Park Pool**, 3704 Verdugo Rd, 323-226-1670
- **Celes King III/Rancho Cienega Pool** (indoor), 5001 Rodeo Rd, 213-847-3406
- **LA84 Foundation/John C. Argue Swim Stadium** (outdoor family pool and competition pool), 3990 S Menlo Ave, 213-763-0129, www.laparks.org/expo/aquaticcenter.htm
- **The Plunge/Urho Saari Swim Stadium**, 219 West Mariposa Ave, El Segundo, 310-524-2738
- **Eleanor G. Roberts Pool** (indoor), 4526 W Pico Blvd, 323-936-8483
- **Roosevelt Pool** (Olympic sized, outdoor), 456 S Matthews, 323-485-7391
- **Santa Clarita Aquatic Center** (outdoor), 20850 Centre Pointe Parkway, 661-250-3700
- **Van Nuys-Sherman Oaks Pool**, 14201 Huston St, Van Nuys, 818-783-6721
- **Venice High School Pool** (indoor), 2490 Walgrove Ave, Venice, 310-575-8260
- **Westwood Pool**, 1350 Sepulveda Blvd, Westwood, 310-478-7019

The **Southern California Aquatic Swim Club**, 310-390-5700, www.swim.net/scaq will help you get your feet wet for recreational swimming. If you're more of a competitive swimmer, there's the Southern Pacific section of United States Swimming, Synchronized Swimming, and Water Polo to try out for, go to www.colasharks.com for prerequisites and more information. For more about local swim clubs, check bulletin board postings at any of the pools listed above. (See **Greenspace and Beaches** chapter for information about area beaches.)

TENNIS/RACQUET SPORTS

Public outdoor tennis and racquetball courts are scattered throughout the city and are open year round. Some courts require a small fee to make a court reservation (these pay-to-play courts are often in better condition than other public courts). The City of LA offers a list of free tennis parks (many of which also have racquetball courts) at www.laparks.org.

For more resources, including information about local clubs, upcoming events, and assistance locating a court, contact the **Southern California Tennis Association**, 310-208-3838, www.scta.usta.com, or **California State Racquetball Association**, 714-966-9329, www.californiaracquetball.org.

The following **tennis parks** charge by the hour (the charge is higher for nonresidents):

- **Billie Jean King Tennis Center**, 1040 Park Ave, Long Beach, 562-438-8509, www.longbeachtennis.com
- **El Dorado Park Tennis Center**, 2800 Studebaker Rd, Long Beach, 562-425-0553, www.longbeachtennis.com
- **Echo Park**, 213-250-3578, Echo Park; six courts
- **La Cienega Park**, 310-550-4765, Beverly Hills; 16 courts

- **Lincoln Park,** 310-394-6011, Santa Monica; six courts
- **Plummer Park,** 323-848-6471, West Hollywood; six courts
- **Riverside Courts,** 323-661-5318, Griffith Park
- **Studio City Recreation Center/Beeman Park,** 818-769-4415, Studio City; six courts
- **Westwood Recreation Center,** 310-473-3610, Westwood; 12 courts
- **Van Nuys-Sherman Oaks Park,** 818-756-8400, Sherman Oaks; 10 courts

VOLLEYBALL

Several beaches offer beach volleyball courts, including **Zuma, Malibu Lagoon, Will Rogers, Santa Monica State, Venice,** and the granddaddy of them all, **Manhattan Beach,** which has more than 100 courts. Additionally, many parks have volleyball courts, including the **West Wilshire Recreation Center,** 323-939-8874, **Palisades Recreation Center,** 310-454-1412, **Barrington Recreation Center,** 310-476-4866, and **Westwood Recreation Complex,** 310-473-3610.

To join a group, contact any of the following:

- **California Beach Volleyball Association,** 800-350-2282, www.cbva.com
- **San Gabriel Volleyball Club,** 323-254-8476, www.sangabrielvbc.org
- **South Bay Volleyball Club,** 310-328-7282, www.southbavbc.com
- **Southern California Volleyball Association,** 714-917-3595, www.scvavolleyball.org
- **Southern California Volleyball Club,** 310-316-4264, www.goscvc.com

YOGA

Namaste! Hatha, Kundalini, Bikram...you name it and there is a center in Los Angeles that teaches it. Many accomplished gurus have made their home here, including Paramahansa Yogananda, who founded a self-realization fellowship and lived and wrote near downtown Los Angeles for 30 years. Explore the various styles, levels, and teaching techniques to find one that best suits you. Always ask for a free demo clinic or class before joining. Most centers that offer classes also sponsor retreats. You should also know about *LA Yoga* Magazine, a free bimonthly, www.layogamagazine.com. Here's a sampling of area yoga centers:

- **Bikram's Yoga College of India,** 1862 S La Cienega Blvd, 310-854-5800, www.bikramyoga.com
- **Center for Yoga,** 323-464-1276, www.centerforyoga.net, the city's oldest studio
- **City Yoga,** 1067 N Fairfax Ave, 323-654-2125, www.cityyoga.com
- **Golden Bridge Yoga,** 6322 De Longpre Ave, 323-936-4172, www.goldenbridgeyoga.com

- **LA Sivananda Yoga Center**, 13325 Beach Ave, Marina Del Rey, 310-822-9642, www.sivananda.org/la; founded by Swami Vishnu-Devananda, specializes in Sivananda yoga
- **Los Angeles Yoga Studio**, 11740 San Vicente Blvd Ste 202, 310-826-YOGA, www.yogalosangeles.org
- **Yoga Works**, 323- 464-1276, www.yogaworks.com; seven locations.

HEALTH CLUBS

Los Angeles is the fabled land of "the beautiful people," and you may notice that physiques are trimmer and fitter here than elsewhere in the USA. The good weather makes it pleasant to exercise outdoors…and, alas, not so easy to hide under layers of clothing.

There are **YMCAs** located throughout the city (check the telephone directory or www.ymca.net for one near you), which traditionally offer good workout options at reasonable prices. On the other end of the spectrum, the most luxurious fitness complex in town is **The Sports Club/LA**, 310-473-1447, www.thesports clubla.com, which offers everything from personal trainers and top-of-the-line equipment to a gourmet grill restaurant in its 100,000 square-foot complex. Unfortunately, the health club industry is one with few fixed, publicly available prices, so words like "sale" and "discount" have little meaning. Take everything with a grain of salt. The person on the treadmill next to you may have paid half—or double—what you paid. Also, before you fork over money for a membership, ask for a free pass. Find out if this is the right place for you; skull-pounding music and grunting weight lifters may not be as healthful as you had imagined.

Major health clubs, some local, some national, include the following. (Check the telephone directory for additional listings, including small neighborhood gyms and fitness centers.)

- **Bally's Total Fitness**, 800-FITNESS, www.ballyfitness.com; many locations
- **Bodies in Motion**, www.bodiesinmotion.com; LA-based chain with numerous locations
- **Boot Camp LA**, 323-938-6179, www.bootcampla.com; a military-style training regimen
- **Circuitworks**, 1410 Abbot Kinney Blvd, Venice, 310-664-1017, www.circuit worksla.com
- **Core Pilates NYC**, 5225 Wilshire Blvd, 323-939-6333, http://corepilatesnyc. com
- **Crunch Fitness**, 8000 W Sunset Blvd, 323-654-4550, www.crunch.com
- **Curves**, 800-848-1096, www.curvesinternational.com; numerous locations, specializes in 30-minute workouts for women only
- **Equinox Fitness Clubs**, 8590 W Sunset Blvd, West Hollywood, 310-289-1900
- **Gold's Gym**, 310-392-3005, www.goldsgym.com; the original Gold's Gym started in Venice, California in 1965. It was *the* place for serious, no-frills workouts.

- **Hollywood Gym**, 323-845-1420, www.hollywoodgym.com, 1551 N La Brea Ave, Hollywood; open 24 hours
- **KOR Health & Fitness**, 815 N La Brea Ave, 323-933-3744, www.kor4life.com
- **LA Fitness Sports Clubs**, 888-889-0984, www.lafitness.com; numerous locations
- **Spectrum Athletic Club**, 310-829-4995, www.spectrumclubs.com; numerous locations
- **Studio B Pilates**, 215 N Larchmont Blvd, 323-461-8663, www.studiobpilates.com
- **Total Woman Day Spa & Gym**, 818-552-2027, www.totalwomanspa.com; four in the Valley
- **Venice Beach Recreation Center**, 1800 Ocean Front Walk, Venice, 310-399-2775, www.laparks.org
- **World Gym**, 310-827-7705, www.worldgym.com; numerous locations, all World Gym fitness centers are a minimum of 9,500 square feet

LOS ANGELES IS NOTORIOUS FOR ITS URBAN SPRAWL. WHAT IS LESS evident, until you live here, is that this area is rich with open spaces including parks, both urban and rural, and of course, beaches, lots and lots of beaches. The County of Los Angeles Department of Parks and Recreation, 213-738-2961 or www.lacountyparks.org, is responsible for the county's 63,000 acres of parks, gardens, lakes, trails, natural areas, and the world's largest public golf course system. The City of LA Department of Recreation and Parks, 888-LAPARKS, www.laparks.org, maintains the city parks and gardens. In Orange County, it's the Harbors, Beaches, and Parks Division, 714-973-6865 or 866-OCPARKS, www.ocparks.com, that maintains its beaches and open spaces. (Information about California State parks and beaches can be found at www.parks.ca.gov.)

CITY PARKS AND GARDENS

PARKS

Like mini-oases, urban parks dot the City of Los Angeles, offering amenities such as tennis courts, baseball diamonds, basketball courts, and plenty of grass on which to stretch out and relax. For a listing of the parks in your neighborhood, check the front of the Yellow Pages or call the recreation and parks department for your area (see **Sports and Recreation**). Two of the largest urban parks in Los Angeles are **Griffith Park** and **Cheviot Hills**.

Located in the Hollywood Hills, **Griffith Park**, 323-913-4688, www.laparks.org, is the largest municipal park in the United States, occupying 4,100 acres and featuring the Los Angeles Zoo, the Griffith Park Observatory and Planetarium (reopened in 2006 after a four-year renovation), Travel Town Train Park, and the Autry Museum of Western Heritage. There are also pony rides, tennis courts, a soccer field, merry-go-round, picnic areas, and 50 miles of hiking and horseback riding trails.

Cheviot Hills Park, 310-837-5186, www.laparks.org, located in West LA near Cheviot Hills, offers 14 lit tennis courts, a pro shop, archery, swimming, basketball courts, soccer fields, baseball diamonds, a par course, a driving range, and what is reputed to be one of the busiest public golf courses in the country, Rancho Park (see **Sports and Recreation** for contact information).

If you're looking to be near some water but don't want to head for the beach, East Los Angeles's **Silverlake**, 323-644-3946, www.laparks.org, or **Echo Park**, 213-250-3578, www.laparks.org, in downtown LA, might do the trick. While Silverlake is actually a reservoir, so no water access is allowed, it offers basketball courts, a playing field, and a gymnasium for children, and is a pretty respite from the hustle and bustle of city life. At Echo Park you can rent canoes or paddle boats, use the tennis courts, baseball diamonds, and swim in its two pools, one indoor Olympic-sized, the other outdoor and shallow. Fishing is possible at Echo Park's stocked lake. Also downtown, the **Walt Disney Concert Hall** sports a small urban park, wonderful for an impromptu break if you're in the area.

Nestled beneath the famed Hollywood sign is **Lake Hollywood**, 323-913-4688, www.laparks.org, which is not really a lake at all but an emergency water reservoir managed by the LA Department of Water and Power. Nonetheless, it features open space, a jogging and pedestrian path around the lake, a children's play area, and a great view of the Hollywood sign.

The largest recreational park in the Valley, just off the 405 Freeway, is the **Sepulveda Basin Recreational Area**, 818-756-8060, www.laparks.org. Spanning over 2,000 acres, it includes a lake where you can paddleboat or fish. There are three golf courses, an archery range, 10 soccer fields, and three cricket fields, and tennis, handball, and basketball courts abound. In addition, there are paved jogging and biking trails. Nearby, at the Donald C. Tillman Water Reclamation Plant, is the Japanese Garden. It is open for tours; call 818-756-8166 or go to www.lajapanesegarden.org to check for times.

The **Van Nuys-Sherman Oaks Park**, 818-783-5121, www.laparks.org, is a grassy, tree-shrouded neighborhood recreation area, featuring six baseball fields, lighted tennis courts, and walking trails. Additional intimate neighborhood parks perfect for a quiet picnic include the **Johnny Carson Park**, 818-238-5300, www.ci.burbank.ca.us, in Burbank, and **Verdugo Park**, 818-548-2000, www.ci.glendale.ca.us, in Glendale.

GARDENS

In the hills of Bel Air lies a peaceful excursion possibility at the two-acre **UCLA Hannah Carter Japanese Garden**, 310-794-0320, www.japanesegarden.ucla.edu. Reservations are required (open only three days a week) and your 50-

minute visit is self-guided. Ancient pagodas and bridges, koi fish, devil-casting stones, a teahouse, and a mix of indigenous Japanese trees and plants complement delightful views.

On the other side of the 405 Freeway in West LA is the **Getty Center** with a wooded walkway that leads to a spiral-shaped "floating" garden, designed to reflect the personality of each season. Guided tours of the garden are available: 310-440-7300, www.getty.edu.

Hidden in Ranchos Palos Verdes is the **Wayfarers Chapel Garden**, 310-377-1650, www.wayfarerschapel.org, 3.5 acres of rolling grass and trees framed by sweeping views of the ocean. The Frank Lloyd Wright–designed chapel is made almost entirely of tall glass windows for unobstructed views of the redwood forest setting. The Chapel also hosts an annual concert series and art show.

The lush 207-acre **Huntington Library, Art Collections and Botanical Gardens**, 626-405-2100, www.huntington.org, in San Marino is a spectacular treat for garden lovers. Meander through the sculpture garden, view a towering cactus garden, and be transported to another land in the nine-acre Japanese garden. A dreamy 12-acre Chinese garden, opened in 2008, is one of the largest classical Chinese gardens outside of China. The Huntington is also home to a giant Corpse Flower, one of the world's most unpleasant smelling and biggest flowers (if in bloom—which is about once every one to three years). Along with an afternoon tea room and mansion-turned-museum, which houses English and French art of the 18th and 19th centuries, the most famous of which is Gainsborough's *Blue Boy*, it is easy to spend a whole day at the Huntington.

Lest we forget, in this land of roses, out-of-town visitors and locals alike delight in the **Virginia Robinson Gardens**, viewable by appointment only, 310-276-5367, www.robinson-gardens.com or http://parks.co.la.ca.us, in Beverly Hills, as well as the **Exposition Park Rose Garden**, 213-763-0114, www.laparks.org, across the street from the University of Southern California—a true urban oasis that consists of a romantic seven and a half acres of roses.

STATE/COUNTY PARKS

Outside of LA proper, garden aficionados will want to visit the **Los Angeles County Arboretum & Botanic Garden** in Arcadia, 626-821-3222, www.arboretum.org, a 127-acre garden that features free-roaming peacocks, an extensive horticultural library, an orchid greenhouse, and several national and state historical landmarks from the 1880s: the Queen Anne Cottage, the Coach Barn, and the Santa Anita Railroad Depot.

Nestled in the Santa Monica Mountains near Pacific Palisades is **Will Rogers State Historic Park**, 310-454-8212, www.parks.ca.gov. The former ranch of actor, humorist, and columnist Will Rogers, the park features tours through the 31-room ranch home, a large grassy hill for picnics, and miles of trails behind the house. On weekend mornings you can sit alongside the polo field and enjoy the matches.

Other beautiful canyon parks are **Malibu Creek State Park**, 818-880-0367, www.parks.ca.gov, with more than 15 miles of hiking trails; **Temescal Gateway Park**, a 20-acre site that includes a trail that travels more than 12 miles north to the Backbone Trail; **Topanga State Park**, 310-455-2465, www.parks.ca.gov, with 10,000 acres and 36 miles of hiking trails; **Brookside Park**, 626-744-4385 or 626-744-7275, www.ci.pasadena.ca.us, in Pasadena (home to the Rose Bowl, as well as a great gorge called the Arroyo Seco, and a golf course); and Newhall's 350-acre **Placerita Canyon Park and Nature Center**, 661-259-7721, www.placerita.org, with 10 miles of hiking trails, a nature center with live animal exhibits, and sites for picnicking and camping. Visit any of these parks in the spring or early summer for a delightful traipse along trails in flower-strewn fields and valleys.

The **Kenneth Hahn Recreation Area**, 323-298-3660, http://parks.lacounty.gov, in Los Angeles, is a 370-acre respite with hiking trails and a manmade lake, best known as the site of the 10th Olympiad (in 1932). The **Whittier Narrows Recreation Area**, 626-575-5526, http://parks.lacounty.gov, offers lakes, trails, an equestrian center, and an athletic complex sprawled over 1,000 acres. And in Rowland Heights is **Schabarum Regional Park**, 626-854-5560, http://parks.lacounty.gov, with over 600 acres of open space and an equestrian center.

Campsites take a little digging to locate within Los Angeles County, but camp grounds can be found at **Malibu Creek State Park**, 818-880-0367, **Leo Carrillo State Park** (just north of Malibu), 818-880-0363, and **Saddleback Butte State Park** (near Lancaster), 661-942-0662 (campsites are first-come, first-served), and in the national parks described below. For more information on any of the above-listed state parks, go to www.parks.ca.gov.

A warning, some of the parks mentioned here are proposed for closure in 2008 to balance the state budget. Call before going to make sure your park-of-choice is still open.

NATIONAL PARKS

The canyon parks offer a much different experience from what can be found in the immediate vicinity of LA. With only a short drive you'll leave the city behind, and a few minutes along a hiking trail can find you in a spot where cars can't be heard, houses can't be seen, and you're about as likely to meet a lizard or jackrabbit as a human being. The largest area of canyon parkland is the **Santa Monica Mountains National Recreation Area**. The Santa Monica Mountains stretch almost 50 miles across Los Angeles, and most of the trails here are part of, or hook up to, the Backbone Trail (see **Sports and Recreation**). For more information about parks throughout these mountains, call 310-589-3200 or 323-221-8900, or go online to http://smmc.ca.gov or www.lamountains.com.

Located on the northeastern edge of the San Fernando Valley is **Angeles National Forest**, one of seventeen national forests in California. Though accessible at many different points, the nearest point of entry for most Los Angeles residents is adjacent to Pasadena, in the San Gabriel Mountains. Here you'll find campgrounds, picnic sites, lakes, streams, and miles of hiking trails. For more information, call 626-574-5200 or go to www.fs.fed.us/r5/angeles.

Channel Islands National Park, 805-658-5730, www.nps.gov/chis, is 70 miles north of Los Angeles, off the coast of neighboring Ventura County. It comprises five of the eight California Channel Islands and is accessible only by boat. One hundred forty-five species of plants and animals are unique to the islands and found nowhere else in the world. Camping, hiking, snorkeling, bird watching, and marine mammal observation are some the activities possible here. Think of it as California's Galapagos Islands.

BEACHES

LOS ANGELES COUNTY BEACHES

Los Angeles is famous for its golden beaches, and they too provide an alluring place to get away from it all. There's nothing quite like standing at the edge of the continent, comforted by the knowledge that, although there may be millions of people and a bustling civilization behind you, there are no such distractions in front of you as far as the eye can see. Go to the **Los Angeles County Department of Beaches and Harbor** web site, http://beaches.co.la.ca.us, or call them at 310-305-9503 for detailed information about local beaches, including surf reports, upcoming events, and permit applications. The **California Department of Parks and Recreation**'s web site, www.parks.ca.gov, also has information about state beaches.

First, some safety advice: If you plan on swimming, swim in front of the nearest manned lifeguard tower. Take care to protect your eyes and skin; cover up with UV-safe glasses, hats, or clothing if necessary, and use sunscreen. Finally, being alone or even in a small group on the beach after dark is not safe; stick to beachcombing as a daytime activity.

At Malibu's northwestern-most end is **Leo Carrillo State Beach**, 818-880-0363, www.parks.ca.gov, named for the LA-born actor, preservationist, and conservationist. The 1,600-acre beach features nature trails, some of which lead to tide pools, and three campgrounds. The water is good for surfing and swimming, and you can explore Sequit Point, which has sea caves and a natural tunnel. Also in Malibu is the **Malibu Lagoon State Beach**, 818-880-0363, www.parks.ca.gov, located just west of the Malibu Pier. It consists of 22 acres of saltwater marsh, flower gardens, and sandy beach. Guided tours of the wetlands for grunion, the monarch butterfly, and the gray whale are scheduled seasonally; call the number provided for tour information. At the end of the Malibu Pier is **Surfrider Beach**, 310-305-9546, http://beaches.co.la.ca.us, famous for its good surfing conditions; it also features volleyball courts.

Further southeast is **Zuma Beach**, 310-305-9546, http://beaches.co.la.ca.us, which is known for its scenic views and rough surf. It also features volleyball, swimming, fishing, diving, and a children's playground. At nearby **Point Dume**, 310-305-9546, http://beaches.co.la.ca.us, you can explore tide pools and perhaps catch a glimpse of the migrating California gray whales, which travel through the area from November through May.

At the foot of Topanga Canyon are the small **Las Tunas Beach**, 310-305-9546, http://beaches.co.la.ca.us, and **Topanga State Beach**, 310-305-9546, http://beaches.co.la.ca.us. Although Topanga State Beach covers almost 22 acres, its most frequented site is a mile-long sandy stretch near Topanga Creek. Further south is **Will Rogers State Beach**, 310-305-9503, www.parks.ca.gov, a popular spot for board and body surfing and swimming. It too has volleyball courts and a playground.

Santa Monica State Beach, 310-458-8411, www.smgov.net, is one of the largest and most popular beaches in California, due to its proximity to the City of LA and its amusement amenities, which include the Santa Monica Pier, playgrounds, and basketball and volleyball courts. Though you will see many people swimming here, reports on the water quality at local beaches often rate this one poorly. For the most up-to-date water conditions, call the **Department of Beaches and Harbors**, 310-305-9503, http://beaches.co.la.ca.us, or read up on the beach report cards put out by **Heal the Bay** (a volunteer advocacy group), 310-451-1500, www.healthebay.org. Clean-up efforts and diligent monitoring will some day pay off, and actually the bay is safer now than in years past, though there are often swimming advisories near the major storm drains.

Just south of Santa Monica is **Venice Beach**, which features 238 acres of sand, but it's the adjacent boardwalk that has made it famous and brings more visitors. (See **Venice** in the **Neighborhoods** chapter.) Bicycles can be rented at several vendors along the beachfront, and there's a nice children's playground. For people watching, it can't be beat.

Marina del Rey's **Dockweiler Beach**, 310-305-9546, http://beaches.co.la.ca.us, is a quieter area that is popular with families and young singles. Features here include three miles of shoreline, swimming, surfing, a picnic area, and a campground.

Busy **Manhattan Beach** boasts more than 100 volleyball courts. One of the main attractions here is The Strand, a concrete promenade for jogging, skating, and walking…and a whole lot of watching.

Long Beach, in Long Beach, is a long, long, long strip of waterfront. Here are just some of the local beaches that make up its 11 miles of oceanfront property: Alamitos Beach, Bayshore Beach, Belmont Plaza Beach (and Belmont Pier), Belmont Shore Beach, Peninsula Beach, Colorado Lagoon, Junipero Beach, and Marine Park. Long Beach's Marine Bureau, 562-570-1582, www.ci.long-beach.

ca.us, oversees these beaches, as well as the largest municipally operated marina system in the nation.

ORANGE COUNTY BEACHES

The "O.C." offers over 42 miles of coastline. Glamorized by a TV series of the same name, the glistening beaches of Orange County are a surfer's paradise and the stuff of dreams. The **Orange County Harbors, Beaches and Parks Division**, which oversees 37,000 acres of parkland and open space, including regional and wilderness parks, nature preserves and recreational trails, historic sites, as well as harbors and beaches, is the place to contact for information about its water-side facilities: 714-973-6865, www.ocparks.com.

On the north end of Orange County, **Seal Beach**, 562-431-1383, www. ci.seal-beach.ca.us, is at the opening of Alamitos Bay, providing access for boats and yachts entering the Pacific Ocean from Huntington Harbor. Fishing and strolling are just some of the activities to be enjoyed along the Seal Beach Pier. A little further south is **Sunset State Beach**, 831-763-7062, which offers bike paths and volleyball. **Crystal Cove State Park**, 714-661-7013, is just one of more than a handful of beaches to be found in the City of Laguna Beach. The park is made up of three and a half miles of shoreline and 2,000 acres of undeveloped woodland for hiking and horseback riding. Also within the Laguna Beach shoreline is the **Thousand Steps Beach**, where a long, steep staircase in South Laguna between 9th and 10th streets rewards persistent individuals with great surfing.

Farther down the Pacific Coast Highway is another popular surfing beach called Salt Creek Beach, 949-923-2280, www.ocparks.com, where a small reef creates some fine swells. **Dana Point Harbor**, 949-923-2255, www.danaharbor.com, is home to 2,500 pleasure craft, restaurants and shops, tide pools, and the Orange County Marine Institute. Neighboring to the south is **Capistrano Beach**, 949-923-2280, www.ocparks.com. This 62-acre stretch of beach is ideal for volleyball. Next door is the county's most popular oceanside campground, **Doheny State Beach**, 949-496-6172, www.dohenystatebeach.org, with picnic tables, volleyball courts, and a palm leaf–lined "Palapa" gazebo that's popular for weddings on the beach. The beach is most popular for its 100+ campsites. **Sunset Beach**, 949-923-2220, spans 45 acres of sand, dotted by facilities that range from children's playgrounds to volleyball courts to lifeguard towers. **Newport's Municipal Beach**, 949-673-3371, www.city.newport-beach.ca.us, is set in a backdrop of world-class shops, golfing greens, and yachts (in the very photogenic Newport Harbor). **Huntington State Beach**, 714-536-1454, www.parks.ca.gov, a.k.a. "Surf City," is popular with bikers, skaters and, of course, surfers. Nearby is the 114-acre Huntington Beach Wetlands, which serves as a nesting sanctuary for threatened and endangered species. And sitting near the southern point of Orange County is **San Clemente State Beach**, 949-492-3156, www.parks.ca.gov. The north end of this one-mile beach is popular with surfers. Trails lead from the bluffs down to the beach, where skin diving is popular, and hiking opportunities along the bluff trails abound.

A final note: California was the first state in the nation to ban smoking in its restaurants and bars, and this restriction continues to expand to greenspaces in LA and Orange County. Beginning in 2004, this fineable offense extended to parts of the state's coastline. Beaches in the cities of Santa Monica and Malibu, Los Angeles, and state beaches in Orange County now have smoking bans in place. And in an effort to reduce secondhand smoke exposure to children and prevent wildfires, smoking is banned from all LA city parks (except for designated smoking areas) as of 2007. In Orange County, the cities of Laguna Hills, Irvine, and Seal Beach have instated smoking prohibitions in their parks, with more cities expected to follow suit.

G IVING BACK TO THE COMMUNITY IS A REWARDING EXPERIENCE. Whether you are skilled at building houses, caring for the elderly, tutoring underprivileged children, or canvassing neighborhoods (having bilingual skills in any of these areas can be particularly useful), you can find a volunteer project that suits your talents and beliefs. This chapter discusses the many ways you can get involved with the community via volunteering, clubs, and places of worship.

COMMUNITY INVOLVEMENT

Helping out in your new community is a great way to meet people and can make the transition to an unfamiliar place less stressful.

VOLUNTEER MATCHING AND PLACEMENT

The following organizations coordinate much of LA's volunteer activity, from feeding the hungry to counseling fire victims to providing mediation for the City Attorney's Office. Give them a call and they'll direct you to where help is most needed. **LA Works** is a clearinghouse for local short- and long-term volunteer opportunities; contact them at 323-224-6518 or go to www.laworks.com. **Volunteer Match**, www.volunteermatch.org, is a national service.

- **Retired and Senior Volunteer Program** (**RSVP**), 310-253-6704, www.culver city.org/senior/rsvp.asp?sec=res
- **Senior Corps**, 319-235-7421, www.seniorcorps.org
- **Volunteer Center of Los Angeles**, 818-908-5066, www.vcla.net
- **Volunteers of America, Greater Los Angeles**, 213-389-1500, www.voala.org

OTHER CONNECTIONS

- **Check bulletin boards** at your office, church, neighborhood grocery store, laundries, and school.
- Walk into local **churches, temples, community organizations**, and/or **libraries**.

AREA CAUSES

Once you've settled in, you may want to be a good neighbor by getting involved in some of the many charitable organizations in Los Angeles. The list below is just a small sampling of the numerous worthy organizations and causes that would appreciate your support. When calling, ask to speak to their volunteer coordinator and be sure to mention any special skills you might have.

AIDS & HIV

- **AIDS Project Los Angeles (APLA)**, 213-201-1600, www.apla.org
- **Lifegroup LA**, 888-208-8081, http://thelifegroupla.org
- **LA Gay and Lesbian Center**, 323-993-7400, www.lagaycenter.org
- **Minority AIDS Project**, 323-936-4949, www.map-usa.org
- **Out of the Closet Thrift-Store**, 323-860-0173, www.outofthecloset.org

ALCOHOL AND DRUG DEPENDENCY

- **Alcohol-Drug Council, West**, 310-451-5881, www.adcwa.org
- **Alcoholics Anonymous**, 323-936-4343, www.lacoaa.org
- **Addictions Referral Network**, 800-577-4740
- **Focus on Recovery Helpline**, 800-374-2800
- **Families Anonymous**, 800-736-9805, www.familiesanonymous.org
- **Narcotics Anonymous**, 310-390-0279, www.na.org
- **National Alcohol and Drug Abuse Hotline**, 800-252-6465

ANIMALS

- **Animal Regulations Department & Shelters**, City of Los Angeles, 888-452-7381, www.laanimalservices.com
- **Last Chance for Animals**, 310-271-6096, www.lcanimal.org
- **Pets are Wonderful Support (PAWS)**, 323-464-7297, www.pawsla.org
- **ResQPet**, 888-738-7377, www.resqpet.com

- **Society for the Prevention of Cruelty to Animals (SPCA)**, 323-730-5300, www.aspcala.org

CHILDREN & YOUTH

If involvement with children is especially appealing, you can tutor in and out of schools, be a big brother or sister, teach music and sports in shelters or at local community centers, run activities in the parks, entertain children in hospitals, and accompany kids on weekend outings. Schools, libraries, community associations, hospitals, and other facilities providing activities and guidance for children are all worth exploring.

- **Angel's Flight**, 800-833-2499, www.catholiccharitiesla.org
- **Big Brothers of Greater Los Angeles**, 213-481-3611, www.bigbrothersbigsis terslaie.org
- **Big Sisters of Greater Los Angeles**, 213-481-3611, www.bigbrothersbigsis terslaie.org
- **Catholic Big Brothers and Big Sisters**, 213-251-9800, www.catholicbigbroth ers.org
- **Children of the Night**, 818-908-4474, www.childrenofthenight.org
- **Exceptional Children's Foundation**, 310-204-3300, www.ecf.net
- **Fathers' Heartline,** 877-716-8000
- **Girls & Boys Town**, 800-448-3000, www.girlsandboystown.org
- **Jewish Big Brothers**, 323-761-8675, www.jbbbsla.org
- **Los Angeles Youth Network**, 323-957-7757, www.layn.org
- **Make-A-Wish Foundation**, 310-788-9474, www.wishla.org
- **My Friends Place**, 323-908-0011, www.myfriendsplace.org
- **Runaway Adolescent Project**, 323-466-7776
- **School Volunteer Program of the Los Angeles Unified School District**, 213-241-6900, https://lausd.volunteermatch.org
- **Starlight Starbright Children's Foundation**, 310-479-1212, www.starlight.org
- **Youth Mentoring Connection**, 323-731-8080, www.youthmentoring.org

CULTURE AND THE ARTS

Most museums, theaters, symphonies, chorus groups, and opera and dance companies routinely round up volunteers to help their programs run. Here are just a few to consider (check the **Cultural Life** chapter for more):

- **Hollywood Bowl**, 323-850-2000, www.hollywoodbowl.com

- **Huntington Library, Art Collections, and Botanical Gardens,** 626-405-2100, www.huntington.org
- **Los Angeles County Museum of Art,** 323-857-6000, www.lacma.org
- **Los Angeles Philharmonic,** 323-850-2000, www.laphil.org

DISABILITY

You can read to the blind, help teach the deaf, work to prevent birth defects, and help the retarded and developmentally disabled, among others. You can also make regular visits to the homebound elderly, bring hot meals to their homes, and teach everything from nutrition to arts and crafts in senior centers and nursing homes.

- **Association for Retarded Citizens,** 562-803-4606, www.thearc.org
- **Braille Institute,** 323-663-1111, www.brailleinstitute.org
- **Easter Seal Society of Los Angeles and Orange Counties,** 714-834-1111, http://southerncal.easterseals.com
- **Greater Los Angeles Agency on Deafness,** 323-478-8000, www.gladinc.org
- **Independent Living Center of Southern California,** 818-785-6934, www.ilcsc.org
- **Los Angeles Caregiver Resource Center,** 800-540-4442, www.losangelescrc.org
- **The Mission of the Disability Rights Legal Center,** 213-736-1479, www.disabilityrightslegalcenter.org
- **Ryan Dyslexia Center,** 818-506-1111
- **Westside Center for Independent Living,** 888-851-9245, www.wcil.org

ENVIRONMENT

- **Audubon Society,** 323-876-0202, www.laaudubon.org
- **California Conservation Corps,** 323-231-8248, www.ccc.ca.gov
- **Heal the Bay,** 310-451-1500, www.healthebay.org
- **Oceana,** 877-7-OCEANA, www.oceana.org
- **Sierra Club,** 213-387-4287, http://angeles.sierraclub.org
- **TreePeople,** 818-753-4600, www.treepeople.org

GAY, LESBIAN, BISEXUAL, TRANSGENDER

- **Gay and Lesbian Alliance Against Defamation,** 323-933-2240, www.glaad.org
- **Los Angeles Gay & Lesbian Center,** 323-993-7400, www.laglc.org

- **Los Angeles Gender Center**, 310-475-8880, www.lagendercenter.com
- **Parents, Friends & Families of Lesbians & Gays (PFLAG)**, 310-472-8952, www.pflag.org
- **The Spot**, 323-993-7440

HEALTH AND HUMAN SERVICES

The need for volunteers in both city-run and private hospitals is manifold: From interpreters to laboratory personnel to admitting and nursing aides, many volunteers are required. Assistants in crisis medical areas—emergency rooms, intensive care units, and the like—are wanted if you have the skills, as are volunteers to work with victims of sexual abuse. If you just want to be helpful, you might assist in food delivery or work in the gift shop. Most city hospitals are large and busy, and many are in need of help.

Refer to the **Useful Phone Numbers and Web Sites** chapter for contact information for local crisis centers, hospitals, and other health care organizations that are always in need of qualified volunteers for a host of jobs, from fundraising to manning call centers, to providing a listening ear and caring touch. Nationally, foundations that continually look for volunteers include the American Cancer Society, March of Dimes, United Way, and Visiting Nurse Service (you don't have to be a nurse). The list goes on.

Scores of volunteers concern themselves with shelter for the city's homeless. Jobs include monitoring and organizing the shelters, providing legal help, ministering to psychiatric, medical, and social needs, raising money, manning phones, and caring for children in the shelters. Many people solicit, organize, cook, and serve food to the destitute at sites throughout the city. Still others deliver meals to the homeless and the homebound. Many soup kitchens tend to be overwhelmed with well-meaning volunteers during the winter holidays, when they can use help year round. So consider pitching in "off season."

Locally, contact one of the following:

- **American Red Cross of Greater Los Angeles**, 310-376-1724, www.redcrossla.org
- **Bob Hope Hollywood USO at LAX**, 310-645-3716, www.bobhopeuso.org
- **Catholic Charities**, 213-251-3400, www.catholiccharitiesla.org
- **Chrysalis Works**, 213-806-6300, www.changeslives.org
- **Habitat for Humanity Greater Los Angeles**, 310-323-4663, www.habitatla.org
- **Los Angeles Community Action Network,** 213-228-0024, www.cangress.org
- **Los Angeles Mission**, 213-629-1227, www.losangelesmission.org
- **Los Angeles Regional Food Bank**, 323-234-3030, www.lafoodbank.org

- **Meals on Wheels West**, 310-394-7558, www.mealsonwheelswest.org
- **People Assisting the Homeless (PATH)**, 323-644-2200, www.epath.org
- **Project Angel Food**, 323-845-1816, www.angelfood.org
- **Saint Joseph Center**, 310-396-6468, www.stjosephctr.org
- **St. Vincent Meals on Wheels**, 213-484-7494, www.stvincentmow.org
- **The Salvation Army**, 213-553-3295, 818-361-6462, www.salvationarmy-socal. org
- **SOVA Food Pantry**, 818-988-7682, http://jfsla.org/sova/
- **Step Up on Second**, 310-394-6889, www.stepuponsecond.org
- **Union Station Foundation**, 626-240-4550, www.unionstationfoundation.org
- **Westside Food Bank**, 310-828-6016, www.westsidefoodbankca.org

INTERNATIONAL RELIEF AND DEVELOPMENT

- **EF Foundation for Foreign Study Cambridge**, 800-447-4273, www.effound ation.org
- **Travelers Aid Society of Los Angeles**, 323-468-2500, www.tasla.org

LEGAL

- **American Civil Liberties Union of Southern California (ACLU)**, 213-977-9500, www.aclu-sc.org
- **Bet Tzedek Legal Services**, 323-939-0506, www.bettzedek.org
- **Legal Aid Foundation of Los Angeles**, 800-399-4529 www.lafla.org

LITERACY

- **Literacy Network of Greater Los Angeles**, 213-237-4350, www.literacynet work.org
- **Los Angeles Central Library**, 213-228-7542, www.lapl.org

MENTORING AND CAREER DEVELOPMENT

- **Dress for Success Los Angeles**, 213-629-3537, www.dressforsuccess.org
- **Forty Plus of Southern California**, 213-388-2301, www.40plussocal.org
- **Latin Professional Network**, 213-792-0877, www.lpnonline.com
- **Los Angeles Urban League Young Professionals**, 323-299-9660, www.la ulyp.org
- **SCORE Los Angeles**, 818-552-3206, www.scorela.org
- **Women in Film**, 310-657-5144, www.wif.org

MEN'S SERVICES

- **American Coalition for Fathers & Children**, 800-978-3237, www.acfc.org
- **Domestic Abuse Hotline for Men & Women**, 207-683-5758, www.dahmw. org
- **Men's Activism News Network**, http://news.mensactivism.org
- **My Child Says Daddy**, 310-642-8816, www.mychildsaysdaddy.org
- **National Coalition of Free Men**, LA Chapter, 818-907-9383, www.ncfmla.org
- **YMCA of Metropolitan Los Angeles**, 310-380-6448, www.ymcala.org

POLITICS

Many of the large and small political parties are active here and happy to welcome proponents of their ideals. Activism in more specific categories can be found throughout this chapter. The following groups are more generalized in public affairs:

- **Amnesty International - Southern California Cluster**, 310-815-0450, www. amnesty-volunteer.org/usa/scal/glad.html
- **League of Women Voters Los Angeles**, 213-368-1616, www.lwvlosangeles. org
- **LA County Registrar of Voters**, **Voter Registration and Poll workers**, 562-466-1323, http://regrec.co.la.ca.us
- **Orange County Registrar of Voters**, 714-567-7600, www.ocvote.com

REFUGEES AND IMMIGRANTS

- **Coalition for Humane Immigrant Rights of Los Angeles** (CHIRLA), 213 353-1333, www.chirla.org
- **International Institute of LA, Immigrant & Refugee Services**, 323-224-3800, www.iilosangeles.org
- **Los Angeles County Bar Association, Immigration Legal Assistance Project**, 213-485-1873, www.lacba.org
- **US Citizenship & Immigration Services**, 800-375-5283, www.ucis.gov

SENIORS

- **American Association of Retired Persons**, 888-687-2277, www.aarp.org
- **Jewish Family Service of Los Angeles**, 323-761-8800, www.jfsla.org
- **Los Angeles County Community and Senior Services**, 213-738-2600 or 800-510-2020, www.ladcss.org

- **Retired Senior Volunteer Program**, 310-394-9871, 818-908-5070, www.senior corps.org

WOMEN'S SERVICES

- **Asian Pacific Women's Center,** 213-250-2977, www.apwcla.org
- **Equal Rights Advocates,** 800-839-4372, www.equalrights.org
- **LA Commission on Assaults Against Women**, 213-955-9090, http://peace overviolence.org
- **Planned Parenthood of Los Angeles**, 800-576-5544, www.plannedparent hood.org/los-angeles
- **Progressive Health Services & Holistic Health for Women**, 323-650-1508, www.progressivehealth.org
- **Safe Harbor Women's Clinic**, 213-622-4073
- **Santa Monica Hospital Rape Treatment Center**, 310-319-4000, www.ucla health.org
- **YWCA of Greater Los Angeles**, 213-365-2991, www.ywcagla.org

CHARITABLE GIVING

If your time is too limited to contribute, charities always welcome monetary donations. Some donations are partially or entirely tax deductible too, so make sure to get a receipt and consult with your tax advisor. If you'd like to conduct some due diligence on a charity's fiscal responsibility to ensure that the bulk of contributions are spent on projects and not fund raising, there are a number of watchdog sites to help. The **Better Business Bureau's Wise Giving Alliance** (www.give.org), **Charity Navigator** (www.charitynavigator.org), and **Guidestar** (www.guidestar.org) are some useful resources.

MEETING PEOPLE

Los Angeles attracts such a diverse group of people, odds are that many others living here share your interests. Finding them is the challenge. Many profession-als are career driven, and whatever time they have for socializing is devoted to career networking. Even platonic friends are rated on their geographic desirabil-ity (who wants to sit in another 40 minutes of traffic to meet someone after a long day working). How do you meet people outside of your job, especially if you're not into the bar/nightclub scene? There are excellent opportunities for making new friends at volunteer organizations (see "Community Involvement" above), cultural events (see **Cultural Life**), recreation sports clubs (see **Sports and Recreation**), and religious groups (see "Places of Worship" below). Social networking sites like MySpace, Facebook, and Craigslist are popular for meeting new people. So are online dating and matchmaking services; in fact, eHarmony. com is based in Pasadena.

LA People Connection is a free group originally started in Los Angeles to help people make new friends in LA. Now called **My People Connection** (www. mypeopleconnection.com), it is entirely run by volunteers who organize many activities around the city. Similar groups include **Young Active Professionals** (YAP) **Los Angeles** (www.yapclub.com/la) and **Meet in LA** (www.meetin.org).

Finally, just going out and running errands is an underrated but effective method of meeting friends-to-be. *LA Magazine* recently observed in their Dating issue that singles aren't just shopping for groceries at the local Trader Joe's.

ALUMNI GROUPS

Most local, regional, and large national colleges and universities have alumni groups here in Los Angeles. If by some small chance there isn't, check with your alma mater's alumni office to help locate other graduates from your school who may be living in your area.

BUSINESS GROUPS

Numerous careers are represented by various professional groups here. Since they exist for networking purposes, many hold regular, frequent events. See "Mentoring and Career Development" above for a sampling.

POLITICAL GROUPS

Got strong political leanings? There are certainly groups of likeminded individuals who meet regularly. The organizations listed above in "Politics" under "Area Causes" may offer you a starting place.

OUTDOOR ADVENTURES

Constant great weather here is a magnet for outdoor enthusiasts. **The Outdoors Club** (www.outdoorsclub.org), **Outdoor Los Angeles** (http://outdoorla.org), and **Jewish Outdoor Adventures** (310-858-6875, http://jewishoutdooradventures. com) are just some of the local organizations you can join if you're a lover of the great outdoors. The **Extreme Things Adventure Club** (866-831-8314, www.ex tremethings.com) organizes discounted events for its members within a 40-mile radius of downtown LA.

SPECIAL INTERESTS

If this chapter is any indication, there's a group dedicated to just about any hobby. Classes and seminars are another way to meet people interested in cooking, arts and crafts, etc. Online gaming sites, foodie blogs—the internet has made it easy for people to interact about their favorite subject…so if those special someones aren't gaming or updating their YouTube content, you might even chance meeting them in person.

The civic minded shouldn't forget those who support us, such as our firemen and police. Also, civilians who want to receive special training to help their fellow citizens with on-scene crisis assistance can take classes for the following. Bilingual volunteers are especially needed.

- **Adopt a Firestation**, 213-978-3820, www.lafd.org/adopt.htm
- **Community Emergency Response Team** (**CERT-LA**), 818-756-9674, www. cert-la.com
- **Crisis Response Team** (**CRT**), 213-978-0697, www.lacity.org
- **LAPD Volunteer Program**, 213-485-4097, www.lapdonline.org
- **Neighborhood Watch Programs**, 213-485-3134, www.lapdonline.org

PLACES OF WORSHIP

The Los Angeles area is home to a variety of faiths. It is host to substantial Roman Catholic and Protestant communities, the second largest Jewish population in the USA (behind the New York City metropolitan area), and is well represented by Muslims as well as Hindus and Buddhists, among others.

Finding a suitable church, synagogue, mosque, or temple may be as simple as getting a suggestion from an acquaintance, or it may be as intensely personal and complex as choosing a spouse. The houses of worship described below are included for a variety of reasons, whether they are of historic or architectural note, renowned for their strong outreach programs, or host a popular music series. Certainly it is not a comprehensive list. A quick look at the Yellow Pages, listed by denomination, should provide you with all of the religious centers in your neighborhood; as well, www.losangeleschurches.com describes the various meeting places/faiths within Los Angeles County and includes user ratings. Nationally, you can contact the **National Council of Churches**, 212-870-2228, www.ncccusa. org, which publishes the *Yearbook of American & Canadian Churches*, a directory listing thousands of Christian churches. (Order one for $50 at 888-870-3325 or browse the directory links at www.electronicchurch.org.) Other national online directories of churches—generally limited to Christian denominations—include www.churchangel.com, www.usachurch.com, http://netministries.org, http:// churches.net, www.forministry.com, and www.adherents.com. Synagogues serving all branches of Judaism are listed at www.lajewishguide.com.

BAHÁ'Í

Although Bahá'í houses of worship may differ from one another in architectural styles, they are often stunning, and are recognizable by their nine sides and central dome, which symbolize "the diversity of the human race and its essential oneness." For more information, go to www.bahai.org. The local Bahá'í community worships at the **Bahá'í Faith Los Angeles Center**, 5755 Rodeo Road, 323-933-8291 or go to www.labc.org.

BUDDHIST

Buddhism dates back over two millennia, and today over 350 million people across the globe consider themselves Buddhists. There are many different sub-traditions, including **Zen, Tibetan, Tantric (Vajrayana)**, and **Mahayana**.
Area temples include:

• **Wat Thai Temple** of Los Angeles, 8225 Coldwater Canyon Ave, North Hollywood, 818-785-9552, www.watthaiusa.org; the largest Thai Theravada Buddhist Temple in the United States. Many festivals are celebrated by the monks residing here, including "Taleung Sok Day" (Thai New Year's Day) in April. The temple complex is a major social hub for local Thais. Almost every weekend, Wat Thai's lower level turns into a busy, noisy Bangkok-style street scene where vendors sell Thai household wares, fabrics, and foods, including fiery spices and traditionally prepared foods.
• The **Zen Center** of Los Angeles, 923 South Normandie Avenue, 213-387-2351, www.zencenter.org

CHRISTIAN

Christian houses of worship, prayer retreat centers, and monasteries can be found throughout Southern California. While Roman Catholicism predominates, Christian churches of all persuasions are well represented.

One nondenominational church, while not exactly a house of worship in the traditional sense, has an interesting history and is where many love-struck couples have found themselves. The small (seats 150) **Little Brown Church**, 4418 Coldwater Canyon Avenue, Studio City, 818-761-1127, www.covtoday.org, was built in the late 1930s. Open 24/7, this intimate and homey wood chapel with its white trim, pine interior, and hand-hewn pine pews, has hosted over 22,500 weddings. One of California's most famous couples to marry within the chapel was former President Ronald Reagan and his wife Nancy in 1952.

What follows are just some of the Christian faith groups in Los Angeles.

CATHOLIC CHURCHES

ORTHODOX (COPTIC, EASTERN, GREEK, ALBANIAN, MOROVIAN, RUSSIAN, ETC.)

In Los Angeles, the **St. Sophia Greek Orthodox Cathedral**, 1324 South Normandie Avenue, LA, 323-737-2424, www.stsophia.org, is a visual delight. Its stunning interior—gilded arches, lofty frescoes, ornate chandeliers, complete with a choir loft—seats 850. St. Sophia's Sunday school and youth programs are popular, as well as its camp and retreat center located in Crestline.

Contact information for Orthodox churches in the USA includes:

- **Greek Orthodox Church of America**, www.goarch.org/en/archdiocese
- **Moravian:** Moravian Church in America, 800-732-0591, www.moravian.org
- **Orthodox Christian Foundation**, www.ocf.org
- **Orthodox Church in America**, www.oca.org

ROMAN CATHOLIC

Given the history of Southern California's early Spanish settlers and the continued Latino influence, it is no wonder that Roman Catholicism dominates the LA landscape. Roman Catholics should contact the **Roman Catholic Archdiocese of Los Angeles**, 213-637-7000, www.la-archdiocese.org, 3424 Wilshire Boulevard, Los Angeles, for a list of churches for each town as well as information about the Vatican, Catholic charities, marriage preparation, Catholic Social Services, and job opportunities. Another resource is the Catholic Information Center at www.catholic.net.

Roman Catholic churches of note include:

- The **Cathedral of Our Lady of Angels** at 555 W Temple St (213-680-5200, www.olacathedral.org) in downtown Los Angeles; opened in 2002, the Cathedral of Our Lady of Angels is visually striking from the nearby 101 Freeway. Designed by Spanish architect Rafael Moneo, its amber-colored contemporary lines feature virtually no right angles. Construction of this $189 million cathedral began in 1994, after the Northridge earthquake severely damaged the 120-year-old St. Vibiana's Cathedral and displaced the Archdiocese of Los Angeles. Tourists and locals alike can call to reserve a tour of the cathedral or casually drop by to enjoy the open plaza and even grab lunch from the café.
- The **Our Lady Queen of Angels Catholic Church,** 535 N Main St (in El Pueblo de Los Angeles Historic Park), 213-629-3101, www.laplacita.org or www.la-archdiocese.org; originally called the La Iglesia de Nuestra Senora de Los Angeles, it is the oldest church in the city. In 1781 about 40 settlers established a farming community here upon what is now considered the founding site of the City of LA. Currently consisting of 44 acres of city land (bounded by Alameda, Arcadia, Spring, and Macy streets), these grounds house this lovely

Spanish-style church, founded and built by the Franciscans in the early 1800s. Still an active church of the Roman Catholic Archdiocese of Los Angeles, it is within walking distance of the famed Mexican Marketplace on Olvera Street. If you pay a visit, be sure to stroll the northwest corner of Olvera Street; this is the oldest thoroughfare in Los Angeles.

- The **San Gabriel Mission**, 428 South Mission Drive, San Gabriel, 626-457-3035, www.sangabrielmission.org, is the oldest structure of its kind south of Monterey, California, founded on September 8, 1771, by Father Junipero Serra. The fourth mission in the 21-mission chain in California, it grew so prosperous that it earned another name, "Pride of the Missions." The early fathers planted orange trees and grapevines, crops of corn and beans, and raised cattle and sheep. The mission became known for its production of fine wines, soaps, and candles, which were used by the other missions and given to passing travelers. Catholic services are still performed at the mission's church, and outreach continues toward those in need, particularly recent immigrants. A museum as well as a gift shop is on site.

PROTESTANT CHURCHES

AMERICAN METHODIST EPISCOPAL (AME)

The **First AME Church** (FAME-Los Angeles), 2270 South Harvard Boulevard, South Los Angeles, 323-730-7750, www.famechurch.org, is the oldest African-American congregation in the City of Los Angeles. Former LA Mayor Tom Bradley and the Reverend Jesse Jackson are frequent guest speakers. FAME-Los Angeles was founded in 1872 by former slave Biddy Mason and housed the city's first black school. Several of the earliest African-American movie stars, including Hattie McDaniel and Ethel Waters, resided just north of the church. FAME-Los Angeles is an active church with a host of community outreach programs, including FAME Renaissance, a social and business development program that benefits impoverished communities in LA County. During his presidency, George H.W. Bush declared First AME Church the 177th Point of Light for its outreach in community services. Reverend Cecil L. "Chip" Murray, who was largely responsible for spearheading the church's community outreach, retired in 2004, after 27 years of tireless service.

If you'd like to find an AME or Episcopal Zion church in your neighborhood, you can go to the directory link at the official AME site, www.ame-church.com.

ANGLICAN/EPISCOPAL

The **Episcopal/Anglican Diocese of Los Angeles** can be reached at 213-482-2040 (toll free 800-366-1536); online at www.ladiocese.org. For general information about the Episcopal Church of the USA, visit www.episcopalchurch. org; and for the Anglican Church, go to http://anglicansonline.org.

ASSEMBLY OF GOD

Assemblies of God are the largest Pentecostal denomination of the Protestant church in the USA. Their homepage, www.ag.org, is informative and provides a complete directory of its churches nationwide. **Assembly of God, Southern California District**, can be contacted at 949-252-8400, www.socalag.org, or www. ag.org.

BAPTIST

To find out more about the **American Baptist** community, contact the American Baptist Churches Mission Center, www.abc-usa.org, 800-ABC-3USA. To find out more about **Southern Baptists** in Los Angeles, go to www.sbc.net.

CHRISTIAN SCIENCE

Christian Science Churches and Organizations, 949-494-5071, www.cssocali fornia.com, can provide more information about this group. *The Christian Science Journal*, www.csjournal.com, is another resource.

CHURCH OF JESUS CHRIST OF LATTER-DAY SAINTS (MORMON)

For more information on the Church of Jesus Christ of Latter-day Saints, contact the **Los Angeles California Stake**: 1209 S Manhattan Place, Los Angeles, 323-731-1350, www.lds.org.

CHURCH OF THE NAZARENE

Church of the Nazarene is the largest denomination in the Wesleyan–holiness tradition. For information about the Church of the Nazarene and a church locator service, go to the church's national web site, www.nazarene.org.

CONGREGATIONAL/UNITED CHURCH OF CHRIST

The Congregational Church is also known, since the 1950s, as the United Church of Christ (UCC). For more information on the local Congregational community, try the **Los Angeles Congregational Church of Christian Fellowship UCC**, 323-731-8869, www.churchofchristianfellowship.org; nationally at 800-537-3394, www.ucc.org.

FRIENDS (QUAKER)

Members of the **Society of Friends** (a.k.a. Quakers) can trace their church's roots back to some of the first Europeans to settle in the Americas. Contact the **Southern California Religious Society of Friends** at 800-962-4766 or go online: http://scqm.org or www.quaker.org.

JEHOVAH'S WITNESS

For information about Jehovah's Witness or to find a kingdom hall, you can call their local office at 323-660-1386 or visit www.watchtower.org or www.jw-media.org.

LUTHERAN

Lutherans of the **Evangelical Lutheran Church in America** (**ELCA**), 800-638-3522, www.elca.org, and the **Missouri Synod** are both represented in LA. Contact one of the following for assistance with finding a church near you.

- **ELCA**: Southwest California Synod, 818-507-9591, www.socalsynod.org
- **Missouri Synod**: Pacific Southwest District, 949-854-3232, www.psd-lcms.org, or 888-773-5267, www.lcms.org

MENNONITE

Until the 19th century, most Mennonites were concentrated in rural farming communities, speaking German, and leaving alone much of the secular world. Since the 1800s, there have been divisions in the church, yielding the Old Mennonite Church, General Conference Mennonite Church, Mennonite Brethren, and Old Order Amish. The regional office of the **Pacific Southwest Mennonite Conference** can be reached at 626-720-8100, www.pacificsouthwest.org.

METHODIST (UNITED)

The **United Methodist Church Los Angeles District** can be reached at 626-568-7300 or 800-244-UMCC, www.cal-pac.org or www.umc.org. Search their web sites for a church near you.

METROPOLITAN COMMUNITY CHURCH

The **MCC of Los Angeles**, 310-854-9110, www.mccla.org, welcomes all but specifically reaches out to the gay, lesbian, bisexual, and transgender Christian community. The founding church of the MCC movement, the MCC of Los Angeles has been blessing the unions of same-sex couples for more than 35 years.

Along the same lines, the **Unity Fellowship of Christ Church**, 5148 West Jefferson Blvd., 323-938-8322, www.ufc-usa.org, serves a predominantly gay and African-American community. Their motto is "God is Love and Love is for Everyone."

PENTECOSTAL/CHARISMATIC

Some local Charismatic churches are organized through the offices of the **Southern California Renewal Communities**: 818-771-1361, www.scrc.org. Pentecostal contacts include the **Pentecostal Church of God in Christ**: First Jurisdiction of Southern California, 323-733-8300, www.cogic.org; and **International Pentecostal Holiness Church**, World Agape Mission Church, 213-384-1882, www.iphc. org. For more information about the Pentecostal/Charismatic Churches of North America and to find a local church, visit www.pccna.org.

PRESBYTERIAN (USA)

A Protestant church with its roots in 17th-century England, Presbyterianism was brought by the Scottish and Irish to the USA in the late 1600s. The largest Presbyterian branch in the USA is the **Presbyterian Church** (**USA**); find them on the web at www.pcusa.org or call 800-872-3283. Of particular note in Los Angeles is the towering, neo-gothic structure that houses the **Hollywood First Presbyterian Church** (**FPCH**) at 1760 North Gower Street, Hollywood, 323-463-7161, www.fpch.org. The FPCH reaches out to the local community, which, being in Hollywood, has much to do with the entertainment industry. Beginning with the Actors Co-op in 1987, it now operates two theaters on its campus under a contract with Actors Equity Association. The Actors Co-op stages four plays each season and has received numerous Drama-Logue awards. Not to leave out writers, the church runs a month-long training program (Act One: Writing for Hollywood) for Christian scriptwriters.

REFORM CHURCH OF AMERICA (RCA)

The **Crystal Cathedral** in Orange County, 13280 Chapman Avenue Garden Grove, 714-971-4000, www.crystalcathedral.org, is a magnificent modern structure. More than 10,000 windows of silver glass are laced together by white steel trusses. Two 90-foot-tall doors open electronically behind the pulpit to allow the morning sunlight and breeze in during worship services, and the bell tower houses a 52-bell carillon. The Cathedral's pipe organ is world renowned for its size and quality, and is among the five largest pipe organs in the world. This is a large church: Over 1,000 singers and instrumentalists can perform in the 185-foot long chancel area, and a giant indoor Sony "Jumbotron" television screen broadcasts the service. Programs include the internationally televised

"Hour of Power," and its Christmas and Easter services are popular, large-scale productions that are frequently televised. Smaller "houses of power," which meet weekly in congregants' homes, are organized to meet the needs of its far-reaching congregation.

To locate a Reform Church of America near you, go to www.rcawest.org and use its locator service.

SEVENTH DAY ADVENTIST

Contact the **Seventh Day Adventist**: **Southern California Conference**, 818-546-8400, http://scc.netadventist.org (nationally at www.adventist.org), for a church near you.

UNITARIAN UNIVERSALIST ASSOCIATION (UUA)

The Unitarian Universalist Association (UUA) dates back to 1961, when the Universalism and Unitarianism movements officially merged. The **First Unitarian Church of Los Angeles** can be reached at 213-389-1356, www.uula.org (nationally at www.uua.org).

UNITY CHURCHES

For information about local Unity Churches, go online to the **Association of Unity Churches** at 816-524-7414, www.unity.org.

WESLEYAN

The local Wesleyan Church is part of the **Pacific Southwest District**: 619-660-0102, www.wesleyanpsw.org or www.wesleyan.org. Contact them for a directory of area churches.

ETHICAL SOCIETIES

Not a conventional religious organization, ethical societies offer a meeting place and fellowship to members and visitors. Their "focus is on core ethical values that people have in common." Acknowledging that humans are both individualistic and social in nature, the society explores what it means to understand the inner workings of self and how to relate to each other in a respectful/ethical/moralistic way. For more information go to www.ethicalsociety.org or contact the **Ethical Culture Society of Los Angeles** at 818-784-9107 or online at www.ethicalsocietyla.org.

HINDU

Hinduism is as complex and multifaceted as the many gods it incorporates. Nearly 13% of the world's population is Hindu. Although most Hindus reside in India, there are roughly one million in the United States. In Los Angeles, contact the **Hindu Temple of Southern California**, 1600 Las Virgenes Canyon Road, Calabasas, 818-880-5552, www.hindutemplesoutherncalifornia.org. Designed by master architect Muthiah Sthapathi from India, this temple is one of the largest and most architecturally authentic Hindu temples in the western hemisphere. Built in the Malibu hills, the ornate temples, called shastras, comply with the strict architectural codes of the Silpa Shastra in the Chola style of temple architecture.

ISLAMIC

To tap into the local Islamic community try the **Islamic Center** at 434 South Vermont Avenue, between 4th and 5th streets in Los Angeles, 213-382-9200, www.islamctr.org; or go to www.islamicfinder.com.

JEWISH

Unlike most of the country, Los Angeles has a sizable Jewish population, with the heaviest concentrations in the Fairfax District. The local media outlet is the *Jewish Journal of Greater Los Angeles*, which you can subscribe to online at www.jewishjournal.com or by calling 213-368-1661. Newcomers in particular may want to contact the **Westside Jewish Community Centers** at 5870 W Olympic Boulevard, in LA. Call them at 323-938-2531 or go online to www.westsidejcc.org or www.jcca.org for information about educational, cultural, and social opportunities. If you are a student, professor, or otherwise affiliated with one of the many area colleges and universities, you can likely attend your school's Hillel or Chabad house.

Of note, the **Wilshire Boulevard Temple**, 3663 Wilshire Boulevard, 213-388-2401, www.wilshireboulevardtemple.org, is home to a prominent Jewish Progressive Reform congregation. Originating as Congregation B'nai Brith in 1862, it was the first synagogue in Los Angeles, with Rabbi Abraham Wolf Edelman as the first full-time rabbi in Southern California. Ten years later, they built their first temple. As membership grew, the congregation moved several times, eventually settling on Wilshire Boulevard in 1929. The Byzantine-inspired architecture was designed by A.M. Edelman, S. Tilden Norton, and David C. Allison; interior features include murals by Hugo Ballin. The Wilshire Temple is listed in the United States Register of Historic Places.

Contact information for branches of Judaism in Southern California includes:

- **Conservative**: United Synagogue of Conservative Judaism, Pacific Southwest Region, 818-986-0907, http://pacsw.uscj.org
- **Orthodox**: Orthodox Union, 310-229-9000, www.ou.org/west
- **Reconstructionist**: Jewish Reconstructionist Federation, www.jrf.org, Kehillat Israel, 310-459-2328, www.kehillatisrael.org
- **Reform**: Union of American Hebrew Congregations, www.urj.org, 212-650-4000

SIKH

Although there are over 20 million Sikhs throughout the world, only 220,000 live in America. There is enough of a Sikh population in Los Angeles for several gurdwaras. In 1989 the **Sikh Sangat of Los Angeles** founded the gurdwara located at 7640 Lankershim Boulevard, North Hollywood, 818-765-9399; and the **Guru Ram Das Gurdwara** is at 1649 South Robertson Boulevard in Los Angeles, 310-201-0954. For more information, go to www.sikhs.org.

KEEPING THIS INCREASINGLY CROWDED CITY LIVABLE REQUIRES SEN-sitivity to our environs. As a result, economizing measures permeate many aspects of LA life. Restaurants may serve customers tap water only upon request; in summer months, residents are constantly reminded by the state to avoid using non-essential electrical appliances during peak hours; and blue recycling bins are regular home and office fixtures. Residents are helping to increase LA's tree canopy cover (currently at 21%) to meet the national average of 27% by planting a tree and registering it with the Mayor's Million Trees LA initiative (www.milliontreesla.org).

The concepts of "green living" and "sustainability" are en vogue among city leaders, and conservation efforts are paying off. Water consumption has remained steady since 1990 despite a 15% increase in the population. LA leads other U.S. cities with Energy Star–certified green large office buildings. In 2006, the SustainLane media company ranked Los Angeles number 4 out of 50 cities surveyed for energy and climate-change policies that are environmentally friendly and economically competitive.

Individuals too can do their part to get closer to carbon-neutral living, but there are trade-offs to consider. Compact fluorescent light bulbs, for example, are touted for their energy-saving properties, but because they contain mercury, CFLs must be treated as hazardous waste for disposal in California and are an exposure hazard if you accidentally break one because they release mercury in your home. Likewise, using a hybrid car may reduce carbon emissions coming from the car, but the production and disposal of the battery presents a hazardous waste issue, not to mention the emissions produced from generating the electricity for charging the battery. Responsible environmental awareness should include due diligence on the unintended consequences of your actions…some popular options are presented below.

GREENING YOUR HOME

A green home is well-insulated and energy-efficient, incorporates nontoxic and sustainably produced materials, and/or has sustainable features like solar-assisted hot-water heating. Unfortunately, green materials and features tend to cost more upfront (sometimes significantly) than non-green. Sometimes, and depending on the feature, the savings gained over the lifespan of the efficiency product will recoup the premium paid in the beginning; other times, a clearer conscience is the primary reward. The cost gap between the idealistic and practical should close as green technology continues to advance. Whether social consciousness or financial savvy motivates a homeowner, there are many features one can add to an existing home to make it greener.

GREEN REMODELING

The City of LA web site has an **Environmental Affairs Department** that offers plenty of informative links for local sustainability resources and publishes a *Sustainable Building Guidebook* that can be downloaded for free at www.lacity. org/ead/index.htm. The City of Santa Monica also publishes a *Green Building Designs and Construction Guidelines* booklet online at http://www.greenbuildings. santa-monica.org. Likewise, the **California Integrated Waste Management Board** offers free fact sheets, case studies, and other information on green building practices at www.ciwmb.ca.gov/GreenBuilding/ToolKit.htm. Remodelers in the planning stages may want to visit the **Green Building Resource Center** (2218 Main Street, Santa Monica, 310-452-7677, www.globalgreen.org/gbrc) to view samples of green building materials and get additional ideas.

Once you're ready to go shopping, browse the **Builder's Surplus Store** (770 North Fair Oaks Avenue, Pasadena, 626-792-3838, www.sgvhabitat.org/TheRe Store/Index.html) for salvaged material from windows to cabinets to plumbing. **Habitat for Humanity's Home Improvement Store** (17700 South Figueroa Street, Gardena, 310-323-5665, www.shophabit.org) keeps an impressive inventory of lighting, flooring, gardening fixtures and just about anything you could save from a demo or remodel. And if you can't find what you need at an architectural salvage store, **LACoMax**, http://ladpw.org/epd/lacomax, is a free searchable online exchange service to locate or sell recycled materials within the county.

New but green materials are now regularly offered at major hardware stores. **LivinGreen** (10000 Culver Boulevard, Culver City, 310-838-8442, www1.livin green.com) specializes in sustainable flooring, carpeting, salvage lumber and all the housewares you'd need to furnish a green home such as furniture, light bulbs, and cleaners. **Cisco Home** stores (multiple locations, www.ciscohome.net) carry a line of sustainable furniture. Low VOC or Zero VOC paints can be purchased at any major building supply store, but local options include **Architectural Coatings & Design Center** (18424 Ventura Boulevard, Tarzana, 818-757-3900, www.

acplusdc.com), **Par Paint**, 1801 Sunset Boulevard, 213-413-4950, www.parpaint. com), **Dunn Edwards** (multiple locations, www.dunnedwards.com) and **Sherwin-Williams** (multiple locations, www.sherwin.com).

Don't forget that you can give back as well while fixing up your home. **The California Integrated Waste Management Board** web site (www.ciwmb. ca.gov) has a searchable C&D database listing companies that reuse or recycle construction and demolition debris. Both the Builder's Surplus Store and Habitat for Humanity's Home Improvement Store accept donations of your salvageable home materials.

ENERGY EFFICIENCY

The California Energy Crisis that started in 2000 officially ended with the gubernatorial state of emergency status ending in November of 2003. However, the California electrical grid is in danger of being stretched beyond maximum capacity each summer. Every resident is strongly encouraged to help reduce energy consumption and increase energy efficiency. California has entire web sites devoted to this topic: www.fypower.org, 866-431-FLEX, and the California Energy Commission's Consumer Energy Center, www.consumerenergycenter.org, 800-555-7794, are the most thorough.

The following are typical recommendations for boosting your home's energy efficiency:

- **Insulate and weatherize your home.** Poorly insulated walls, ceilings, and floors allow heated or cooled air to escape from your house, needlessly raising your energy use (and energy bill). Also seal ductwork, insulate hot water pipes in non-conditioned spaces, and seal or caulk leaks around doors, windows, pipes, vents, attics, and crawlspaces. Replace leaky old windows with insulated windows. These steps will also reduce drafts and increase comfort levels in your home.
- **Upgrade your heating and cooling systems.** Old furnaces and air conditioning units are usually much less efficient than new models. Once you've insulated and weatherized your home, consider replacing old units with new, efficient units, and make sure that they are properly sized for your home. A programmable thermostat can also help reduce energy consumption by automatically maintaining the inside temperature for you. For summer, utility companies suggest setting the thermostat for 78 or higher, and in winter setting it to 68 or cooler.
- **Upgrade inefficient appliances.** Replacing old, inefficient washing machines, dishwashers, water heaters, and especially refrigerators with more efficient models can have a major effect on your energy consumption (and, in the case of washing machines and dishwashers, on your water consumption, too). For-

go using the appliance completely if possible: let washed dishes and clothes air dry instead of using the dishwasher or clothes dryer.

- **Install efficient lighting.** Compact fluorescent light bulbs use 75% less energy and last up to ten times longer than standard incandescent bulbs. They also generate less heat. For an assurance of quality, choose ENERGY STAR® bulbs. (As mentioned at the beginning of this chapter, CFL bulbs do contain mercury and require special handling if they break. The state requires you to dispose of these bulbs at hazardous waste collection centers.) Another option are solar light pipes (commonly sold as Solatubes); these are sky lights installed in the roof that reflect sunlight through a tube into rooms during the day.

- **Turn off appliances when not in use.** Many home electronics such as the TV, DVD player, computer printer, and microwave oven are actually in standby mode and continue to draw a small amount of power even when "off." Plug these appliances into a power strip and turn off the power strip when not in use to completely cut off the drain.

The LA DWP's (and other local utilities') monthly bills frequently include tips on how to make your home more energy efficient. Their web site (www.ladwp. org) lets you conduct an online audit of your own home. They also list rebates and incentives to assist with energy-saving improvements for your home. For a comprehensive whole-house energy assessment and energy recommendations, consider hiring an Energy Trust–certified contractor to do a Home Performance with ENERGY STAR analysis.

California used to offer tax credits for solar and wind energy, but no longer. However, federal tax credits are available; visit the federal government's **Energy Star** web site (www.energystar.gov) or the **Tax Incentives Assistance Project** (www.energytaxincentives.org) to review homeowner incentives, or talk to your accountant for details.

RENEWABLE ENERGY

Consider buying green power from your local utility; look in the "Utilities" section of the **Getting Settled** chapter for details. You can also make your own energy. With constant sunshine here, **solar energy**, including solar water heating and photovoltaic electricity, has long been a power source for heating backyard pools and residential water. Depending on your home's location, wind power or geothermal heating systems may also be potential options. LADWP customers who choose to purchase and install their own solar power system can take advantage of the utility's **Solar Photovoltaic Incentive Program.** Currently, the LADWP offers an additional incentive payment for systems using photovoltaic modules manufactured in the City of Los Angeles. Visit their web site to download the forms. They also list resources for getting loans to install a solar electric system at home. The **California Solar Center** (www.californiasolarcenter.org) is a great clearinghouse of information, from how solar power works to how to implement this plentiful resource. And **HomePower.com** is an in-depth online magazine that features the many ways handy homeowners can build their own means of harnessing natural power resources.

WATER CONSERVATION

Very dry weather conditions have brought water levels low enough to require conservation. Homeowners in the county should be aware of water use prohibitions listed on the **County of Los Angeles Department of Public Work**'s web site (http://ladpw.org) including:

- no water hosing of sidewalks
- no watering of landscaping between 10 a.m. and 5 p.m. during April through September, and between 11 a.m. and 3 p.m. during October through March; plants cannot be watered more than once a day
- no washing of one's car with a hose unless it has an auto shut-off handle

And if you're shopping for a house or condo, note that the seller is required (by Los Angeles Municipal Ordinance No. 172075) to replace all non–water conserving shower heads and toilets with low-flow shower heads and ultra-low-flush toilets before close of escrow. Apartment dwellers are also required to live with these water-saving appliances installed by their landlord.

Exhaustive water conservation advice, like washing full loads of laundry and taking shorter showers, can be found at www.bewaterwise.com. This same web site lists many rebates for installing ultra-low-flush toilets, rotating head sprinklers, and high-efficiency clothes washers. Check the web site to see if you qualify.

LANDSCAPING

Growing native southern California plants is the best way to make your front and/or back yard more Earth friendly. The **Theodore Payne Foundation Nursery** (10459 Tuxford St, Sun Valley, 818-768-1802, www.theodorepayne.org) specializes in selling California native plants and seeds. This nonprofit retail nursery also has demonstration gardens and exhaustive links on their web site promoting native flora. Click "The Garden Spot" tab on www.bewaterwise.com to get ideas on how to convert your existing garden to a water-wise landscape. It lists thousands of plants, shrubs, and trees that are native to the state and drought tolerant. This same web site also has a watering index and calculator to help you adjust your watering schedule so that it is appropriate to the climate as it changes through the seasons. Experts claim homeowners tend to over-water their gardens by twice the amount necessary.

If you live in an area with a wildfire hazard, planting fire-resistant greens is simply a good investment. The **LA County Fire Department** lists such plants at http://fire.lacounty.gov.

Finally, investigate organic gardening practices like composting and replace pesticides with natural pest barriers (such as diatomaceous earth), releasing beneficial insects, and companion planting (such as planting spearmint to repel ants from a vegetable garden). **The Invisible Gardener** (http://invisiblegardener. com) is a solid starting point on these topics.

ENVIRONMENTALLY FRIENDLY PRODUCTS AND SERVICES

The best way to encourage the proliferation of environmentally friendly products and services is to support them. For businesses concerned about the bottom line, customer demand is the most compelling motivation to change. Here are a few resources for finding green products and services.

- **Urban Dweller's Guide to Green Living** describes sustainable products and services from Los Angeles–based businesses; visit www.greenopia.com/la.
- **LA Green Living** profiles local green businesses and events at www.lagreen living.com.
- **The Consumers Union guide to environmental labeling** is online at www. eco-labels.org; the site includes a report card for various environmental claims, and labels and assesses whether the claim is meaningful and/or verified.
- **Consumer Reports** maintains a web site that assesses the environmental soundness of various products; visit www.greenerchoices.org.

FOOD

The weekly farmers' markets are convenient and popular outlets for locally grown organic produce and products. In addition to fruits and vegetables, these markets typically offer locally produced honey, eggs, cheeses, meat, and breads. Consumers who buy local reduce traffic and pollution by shopping in proximity as well as support local agriculture and artisans. **Farmer Net** (www.farmernet. com) lists all the certified farmers' markets in California. To read up on local food issues, look in the weekly food section of the *LA Times* or the new quarterly magazine, **Edible Los Angeles** (www.ediblelosangeles.com).

Many grocery stores in LA have an organic produce section. In addition to seeking out organic labels, certifications such as **Salmon Safe** (www.salmon safe.org) will assure that the source farm or vineyard uses watershed-friendly practices; the **Marine Stewardship Council** (www.msc.org) certifies seafood as being from sustainable fisheries; and the **Food Alliance** (www.foodalliance.org) certifies farms and ranches for sustainable and humane practices.

Finally, because livestock production is resource intensive and can result in their mistreatment, the earth conscious and animal compassionate suggest reducing the amount of meat in your diet. Beginners and veterans will want to investigate **Southern California Vegetarians** (310-289-5777, http://socalveg. org) for helpful information. **Vegetarians in Paradise** (www.vegparadise.com) is a local web magazine that supports non-meat eaters. The raw (uncooked vegan diet) and "conscious food" movement is active in Los Angeles. **Euphoria Loves RAWvolution** (2301 Main Street, Santa Monica, 310-392-9501, http://euphoria lovesrawvolution.com) is the first and only raw, vegan market in the USA. Lots of raw food spots are listed at **We Like It Raw'**s web site (http://restaurants.we likeitraw.com/guides/la).

GREEN MONEY

Some banks, including large national banks, are making efforts to become greener in their operations and lending practices. **Wachovia** has pledged to build only green branches in Los Angeles. **Bank of America** and **CitiCorp** too have promised to invest millions of dollars to go green. But the simplest way for consumers to conserve paper and fuel is to do all of their banking online.

For those looking to invest their money in a socially conscious manner, start your research with **GreenMoneyJournal** (www.greenmoneyjournal.com) or **The Progressive Investor** (www.sustainablebusiness.com/progressiveinvestor/).

GREENER TRANSPORTATION

Living closer to work, telecommuting, combining short trips, carpooling, and relying more on walking, biking, and public transportation are tried-but-true ways to reduce congestion and pollution. The **Transportation** chapter covers these alternatives. The **Drive Less/Save More** web site (www.drivelesssavemore.com) offers additional ideas, discusses how reducing the amount you drive can benefit you, and has a handy driving-cost calculator.

If these options are not practical for your situation, consider owning a more fuel-efficient vehicle. The most popular and efficient mass-production cars are gas-electric hybrids like the Toyota Prius or the Honda Civic hybrid. A hybrid car consumes less fuel, and you may be entitled to federal tax credits if you buy one. The **Drive Clean** web site (www.driveclean.ca.gov) will help you research zero and near-zero emission vehicles as well as incentives. If you managed to purchase an Electric Vehicle (EV) before they stopped selling them, be aware that EVs may currently park for free at LAX charging stations. Vehicles that are 100% electric, 100% compressed natural gas (CNG), or hybrid and carrying a Clean Air Decal may park at any meter in the City of Santa Monica for free. The City of Los Angeles has not yet decided to renew their free-parking program, which expired at the end of 2007. To see if your car qualifies you to obtain a California Clean Air Decal, visit http://www.dmv.ca.gov/vr/decal.htm.

And there are more incentives. Los Angeles–based Farmers Insurance is offering a 10% discount on auto insurance to customers who own a hybrid-electric or alternative-fuel vehicle. Owners of qualifying hybrid cars are also allowed to use the carpool lane if they requested a sticker, good thru 2011. The allotment of stickers has all sold out, however, and there are no plans to extend the program.

No matter what car you own, routine maintenance ensures that the engine runs as efficiently as possible. The nation's only environmentally friendly auto club, **Better World Club** (866-238-1137, www.betterworldclub.com), can provide roadside assistance and travel advice. They offer the full menu of auto-club services, along with discounts on hybrid rentals, bicycle roadside assistance, and an electronic newsletter, *Kicking Asphalt*.

ALTERNATIVE FUELS

You can buy or modify cars to run on alternative fuels like pure ethanol, hydrogen, compressed natural gas, or biodiesel (diesel fuel made from vegetable oil). The Honda Civic GX runs entirely on CNG and was named "America's Greenest Car" in 2007. Natural gas cars are the alternative fuel car of choice in Los Angeles.

Alternative fuel stations are somewhat rare finds in LA, and you'll need to use the web to locate them. For CNG, visit www.cleancarmaps.com or the California Natural Gas Vehicle Coalition at www.cngvc.org. And if you're considering installing a CNG station at home, look at www.myphill.com. To top off on your ethanol, aka E85, go to www.e85refueling.com. For biodiesel, www.labiodiesel coop.org lists local stations. And your nearest hydrogen fueling centers can be located through www.fuelcells.org.

GREEN RESOURCES

The following are just a fraction of the available resources on sustainability and environmental protection:

- **The Los Angeles Chapter of the Sierra Club**, 3435 Wilshire Blvd #320, 213-387-4287, http://angeles.sierraclub.org, is a wealth of well-organized information on local environmental issues.
- **EcoGeek**, www.ecogeek.org; web site analyzes earth-friendly technology.
- **Carbon offsets** relies on the theory that you can neutralize the carbon dioxide you generate by funding anti-CO_2 measures. Carbon offsets funds projects that store carbon or reduce carbon emissions from other sources, such as tree-planting projects, energy-efficiency projects, and alternative-energy investments. You can calculate how much CO_2 you're producing at www.Live Neutral.org. Offsets are available from sources like Terra Pass (877-210-9581,

TerraPass.com), Green Tags (503-248-1905, www.greentagsUSA.org) and My Climate (www.myclimate.org).

- **Sustain LA** is a city-run clearinghouse of web-based green information for both residents and businesses at www.sustainla.org.
- **City of LA's Environmental Affairs Department**, 200 N Spring St, Ste 2005, 213-978-0888, www.lacity.org/ead/index.htm, offers information for local sustainability resources and environmental affairs.
- **The California Environmental Protection Agency**, 916-323-2514, www.calepa.ca.gov, oversees a wide range of environmental topics that affect Californian residents.
- **The Regional Environmental Information Network (REIN)**, www.rein.org, an online clearinghouse of environmental information, is part of the Metro regional government's Nature in Neighborhoods program.
- **The United States Department of Energy's Energy Efficiency and Renewable Energy** web site, www.eere.energy.gov, informs consumers about renewable energy.

I N LOS ANGELES, WHERE THERE IS APPROXIMATELY ONE CAR FOR EVERY 1.8 persons, it is easy to understand why the city consistently ranks number one in the nation for traffic congestion. Los Angeles sprawls across 467 square miles and, while technically it is possible to get around by foot, bicycle, bus, and Metro light rail or subway, in most cases it is quicker and more convenient to drive. According to the Texas Transportation Institute, Los Angeles commuters spend an average of 90 hours a year sitting still in traffic—something to think about when choosing a place to live relative to where you work. To combat LA's reliance on the auto, the **South Coast Air Quality Management District (AQMD)** is doing its best to encourage use of public transportation, carpooling, bicycling, and walking, and many smog-conscious residents are trying to cut down on their driving, especially during peak commute hours. (There's even a hotline that you can call, 800-CUT-SMOG, to report a vehicle that you see emitting visible exhaust for more than 10 seconds.) In addition, the AQMD has mandated that companies with 100 or more employees must encourage smog-cutting transportation alternatives. In consideration of these mandates, some companies operate on flex time, which allows employees to work a compressed schedule of nine out of ten working days or to telecommute in certain situations, creating fewer cars on the road. To find out more about AQMD's initiatives, call 909-396-2000 or go to www. AQMD.gov. The **Los Angeles County Bicycle Coalition** (213-629-2142, www.la bike.org) has tips on commuting by bike. (If this interests you, consult with the LA County Bike Map Hotline, 213-244-6539 for route information. For personalized bike route information in LA and OC counties, try www.bikemetro.com.)

California law requires that everyone be buckled up, and children under age six or weighing less than 60 pounds must use a car safety seat. Drivers are required to use a hands-free device when using their cell phone while driving. And smoking in a vehicle with a minor present is prohibited.

GETTING AROUND

BY CAR

A quick glance at the map will tell you that Los Angeles and Orange County are the land of freeways. Any which way you look at it, morning (7:30 a.m. to 10:30 a.m.) and evening (3 p.m. to 6 p.m.) rush hours are a bear. If avoiding driving during these hours is not possible, be sure to check the electronic freeway condition signs along the road and heed any "**Sig-Alerts**" when driving (named after their inventor, the alert refers to any unplanned event that causes at least one lane of traffic to close for 30 minutes or more). A check of real-time traffic condition maps on the internet, www.sigalert.com (freeway) and http://trafficinfo.lacity.org (surface streets), as they're getting off work, is a popular way for natives to plan their commute home. On the road, two local radio stations, AM 1070 and AM 980, broadcast traffic reports every 5 minutes and "on the ones" (9:01, 9:11, etc.) respectively. **Caltrans**, the city crews responsible for maintaining Los Angeles' and Orange counties' massive freeway network, posts real-time road incidents on the internet via a Statewide Travel Information Map at www.dot.ca.gov/travel/index.php. The **California Highway Patrol** (**CHP**) also posts real-time road alerts at http://cad.chp.ca.gov. The **California Department of Transportation** lets you view live streaming of freeway traffic cams at www.dot.ca.gov/hq/roadinfo; and the **Travel Advisory News Network**'s site, http://traffic.tann.net/maps/lartraffic.jsp, also covers Orange County.

So, what is the best way to get around? In general, the freeways are a good choice if you need to go long distances. However, some savvy road jockeys swear by surface streets if gridlocked freeways are moving at under 30 mph. **Interstate 5** runs north-south, and is the fastest, though not the prettiest route, to the San Francisco Bay Area and other parts of Northern California. It is also the primary artery into Orange County. **US-101**, a more scenic route through the state, cuts through the San Fernando Valley and Hollywood. **Highway 1**, known as the **Pacific Coast Highway** (**PCH**) in the Los Angeles area, runs up and down the entire California coast. Most agree that, at some point, it's worth the extra hours on the road to take Highway 1 to or from northern California, as it covers some of the most beautiful terrain in the country.

Locally, **I-10** runs east-west, and is the most common way to get from West LA to downtown and points in between. The **I-405** runs north-south between the Valley and West LA, and down through the South Bay, and can have punishing traffic. Going north-south in south-central LA is the **I-110** freeway, which features an impressive elevated carpool lane. The **I-105** provides quick access from south-central LA to the west, ending at LAX. The **I-101** runs north-south in LA (called the **Hollywood Freeway**), but heads west in the Valley (and becomes the **Ventura Freeway**). **Highway 134** runs east-west and begins in Toluca Lake, then becomes the **I-210** in Pasadena.

Some of the stickiest interchanges in LA include the "four-level" in downtown, which is where on-ramps to the 110, 101, 10, and 5 freeways are clustered within a mile of each other. The interchange between the 405 and 101 is also tough, especially from the 405 to the 101. The American Highway User's Alliance ranked this interchange the worst bottleneck in the nation. A $46 million revamp of this interchange completed in 2007 has eased congestion somewhat. The 405 near LAX is another trouble spot, especially on Friday and Sunday evenings. Ditto for the junction where the 405 funnels into the 5 (sometimes called the "El Toro Y") in Orange County. Where the 5 meets the **SR-22** (**Garden Grove Freeway**) and **SR-57** (**Orange Freeway**) is appropriately nicknamed the "Orange Crush." The notorious crush was listed in the 2002 Guinness Book of World Records as the most complex road interchange in the world. **SR-73** (**San Joaquin Hills Transportation Corridor**) is a toll road that parallels the 405 and can be a time-saving shortcut between the 5 in San Juan Capistrano and the 405 in Costa Mesa. Seemingly constant freeway improvements in the OC continue to make these roads more efficient, but they do translate into intermittent inconveniences for commuters. The I-5 Gateway, a two-mile stretch from the **SR-91** (**Riverside Freeway**) to the LA County line, is scheduled to complete its lane-widening project in 2010. The **Orange County Transportation Authority** (www.octa.net) estimates that nearly 2 million people cross the OC/LA border daily.

During rush hour and rainy weather most major LA and OC surface streets are overwhelmed. The intersection of Wilshire and Westwood Boulevards (in Westwood) is the busiest in LA. The junction of Wilshire and Santa Monica Boulevards (in Beverly Hills) is also bad. In the OC, MacArthur Boulevard and Campus Drive tends to be gridlocked. The three-street junction of Yorba Linda Boulevard, SR-90 (Richard Nixon Freeway), and Lakeview Avenue can be very frustrating to navigate in Yorba Linda.

The availability of GPS with real-time traffic reports has been a true time-saver for many SoCal drivers. In addition, most locals have their tried and true shortcuts around town (remember Steve Martin's cruise through alleys, parking lots, and front lawns in *LA Story*?), but they may be stingy about telling you what they are. After all, too much traffic on the shortcut defeats the purpose! It's worth experimenting yourself to see which byways move and which do not.

CARPOOLING

Most cars on local freeways hold one person—you guessed it, the driver. Local and statewide agencies are trying to change that. Carpooling diamond lanes, also called HOV (high occupancy vehicle) or diamond lanes, located in the far left lane and marked by white diamonds and carpooling signs, are for the exclusive use of cars with two or more people (some diamond lanes require a minimum of three people). Check with your human resources office at work for carpooling in-centives. Many employers offer gas coupons, parking spaces, and other freebies to those who make the trip with co-workers. For more information on commuter carpools and vanpools, visit Commutesmart.info or call 800-266-6883.

For additional information on transportation around Los Angeles, call the **Regional Transportation Information Network** at 800-2LA-RIDE.

PARK & RIDE LOCATIONS

Too many to list here (see your *Thomas Guide* index or www.commutesmart.info/lotslaneslinks/parkridelots.asp for a full list). A few include (located in Los Angeles unless otherwise noted):

- **Burbank Metrolink Station**, 201 N Front St, Burbank
- **Del Mar Gold Line Station**, 230 S Raymond Ave, Pasadena
- **Glendale Transportation Center**, 400 W Cerritos Ave, Glendale
- **Harbor Freeway Green Line Station**, 11500 Figueroa St
- **Riverton Park & Ride**, Riverton Ave and Ventura Blvd, Studio City
- **Santa Clarita Metrolink Station**, 22122 Soledad Canyon Rd, Santa Clarita
- **Sierra Madre Park & Ride**, Sierra Madre Blvd. and I-210, Pasadena
- **Sepulveda Pass Park & Ride**, 2350 Skirball Center Dr, Brentwood
- **South Pasadena Park & Ride**, 435 S Fairoaks Ave, South Pasadena
- **Van Nuys Metrolink Station**, 7720 Van Nuys Blvd, Van Nuys
- **Union Station**, 800 N Alameda St, Los Angeles

CAR RENTALS

There are numerous car rental agencies near the airports, and throughout the city. Call the following phone numbers for information, reservations, and locations:

- **Alamo**, 800-327-9633, www.alamo.com
- **Avis**, 800-331-1212, www.avis.com
- **Budget**, 800-527-0700, www.budget.com
- **Dollar**, 800-800-4000, www.dollar.com
- **Enterprise**, 800-325-8007, www.enterprise.com
- **Hertz**, 800-654-3131, www.hertz.com
- **National**, 800-227-7368, www.nationalcar.com
- **Payless**, 800-729-5377, www.paylesscarrental.com
- **Rent-a-Wreck**, 800-535-1391, www.rentawreck.com
- **Thrifty**, 800-367-2277, www.thrifty.com

TAXIS AND SHUTTLES

Unlike New York or Chicago, Los Angeles is not a major taxi town. You will not, for instance, be able to step out of any building and flag down a cab. Nonetheless, there are taxis at airports, hotels, and tourist attractions. If you need a cab at a specific time, your best bet is to call and order one in advance. Group shuttles are almost always cheaper than cabs for one passenger, and may still be cheaper for groups. The listing here includes both taxis and shuttles:

- **Checker Cab**, 800-300-5007, www.lacheckercab.com
- **Prime Time Shuttle**, 800-733-8267, www.primetimeshuttle.com
- **Super Shuttle**, 800-258-3826, www.supershuttle.com
- **Super Airport Shuttle**, 310-263-7072, www.superaiportshuttle.com
- **United Taxi**, 800-822-8294, www.unitedtaxi.com
- **VanGo**, 800-275-8264 www.askvango.com
- **Yellow Cab**, 877-733-3305, www.layellowcab.com

LIMOUSINES

Check the Yellow Pages under "Limousine" for a listing of the many companies that provide limo service—just don't expect to get a limo on the day of the Academy Awards.

BY PUBLIC TRANSPORTATION

METROPOLITAN TRANSPORTATION AUTHORITY—METRO

LA County's **Metro** serves the greater Los Angeles area with more than 190 bus, rail, and light-rail routes. Base fare is $1.25; the unlimited local travel monthly pass is $62 (available in advance on the 25th of each month). For more on fares and passes, as well as routes and maps, visit www.mta.net or call 800-COMMUTE; TTY 800-252-9040, 6 a.m. to 8:30 p.m., Monday-Friday, and 8 a.m. to 6 p.m., Saturday and Sunday (outside of Los Angeles, call 213-922-6235, 8 a.m. to 4:15 p.m., Monday–Friday, or write to: Los Angeles County Metropolitan Transportation Authority, One Gateway Plaza, Los Angeles, CA 90012-2952). Metro also operates a web-based trip planner to help you navigate the county's massive public transportation network: www.taketransit.net.

Metro's light rail and buses are ADA-compliant for passengers with hearing, mobility and visual impairments, and reduced fares are available to disabled passengers. If a disability prevents you from using regular bus or rail service, you may hire Access Paratransit for curb-to-curb service 24-hours-a-day. Contact Access Services' information specialists at 800-827-0829, TDD 800-827-1359, or online at www.asila.org to obtain information for this and all accessible transportation options in Los Angeles County.

SUBWAY AND LIGHT TRANSIT

Los Angeles has an interesting history with public transportation. Until the 1940s, like most major American cities, LA had an extensive system of electric trolley cars run by the Pacific Electric Railway, known as "Red Cars." The old tracks can still be seen in Santa Monica and Beverly Hills. The system was famed for its efficiency and affordability. There's a long-held myth perpetuated by the movie "Who Framed Roger Rabbit" that car and tire manufacturers killed the railway in the interest of big business. But the less glamorous and more likely cause for the demise of the system included the growing popularity of automobiles, lack of public support, and unrecoverable losses in ridership from the Great Depression. Today you can relive a bit of history: The Port of Los Angeles has restored two Red Cars from the 1920s and operates them along a 1.5-mile route that retraces a portion of the original Red Car line in Long Beach. For schedule information: 310-732-3473, http://portoflosangeles.org.

LA's first subway was rolled out in the form of the **Metro's Red Line**. The project, delayed by shoddy workmanship and cost overruns, was unpopular with Angelenos ("A subway in earthquake country?" was the question commonly asked by those opposed to it). It was so unpopular, in fact, that in 1998 a proposition to outlaw the use of tax dollars to fund the Metro passed by a 68% majority. Today, however, ridership on the Metro subway continues to grow as commuters are taking advantage of this clean, predictable, and well-patrolled mode of transport. Currently, the Metro has five lines: the **Blue Line** (light rail) runs from downtown to Long Beach; the **Red Line** (subway) originates from Union Station in downtown and runs through Hollywood, finishing in North Hollywood; the **Green Line** (light rail) takes commuters through south-central communities, between Redondo Beach and Norwalk; and the **Gold Line** (light rail) connects Union Station to Pasadena. The **Purple Line** (subway) runs from Union Station to Mid-Wilshire. Fares at press time were $1.25 per boarding. An unlimited local travel monthly pass may be purchased for $62. Maps, timetables, tickets, and passes may be purchased in person at the Metro customer service center at Union Station, downtown, 800 North Alameda Street, or by calling 800-COMMUTE (out of state, call 213-922-6059 to purchase passes; 213-922-6235 for customer service). Online, go to www.mta.net for Metro and bus timetables and to download the "Rider's Guide."

BUS

Due to the limited range of the Metro light rail lines, most residents who use public transportation rely on Metro buses to get around. For more information on using the bus in LA, call Metro's 800-COMMUTE line, an automated phone system that connects callers to over 40 transportation agencies serving Los Angeles and Orange counties. Also download Metro's "Metro Bus & Rail Rider's Guide" at www.mta.net. The *Transit Guide* ($12.50), published by the **Southern Califor-nia Transit Advocates**, 3010 Wilshire Boulevard #362, Los Angeles, CA 90010, 213-388-2364, www.socata.net, lists over 50 fixed-route public transit agencies operating in Southern California, with tips on using the systems. **Transit-rider. com** (www.transitrider.com) is another comprehensive resource for getting around Los Angeles, Orange, and San Diego counties.

Seniors and the mobility impaired can utilize the Los Angeles Department of Transportation's **CityRide** (see LADOT contact information below), a service that provides substantial discounts on Metro passes, taxi rides, private lift van services, and dial-a-ride trips to those who qualify.

Additional bus service options in and around LA include:

- The **City of LA Department of Transportation (LADOT)** operates **Commuter Express** and **DASH**. The Commuter Express links the San Fernando Valley with other parts of LA, including downtown, Burbank, Glendale, Pasadena, and LAX, with a limited number of stops. The DASH is a shuttle bus that runs short hops in the Valley and greater LA. Call 818/213/323/310-808-2273 or visit www. ladottransit.com for more information.

- The **Metrolink** is a long-distance commuter train connecting Los Angeles to surrounding counties, including Orange, Ventura, and San Diego. There is also a Ventura County Line that takes riders from Union Station to Northridge, Van Nuys, Burbank, and Glendale. Fares are determined by distance traveled. Call 800-371-5465 or visit www.metrolinktrains.com for more information.

- The **Culver City Bus**, 310-253-6510 (recorded information), www.culvercity. org/bus/bus.asp?sec=res; provides local service in Culver City and to Los An-geles, LAX, Marina del Rey, UCLA, Venice, and the Westside. Adult base fare is $.75.

- **Foothill Transit**, 626-967-3147, www.foothilltransit.org; operates local and ex-press buses within the Foothills area.

- Get around Glendale via the **Glendale Beeline**: 818-548-3960, www.glendale-online.com/transportation/beeline

- **Orange County Transportation Authority (OCTA)**, 714-560-OCTA or www. octa.net; serves Orange County. Light rail projects have not yet been able to get traction.

- **Santa Clarita Transit (SCT)**, 661-294-1287, www.santa-clarita.com/cityhall/ field/transit; offers local bus service in the Santa Clarita Valley, as well as ex-press buses to downtown LA, Westwood, and the Valley.

- **Torrance Transit**, 310-618-6266 or www.ci.torrance.ca.us; serves the South Bay area of LA County.

- **Santa Monica Municipal Bus Lines (Big Blue Bus)**, 310-451-5444, www.big bluebus.com; services Santa Monica and the Westside, some routes extend to UCLA, LAX, and downtown.

- The **West Hollywood CityLine/DayLine** services the city of West Hollywood, fares are $ .25 or free with a Metro pass. Call 323-848-6375 or go to www.weho. org for route and schedule information.

NATIONAL TRAIN AND BUS SERVICE

- **Amtrak**, 800-872-7245, www.amtrak.com; Los Angeles's Union Station is downtown at 8090 N Alameda St. Amtrak offers a variety of departure times for San Diego commuters. Discount fares and promotions can be found on its web site.
- **Greyhound**, 800-231-2222, www.greyhound.com; the Los Angeles terminal is downtown at 1716 E 7th St, 213-629-8402.

AIR TRAVEL

AIRPORTS

Several airports serve this teeming metropolitan area. **Los Angeles International Airport (LAX)**, 310-646-5252, www.lawa.org, is the largest and busiest airport on the West Coast. It is located just south of Playa del Rey.

Numerous public transportation service options to and from LAX are available. The Metro Rail Green Line stops at Aviation Station and provides free shuttle service to and from LAX. The Metro bus route #42 travels from LAX to downtown Los Angeles and to Union Station (train), which is about two miles from the Los Angeles Greyhound Bus Terminal. Board the bus at the LAX City Bus Center located in remote Parking Lot C on 96th Street and Sepulveda Boulevard.

If you drive, LAX has almost 8,000 parking spaces in eight parking structures surrounding the passenger terminals, plus an additional two satellite lots (Parking Lot C at 96th Street and Sepulveda Boulevard and Parking Lot B at 111th Street and La Cienega). Check traffic flow to the airport on the web at http://trafficinfo.lacity.org/html/lax.html, or tune into 530AM, the LAX Travelers Information Service radio station.

For lost or misdirected luggage from your flight, you should contact your airline. To retrieve items left behind at any of the passenger screening stations at LAX, contact the TSA Lost and Found in Terminal 6 at 310-665-7382. For assistance with items lost elsewhere at the airport, contact the LAX Lost and Found at 310-417-0440.

Airlines serving LAX include (see further below for contact information):

- **Terminal 1**: Southwest and US Airways
- **Terminal 2**: Air Canada, China, Air France, Air New Zealand, Hawaiian, Northwest, Virgin Atlantic, and others

- **Terminal 3**: Alaska, Frontier, Midwest, and others
- **Terminal 4**: American Airlines, Qantas
- **Terminal 5**: Aeromexico, Air Jamaica, and Delta Air Lines plus partner airlines
- **Terminal 6**: Continental Airlines, United (Premiere, First class, Business class only), and others
- **Terminal 7**: United Airlines
- **Terminal 8**: TED Airlines and United Express
- **Terminal B** is The Tom Bradley International Terminal and serves most non-US airlines, including Air India, British Airways, Cathay Pacific Airways, Japan, and Mexicana.

Additional **regional airports** include:

- **Bob Hope (Burbank/Glendale/Pasadena) Airport**, 2627 N Hollywood Way, 818-840-8840, www.bur.com: Alaska, American, America West, SkyWest, Southwest, and United airlines offer domestic service.
- **Long Beach Airport** is located at 4100 E Donald Douglas Dr, 562-570-2600, www.longbeach.gov/airport. For information on parking, call 562-570-2683. Commercial airlines servicing this airport include Alaska, Delta, Jet Blue, and U.S. Airways.
- **LA/Ontario International Airport** is located about an hour southeast of Los Angeles at Airport Dr and Vineyard Ave in Ontario. For general information, call 909-937-2700 or go to www.LAWA.org. Major airlines servicing LAX, as well as Jet Blue, also fly into Ontario.
- **LA/Palmdale Regional Airport** is located in the northern tip of LA County at 41000 20th St E, Palmdale, 661-266-7602 www.LAWA.org. United is the only passenger airline operating limited flights to San Francisco currently.
- **Orange County's John Wayne Airport** is at 18741 Airport Way in Santa Ana, 949-252-5200, www.ocair.com; parking, dial the airport and press 0. Airlines include Alaska, Aloha, American, Continental, Delta, Frontier, Northwest, Southwest, United, and US Airways.
- **Santa Monica Airport**, 3223 Donald Douglas Loop S, 310-458-8591, www.santa-monica.org/airport; no commercial flight service. For the exclusive use of private planes and helicopters.
- **Van Nuys Airport**, 16461 Sherman Way, 818-785-8838, www.LAWA.org; for corporate and private planes and helicopters, no commercial flights.

Contact information for the **Major Airlines** serving Greater Los Angeles:

- **AeroMexico**, 800-237-6639, www.aeromexico.com
- **Air Canada**, 888-247-2262, www.aircanada.ca
- **Alaska**, 800-252-7522, www.alaskaair.com
- **American**, 800-433-7300, www.aa.com
- **British Airways**, 800-247-9297, www.britishairways.com
- **Cathay Pacific**, 800-233-2742, www.cathaypacific.com

- **Delta**, 800-221-1212, www.delta.com
- **Continental**, 800-525-0280, www.continental.com
- **Japan Airlines**, 800-525-3663, www.japanair.com
- **Jet Blue**, 800-538-2583, www.jetblue.com
- **Mexicana**, 800-531-7921, www.mexicana.com
- **Northwest-KLM**, 800-225-2525, www.nwa.com
- **Qantas**, 800-227-4500, www.qantas.com.au
- **Southwest**, 800-I-FLY-SWA, www.southwest.com
- **US Airways**, 800-428-4322, www.usairways.com
- **United**, 800-241-6522, www.ual.com

FLIGHT DELAYS

Information about flight delays can be checked online on your airline's web site, or at www.fly.faa.gov. Similarly, the site www.flightarrivals.com offers real-time arrival, departure, and delay details for commercial flights.

CONSUMER COMPLAINTS—AIRLINES

To register a complaint against an airline, the Department of Transportation's Aviation Consumer Protection Division is the place to call or write: 202-366-0511, Aviation Consumer Protection Division, C-75, U.S. Department of Transportation, 1200 New Jersey Avenue, Washington, DC 20590. There is also the option of filing a complaint online at their web site: http://airconsumer.ost.dot.gov.

L OS ANGELES AND THE GREATER METROPOLITAN AREA HAVE A GOOD selection of hotels and motels. Accommodations run the gamut from utilitarian to ultra-luxurious. When reserving a room, be sure to ask about discounts or weekend packages. Some hotels offer senior citizen and/or automobile club discounts. Always inquire about specials to check for unadvertised discounts. Keep in mind that summer rates can be higher than the rest of the year, and that big conventions, or other area events, will cause hotels to fill up fast and rates to rise.

Once you've found the hotel, motel, inn, or other option that suits your fancy, you've got to decide how you want to reserve your room. Do you want to call and reserve directly or go through a reservation service? You will get more liberal cancellation policies if you contact the hotel directly. And don't forget to ask about packages and weekend specials. Here are a few reservation services and online travel agents that can assist you with finding a place to stay:

- **Cheap Tickets**, www.cheaptickets.com
- **Expedia**, 800-EXPEDIA, www.expedia.com
- **Hotel Locators**, 800-576-0003, www.hotellocators.com
- **Hotels.com**, 800-964-6835, www.hotels.com
- **LowestFare.com**, www.lowestfare.com
- **Orbitz**, www.orbitz.com
- **Priceline**, www.priceline.com
- **Quikbook**, 800-789-9887, www.quikbook.com
- **Tom Parsons' Best Fares**, www.bestfares.com
- **Travelocity**, www.travelocity.com
- **TurboTrip.com**, www.turbotrip.com

A word of advice: When making reservations through any discount site it is always wise to ask about its cancellation policy and if the rate quoted includes the hotel tax, which in LA is a whopping 14%. Also, some services require a full payment when making the reservation.

The following list of hotels and motels is by no means complete. For more listings, check the telephone directory under "Hotels and Motels." If you are traveling and know the area in which you wish to book a room, you might call the local Chamber of Commerce or visit the city's web site for a list of what's available. The **LA Visitors Bureau**, 800-228-2452, www.discoverlosangeles.com, and **California Tourism** web site, http://gocalif.ca.gov, also offer a few recommendations. While you're at the LA Visitors Bureau web site, request the *LA Official Visitor's Guide* to get a quick introduction to the city.

Unless otherwise noted, the following establishments are located in Los Angeles.

LUXURY LODGINGS

There is no shortage of luxury hotels in Los Angeles and the sky's the limit in terms of room rates ($5,000 a night for a suite at the Century Plaza Hotel, where visiting presidents and dignitaries stay). What follows are just a few in the $200- to $500-a-night range:

- **Beverly Hills Hotel**, 9641 Sunset Blvd, Beverly Hills, 310-276-2251, www.beverlyhillshotel.com
- **Chateau Marmont**, 8221 Sunset Blvd, Hollywood, 323-656-1010, www.chateaumarmont.com
- **Four Seasons Los Angeles**, 300 South Doheny Dr, 310-273-2222, www.fourseasons.com
- **Hyatt Regency Century Plaza Hotel & Spa**, 2025 Avenue of the Stars, Century City, 310-228-1234, http://centuryplaza.hyatt.com
- **Hotel Bel Air**, 701 Stone Canyon Rd, Bel Air, 310-472-1211, www.hotelbelair.com
- **Loews Santa Monica Beach Hotel**, 1700 Ocean Ave, Santa Monica, 866-210-9156, www.santamonicaloewshotel.com
- **Raffles L'Ermitage Beverly Hills**, 9291 Burton Way, Beverly Hills, 310-278-3344, http://beverlyhills.raffles.com
- **Sofitel Los Angeles**, 8555 Beverly Blvd, 310-278-5444, www.sofitel.com
- **The Peninsula**, 9882 Santa Monica Blvd, Beverly Hills, 310-551-2888, http://beverlyhillspeninsula.com
- **Beverly Wilshire Four Seasons**, 9500 Wilshire Blvd, Beverly Hills, 310-275-5200, www.fourseasons.com
- **Langham Huntington**, 1401 South Oak Knoll Ave, Pasadena, 626-568-3900, whttp://pasadena.langhamhotels.com
- **Ritz Carlton Marina del Rey**, 4375 Admiralty Way, Marina del Rey, 310-823-1700, www.ritzcarlton.com

MIDDLE-RANGE LODGINGS

For hotels with multiple locations, call and inquire about their rates, as prices will vary according to location. The following hotels offer rooms that range between $100 and $300.

- **Sunset Tower Hotel**, 8358 Sunset Blvd, West Hollywood, 323-654-7100, www.sunsettowerhotel.com
- **Marriott Courtyard/Hotels/Inns**, 800-228-9290, www.marriott.com; Marriotts are located in Burbank, Century City, Long Beach, LAX, Marina del Rey, Sherman Oaks, Torrance, and Woodland Hills.
- **Hilton Hotels**, 9 in the LA area, call 800-445-8667, www.hilton.com
- **Hyatt Hotels**, 800-233-1234, www.hyatt.com; locations in LA, Century City, West Hollywood, and Long Beach
- **Omni Hotel**, 251 South Olive St, 213-617-3300, www.omnihotels.com
- **Radisson Hotels;** 800-333-3333, www.radisson.com, locations in Culver City, LAX, Whittier, and Covina
- **Hotel Shangri-La**, 1301 Ocean Ave, Santa Monica, 310-394-2791, www.shangrila-hotel.com (set to reopen in 2008)
- **The Standard**, www.standardhotels.com, two locations: Hollywood, 8300 W Sunset Blvd, 323-650-9090; and downtown LA at 550 S Flower St, 213-892-8080
- **Hilton Checkers Hotel**, 535 S Grand Ave, 213-624-0000, www.hiltoncheckers.com
- **Westin** and **Sheraton Hotels**, 800-937-8461 or 800-325-3535, www.starwoodhotels.com; locations in Pasadena, LAX, Universal City, Culver City, Long Beach, and downtown. Their most famous hotel is the Westin Bonaventure Hotel & Suites at 404 S Figueroa St, 213-624-1000; their glass elevators have been featured in many films.

INEXPENSIVE LODGINGS

For hotels with multiple locations, call and inquire on their rates and reservations; prices will vary according to location. The following generally range between $22 and $150.

- **Best Western**, 800-780-7234, www.bestwestern.com; various locations in LA, including Santa Monica, Pasadena, and Westwood
- **The Beverly Laurel Motor Hotel**, 8018 Beverly Blvd, 800-962-3824
- **Beverly Terrace**, 496 N Doheny Dr, 310-274-8141, www.hotelbeverlyterrace; offers pleasant if small rooms in a great location
- **Comfort Inn**, 877-424-6423, www.comfortinn.com, **Econo Lodge**, 877-424-6423, www.econolodge.com, **Clarion Hotel**, 877-424-6423, www.clarionhotel.com, and **Rodeway Inn**, 877-424-6423, www.rodewayinn.com are all run by Choice Hotels International; there are 100+ locations throughout LA, includ-

ing downtown, Burbank, Hollywood, Glendale. Accommodations are basic, but inexpensive.

- **Days Inn**, 800-329-7466, www.daysinn.com; various locations
- **Farmer's Daughter Hotel**, 115 S Fairfax Ave, 323-937-3930, www.farmers daughterhotel.com
- **Holiday Inn**, 888-HOLIDAY, www.ichotelsgroup.com; there are many Holiday Inns and Holiday Inn Expresses in the Los Angeles area. Call for reservations and information.
- **Hotel Figueroa**, 939 S Figueroa St, 213-627-8971, www.figueroahotel.com
- **Howard Johnson**, 800-446-4656, www.hojo.com; there are four in the Los Angeles area.
- **The Magic Castle Hotel**, 800-741-4915, www.magiccastlehotel.com; 7025 Franklin Ave, Hollywood; cheery two-story lodge-type building located near Hollywood tourist attractions.
- **Motel 6**, 800-466-8356, www.motel6.com; various locations, including Hollywood
- **Orbit Hotel** & **Hostel**, 7950 Melrose Ave, Hollywood, 877-672-4887, www.orbit hotel.com; six-person dorm-type rooms and some private rooms available with baths; no individual telephone lines
- **Ramada Inn**, 800-272-6232, www.ramada.com; multiple locations, including West Hollywood
- **Vibe Hotel**, 5922 Hollywood Blvd, Hollywood, 866-751-8600, www.vibehotel. com. Hostel-type accommodations are also available.

BED & BREAKFAST INNS

The majority of B&Bs in Los Angeles are hosted, usually by the proprietors, and are reminiscent of a stay at a mini-hotel with a dash of an overnighter at grandma's house. Nearly all require a minimum stay of two nights. It is possible to book reservations through a B&B directly, though some only list with an agency. In comparison with the number of hotels in LA, the selection of B&Bs is very limited. The following guides can assist you with locating a B&B that suits your needs and budget. Commissions, if any, are included in the price of the reservation.

- **California Association of Bed and Breakfast Inns**, 800-373-9251, www.cab bi.com
- **California B&B Travel Directory**, www.bbtravel.com; comprehensive listings
- **Bed and Breakfast Explorer**, www.bbexplorer.com
- **LA Convention & Visitors Bureau**, 333 S Hope St, 18th floor, Los Angeles, CA 90071, 800-228-2452, www.discoverlosangeles.com; search its web site or call for referrals to local B&Bs.

EXTENDED-STAY HOTELS

Extended-stay hotels may be a good option for those simply needing more time in their search for permanent housing, although finding a summer sublet near a university will probably cost far less (see the **Finding a Place to Live** chapter for more information). Nightly, weekly, or monthly leases can be had, though a monthly lease may be the minimum at some extended-stay chains. These fully furnished suites are large and offer more privacy than a standard hotel room. They also come with a fully equipped kitchen, data port, and on-premise laundry facilities. Some even offer gym and pool privileges.

- **Marriott Execustay Inc.**, 888-340-2565, http://execustay.com
- **Extended Stay America** and **Studio Plus Deluxe Studios**, 800-804-3724, www.extendedstay.com; various locations, including: 2200 Empire Ave, Burbank, 818-567-0952; 18602 S Vermont Ave, Gardena, 310-515-5139; 19200 Harbor Gateway, Torrance, 310-328-6000; 6531 S Sepulveda Blvd, near LAX, 310-568-9337; 4105 E Willow St, Long Beach, 562-989-4601
- **Homestead Studio Suites Hotels**, 800-804-3724, www.homesteadhotels. com: various locations, including 1377 W Glenoaks Blvd, Glendale, 818-956-6665; 1910 E Mariposa Ave, near LAX, 310-607-4000; 930 S Fifth Ave, Monrovia, 626-256-6999
- **Oakwood Apartments**, 877-902-0832, www.oakwood.com; corporate apartments throughout Los Angeles
- **Residence Inn by Marriott**, 800-321-2211, www.marriott.com

HOSTELS

There are three **Hostelling International** locations in the Los Angeles area (go to www.hiusa.org for more information about this organization):

- **Fullerton**, 1700 N Harbor Blvd (nearest to Disneyland), 714-738-3721
- **South Bay**, 3601 S Gaffey St, #613, 310-831-8109
- **Santa Monica**, 1436 2nd St, 310-393-9913

YMCAS

Although there are multiple YMCAs (www.ymca.net) in Los Angeles, the Glendale location at 140 North Louise, 818-240-4130, is the only one that offers lodging. Dormitory rooms are for single men only and are $125 per week. Vacancies are rare and you must inquire in person.

EXCHANGES

Believe it or not, there are strangers willing to exchange their house or room with yours for a mutually beneficial amount of time for free. These home swap services require a membership fee and are typically used for vacations, but it could work for when you're still scouting out a more permanent living situation. When using these services, it's up to you and the other party to build trust and negotiate terms that are acceptable to both.

- **Room Exchange**, www.roomexchange.net
- **Home Exchange**, www.homeexchange.com

HAVE CAR, WILL TRAVEL. MANY ANGELENOS USE THE WEEKEND AS AN opportunity for a quick escape from the city. San Francisco, Las Vegas, San Diego, Santa Barbara, and Mexico are popular weekend destinations, as are Catalina and Palm Springs. But with LA as big as it is, just driving to a different community like Long Beach can be a quick getaway in itself. Don't forget to review the **Greenspace and Beaches** chapter of this book for other relaxing ways to fill up a weekend. Also, contact the **California Travel and Tourism Commission** (800-862-2543, www.visitcalifornia.com) and request their fact-filled Visitor's Guide on popular California getaway destinations. For more ideas on quick getaways and packages, go online to http://travel.latimes.com.

CATALINA ISLAND

Catalina Island is approximately 22 miles west of Long Beach, and is accessible only by a two-hour boat ride (or a helicopter ride) across the Pacific Ocean. Although getting to this resort town requires a little bit of planning, it is worth the effort. Once you land in Avalon, the island's port, scan the waters of the bay to receive greetings from the bright orange fish, called garibaldi, native to the waters here. Since the island is so small, 28 miles long and only eight miles wide, rented golf carts are the only means of transportation for visitors who don't want to walk. Take your cart on a loop around the island for a self-guided tour. Over 80% of the land has been set aside for the preservation of native flora and fauna. Most hotels require a two-night minimum stay on the weekends, but you can also rough it at a campground. Contact the **Catalina Island Visitors Bureau** (310-510-1520, www.visitcatalina.org) for trip-planning assistance.

PALM SPRINGS

Palm Springs is a popular golf and spa resort destination located in the upper Colorado Desert. National golf tournaments are frequently held here, making it a favorite destination for golf lovers. Upscale shopping is another prime activity. Don't miss the Palm Springs Tram, which whisks you from desert country to an alpine forest within 15 minutes and provides a beautiful birds-eye view of the city. Contact the **Palm Springs Tourism Center** (760-778-8418, www.palm-springs.org) for more information. Palm Springs is also a popular LGBT destination; indeed, the web site www.gaypalmspringsca.com terms it "America's Gay Oasis."

SAN FRANCISCO

San Francisco, charming and fresh, in spite of the crowds. Popular sightseeing destinations include Fisherman's Wharf, the Golden Gate Bridge and Park, the Presidio, Alcatraz Island, Coit Tower, Chinatown, Union Square, and of course, the old-fashioned cable cars. A word to the wise, much of your sightseeing time can be spent seeking out street parking, especially on weekends. You're better off shelling out the bucks for garage parking. Contact **San Francisco's Visitor Bureau** (415-391-2000, www.onlyinsanfrancisco.com) for planning assistance.

With frequent and inexpensive flights out of LAX and Burbank airports to San Francisco, San Jose, or Oakland, you may opt to skip the seven- to eight-hour drive north and fly instead. But if you do drive and have the time for a detour, halfway between LA and SF is the coastal town of **San Simeon**, where the main attraction is the opulent Hearst Castle. The mansion of newspaper-tycoon William Randolph Hearst is so large it takes more than half a day to walk all the different tours offered.

LAGUNA BEACH

Laguna Beach, about an hour south of Los Angeles, is a picturesque resort town and artists' colony. Art collectors spend entire weekends just checking out the local artists at the town's popular summer Sawdust Festival (from July to August). The consistently sold-out Pageant of the Masters, a live-stage recreation of famous works of art by community actors set to live music, is a unique must-see as well. Many area hotels offer overnight packages that include tickets to the show; be sure to ask. **Laguna Beach Visitor Services** (800-877-1115, www.lagunabeachinfo.com) can provide more information.

SAN DIEGO AND MEXICO

Two-and-a-half hours south and you'll be in San Diego. Though now the second largest city in California, San Diego has still managed to maintain a laid-back beach-town feel. In addition to being the largest naval air station on the West

Coast, it is host to the world-renowned San Diego Zoo and Sea World Marine Park. The charming communities of La Jolla, Old Town, and Coronado Island are also popular with families. After a day of shopping and sightseeing, head over to downtown's Fifth Avenue, a popular street for nighttime dining, dancing, and people watching.

On the southern edge of San Diego are two international border crossings into Mexico. Young people jam the borders on long weekends and head into Tijuana's main drag, Avenida de Revolution, for serious bar hopping and partying. Don't forget to bring your passport to get back into the U.S. And be aware of travel advisories when going to Mexico, available at: http://travel.state.gov. Expect a one-hour minimum wait during peak travel times when crossing the border by car. Visit www.traffic.com to view the estimated wait time at the border crossing. The **San Diego Convention and Visitors Bureau** (800-892-VALU, www.sandiego.org) can provide additional information about San Diego as well as trips into Mexico.

SANTA BARBARA AND SURROUNDING TOWNS

Santa Barbara is another coastal community, located two hours north of Los Angeles. Highlights of this historically rich town include El Presidio State Historic Park, Mission Santa Barbara, the Zoological Dens, Sea Center, and downtown's State Street for its long thoroughfare of shops and restaurants. Antique collectors and flea market junkies should keep an eye out for **Summerland**, a tiny little town just five miles south of Santa Barbara. Many of the buildings along the town's main strip, Lillie Avenue, feature antique shops, cafés, and houses constructed in the late 1800s. The **Santa Barbara Visitor's Bureau** (805-966-9222, www.santabarbaraca.com) can assist you with your vacation plans in both towns. Less than an hour north of Santa Barbara is **Solvang**, a city that gives a sense of visiting Denmark. A visit to this quaint, old-world village is a full-immersion experience of Danish restaurants, shops, and windmills. The **Solvang Visitors Bureau** will help with trip-planning assistance: 800-468-6765, www.solvangusa.com.

Just off the coast of Santa Barbara are the **San Miguel** and **Santa Cruz Islands**, which offer scenic hiking, kayaking, caverns, and a petrified forest. Both islands are accessible only by chartered boat. Contact the **Channel Islands National Park** (805-658-5730, www.nps.gov/chis/homepage.htm) for additional information.

LOMPOC

From May through September flower lovers head in droves to the flower beds of **Lompoc**, which is located about an hour's drive northwest of Santa Barbara. Many of the nation's flower seeds are harvested here, and the colorful flower fields are the primary attraction in this picturesque town. Its normal population of 37,000 multiplies by three during the Lompoc Valley Flower Festival, held over a weekend in late June. Formal bus tours are arranged for the many tourists. Contact the **Lompoc Valley Chamber of Commerce** (805-736-4567, www.lompoc. com) for more information.

BIG BEAR

An easy two-hour drive east of Los Angeles, Big Bear is a popular ski destination in the winter, and is one of the largest year-round recreational areas in the state. There are seven ski resorts here, offering a good selection of slopes with varying degrees of difficulty. Come summer, you can rent a boat, go horseback riding, hiking, camping, or picnicking. Quaint bed and breakfasts, perfect for romantic getaways, abound. Contact the **Chamber of Commerce** (909-866-4607, www. bigbearchamber.com) for more vacation ideas.

LAS VEGAS

And, on a completely different note, if you're in the mood for glamour and gambling, **Las Vegas**, Nevada, is a mere four-hour drive away and the top destination for Angelenos on holidays. With popular themed mega-hotels in constant construction on the Strip, this city may have more hotel rooms clustered in one town than anywhere else in the world. The best room rates can be found on the weekdays, and many hotels require a two-night minimum on weekends. This glittering, restless city offers one of the most economical vacations around—unless you lose it all at the tables. Non-gaming options include the Bellagio's Art Museum, the MGM Theme Park, the spectacular Red Rock Canyon, and the Hoover Dam. Fine dining is another draw since many upscale restaurants are run by celebrity chefs. Call the **Las Vegas Convention and Visitors Authority** (877-847-4858, www.visitlasvegas.com) for more information.

LAKE TAHOE

The largest alpine lake in North America, Lake Tahoe straddles the border between California and Nevada. It spans 12 miles wide and is 22 miles long. South Lake Tahoe has a population of 34,000. The lake water is so pure, it sparkles a brilliant blue and is popular for summer recreation such as hiking, boating, fishing, and camping. Casinos can be found on the Nevada side of the lake for those who want an alternative to Las Vegas. But what Lake Tahoe is most known for is its world-class skiing and resorts, located in the northern end of the lake. It's a good seven-hour drive by car, but if you do drive in the winter, carry snow chains. Some choose to fly into Reno, Nevada, then drive an hour to reach the lake. The **Tahoe Visitor Bureau** can help you with your vacation plans: 775-588-5900, www.vis itinglaketahoe.com.

STATE AND NATIONAL PARKS AND FORESTS

Nature lovers should consider the five-hour drive out to **Sequoia & Kings Canyon National Parks**. Among the park's lush old-growth pines, firs, and cedars are some of the world's oldest sequoia trees. In addition to camping in log cabins, there's hiking, fishing, climbing, and horseback riding in the spring and summer. During the winter, cross-country skiers delight in trekking through the snow-frosted sugar pine forest. Contact the **Sequoia-Kings Canyon Park Services Company** (559-565-3341, www.nps.gov/sek) for camping reservations and trip-planning information.

Much closer to home is the **Malibu Creek State Park** (818-880-0367, www.parks.ca.gov). It consists of over 4,000 acres for hiking, fishing, and bird watching. Malibu Creek runs 25 miles through the park; a trail runs about 15 miles along-side the stream through oak and sycamore woodlands and chaparral-covered slopes. The park looks so convincingly remote that TV shows like "Planet of the Apes" and "M*A*S*H" were shot here.

There's also **Topanga State Park** (310-455-2465, www.parks.ca.gov), a 10,000-acre park that's located entirely within the Los Angeles city limits and is considered the world's largest wild lands within a major city. Visitors should start at Trippet Ranch to head out on one of the many hiking trails (36 miles' worth) through oak trees and open grasslands.

The **Santa Monica Mountains National Recreation Area** (818-597-1036, http://smmc.ca.gov or www.lamountains.com) encompasses a mind-boggling variety of parks and beaches. The Santa Monica Mountains stretch almost 50 miles across Los Angeles. Within this recreational area are over 20 parks, including the **Will Rogers State Historical Park** in Pacific Palisades (310-454-8212, www.parks.ca.gov); **Griffith Park** (323-913-4688, www.lacity.org/rap/dos/parks/griffithPK/griffith.htm), which is one of the largest municipal parks in the United States; **Laurel Canyon Park** (818-762-7246, www.lamountains.com), best known for its three-acre off-leash dog park in Studio City; and the popular **Coldwater Canyon Park** (818-753-4600), headquarters to the urban forest advocacy group TreePeople in Beverly Hills.

A number of parks mentioned here have been proposed for closure in 2008 to balance the state budget, so call before going to make sure a particular park is still open. For additional information on city parks, refer to the **Sports and Recreation** and **Greenspace and Beaches** chapters.

WEATHER AND CLIMATE

YEAR-ROUND SUNSHINE MEANS WHEN OTHER PARTS OF THE COUNTRY are knee deep in snow or rain, you'll see at least one person walking around here in shorts. The period between July 2006 and July 2007 was declared by the National Weather Service as the driest rain season *ever* for downtown LA—and rain records started in 1877. Only 3.21 inches of rain were recorded for that time period. And rain fell on only 21 days out of the entire year.

But that's the exception. Normal precipitation in a year totals a little over 15 inches. They don't call it Sunny California for nothing. Have a look at the precipitation chart from the National Weather Service below:

NORMAL PRECIPITATION (IN INCHES)

JAN	3.33
FEB	3.68
MAR	3.14
APR	0.83
MAY	0.31
JUN	0.06
JUL	0.01
AUG	0.13
SEP	0.32
OCT	0.37
NOV	1.05
DEC	1.91
Yearly Total:	15.14

Come summer, we're reminded that it's possible to have too much of a good thing. This season is often associated with high air-conditioning bills since temperatures can soar to the 100s, especially in the Valley and northern parts of LA County, and stay there for consecutive days. Woodland Hills broke a record in July 2006 with 21 consecutive days of 100+ degree temperatures. However, just because it's boiling in the Valley doesn't mean the same for coastal areas such as Santa Monica or Long Beach. Television news reporters frequently deliver the weather outlook in three zones: downtown, Valleys, and the coast. Below is a sampling of the possible ranges:

	Ave High	Ave Low	Ave Month
Downtown LA	89.7	70.1	79.9
L.A. Airport	80.5	68.0	74.3
Long Beach Airport	87.1	67.9	77.5
UCLA	83.4	66.3	74.9
Burbank Airport	93.9	70.0	82.0
Woodland Hills	103.1	64.5	83.8

Here is a month-by-month breakdown of average temperatures for downtown LA:

	High	Low
Jan	68.1	48.5
Feb	69.6	50.3
Mar	69.8	51.6
April	73.1	54.4
May	74.5	57.9
Jun	79.5	61.4
July	83.8	64.6
Aug	84.8	65.6
Sept	83.3	64.6
Oct	79.0	59.9
Nov	73.2	52.6
Dec	68.7	48.3

Keep in mind, the temperature can vary by several degrees in either direction depending on what part of town you're in. For comparison purposes, here is a month-by- month for Santa Monica, located on the coast, about 16 miles southwest of downtown:

	High	Low
Jan	63.7	50.2
Feb	63.4	51.3
Mar	62.1	52.1
April	63.4	53.9
May	63.6	56.5
Jun	65.9	59.4
July	68.8	62.1

Aug	70.3	63.1
Sept	70.5	62.6
Oct	69.6	59.4
Nov	67.3	54.3
Dec	64.8	50.5

Every three years or so in local winter-time weather reports you'll hear references to "El Niño" or "La Niña." Both refer to a weather cycle of stronger than normal trade winds and below- or above-normal (respectively) sea-surface temperatures in the Pacific Ocean. The causes of El Niño/La Niña are not clearly understood but many lengthy theories abound within the scientific community because it impacts the world's climate and fishing. To put it simply, the presence of El Niño can mean wetter and cooler winters and La Niña can mean dryer, cooler winters for Southern California. According to NASA, La Niña started in February of 2007 and is expected to peak in early 2008.

The **Santa Ana** winds are phenomena that you're bound to experience at least a couple times a year. Blowing between fall and winter, these winds pose a hazard because they increase fire risk significantly in areas with dry chaparral (and that's pretty much anywhere there's a mountain). Mixing a wildfire with a Santa Ana is a firefighting nightmare. These strong, dry winds, which can be cold or hot, are unique to Southern and Baja California. They can blow at sustained speeds of 40 mph and gust up to 115 mph. These gusty winds are responsible for fueling the seemingly unstoppable wildfires that ravaged areas in Los Angeles in late 2007. The Santa Anas make driving with a high-profile vehicle difficult, especially in windy mountain passes. They also kick dust, pollen, and debris around. It's not unusual to find streets littered with palm tree leaves after a Santa Ana. For many with allergies, Santa Ana conditions mean keeping a box of tissues nearby. Definitely a bad hair day, but life continues as normal otherwise. And there's even a positive—smog is nonexistent this time of the year, thanks to the gusts that clear the horizon.

For more detailed information about these seasonal anomalies and Los Angeles climates, visit the **National Weather Service Western Regional Headquarters**: www.nwsla.noaa.gov.

AIR QUALITY

The South Coast Air Quality Management District is the air pollution agency for the City of Los Angeles and all of Orange County. The AQMD's web site (www.AQMD.gov) contains a color-coded (green through maroon) Air Quality Index (AQI) that tells you how clean or polluted your outdoor air is, and what associated health effects, if any, may affect you.

The bad news, according to the American Lung Association's 2007 State of the Air report, is that Los Angeles is the most polluted city in the nation. It had 158 days of code orange smog (unhealthy air for sensitive groups such as children, the elderly, and people with asthma or other heart/lung disease), 35 code red days (unhealthy to all for long exposure), and 16 code purple days (very unhealthy to all). When the AQI reaches the purple stage, the AQMD issues a stage-one smog alert that is filtered through the media advising people to stay indoors.

The good news is that city leaders and residents are constantly working to improve LA air quality. The year 2007 was also the cleanest on record in Southern California history according to the AQMD. For perspective, there were 121 stage-one smog alerts for LA in 1977. Also remember that coastal cities see much less smog than the inland. And for the general population, a red or purple day simply means rescheduling outdoor exercise or work for another day.

For current air quality conditions and forecasts, visit the AQMD web site, www.AQMD.gov, or call for additional information, 909-396-2000. Another resource is the government's web site, www.Airnow.gov, which allows you to view past and current ozone maps for the county and nationwide.

Indoor air purifiers have become a popular way to clean indoor air in the home, but some purifiers produce ozone (a component of smog), which is what you're trying to get away from in the first place. The California EPA Air Resources Board has advised consumers against using these ozone generators and lists specific "air purifiers" to avoid and how to select a safe purifier at http://www.arb. ca.gov/research/indoor/ozone.htm. The EPA web site, www.epa.gov/iedweb00/ pubs/ozonegen.html, also has detailed information discussing the pros and cons of air-cleaning devices.

One final bit of advice if you encounter a bad smog day: the American Lung Association advises you refill your gas tank after dark so that ozone can't form because gap vapors require sunlight to form ozone.

NATURAL DISASTERS

Fortunately, natural disasters such as earthquakes, wildfires, landslides, and floods happen infrequently. These disasters may be localized, such as the wildfires, or citywide like a temblor. The unpredictability of a natural or manmade disaster illustrates the importance of establishing a family emergency plan and stockpiling emergency supplies. If a calamity is on a large-enough scale, you should expect public emergency services to be overwhelmed and fend for yourself until help can reach you. This is why disaster preparedness experts advise having enough supplies to sustain you and your loved ones for at least three days. Preparedness is so important to the government that they have a web site devoted to being ready: www.ready.gov.

To become better informed on what to do *during* and how to help *after* a disaster strikes, consider getting **Community Emergency Response Team** (CERT) certified. A series of free classes is put on by the LA fire department to teach residents how to help themselves and others in various disaster scenarios before first responders can arrive. These classes can even be hosted at your choice of venue if you organize it. Call or visit their web site for more info: 818-756-9674, http://lafd.org/cert.htm.

EARTHQUAKES

One of the biggest fears about living in California is earthquakes. While natives are quick to dismiss the swaying or bumps of a small temblor, no one relishes the thought of the proverbial "big one." The 6.8 Northridge earthquake that rocked LA in 1994 killed 57 people, with 1,500 more suffering serious injuries. It is believed that casualties would have been much greater had it struck in the middle of the day when the collapsed stores would have been filled with shoppers and the failed freeways crowded with cars. Twenty-two-thousand people were forced to leave their homes (either permanently or while repairs were made) due to quake damage, and more than 3,000 buildings were declared unsafe for reentry. Yet, when you consider the millions of people who felt the quake that early morning, the number of people affected in more than a casual way was relatively small.

While only chance dictates who will be in the wrong place at the wrong time during a quake, there are precautions you can take to aid your survival in an earthquake. Here are some for you to consider.

In your home:

- Place your bed away from windows and bookshelves, and don't hang heavy objects above it.
- Heavy ceiling fans and lights should be supported with a cable that is bolted to the ceiling joist. The cable should have enough slack to allow it to sway.
- Be sure to store flashlights, a radio, and batteries and a crowbar (in case your door gets jammed shut) in your bedroom.
- Store a disaster kit somewhere accessible. Local home improvement and specialty stores sell earthquake preparedness kits (see below).
- Heavy objects should always be placed on lower shelves.
- Use brackets to bolt bookshelves, file cabinets, and other heavy pieces of furniture to the walls. Be sure to connect brackets to wall studs.
- Brace chimneys (usually a professional will need to do this for you).
- Fasten down lamps, TVs, computers, printers, and other objects that can become projectiles in a large quake. Use earthquake putty to hold breakables in place.
- Be sure your home is bolted to its foundation.
- Strap your water heater to the wall.
- Put latches on cabinet doors.
- Know where your water and gas valves are located, and how to shut them off.

In your car:

- Store the following: flashlight, batteries, portable battery-powered or hand-crank radio, first-aid kit, food such as trail mix or non-melting energy bars, water, cash, work gloves, and tennis shoes. In the event of an earthquake during your commute, damaged roads and fallen debris may make it impossible to continue driving to your destination. Sturdy shoes and gloves can make it easier for you to walk home.

In your office:

- Store the following: a portable battery-powered or hand-crank radio, flashlight with spare batteries, first-aid kit, leather gloves, and tennis shoes. If your company does not have emergency procedures in place, ask that some be developed.

The Southern California region offers a wealth of disaster preparedness programs, from natural disasters to terrorist attacks. To find out more about real-time earthquake activity, recent temblors, locations of fault lines, flooding zones, and fire activity, you can consult with the following **disaster preparedness** resources:

- **City of LA Fire Department**, www.lafd.org
- **City of LA Health and Human Services**, 800-339-6993, www.211LACounty.org
- **US Geological Survey's Earthquake Hazards Program—Southern California**, 650-329-4668, http://earthquake.usgs.gov/regional/sca
- **Office of Emergency Management for the County of Los Angeles**, 323-980-2260, http://lacoa.org
- **LA County Fire Department**, http://fire.lacounty.gov
- **Southern California Earthquake Center**, 213-740-5843, www.scec.org

DISASTER KITS

Bottom line, if you live in LA, you should have a disaster kit ready. You may elect to purchase a prepared kit (see list of stores below) or do like most Angelenos, make your own. Any waterproof plastic container that's big enough to store all the items will do, but using a plastic trashcan with wheels will make transportation in the event of an evacuation easier. The items on your list should be customized according to your specific needs. Generally, here is what the experts recommend:

- Portable radio and batteries or hand-crank radio
- Flashlights and batteries or hand-crank flashlight
- Candles and matches
- Medical and personal hygiene supplies
- Canned and/or dehydrated food

- Can opener
- Sleeping bags or blankets and sturdy shoes
- Three gallons of drinking water per person in your household
- Barbecue or camp stove
- Toiletries, including diapers for those with little ones
- Plastic sheeting and duct tape

Store your kit in a place that's easily accessible to the entire family. Don't forget to rotate your water and food every six months. And check that your batteries and first-aid supplies are still fresh.

Military supply and surplus stores are a great resource for stocking a kit; turn to the Army and Navy Goods section of your Yellow Pages for a list of stores or look on the web. Here are some mail order and walk-in stores that specialize in **earthquake supplies**:

- **Grabbit Emergency Pack**, 310-471-8608, www.grabbit.com
- **Quake Kare Inc.**, 800-2-PREPARE, www.quakekare.com
- **Safe-T-Proof Disaster Preparedness Co.**, 800-377-8888, www.Safe-T-Proof.com
- **SOS Survival Products**, 800-479-7998, www.sosproducts.com

FIRES, LANDSLIDES, FLOODS, ETC.

While massive fires, landslides, and floods are seldom issues for people living in the most populated areas of Los Angeles, summer brush fires are a normal occurrence in Southern California, especially in hilly canyon areas where there is a good deal of vegetation. If you live in the foothills of a mountain or a canyon (for instance Malibu, Topanga Canyon), be sure to clear the brush around your home year round. A fire hazard condition is made worse when it occurs during the Santa Anas mentioned earlier. The media passes along high wind and/or high fire danger advisories when issued by the National Weather Service.

Check with wildfire specialists on how to shield your home, especially in areas of high fire danger. Expect to keep a clearing between your house and the surrounding brush, and invest in a fireproof roof for peace of mind. The **California Department of Forestry and Fire Protection's** web site provides specific tips on creating "defensible space" around your home. The **Los Angeles City and County Fire Departments**, www.lafd.org and http://fire.lacounty.gov respectively, offer exhaustive tips for fire-proofing a home, as well as free disaster preparedness handbooks.

Despite these efforts, if you find yourself in the path of a fire, you may receive a reverse 911 recorded call notifying you of an evacuation order. Don't wait until the last minute to act, as bottlenecks on narrow roads may make it impossible to drive out in time. Keep the garage closed (to keep out embers), but be ready to disengage the automatic garage door opener and know how to open it manually (a large fire usually results in power failure). Close all doors within the house to slow the fire's spread should your house ignite—it may buy enough time for firefighters to save the structure. Wet the shrubbery around your home. Notify someone of where you are evacuating to and when. Again, the previously mentioned web sites have thorough preparedness information.

Recently burned areas are especially vulnerable to landslides in the rainy season, as the vegetation that normally holds the soil on the hillsides has been burnt away. While we haven't had much rain in recent years, it takes just one major storm to create some headaches. Fire sites are not the only places that landslides occur. The sharp cliffs above the Pacific Coast Highway regularly slide during the rains, and slides are also common in all hilly neighborhoods. Residents often use sandbags to shore up iffy areas, and tarps to cover precarious hillsides. These same neighborhoods are particularly susceptible to flooding. In particular, remote canyon roads may be inaccessible during heavy rains, though not for longer than a few days. Sandbags are made available to residents at neighborhood fire stations should a major storm approach.

Terrorist attacks or pandemics may seem less likely but should be prepared for as well. As a major city with a major port and international airport, metropolitan Los Angeles is considered vulnerable. Many of the resources and advice given here can be useful toward readiness. To research all advisories given by the state, visit the **California Office of Emergency Services Emergency Digital Information Service**: www.edis.ca.gov.

W ITH YEAR-ROUND GOOD WEATHER, IT'S NO WONDER THERE ARE SO many things going on in Los Angeles. Scores of yearly events, including the popular Auto Show and the Home and Garden Expo, take place at the LA Convention Center alone. Museums and individual communities host their own events throughout the year; for more happenings, keep an eye out for flyers and ads in the local publications. The following is just a sample listing of annual festivities:

JANUARY

- **Tournament of Roses Parade**, 626-449-4100, www.tournamentofroses.com; the January 1st parade travels along Orange Grove Blvd in Pasadena. Folks typically camp out on the sidewalks a night (or two) before for the best views. If you don't mind paying a nominal fee to see the floats up close, you can observe construction before the parade or view them after the parade—wear comfortable shoes; even though all the floats are parked nose to nose, you will walk the equivalent of two miles to view them all.
- **The Rose Bowl**, 626-577-3101, www.rosebowlstadium.com; this annual extravaganza hosts the champs of the Pac 10 as they duel with the champs of the Big 10.
- **Martin Luther King Jr. Awareness Day**, 213-473-7700, www.africanameri canla.com; a citywide celebration, featuring poetry, art, films, a gospel fest, and guest lecturers, culminating in the Kingdom Day Parade, 310-537-4240.
- **Marina del Rey Big Boat Show**, 949-757-5959, www.marinadelreyboatshow. com; boating and water sport enthusiasts head down to Burton Chace Park in Marina del Rey to check out the latest in aquatic equipment.
- **Doo Dah Parade**, 626-205-4029, www.pasadenadoodahparade.info; fans of the irreverent or bizarre will want to check out this popular spoof of the

Tournament of Roses Parade in downtown Pasadena. Traditionally held in November, it has moved to January.

- **Restaurant Week**, www.dinela.com; a chance for foodies to dine on discounted prix fixe meals at participating upscale restaurants—contact each restaurant for details and reservations.
- **Los Angeles Art Show**, 310-822-9145, www.laartshow.com; fine-art aficionados can shop for art pieces from the 17th century to the present at Barker Hanger in Santa Monica.

FEBRUARY

- **African-American History Month Celebrations**, 213-473-7700, www.african americanla.com; a citywide event featuring lectures, films, and performances.
- **Chinese New Year Celebrations**, 213-680-0243, www.chinatownla.com; 626-284-1234, www.lunarnewyearparade.com; 213-617-0396, www.lachinese chamber.org; punctuated by noisy firecrackers and lion dancing, a parade, street fair, and carnival are some of the celebrations to take place in Chinatown and San Gabriel Valley.
- **Mardi Gras Celebration**, 213-628-1274 or 213-625-3800 www.cityofla.org/elp; on Fat Tuesday, head downtown to the El Pueblo de Los Angeles Historical Monument for a parade, costume contest, and general revelry.

MARCH

- **Annual Cherry Blossom Festival**, 626-683-8243, www.cherryblossomfes tivalsocal.org; the Japanese-American Cultural & Community Center hosts this annual Japanese spring ritual of viewing blooming cherry trees in Little Tokyo.
- **Celebration of Cesar E. Chavez Day**, 213-624-3660, www.olvera-street.com; a parade, art exhibits, and speakers commemorate the Mexican-American farmlaborer activist.
- **Environmental Education Fair**, 626-821-3212, www.laeef.org; a festival to increase environmental awareness held at the Arboretum of LA County.
- **LA Marathon**, 310-444-5544, www.lamarathon.com; nearly every community the marathon runs through throws a block party along the race route to cheer on the runners. A festival and fair are held downtown, which is the starting and finishing point of the race.
- **Saint Patrick's Day Parade & Pershing Square Celebration**, 311, www.lacity. org/LAFD/stpats.htm; the City of LA hosts a downtown parade that ends at Pershing Square where the fountain water is dyed green in honor of the Irish.

APRIL

- **Art Walk at the Brewery Art Colony**, 213-694-2911, www.breweryartwalk. com, is a biannual event at the world's largest art colony, in downtown LA. The public is invited to browse through local artists' loft studios and view their works. Held again in October.

- **Blessing of the Animals,** 213-628-1274 or 213-625-3800, www.cityofla.org/elp; a Catholic priest will bless your feathered or furry friend at this centuries-old ceremony at the El Pueblo de Los Angeles Historical Monument, downtown.
- **Fiesta Broadway,** 310-914-0015, www.fiestabroadway.la; this popular block party in downtown celebrates Latin-American culture and bills itself as the largest Cinco de Mayo party in the world.
- **Los Angeles Times Festival of Books,** 213-237-6365, www.latimes.com/ex tras/festivalofbooks.com; held the last weekend in April on UCLA campus, this free festival attracts over 100,000 book lovers of all ages. Over 300 booths are set up by booksellers, publishers, and cultural organizations. Events include readings and signings by well-known and not-so-well-known authors and poets.
- **Thai New Year Festival,** 800-921-2597, www.thainewyear.com; go to Holly-wood Blvd and Western Ave to enjoy food booths, performances, ceremonies, and a beauty pageant. This popular festival is attended by Thais from all over California.
- **Renaissance Pleasure Faire,** 800-52-FAIRE, www.renfair.com; starting in late April and running through May, this elaborate recreation of a medieval village takes place about 20 minutes east of downtown in the City of Irwindale. Many people attend in period costume to watch jousting matches, wander the crafts booths, and enjoy a stein of ale with fellow wenches, knights, and royalty.
- **Carnival Primavera Downtown Festival,** 323-585-1155, www.hpchamber1. com; this Spring celebration is held over four city blocks in Huntington Park.
- **Toyota Grand Prix Long Beach,** 562-981-2600, www.gplb.com; streets around the Long Beach Convention Center are converted into a high-speed circuit track for a weekend of Formula One races. Crowds pack the grandstands to watch racing's best drivers at work.

MAY

- **Affaire in the Gardens Arts Show,** 310-550-4796, www.beverlyhills.org; none of the typical costume jewelry or clothing is hawked during this fine week-end event held at the Beverly Gardens Park. Over 200 artists from around the country display fine art from sculpture to paintings for the discriminating art collector. The show takes place again in October.
- **Family Fun Fest,** 213-628-2725, www.jaccc.org; Little Tokyo's Japanese-Ameri-can Cultural and Community Center hosts games, food and crafts booths, and other fun activities in honor of Children's Day.
- **Cinco de Mayo Celebration,** 213-628-1274 or 213-625-3800, www.cityofla. org/elp; celebrate at the El Pueblo de Los Angeles Historical Monument in downtown.

- **Huntington Plant Sale**, 626-405-2141, www.huntington.org; every May, the Huntington Library, Art Collections, and Botanical Gardens has a parking-lot sale of rare and unusual annuals and perennials, many propagated by seeds and cuttings from their botanical collections, a treat for beginning and experienced green-thumbers alike.
- **Museums of the Arroyo Festival**, 213-740-8687 www.museumsofthearroyo. com; six museums in Pasadena—The Gamble House, Heritage Square Museum, The Lummis Home and Garden, Pasadena Museum of History, LA Police Historical Society, and Southwest Museum—offer free admission and shuttles between them for a day.
- **Los Angeles Fire Department Open House**, 213-485-5971, www.lafd.org; every year, on the Saturday before Mother's Day, city firehouses open their garages for visits by the public.
- **NoHo Theater & Arts Festival**, 818-763-5273, www.nohoartsdistrict.com; North Hollywood's arts district, along Lankershim Boulevard in North Hollywood, celebrates with a weekend of music, food and crafts booths, and theatrical performances at area playhouses.
- **Santa Monica Festival**, 310-458-8350, http://arts.santa-monica.org; the city hosts an impressive and eclectic selection of handmade arts-and-crafts booths, workshops, music, and food at Clover Park.
- **UCLA Pow-wow**, 310-206-7513, www.studentgroups.ucla.edu/american indian/powwowpage.htm; Native Americans and friends gather on the college campus to celebrate their heritage with song, dance, food, and displays.

JUNE

- **Annual Salute to Recreation Family Festival**, 888-527-2757, www.laparks. org; a weekend of carnival games, rides, and booths is capped off by an evening of fireworks.
- **Free Fishing Day**, 916-928-5805, www.dfg.ca.gov/licensing/fishing/freefish days.html; no fishing license required to fish in California on two fishing days a year. Contact the Department of Fish and Game to find out the specific day in June (and September).
- **Gay and Lesbian Pride Parade and Celebration**, 323-969-8302, www.lapride. org; the West Hollywood portion of Santa Monica Boulevard is lined with bleachers for thousands of spectators of the gay and lesbian pride parade.
- **Irish Fair and Music Festival**, 919-489-1172, www.irishfair.org; the biggest Irish fair in the Western United States features bagpipes, Gaelic sports, and food.
- **Playboy Jazz Festival**, 323-850-2000, www.hollywoodbowl.com; jazz aficionados flock to the Hollywood Bowl for performances by some of the top names in jazz.

- **Summer Solstice Folk Music, Dance, and Storytelling Festival**, 818-817-7756, www.ctmsfolkmusic.org; this is the country's largest folk festival, featuring workshops, concerts, and exhibits.
- **Valley Fair**, 818-557-1600, www.valleyfair.org; held over a weekend in Santa Clarita, the fair features livestock competitions, carnival rides, game booths, and gardening exhibits.
- **Long Beach Sea Festival**, 562-434-1542, www.longbeachseafestival.com; summer-long events include a food festival on the Belmont Veterans Memorial Pier, movie screenings, and the Mayor's Cup Race; the festival stretches into August to culminate in a sand castle–building contest on the beach.

JULY

- **Fourth of July Celebrations**, 888-527-2757, www.laparks.org; city-wide celebrations with fireworks displays from the Hollywood Bowl to Santa Monica. Contact the above number to locate the nearest fireworks show.
- **Hollywood Bowl Summer Festival**, 323-850-2000, www.hollywoodbowl.com; the Hollywood Bowl begins its summer season each July (through mid-September), featuring varying orchestras and all genres of music from classical to pop. For many Angelenos, bringing a picnic dinner and heading to the bowl for an evening concert is an annual tradition.
- **Lotus Festival**, 888-527-2757, www.laparks.org; the largest lotus bed outside of China is located in Echo Park, which is a fitting host for a weekend filled with dragon-boat races, flower shows, and Pan-Asian food booths.
- **Malibu Arts Festival**, 310-456-9025, www.malibuartsfestival.com; over 200 artists display their wares at the city's civic center.
- **Shakespeare Festival**, 213-481-2273, www.shakespearefestivalla.org; venues around the county pay homage to William Shakespeare by putting on professional productions of the bard's plays.

AUGUST

- **African Marketplace and Cultural Fair**, 323-293-1612, www.africanmarketplace.org; a festival filled with food and entertainment to celebrate African heritage.
- **Children's Festival of the Arts**, 323-871-ARTS, www.hollywoodartscouncil.org; locations vary for this wholesome event but it is filled with performances, food, and crafts for the entire family.
- **Nisei Week**, 213-687-7193, www.niseiweek.org; Little Tokyo celebrates its culture with weeklong festivities including a parade, street fair, taiko drums and ondo street dancing.

- **Watts Towers Jazz and Arts Festivals**, 323-789-7304, www.wattsfestival.org; the Watts Towers Art Center plays host to a three-day event that includes a jazz festival, art exhibits, and fair booths.

SEPTEMBER

- **Los Angeles County Fair**, 909-623-3111, www.lacountyfair.com; this is billed as the world's largest country fair and is held on the Pomona Fairplex grounds.
- **Port of Los Angeles Lobster Festival**, 310-798-7478, www.lobsterfest.com; discounted lobster meals, performances, and shopping, for lobster lovers.
- **Oktoberfest**, 310-327-4384, www.alpinevillage.net; bratwursts, a beer garden, and oompah bands—it must be the annual German celebration.
- **Feria de los Niños**, 888-527-2757, www.laparks.org; a Latin-American festival featuring food, workshops, dances, and mariachi bands in Hollenbeck Park, Boyle Heights.
- **Los Angeles Greek Fest**, 323-737-2424, www.lagreekfest.com; annual opportunity to immerse yourself in Greek food, music, and culture.
- **Coastal Clean Up Day**, 310-305-9503, http://beaches.co.la.ca.us/bandh/main. htm or www.healthebay.org; the Los Angeles County Department of Beaches and Harbors partners with Heal the Bay to organize massive numbers of volunteers to spend the third Saturday of September removing refuse from our coastline.

OCTOBER

- **Edwards Air Force Base Open House**, 661-277-3510, www.edwards.af.mil; annual open house and air show is an opportunity for the public to marvel at the best in aviation exhibits and flight demonstrations.
- **Halloween Harvest Festival**, 818-999-6300, www.halloweenharvestfesti val.com; Angelenos celebrate fall with a corn-stalk maze, hay rides, pumpkin patch, and haunted house at Pierce College.
- **Los Angeles County Arts Open House**, 213-972-3099, www.lacountyarts.org; in honor of the National Arts and Humanities month, the first Saturday of October features free admission to participating museums within LA County. This event is well attended, especially along Museum Row. Wilshire Blvd between Fairfax and Curson, is closed to cars, allowing the crowds to view outdoor performances.
- **West Hollywood's Halloween Carnival**, 323-848-6400, www.visitwestholly wood.com; many might think of Halloween as a child's holiday, but in West Hollywood, adults claim it as their own. An estimated one million people, usually in elaborate costumes, jam Santa Monica Boulevard (west of La Cienega Blvd) to strut their stuff.
- **Port of Long Beach's Annual Open House/Port Fest**, 562-570-6555, www. longbeach.gov; headquartered at the Port Administration building, the public is offered free boat tours of a world-class seaport in action.

NOVEMBER

- **LA Auto Show**, 310-444-1850, www.laautoshow.com; check out the latest models and concept cars at the LA Convention Center. Most of the new cars are open for viewing, touching, photographing, and dreaming.
- **AFI LA International Film Festival**, 323-856-7600, www.afi.com; screenings for one of the largest film festivals in the country, hosted by the American Film Institute, are held in theaters around Hollywood and Santa Monica.
- **Dia de los Muertos**, 213-628-1274 or 213-625-3800, www.lacity.org/elp/index.htm; the Day of the Dead, a traditional Mexican festival to honor the departed, is observed at El Pueblo de Los Angeles Historical Monument, downtown.
- **DWP Light Festival**, 323-665-3051, www.dwplightfestival.com; many families make a tradition of piling into the car for the free, mile-long display of holiday light scenes.
- **Hollywood Santa Parade**, 310-537-4240, www.hollywoodsantaparade.com; formerly the Hollywood Christmas Parade, the Thanksgiving-weekend parade gives residents a reason to flock to Hollywood sidewalks with a thermos of hot chocolate.
- **Beverly Hills Garden & Design Showcase**, 310-285-1000, www.beverlyhills gardenshowcase.org; interior designers and landscape artists show off their stuff at the historic Greystone estate—tours of the English Gothic mansion are also offered.

DECEMBER

- **Downtown on Ice**, 888-LA-Parks, www.laparks.org; skaters flock to this "Rockefeller Center of the West" to enjoy the temporary ice rink and free weekday concerts.
- **Burbank Mayor's Tree Lighting**, 818-238-5320, www.ci.burbank.ca.us; many residents of Burbank attend the mayor's tree lighting ceremony at city hall.
- **Marina del Rey Holiday Boat Parade & Fireworks Show**, 310-305-9545, www.mdrboatparade.org. Crowds gather at Burton Chace Park annually to view fireworks and passing boats decked out in holiday splendor.
- **Huntington Beach Cruise of Lights Holiday Lighted Boat Tour**, 714-840-7542, www.cruiseoflights.com; a boat takes passengers on a tour of decorated shoreline mansions.
- **California African American Museum Kwanzaa Celebration**, 213-744-7432, www.caamuseum.org; this Afro-centric holiday is celebrated via a one-day event full of musical performances, crafts and food booths.
- **LA County Holiday Celebration**, 213-972-3099, www.holidaycelebration.org; the Dorothy Chandler Pavilion is the site of six hours of free annual holiday music and dance performances.

- **Toluca Lake Open House**, 818-761-6594, www.tolucalakechamber.com; shops and restaurants along Riverside Dr in Toluca Lake stay open late the first Friday night of the month to offer free candy canes, cookies, and food samples. The neighborhood caroling truck also makes its rounds, adding to the charm of this holiday evening.
- **Santa Monica Main Street Open House**, www.mainstreetsm.com; similar to the Toluca Lake open house, but held on the first Saturday night of December, along Main St at Ocean Park Blvd

GENERAL NONFICTION

- *The Best Los Angeles Sports Arguments* by J.A. Adane (Sourcebooks Inc); a discussion of the best and worst of the LA sports scene.
- *Curbside L.A.: An Offbeat Guide to the City of Angels from the Pages of the Los Angeles Times* by Cecilia Rasmussen (LA Times)
- *DisneyWar* by James B. Stewart (Simon & Schuster); corporate intrigue behind the Walt Disney Company.
- *Hollywood Dish! Recipes, Tips, & Tales of a Hollywood Caterer* by Nick Grippo (Angel City Press); a unique combination of celebrity gossip and food from a local caterer to the stars.
- *Household Spanish* by William C. Harvey (Barron's Educational Series); English-Spanish guidebook for frequently used phrases in cooking, cleaning, childcare, and gardening.
- *L.A. Story: Immigrant Workers and the Future of the U.S. Labor Movement* by Ruth Milkman (Russell Sage Foundation Publications); in-depth look at blue-collar workers in Los Angeles.
- *The Next Los Angeles: The Struggle for a Livable City* by Robert Gottlieb, et al (University of California Press); latest examination of how activists and idealism have shaped LA into what it is today.
- *Riot on Sunset Strip: Rock'n'Roll's Last Stand in Hollywood* by Domenic Priore (Jawbone Press); a look at the bands that came into prominence on the Sunset Strip in the sixties.
- *Sins of the City: The Real Los Angeles Noir* by Jim Heimann (Chronicle Books); the true-life seedy moments in LA history that spawned popular novels and movies.
- *Six Gun Sound: The Early History of the Los Angeles County Sheriff's Department* by Sven Crongeyer (Linden Publishing); fascinating glimpse into early policing efforts of a wild town.

- *William Mulholland and the Rise of Los Angeles* by Catherine Mulholland (University of California Press); historical account of the man who helped early Los Angeles flourish by building a controversial aqueduct.

ARTS AND ARCHITECTURE

- *Above Los Angeles, Revised Edition* by Robert W. Cameron (Cameron & Co.); incredible aerial views of the city.
- *An Architectural Guidebook to Los Angeles* by Robert Winter and David Gebhard (Gibbs Smith Publishers); local architecture by notable architects.
- *City Observed: Los Angeles* by Charles Willard Moore (Hennessey & Ingalls); classic essays about LA architecture.
- *Dream Town* by Michelle Markel (Heyday Books); a dreamy children's book to pique interest in LA architecture.
- *L.A. 2000+: New Architecture in Los Angeles* by John Leighton Chase (Monacelli); snapshots of original local buildings built since the year 2000.
- *LA Artland: Contemporary Art from Los Angeles* by Chris Kraus (Black Dog Publishing).
- *Los Angeles Art Deco* by Suzanne Tarbell Cooper (Arcadia Publishing); a loving tribute to the many surviving examples of Art Deco in town.
- *Los Angeles: The Architecture of Four Ecologies* by Reyner Banham (University of California Press); an architectural historian examines how Angelenos relate to the beach, freeways, flatlands, and foothills.
- *Picturing Los Angeles* by Jon Wilkman (Gibbs Smith); two hundred years of LA history captured in photographs.
- *Urban Surprises: A Guide to Public Art in Los Angeles* by G. Gerace (Balcony Press).

GUIDES

- *101 Hikes in Southern California: Exploring Mountains, Seashore and Desert* by Jerry Schad (Wilderness Press); a collection of the best hikes from Los Angeles to San Diego.
- *An Actor's Guide: Your First Year in Hollywood* by Michael Nicholas (Allworth Press); advice and tips for newcomers who seek a career on the big screen.
- *Counter Intelligence: Where to Eat in the Real Los Angeles* by Jonathan Gold (LA Weekly Books); deliciously detailed guide to the savory options in town, written by the *LA Weekly's* restaurant reviewer—the first food critic to ever win a Pulitzer Prize.
- *Day Hikes Around Los Angeles* by Robert Stone (Day Hike Books); nearby trails for stretching your legs.
- *Free L.A.: The Ultimate Guide to the City of Angels* by Robert Stock, et al (Corleyguide); fun stuff to do without opening your wallet.

- *Hollywood Creative Directory* by Hollywood Creative Directory Staff; published four times a year, this is the best listing of production companies and contact information for anyone looking to break into Hollywood.
- *Los Angeles A to Z: An Encyclopedia of the City and County* by Leonard Pitt, Dale Pitt (University of California Press); devoted to unique facts about the land, its people, and history.
- *Thomas Guide Los Angeles County; Los Angeles County/Orange County;* and *Los Angeles County/Ventura County* by Rand McNally, Thomas Brothers; a necessary car accessory for getting around this city's sprawling roads.
- *The Underground Guide to Los Angeles* by Pleasant Gehman and Iris Berry (Manic D Press); weird and off-color venues revealed.
- *Zagat Los Angeles Nightlife* by Zagat Survey (Zagat Survey).

FICTION

- *The Assistants: A Novel* by Robin Lynn Williams (Regan Books); five different personalities struggle to stick their proverbial foot in tinsel town's doorway.
- *Hollywood Wives: The New Generation* by Jackie Collins (Simon & Schuster); juicy page-turning frolic amid power, sex, money, and fame.
- *Kill the Messenger* by Tami Hoag (Bantam); thriller set in Los Angeles.
- *L.A. Confidential* by James Ellroy (Grand Central Publishing); 1950s-noir crime tale that was made into a movie in 1997.
- *Less Than Zero* by Bret Easton Ellis (Vintage); cautionary 1980s tale of rich young adults on a cocaine-laden, too-fast trip to nowhere.
- *Little Scarlet: An Easy Rawlins Mystery* by Walter Mosley (Little Brown); shortly after the 1965 Watts riots, a murder investigation threatens to fuel racial tensions further.
- *The Pleasure of My Company* by Steve Martin (Hyperion); the "Saturday Night Live" frequent host/comedian and actor pens a delicious novella about a Santa Monica resident with Obsessive Compulsive Disorder.
- *A Year in Van Nuys* by Sandra Tsing Loh (Crown Publishing Group); struggling thirty-something writer toils in the Valley.
- *Angels Flight* by Michael Connelly (Grand Central Publishing); Hollywood homicide detective investigates a murder at a steep downtown hill.
- *The Big Sleep* by Raymond Chandler (Vintage); the first Philip Marlowe novel of the hardboiled classics set in LA.
- *Day of the Locust* by Nathanael West (Signet Classics); a dark literary classic about a 1930s pursuit of the Hollywood dream.
- *Hollywood* by Charles Bukowski (Ecco); about boozers and brawlers in tinsel town from the author who wrote the screenplay for *Barfly*.
- *If He Hollers, Let Him Go* by Chester Himes (Thunder's Mouth Press); an African- American foreman rages to survive in a Los Angeles shipyard, pre–Civil Rights era.

- ***Imagining Los Angeles: A City in Fiction*** by David M. Fine (University of Nevada Press); an overview of the local fiction scene.
- ***Los Angeles: A Novel*** by Peter Moore Smith (Little Brown and Company); suspenseful noir thriller about an albino living in LA.
- ***Oscar Season: A Novel*** by Mary McNamara (Simon & Schuster); intrigue fogs a hotel's campaign to woo nominated celebrities before the world's most famous award show.
- ***Our Ecstatic Days*** by Steve Erikson (Simon & Schuster); local author writes about post-apocalyptic LA.
- ***Postcards from the Edge*** by Carrie Fisher (Pocket); semi-autobiographical story about an actress struggling with drug addiction.
- ***Running Time*** by Gavin Lambert (Serpent's Tail); a child's determined rise to tycoon starlet during Hollywood's golden era.
- ***Writing Los Angeles: A Literary Anthology*** edited by David Ulin (Library of America); collection of stories and poetry featuring LA.

C ALL 911 FOR ALL POLICE, FIRE AND AMBULANCE EMERGENCIES. FOR 24-hour general information regarding county-wide public assistance, from shelters to food programs, call the **INFO Line of Los Angeles**: 800-339-6993, or go to www.la.infoline.org. The City of LA also has a **24-hour information line** for city services: 213-978-3231 (or 311—works only within city limits); online, go to www.lacity.org.

ALCOHOL AND DRUG DEPENDENCY

- **Alcoholics Anonymous**, 323-936-4343 or 800-923-8722, www.lacoaa.org
- **Alcohol Abuse 24-hour Hotline**, 800-888-9383
- **Cocaine Abuse 24-hour Information and Treatment**, 800-274-2042
- **LA County Alcohol/Drug Helpline**, 800-564-6600
- **Narcotics Anonymous**, 818-773-9999, www.na.org
- **National Alcohol and Drug Abuse Hotline**, 800-252-6465
- **The Watershed**, an Alcohol and Drug Treatment Program 24-hour Hotline, 800-861-1768

ANIMALS

- **Animal Regulations Department & Shelters**, City of Los Angeles, 888-452-7381, www.laanimalservices.org
- **Dead Animal Pick-up**, 800-773-2489
- **Los Angeles County Animal Care & Control**, Downey Shelter, 562-940-6898, http://animalcare.lacounty.gov
- **Los Angeles County Animal Care & Control**, Carson Shelter, 310-523-9566, http://animalcare.lacounty.gov

- **Santa Monica Police Department Animal Control Division**, 310-458-8594, http://animalcare.lacounty.gov
- **Society for the Prevention of Cruelty to Animals**, 323-730-5300, www.lasp ca.com

AUTOMOBILES

- **Automotive Repair Bureau**, Department of Consumer Affairs, 800-952-5210, www.autorepair.ca.gov
- **California Department of Motor Vehicles**, 800-777-0133, www.dmv.ca.gov

PARKING CITATIONS

- **Anaheim**, 800-255-9711, www.anaheim.net
- **Beverly Hills**, 310-285-2553, www.beverlyhills.org
- **Burbank**, 818-238-3120, www.ci.burbank.ca.us/police/parking_enforcement. htm
- **Glendale**, 818-548-3132, www.ci.glendale.ca.us/police
- **Irvine**, 949-724-7000, http://ci.irvine.ca.us/ipd
- **Laguna Beach**, 949-497-3311, www.lagunabeachcity.net
- **Los Angeles City**, 213-623-6533, 310-569-5561, 818-901-7027, www.lacity -parking.org
- **Los Angeles County Sheriff**, 323-526-5541 or 626-458-1722, www.lasd.org
- **Newport Beach**, 949-644-3141, www.city.newport-beach.ca.us
- **Pasadena**, 626-744-6440, http://cityofpasadena.net
- **Santa Clarita**, 661-255-4386, www.santa-clarita.com
- **Santa Monica**, 800-214-1526, http://santamonicapd.org
- **Tustin**, 714-573-3200, www.tustinpd.org
- **West Hollywood**, 800-687-2458 or 323-650-9912, www.weho.org

PARKING PERMITS

- **Beverly Hills**, 310-285-2551, www.beverlyhills.org
- **Burbank**, 818-238-3915, www.ci.burbank.ca.us
- **Glendale**, 818-548-3960, www.ci.glendale.ca.us
- **Irvine**, 949-724-6313, www.ci.irvine.ca.us
- **Laguna Beach**, 714-497-0314, www.lagunabeachcity.net
- **Los Angeles**, 866-561-9742, www.lacity-parking.org
- **Newport Beach**, 949-644-3121, www.newport-beach.ca.us
- **Pasadena**, 626-744-6440, www.ci.pasadena.ca.us

- **Santa Monica**, 310-458-8291, www.santa-monica.org
- **Tustin**, 714-573-3150, www.tustinca.org
- **West Hollywood**, 323-848-6392, www.weho.org

BIRTH AND DEATH CERTIFICATES

- **Los Angeles County Clerk**, 562-462-2137, www.lavote.net
- **Orange County Clerk**, 714-834-2500, www.ocgov.com

CONSUMER COMPLAINTS AND SERVICES

- **Better Business Bureau**, 310-945-3166, 818-401-1480, 562-216-9242, www. bbb.org or www.labbb.org
- **California Public Utilities Commission Consumer Affairs**, 800-649-7570, www.cpuc.ca.gov
- **California Fair Political Practices Commission**, 866-275-3772, www.fppc. ca.gov
- **Los Angeles Consumer Affairs Department**, 213-974-1452 or 800-593-8222, http://dca.lacounty.gov
- **State Bar of California Attorney Complaint Hotline**, 800-843-9053, www. calbar.ca.gov
- **State of California Consumer Affairs Department**, 800-952-5210, www.dca. ca.gov
- **US Consumer Product Safety Commission**, 800-638-2772, www.cpsc.gov

COUNTY OFFICES

LOS ANGELES COUNTY

- **Animal Care and Control**, see web site for individual shelter's phone number, http://animalcare.lacounty.gov
- **Department of Beaches and Harbor**, 310-305-9503, http://beaches.co.la. ca.us
- **Department of Health Services**, 800-427-8700, www.dhs.co.la.ca.us/ hospitals
- **Department of Parks and Recreation**, 213-738-2961, www.lacountyparks. org
- **High Desert Health System**, 44900 N 60th St West, Lancaster, 661-948-8581
- **Housing Authority, LA County**, 323-890-7001, www.lacdc.org
- **INFO Line of Los Angeles**, 211 or 800-339-6993, www.infoline-la.org

- **LA County/USC Medical Center**, 1200 N State St, Los Angeles, 323-226-2622, www.lacusc.org
- **LA County Harbor - UCLA Medical Center,** 1000 W Carson St, Torrance, 310-222-2345, www.humc.edu
- **Library**, 562-940-8415, www.colapublib.org
- **Los Angeles County Government**, 211 or 213-974-1234, http://lacounty.info
- **Martin Luther King Jr. Multi-Service Ambulatory Care Center**, 12021 S Wilmington Ave, Los Angeles, 310-668-4321, www.ladhs.org
- **Office of Assessor**, 213-974-3211, 888-807-2111, http://assessor.co.la.ca.us
- **Office of Education** (**LACOE**), 562-922-6111, www.lacoe.edu
- **Olive View – UCLA Medical Center**, 1445 Olive View Dr, Sylmar, 818-364-1555, www.uclasfvp.org
- **Parks and Recreation**, 213-738-2961, www.lacountyparks.org
- **Police Department**, 323-526-5541, www.lapdonline.org
- **Public Defender**, 213-974-2811, http://pd.co.la.ca.us
- **Public Works, Department of Recycling and Household Hazardous Waste Program**, 888-CLEAN-LA, www.ladpw.org or www.888cleanla.com
- **Registrar-Recorder/County Clerk**, 800-815-2666, http://lavote.net
- **Sanitation District of Los Angeles County**, 562-699-7411 or 562-908-4288, www.lacsd.org
- **Sheriff**, 323-526-5541, www.lasd.org
- **Transportation, Department of** (**LADOT**), 818/213/310/323-808-2273, www.ladottransit.com
- **Treasurer-Tax Collector**, 213-974-2101, http://ttc.lacounty.gov

ORANGE COUNTY

- **Animal Care Services**, 714-935-6848, www.ocpetinfo.com
- **Children's Hospital of Orange County**, 455 S Main St, Orange, 714-997-3000, www.choc.org
- **Department of Education**, 714-966-4000, www.ocde.us
- **Harbors, Beaches, and Parks Division**, 714-973-6865 or 866-OCPARKS, www.ocparks.com
- **Housing & Community Service, Orange County**, 714-480-2900, www.ochousing.org
- **Integrated Waste Management Department** (and Recycling), 714-834-4000, www.oclandfills.com
- **Library**, 714-566-3000, www.ocpl.org
- **Orange County Government**, 714-834-5400, http://egov.ocgov.com
- **Orange County Health Care Agency**, 714-834-4722, http://ochealthinfo.com
- **Police, Anaheim**, 714-765-4311, www.anaheim.net/police

- **Police, Irvine**, 949-724-7000, www.ci.irvine.ca.us/ipd
- **Police, Tustin**, 714-573-3240, www.tustinpd.org
- **Registrar of Voters**, 714-567-7600, www.ocvote.com
- **Sheriff**, 714-647-7000 or 949-770-6011, www.ocsd.org
- **Transportation Authority (OCTA)**, 714-636-7433 or 714-636-6282, www.octa.net
- **Treasurer-Tax Collector**, 714-834-3411, http://egov.ocgov.com

RIVERSIDE COUNTY

- **Animal Control**, 888-636-7387, www.rcdas.org
- **Department of Public Health**, 951-358-5000, www.rivcoph.org
- **Housing Authority**, 951-351-0700, www.harivco.org
- **Library**, 909-685-8121, www.riverside.lib.ca.us
- **Office of Education**, 951-826-6530, www.rcoe.k12.ca.us
- **Parks and Open Space District**, 800-234-7275, www.riversidecountyparks.org
- **Police Department**, 951-787-7911, www.riversideca.gov/rpd
- **Recycling, Waste Management Department**, 951-486-3200, www.rivcowm.org
- **Registrar-Recorder/County Clerk**, 951-486-7000, http://riverside.asrclkrec.com/
- **Riverside Community Hospital**, 4445 Magnolia Ave, Riverside, 951-788-3000, www.rchc.org
- **Riverside County Government**, 951-955-1000, www.co.riverside.ca.us
- **Riverside County Regional Medical Center**, 26520 Cactus, Moreno Valley, 951-486-4111, www.rcrmc.org
- **Sanitation, Local Solid Waste Management**, 951-955-8982, www.rivcowm.org
- **Sheriff**, 951-955-2400, www.riversidesheriff.org
- **Transportation Department**, 951-955-6880, www.tlma.co.riverside.ca.us/trans
- **Treasurer-Tax Collector**, 951-955-3900, www.treasurer-tax.co.riverside.ca.us

SAN DIEGO COUNTY

- **Animal Services**, 619-236-4250, www.sddac.com
- **County Clerk**, 619-238-8158, http://arcc.co.san-diego.ca.us
- **Department of Beaches**, 619-221-8901, www.sdcounty.ca.gov/deh/lwq/beachbay
- **Department of Parks and Recreation**, 858-565-3600, www.sdcounty.ca.gov/parks

- **Health and Human Services Agency,** 619-515-6770 or 800-227-0997, www2. sdcounty.ca.gov/hhsa
- **Housing and Community Development**, 858-694-4801, www.sdcounty.ca. gov/sdhcd
- **Library,** 858 694-2414, www.sdcl.org
- **Metropolitan Transit System,** 619-685-4900 or 858-484-3154, www.sdcom mute.com
- **Office of Education**, 858-292-3500, www.sdcoe.k12.ca.us
- **Police Department**, 619-531-2000 or 858-484-3154, www.sandiego.gov/ police
- **Recycling and Household Hazardous Waste,** 800-237-2583 or 877-713-2784, www.co.san-diego.ca.us/dpw/recycling
- **Registrar of Voters,** 858-565-5800 or 800-696-0136, www.sdvote.com
- **San Diego County Government,** 858-694-3900, www.co.san-diego.ca.us
- **Sheriff,** 858-565-5200, www.sdsheriff.net
- **Trash, Environmental Services,** 858-694-7000, www.sandiego.gov
- **Treasurer-Tax Collector,** 877-829-4732, www.sdtreastax.com

VENTURA COUNTY

- **Animal Care & Control**, 805-388-4341 or 888-223-7387, www.countyofven tura.org/animalreg
- **Department of Harbor**, 805-382-3001, www.countyofventura.org
- **Department of Parks**, 805-654-3951, www.countyofventura.org
- **Environmental and Energy Resources Department** (**Recycling**), 805-658-4321, www.wasteless.org
- **Health Care Agency**, 805-677-5110, www.vchca.org
- **Housing Authority**, 805-480-9991, www.ahacv.org
- **Library**, 805-477-7331, www.vencolibrary.org
- **Police Department**, 805-339-4400, www.ci.ventura.ca.us/depts/police
- **Registrar-Recorder/County Clerk**, 805-654-2263, http://recorder.countyof ventura.org
- **Sanitation Services Division**, 805-584-4829, http://publicworks.countyofven tura.org
- **Sheriff**, 805-654-2380, www.vcsd.org
- **Superintendent of Schools**, 805-383-1900, www.vcss.k12.ca.us
- **Transportation Commission**, 805-642-1591, www.goventura.org
- **Treasurer-Tax Collector**, 805-654-3744, www.countyofventura.org
- **Ventura County Government**, 805-654-3656, www.countyofventura.org
- **Ventura County Medical Center**, 3291 Loma Vista Rd, Ventura, 805-652-6000, www.vchca.org/mc

CHILD ABUSE AND FAMILY VIOLENCE

- **Abducted, Abused, and Exploited Children**, 800-248-8020, www.childquest. org
- **Child Abuse Hotline**, 800-540-4000
- **Childhelp USA**, 800-422-4453
- **Domestic Violence Hotline**, 800- 548-2722
- **Elder Abuse Hotline**, 800-992-1660
- **Father's Heartline**, 877-716-8000
- **Sojourn Services for Battered Women**, 310-264-6644, www.opcc.net/sojourn
- **Victims of Crime Resource Center**, 800-842-8467, www.1800victims.org
- **YWCA Battered Women's Helpline**, 626-967-0658, www.ywcawings.org

CRIME/CRISIS

- **County Central Fraud Reporting Line**, 800-87-FRAUD
- **Crime in Progress**, 911
- **Crime Prevention**, Santa Monica, 310-458-8474
- **Crime Victims Assistance**, 800-777-9229, www.boc.ca.gov
- **Criminal Fraud Reporting**, 800-78-CRIME, www.wetip.com

CRISIS HOTLINES/RAPE AND SEXUAL ASSAULT

- **Boys Town National Hotline**, 800-448-3000
- **LA Rape and Battery Hotline**, 213-626-3393, 310-854-4621, 626-793-3385, www.peaceoverviolence.org
- **Los Angeles County District Attorney Victim-Witness Assistance Program**, 800-380-3811
- **Rape Treatment Center, Santa Monica-UCLA Medical Center**, 310-319-4000, www.911rape.org
- **Sojourn Services for Battered Women**, 310-264-6644, www.opcc.net/sojourn
- **Suicide Prevention Center**, 310-391-1253 or 877-727-4747, www.suicidepreventioncenter.org

DISCRIMINATION

- **California Fair Employment and Housing Department**, 800-884-1684, www.dfeh.ca.gov

- **Los Angeles County Commission on Disabilities**, 213-974-1053, www.lacod. org
- **Gay and Lesbian Alliance Against Defamation**, 323-933-2240, www.glaad. org
- **California Department of Fair Housing and Discrimination**, 800-233-3212, www.dfeh.ca.gov
- **Women's Commission for Los Angeles County**, 213-974-1455, www.laccw. info

ELECTED OFFICIALS AND GOVERNMENT

- **California Governor's Office**, 916-445-2841, http://gov.ca.gov
- **City of Los Angeles Mayor's Office**, 311 or 213-978-0600, www.cityofla.org
- **Federal Citizen Information Center**, 800-688-9889, www.usa.gov
- **LA County Board of Supervisors**, 213-974-7207, http://lacounty.info

EMERGENCY

- **Police, Fire, Medical**, 911
- **American Red Cross Emergency Services**, 800-540-2000, www.redcrossla. org
- **City of LA Storm Water Hotline**, 800-974-9794
- **Earthquake Recovery-Debris Pick-up**, 800-773-2489, www.lacity.org/SAN
- **FEMA Disaster Assistance Information**, 800-621-FEMA, www.fema.gov
- **LA County Office of Emergency Management**, 323-980-2260, www.espfo cus.org

ENTERTAINMENT

- **Audiences Unlimited**, 818-753-3470, www.tvtickets.com
- **City of Los Angeles Cultural Affairs Department**, 213-202-5500, www.cul turela.org or www.lacountyarts.com
- **Ticketmaster** 213-480-3232, www.ticketmaster.com
- **Go Los Angeles (discount card)**, 800-887-9103, www.golosangelescard.com
- **TV Tix**, 323-653-4105, www.tvtix.com
- **Visitor's Bureau, Los Angeles County**, 213-689-8822, www.discoverlosange les.com
- **Visitor's Bureau, Orange County**, 714-278-7491, www.visitorangecounty.net

HEALTH AND MEDICAL CARE

- **AIDS Healthcare Foundation**, 323-860-5200, www.aidshealth.org
- **California Smokers Helpline**, 800-766-2888
- **Healthy Families Information Line**, 888-747-1222 or 800-880-5305, www. healthyfamilies.ca.gov
- **Los Angeles County Health Services Department**, 800-427-8700, www. ladhs.org
- **Los Angeles County Mental Health Services**, 800-854-7771, http://dmh.laco unty.gov
- **Los Angeles County Sexually Transmitted Disease Hotline**, 213-744-3070, http://phps.dhs.co.la.ca.us/std
- **Los Angeles Urban Search and Rescue–Fire Department**, 818-756-9677
- **Medi-Cal Health & Nutrition Line**, 877-597-4777, www.dhcs.ca.gov
- **Minority AIDS Project**, 323-936-4949, www.map-usa.org
- **National Health Information Center**, 800-336-4797, www.health.gov/nhic
- **Nursing Home Information and Referral**, 800-427-8700
- **Poison Control Center**, 800-876-4766 or 800-222-1222, www.calpoison.org
- **South Coast Air Quality Management**, 800-CUT-SMOG, www.aqmd.gov

HOUSING

- **Assisted Housing Authority**, 323-260-2617
- **California Fair Employment and Housing Department**, 800-233-3212, www.dfeh.ca.gov
- **Contractor's State License Board**, 800-321-2752, www.cslb.ca.gov
- **City of LA Housing Department**, 866-557-7368, http://lahd.lacity.org
- **Culver City Housing Division**, 310-253-6000, www.culvercity.org
- **Fair Housing, Santa Clarita**, 818-373-1185, www.santa-clarita.com
- **Fair Housing, Santa Monica**, 310-458-8336, www.smgov.net
- **Fair Housing Congress of Southern California**, 213-387-8400 or 800-477-5977, www.lacity.org/lahd
- **Fair Housing Council of San Fernando Valley**, 818-373-1185, www.lacity.org/lahd
- **Fair Housing Council, Westside**, 310-477-9234, www.lacity.org/lahd
- **Fair Housing South Los Angeles**, 323-295-3302, www.lacity.org/lahd
- **Homeowners and Renters Assistance**, Franchise Tax Board, 800-852-5711, www.ftb.ca.gov
- **HUD Fair Housing Information**, 213-894-8000, 800-767-7468, www.hud.gov
- **US Department of Fair Housing and Discrimination**, 800-233-3212, www.dfeh.ca.gov

LEGAL REFERRAL

- **American Civil Liberties Union of Southern California,** 213-977-9500, www. aclu-sc.org
- **Asian Pacific American Legal Center of Southern California,** 213-977-7500, www.apalc.org
- **Bet Tzedek Legal Services,** 323-939-0506, www.bettzedek.org
- **Legal Aid Foundation of Los Angeles,** 323-801-7991 or 800-399-4529, www. lafla.org
- **Los Angeles County Bar Association Referrals,** 213-243-1525
- **Los Angeles Gay and Lesbian Center Legal Services Department,** 323-993-7670, www.lagaycenter.org
- **Police Misconduct Attorney Referral Service,** 213-387-3325
- **Public Defender Information Line,** 213-974-2811, http://pd.co.la.ca.us
- **San Fernando Valley Neighborhood Legal Services,** 800-433-6251, www. nls-la.org

LIBRARIES

- **Los Angeles Central Library,** 213-228-7272, www.lapl.org
- **Orange County Public Library,** 714-566-3000, www.ocpl.org

See also **Libraries** in **Cultural Life,** and end-listings in the **Neighborhood Profiles.**

MARRIAGE LICENSES

- **LA County Marriage License and Ceremony Information,** 562-462-2137, http://lavote.net
- **Orange County Marriage License Information,** 714-834-2500, www.oc.ca. gov/recorder

MUNICIPALITIES

- **Anaheim,** 714-765-4311, www.anaheim.net
- **Beverly Hills,** 310-285-1000, www.ci.beverly-hills.ca.us
- **Burbank,** 818-238-5850, www.ci.burbank.ca.us
- **City of Bellflower,** 562-804-1424, www.bellflower.org
- **City of Downey,** 562-904-7246, www.downeyca.org
- **City of La Mirada,** 562-943-0131, www.cityoflamirada.org
- **City of Norwalk,** 562-929-5700, www.ci.norwalk.ca.us

- **Costa Mesa**, 714-754-5000, www.ci.costa-mesa.ca.us
- **Culver City**, 310-253-6000, www.ci.culver-city.ca.us
- **Fountain Valley**, 714-593-4400, www.fountainvalley.org
- **Fullerton**, 714-738-5338, www.ci.fullerton.ca.us
- **Glendale**, 818-548-2085, www.ci.glendale.ca.us
- **Irvine**, 949-724-6000, www.ci.irvine.ca.us
- **Laguna Beach**, 949-497-3311, www.lagunabeachcity.net
- **Lakewood City Information Line**, 562-866-9771, www.lakewoodcity.org
- **Long Beach**, 562-570-6555, www.ci.long-beach.ca.us
- **Los Angeles**, 311 or 213-485-2121, www.cityofla.org
- **Malibu**, 310-456-2489, www.ci.malibu.ca.us
- **Newport Beach**, 949-644-3309, www.city.newport-beach.ca.us
- **Pasadena**, 626-744-4000, www.ci.pasadena.ca.us
- **Santa Clarita**, 661-259-2489, www.santa-clarita.com
- **Santa Monica**, 310-458-8411, www.smgov.net
- **South Pasadena**, 626-403-7200, www.ci.south-pasadena.ca.us
- **Tustin**, 714-573-3000, www.tustinca.org
- **West Hollywood**, 323-848-6400, www.ci.west-hollywood.ca.us
- **Westminster**, 714-898-3311 www.ci.westminster.ca.us
- **Yorba Linda**, 714-961-7100, www.ci.yorba-linda.ca.us

PARKS AND RECREATION DEPARTMENTS

- **Beverly Hills Recreation and Parks Department**, 310-285-2537, www.beverlyhills.org
- **Burbank Parks and Recreation Department**, 818-238-5300, www.ci.burbank.ca.us
- **City of LA Department of Recreation and Parks**, 888-LA-PARKS, www.laparks.org
- **Culver City Recreation Department**, 310-253-6650, www.culvercity.org
- **El Segundo Parks and Recreation Department**, 310-524-2300, www.elsegundo.org
- **Glendale Parks Recreation Department**, 818-548-2000, www.parks.ci.glendale.ca.us
- **Irvine Community Services**, 949-724-6600, www.ci.irvine.ca.us
- **Long Beach Parks and Recreation**, 562-570-3232, www.ci.long-beach.ca.us/park
- **LA County Recreation and Parks Department**, 213-738-2961, www.lacountyparks.org
- **Malibu Parks and Recreation Department**, 310-317-1364, www.ci.malibu.ca.us

- **Manhattan Beach Recreation Department**, 310-802-5000, www.ci.manhat tan-beach.ca.us
- **Newport Beach**, 949-644-3151, http://recreation.city.newport-beach.ca.us
- **Orange County Resources and Development Management Department/ Harbors**, Beaches and Parks Division, 949-923-2200 or 866-OCPARKS, www. ocparks.com
- **Pasadena Human Services & Recreation Department**, 626-744-4000, www. ci.pasadena.ca.us
- **Santa Clarita Parks and Recreation Department**, 661-259-2489, www.santa-clarita.com
- **Santa Monica Recreation Division**, 310-458-8411, www.smgov.net
- **Tustin Parks and Recreation Department**, 714-573-3326, www.tustinca. org/parksrec
- **West Hollywood Recreation Department**, 323-848-6400, www.weho.org

POLICE

- **Central Bureau Operations**, 213-458-3101
- **LA County Sheriff**, 323-526-5541, www.www.la-sheriff.org
- **Los Angeles Police Department Divisions**, 877-275-5273, www.lapdonline. org
- **South Bureau Operations**, 213-458-4251
- **Valley Bureau Operations**, 818-756-8303
- **West Bureau Operations**, 213-756-8303
- **Orange County Sheriff**, 714-647-7000, www.ocsd.org

POST OFFICE

For a list of Post Offices with extended hours, see **Mail Receiving and Delivery** in the **Helpful Services** chapter.

- **US Postal Service**, 800-275-8777, www.usps.com

SANITATION AND GARBAGE

- **LA County Sanitation District**, 323-685-5217, http://lacounty.info
- **LA County Recycling and Hazardous Waste**, 888-CLEANLA, http://ladpw. org/epd
- **Orange County Sanitation District**, 714-962-2411, www.ocsd.com
- **Orange County Integrated Waste Management** (recycling), 714-834-4000, www.oclandfills.com

SCHOOLS

See **School Districts** for a listing of LA County and Orange County schools in the **Childcare and Education** chapter.

- **LA County Office of Education**, 562-922-6111, www.lacoe.edu
- **LA School District Boundaries**, 213-241-4500, http://lausd.k12.ca.us
- **LA Unified Parent Resource Network Hotline**, 213-217-5272, www.lausd.k12.ca.us
- **LA Unified School District**, 213-241-1000, www.lausd.k12.ca.us
- **Orange County Department of Education,** 714-966-4000, www.ocde.k12.ca.us

SENIORS

- **Alternative Living for the Aging**, 323-650-7988, www.alternativeliving.org
- **City of LA Department on Aging, Senior Services Referral**, 213-252-4030 or 800-510-2020, www.cityofla.org/doa
- **Elder Abuse Hotline**, 800-992-1660 or 800-677-1116, www.ncea.aoa.gov
- **Elder Care Locator**, 800-677-1116, www.eldercare.gov
- **Jewish Family Service of Los Angeles**, 323-761-8800, www.jfsla.org
- **Long-Term Care Ombudsman, California**, 916-323-6681, www.ltcombudsman.org
- **LA County Area Agency on Aging**, 800-510-2020, www.ladcss.org/aaa/AAA.htm
- **LA County Community and Senior Citizens Services**, 213-738-2600, www.ladcss.org
- **National Council on the Aging**, 415-982-7007, www.ncoa.org
- **Social Security and Medicare Eligibility Information**, 800-772-1213, www.ssa.gov

SHIPPING

- **DHL**, 800-225-5345, www.dhl.com
- **FedEx**, 800-463-3339, www.fedex.com
- **UPS**, 800-742-5877, www.ups.com
- **US Postal Service**, 800-275-8777, www.usps.com

SPORTS

- **Los Angeles Angels**, 888-796-4256, www.angelsbaseball.com
- **Los Angeles Avengers**, 888-AVENGERS, www.laavengers.com
- **Los Angeles Clippers**, 888-895-8662, www.nba.com/clippers

- **Los Angeles Dodgers,** 323-224-1448, http://losangeles.dodgers.mlb.com
- **Los Angeles Kings,** 888-KINGS-LA, http://kings.nhl.com
- **Los Angeles Lakers,** 800-4-NBA-TIXS or 213-480-3232, www.nba.com/lakers
- **Los Angeles Sparks,** 213-929-1300, www.wnba.com/sparks
- **UCLA Bruins,** 310-825-2101, http://uclabruins.cstv.com
- **USC Trojans,** 213-740-GOSC, http://usctrojans.cstv.com

STATE GOVERNMENT

- **California Legislative Information,** www.leginfo.ca.gov
- **California State Senate,** 916-445-9018, www.sen.ca.gov
- **California State Assembly,** 916-319-2856, www.assembly.ca.gov
- **Governor's Office,** 916-445-2841 or 213-897-0322, http://gov.ca.gov/
- **Senate Office of Research,** 916-445-1727, www.sen.ca.gov
- **State of California,** 916-657-9900, www.ca.gov
- **US House of Representatives,** 202-224-3121, www.house.gov
- **US Senate,** 202-224-3121, www.senate.gov

STREET MAINTENANCE

- **Caltrans Highway Information Network,** 800-427-7623, www.dot.ca.gov
- **City of LA Streetlight Repair,** 800-303-5267, www.cityofla.org
- **LA County Road Maintenance,** 626-458-5100, http://lapw.org
- **Pot holes, sidewalk repair,** 626-458-5100, http://ladpw.org
- **Traffic signals, sign repair,** LA County, 800-675-4357, www.lacounty.info

TAXES

- **Internal Revenue Service,** 800-829-1040 or 213-576-3009, www.irs.gov
- **LA County Treasurer-Property Tax,** 213-974-2111, http://lacounty.info
- **State Franchise Tax Board,** 800-852-5711, www.ftb.ca.gov

TELEPHONE

- **AT&T,** 800-222-0300, www.att.com
- **MCI,** 800-444-3333, www.mci.com
- **T-Mobile,** 800-866-2453, www.t-mobile.com
- **Verizon,** 800-483-4000, www.verizon.com

TIME

- **Official US Clock,** www.time.gov

TOURISM AND TRAVEL

- **California State Parks and Recreation**, 800-777-0369, www.cal-parks.ca.gov
- **California Travel and Tourism Commission**, 310-854-7616, www.visitcalifornia.com
- **INFO Line of Los Angeles**, 800-339-6993 or 211
- **Los Angeles Convention and Visitors Bureau**, 213-624-7300, www.greaterlosangeles.com

TRANSPORTATION

- **Cal Trans Highway Conditions**, 800-427-7623, www.dot.ca.gov
- **City of LA Department of Transportation** (**LADOT**), 818/213/323/310-808-2273, www.ladottransit.com
- **Commuter Transportation Services** (carpools), 800-266-6883, www.ridematch.info
- **LA County Metropolitan Transit Authority** (**Metro**), 800-COMMUTE, 213-922-6235, www.metro.net
- **Smart Traveler Information**, www.smart-traveler.info

AIRPORTS

- **Bob Hope (Burbank/Glendale/Pasadena) Airport**, 818-840-8840, www.burbankairport.com
- **Long Beach Airport**, 562-570-2678, www.longbeach.gov/airport
- **Los Angeles International Airport** (**LAX**), 310-646-5252, www.lawa.org
- **Ontario International Airport**, 909-957-2700, www.lawa.org
- **Orange County's John Wayne Airport**, 949-252-5200, www.ocair.com

NATIONAL TRAIN AND BUS SERVICE

- **Amtrak**, 800-872-7245, www.amtrak.com
- **Greyhound**, 800-231-2222, www.greyhound.com

UTILITY EMERGENCIES

- **Anaheim Public Utilities**, 714-765-3300, www.anaheim.net
- **Burbank Water & Power**, 818-238-3700, www.burbankwaterandpower.com
- **Castaic Lake Water Agency**, 661-259-2737, www.clwa.org
- **City of LA City Storm Water Hotline**, 800-974-9794, www.lastormwater.org
- **Glendale Water & Power**, 818-548-2011, www.ci.glendale.ca.us
- **LA County Water District**, 626-458-5100 or 800-675-HELP, www.ladpw.org

- **LA County Waterworks and Sewer**, 626-458-5131, www.ladpw.org
- **Las Virgenes Municipal Water District**, 818-880-4110, www.lvmwd.dst.ca.us
- **Los Angeles Department of Water and Power**, 800-342-5397 or 818-342-5397, www.ladwp.com
- **Newhall County Water District**, 661-259-3610, www.ncwd.org
- **Newport Beach Utilities Department**, 949-644-3011, www.city.newport-beach.ca.us
- **Pasadena Water and Power**, 626-744-4409, www.ci.pasadena.ca.us/waterandpower
- **Santa Clarita Water Division**, 661-259-2737, www.clwa.org
- **Santa Monica Water Department**, 310-458-8999, www.smgov.net
- **South Pasadena Public Works Department**, 626-403-7240, www.ci.south-pasadena.ca.us
- **Southern California Gas Company**, 800-427-2200, www.socalgas.com
- **Southern California Water Company**, 909-999-4033, www.aswater.com/Organization/Company_Links/SCWC/scwc.html
- **Underground Service Alert**, 800-227-2600, www.digalert.com
- **Valencia Water Company**, 661-294-0828, www.valenciawater.com

VOTING

- **California Voter Registration Hotline**, 800-345-VOTE, www.sos.ca.gov/elections
- **LA County Clerk's Voter Registration**, 800-815-2666, www.lavote.net
- **Orange County Registrar of Voters**, 714-567-7600, www.ocvote.com

WEATHER

- **Local Weather**, 213-554-1212, www.nwsla.noaa.gov

ZIP CODE INFORMATION

- **USPS zip codes request**, 800-275-8777, www.usps.com

INDEX

JOAN WAI is a Southern California native and Los Angeles resident since 1987. She has served as a county elections pollworker for several years and is Community Emergency Response Team certified. Favorite LA activities include catching free movie screenings, gourmet grocery shopping, and great conversation. In between her day job and sitting in traffic, she freelances as a screenwriter. Joan is also the author of *100+ Wedding Games: Fun & Laughs for Bachelorette Parties, Showers, & Receptions* and *100+ Baby Shower Games*.

Go Metro

metro.net

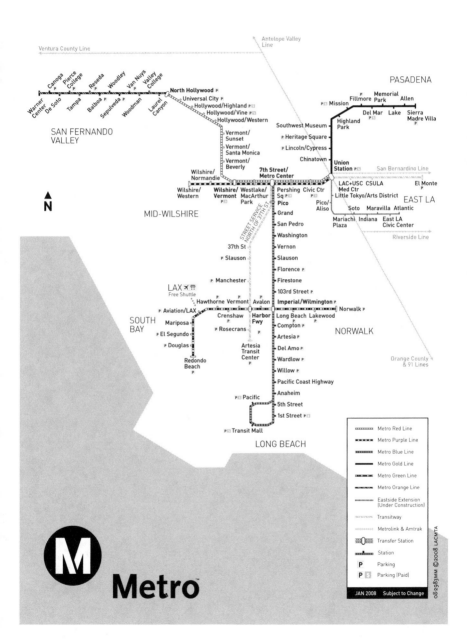

Antelope Valley Line

Ventura County Line

PASADENA

SAN FERNANDO VALLEY

Canoga
Pierce College
Reseda
Woodley
Van Nuys
Valley College
Warner Center
De Soto
Tampa
Balboa
Sepulveda
Woodman
Laurel Canyon

North Hollywood P
Universal City P
Hollywood/Highland P
Hollywood/Vine P
Hollywood/Western

Fillmore
Memorial Park
Allen
P Mission
Del Mar Lake Sierra Madre Villa
Highland Park

Southwest Museum
P Heritage Square
P Lincoln/Cypress
Chinatown
Union Station P

San Bernardino Line

Vermont/Sunset
Vermont/Santa Monica
Vermont/Beverly

7th Street/Metro Center

Wilshire/Normandie
Wilshire/Western
Wilshire/Vermont
Westlake/MacArthur Park P
Pershing Civic Ctr
Sq P
Pico P
Pico/Aliso

LAC+USC CSULA
Med Ctr
Little Tokyo/Arts District
El Monte P

EAST LA

MID-WILSHIRE

Soto Maravilla Atlantic
Mariachi Indiana East LA
Plaza Civic Center

Riverside Line

Grand
San Pedro
Washington
Vernon
Slauson
Florence P
Firestone
103rd Street P
Imperial/Wilmington P

37th St
P Slauson

P Manchester

LAX ✈ 🚌
Free Shuttle
Hawthorne Vermont Avalon
P Aviation/LAX
Crenshaw Harbor Long Beach Lakewood
Mariposa Fwy Compton P
P El Segundo P Rosecrans
P Douglas

Norwalk P

NORWALK

SOUTH BAY

Artesia P
Del Amo P
Wardlow P
Willow P
Pacific Coast Highway
Anaheim

Artesia Transit Center
Redondo Beach P

Orange County & 91 Lines

P ⬚ Pacific
5th Street
1st Street P ⬚

P ⬚ Transit Mall

LONG BEACH

┅┅┅	Metro Red Line
▬▬▬	Metro Purple Line
▬▬▬	Metro Blue Line
▬▬▬	Metro Gold Line
┅┅┅	Metro Green Line
┅┅┅	Metro Orange Line
┄┄┄	Eastside Extension (Under Construction)
┄┄┄	Transitway
┄┄┄	Metrolink & Amtrak
⬚	Transfer Station
▭	Station
P	Parking
P ⬚	Parking (Paid)

JAN 2008   Subject to Change

08-2983MM ©2008 LACMTA

Ⓜ Metro™

371

READER RESPONSE

We would appreciate your comments regarding this fifth edition of the *Newcomer's Handbook® for Moving to and Living in Los Angeles.* If you've found any mistakes or omissions or if you would just like to express your opinion about the guide, please let us know. We will consider any suggestions for possible inclusion in our next edition, and if we use your comments, we'll send you a free copy of our next edition. Please e-mail us at readerresponse@firstbooks.com, or mail or fax this response form to:

Reader Response Department
First Books
6750 SW Franklin, Suite A
Portland, OR 97223-2542
Fax: 503.968.6779

Comments: _____

_____

_____

_____

_____

_____

_____

_____

_____

_____

Name: _____

Address: _____

_____

_____

Telephone: ( ) _____

Email: _____

6750 SW Franklin, Suite A
Portland, OR 97223-2542
USA
P: 503.968.6777
www.firstbooks.com

Utilizing an innovative grid and "static" reusable adhesive sticker format, *Furniture Placement and Room Planning Guide...Moving Made Easy* provides a functional and practical solution to all your space planning and furniture placement needs.

MOVING WITH KIDS?

Look into *The Moving Book: A Kids' Survival Guide*.

Divided into three sections (before, during, and after the move), it's a handbook, a journal, and a scrapbook all in one. Includes address book, colorful change-of-address cards, and a useful section for parents.

Children's Book of the Month Club "Featured Selection"; American Bookseller's "Pick of the List"; Winner of the Family Channel's "Seal of Quality" Award

And for your younger children, ease their transition with our brand-new title just for them, *Max's Moving Adventure: A Coloring Book for Kids on the Move*. A complete story book featuring activities as well as pictures that children can color; designed to help children cope with the stresses of small or large moves.

GOT PETS?

The Pet Moving Handbook: Maximize Your Pet's Well-Being and Maintain Your Sanity by Carrie Straub answers all your pet-moving questions and directs you to additional resources that can help smooth the move for both you and your pets.

"Floats to the top, cream of the crop. Awesome book; I'm going to keep one on the special shelf here." – Hal Abrams, Animal Radio

NEWCOMER'S HANDBOOKS®

Regularly revised and updated, these popular guides are now available for Atlanta, Boston, Chicago, China, London, Los Angeles, Minneapolis–St. Paul, New York City, Portland, San Francisco Bay Area, Seattle, Texas and Washington DC.

"Invaluable ...highly recommended" – Library Journal

If you're coming from another country, don't miss the *Newcomer's Handbook® for Moving to and Living in the USA* by Mike Livingston, termed "a fascinating book for newcomers and residents alike" by the *Chicago Tribune*.

6750 SW Franklin Street
Portland, Oregon 97223-2542
Phone 503.968.6777 • Fax 503.968.6779
FIRST BOOKS   **www.firstbooks.com**

FIRST BOOKS

Visit our web site at

www.firstbooks.com

for information about

all our books.